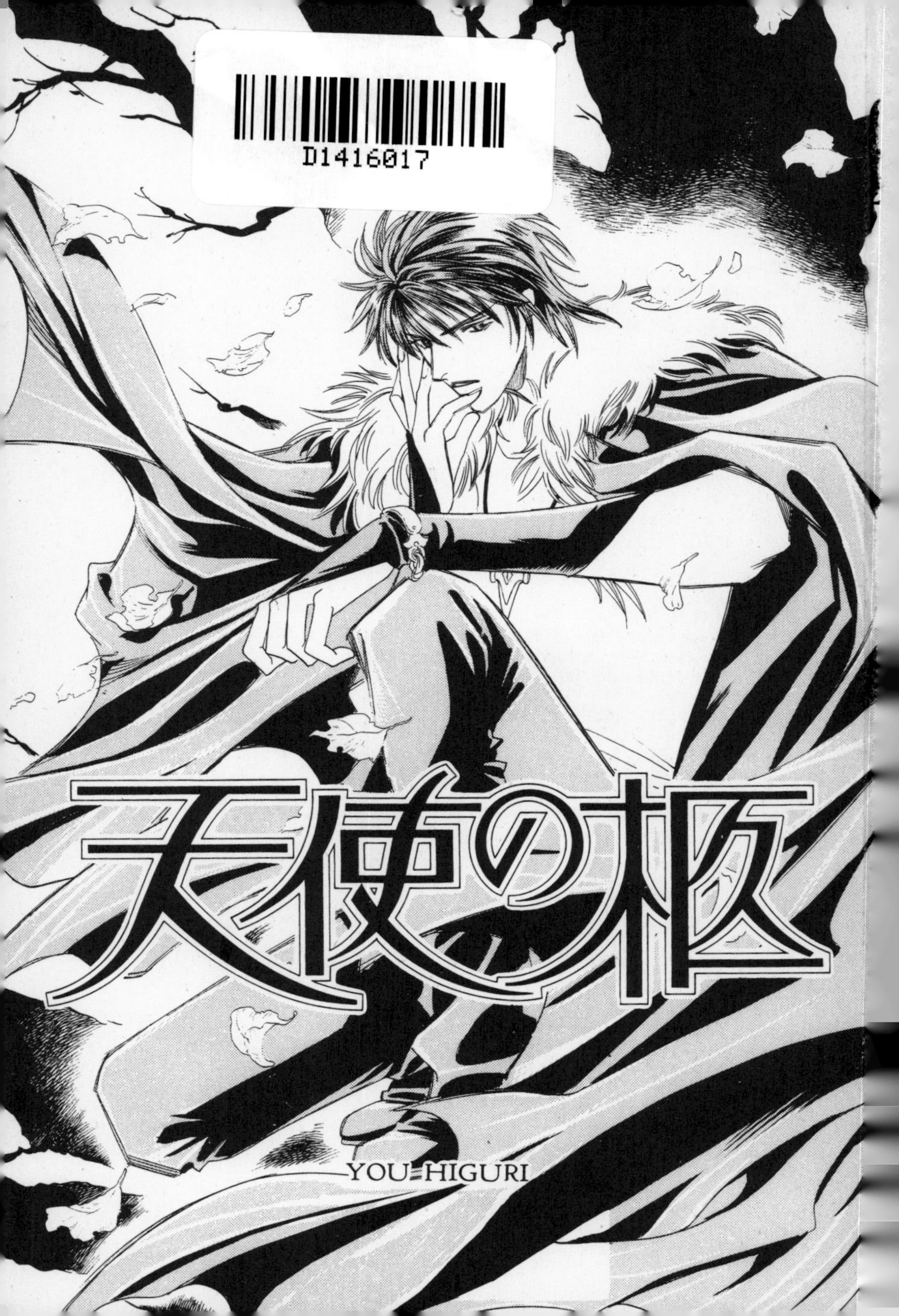
天使の柩
YOU HIGURI

Translation & Adaptation – Christine Schilling
Lettering & Design– John Lo
Production Assistant – Suzy Wells
Editorial Assistant –Mallory Reaves
Production Manager – James Dashiell
Editor – Brynne Chandler


A Go! Comi manga

Published by Go! Media Entertainment, LLC


Tenshi no Hitsugi
© YOU HIGURI 2000
Originally published in Japan in 2000 by Akita Publishing Co., Ltd., Tokyo.
English translation rights arranged with Akita Publishing Co., Ltd. through
TOHAN CORPORATION, Tokyo.

Visit us online at www.gocomi.com
e-mail: info@gocomi.com

ISBN 978-1-933617-68-8

First printed in October 2008

1  2  3  4  5  6  7  8  9

Manufactured in the United States of America

# Angel's Coffin

STORY AND ART BY

## YOU HIGURI

go! comi

# Angel's Coffin

# CONTENTS

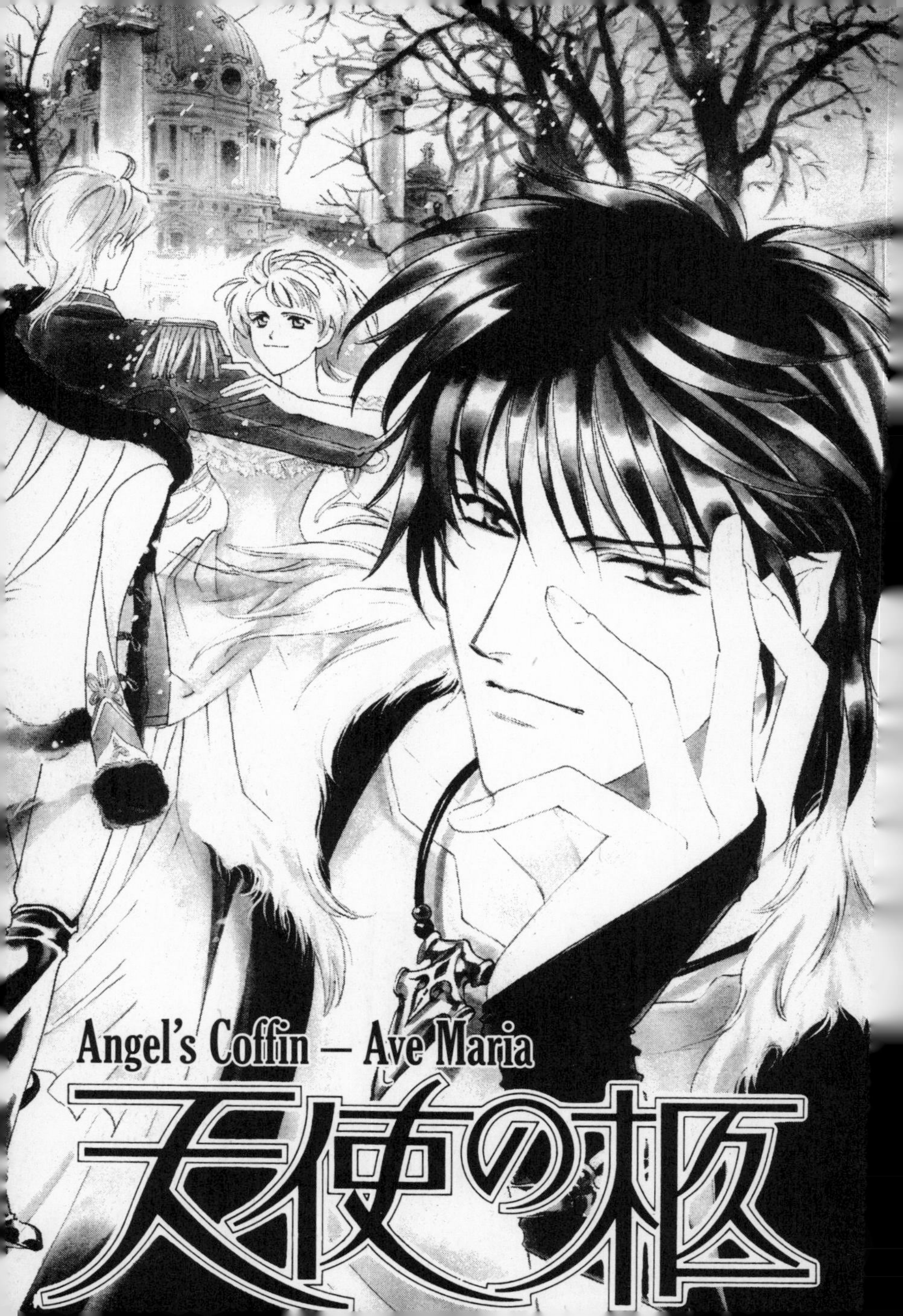
Angel's Coffin — Ave Maria
天使の柩

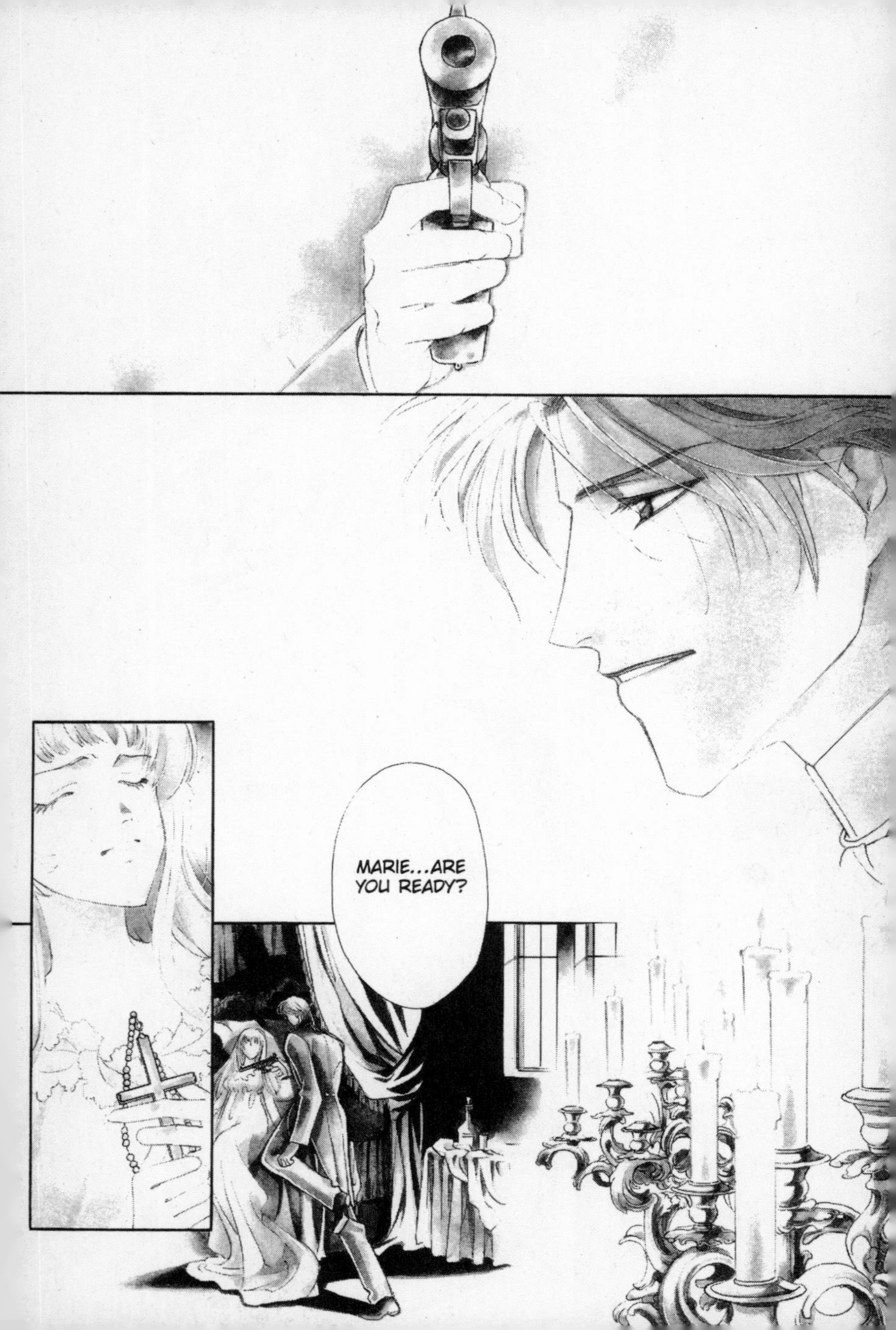
MARIE...ARE YOU READY?

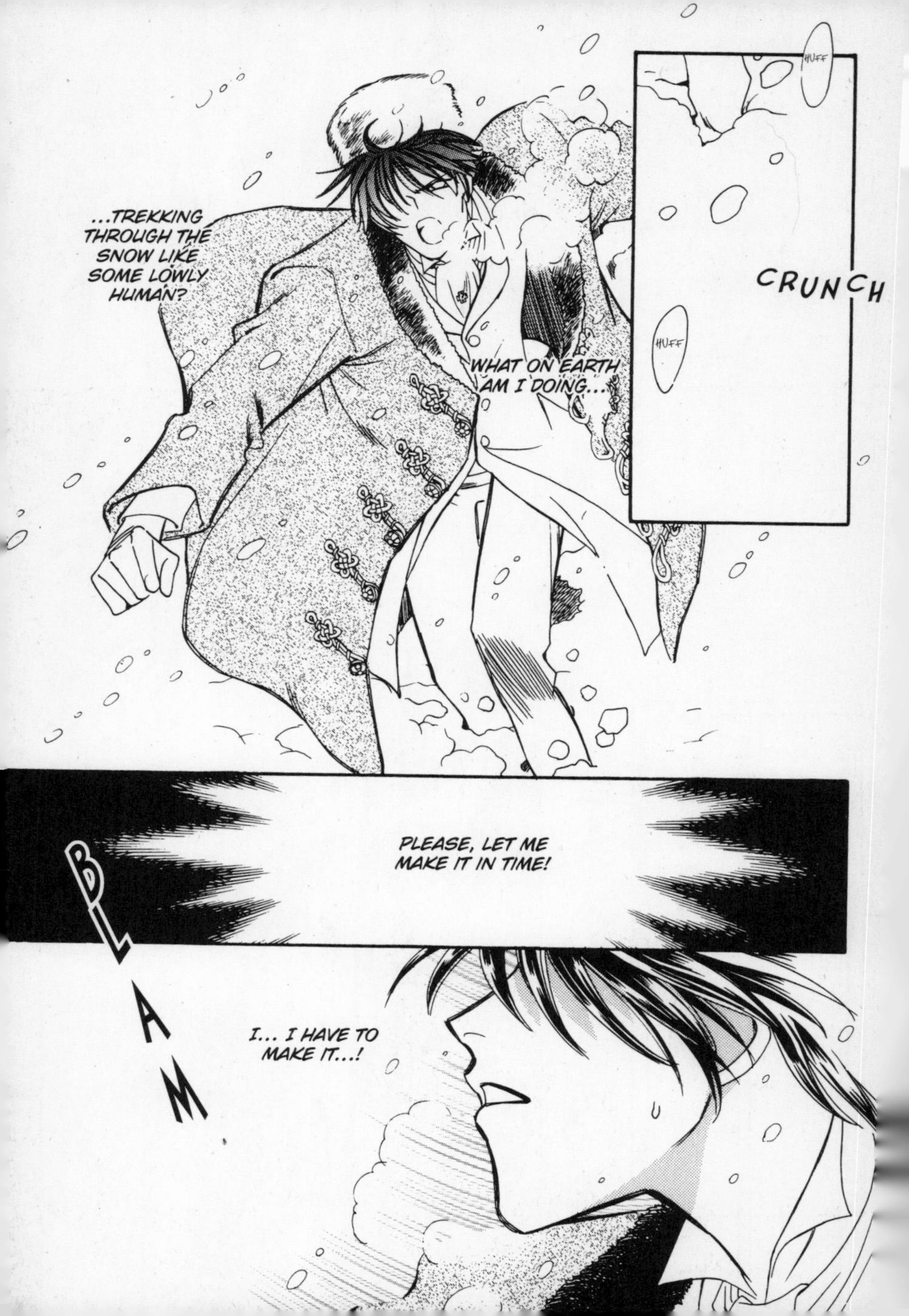
HUFF
CRUNCH
HUFF
WHAT ON EARTH AM I DOING...
...TREKKING THROUGH THE SNOW LIKE SOME LOWLY HUMAN?
PLEASE, LET ME MAKE IT IN TIME!
BLAM
I... I HAVE TO MAKE IT...!

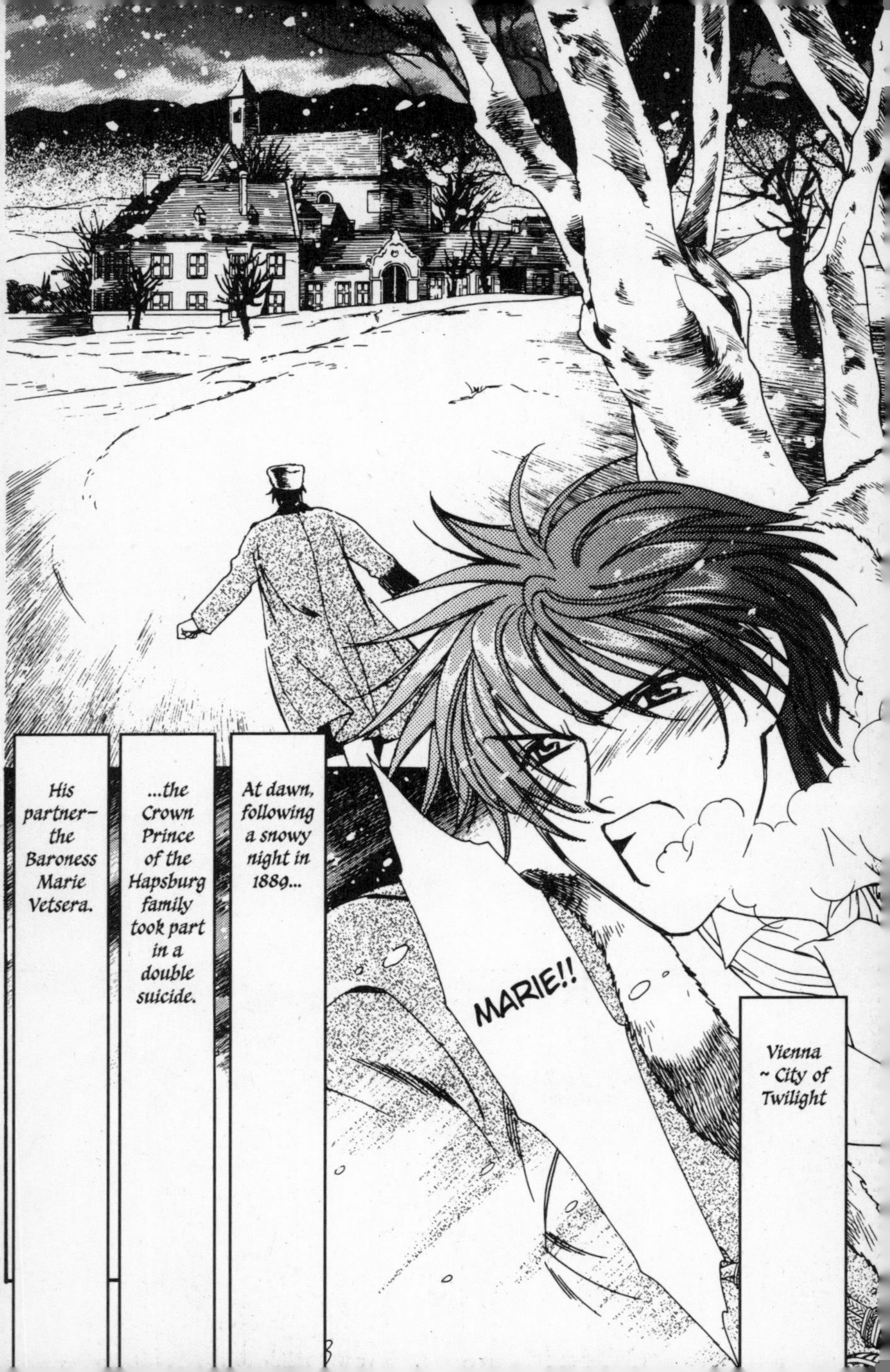
At dawn, following a snowy night in 1889...
...the Crown Prince of the Hapsburg family took part in a double suicide.
His partner—the Baroness Marie Vetsera.
Vienna ~ City of Twilight
MARIE!!

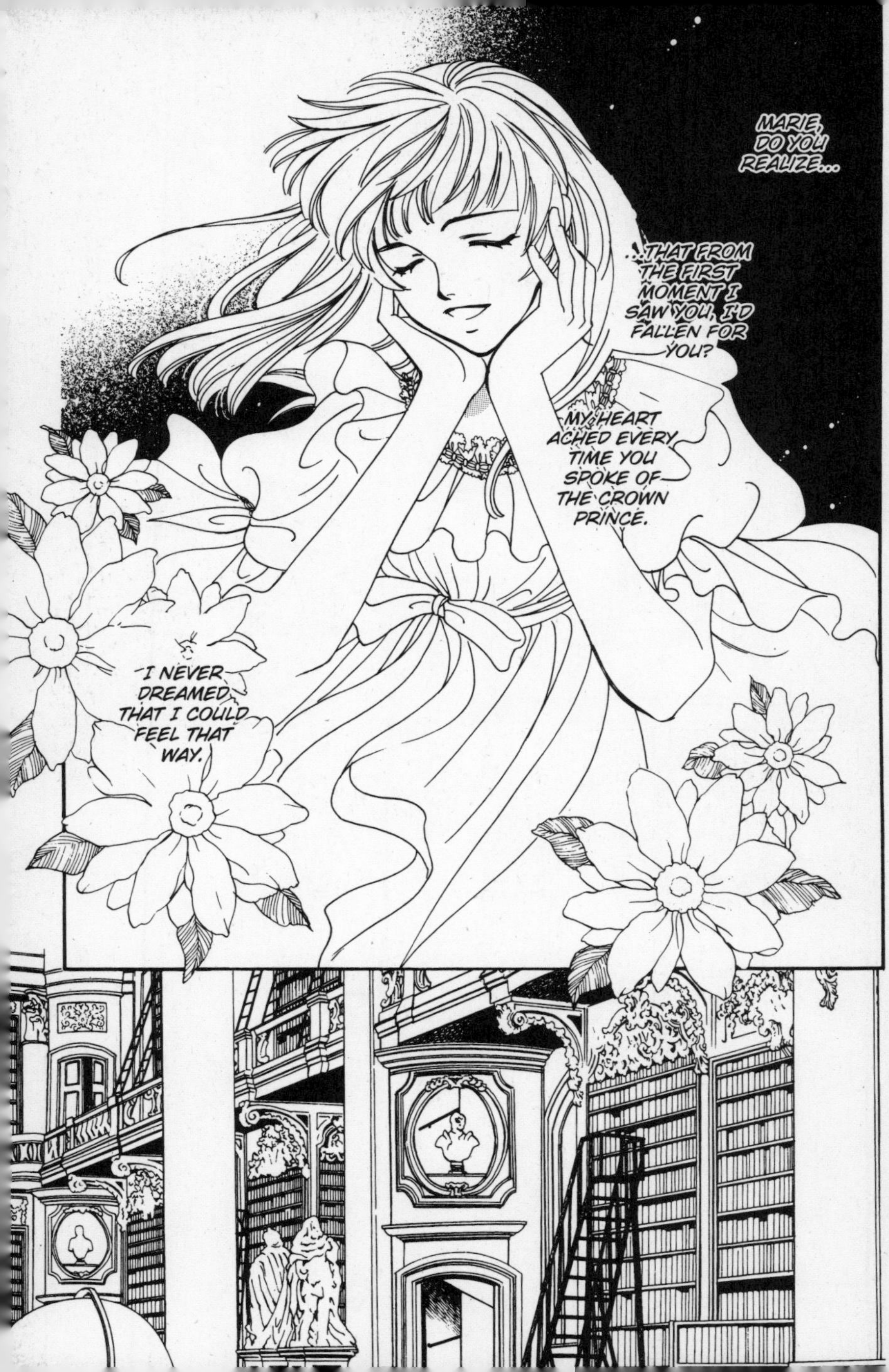
MARIE, DO YOU REALIZE...
...THAT FROM THE FIRST MOMENT I SAW YOU, I'D FALLEN FOR YOU?
MY HEART ACHED EVERY TIME YOU SPOKE OF THE CROWN PRINCE.
I NEVER DREAMED THAT I COULD FEEL THAT WAY.

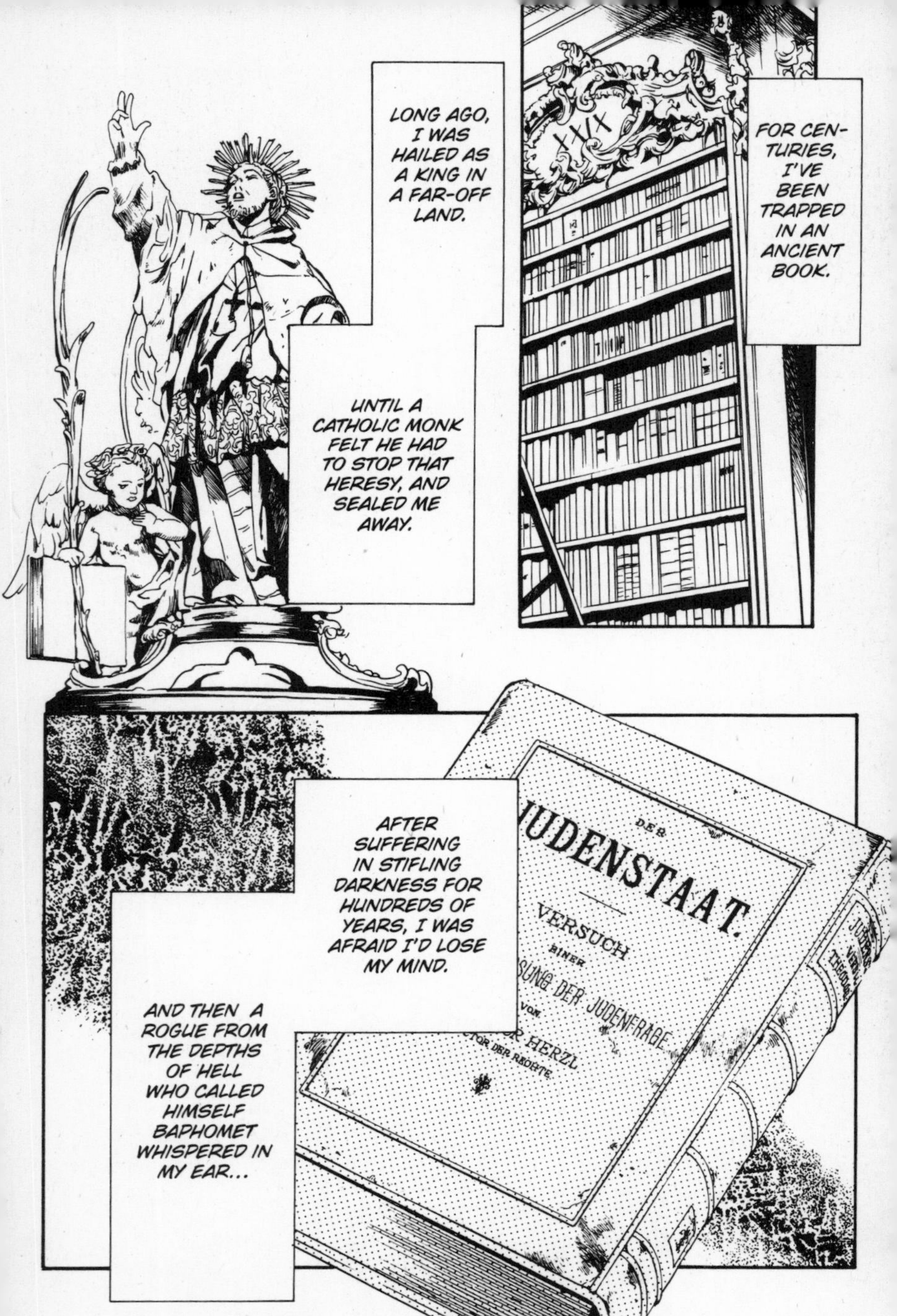
FOR CEN-TURIES, I'VE BEEN TRAPPED IN AN ANCIENT BOOK.
LONG AGO, I WAS HAILED AS A KING IN A FAR-OFF LAND.
UNTIL A CATHOLIC MONK FELT HE HAD TO STOP THAT HERESY, AND SEALED ME AWAY.
DER
JUDENSTAAT.
VERSUCH
EINER
VON
AFTER SUFFERING IN STIFLING DARKNESS FOR HUNDREDS OF YEARS, I WAS AFRAID I'D LOSE MY MIND.
AND THEN A ROGUE FROM THE DEPTHS OF HELL WHO CALLED HIMSELF BAPHOMET WHISPERED IN MY EAR...

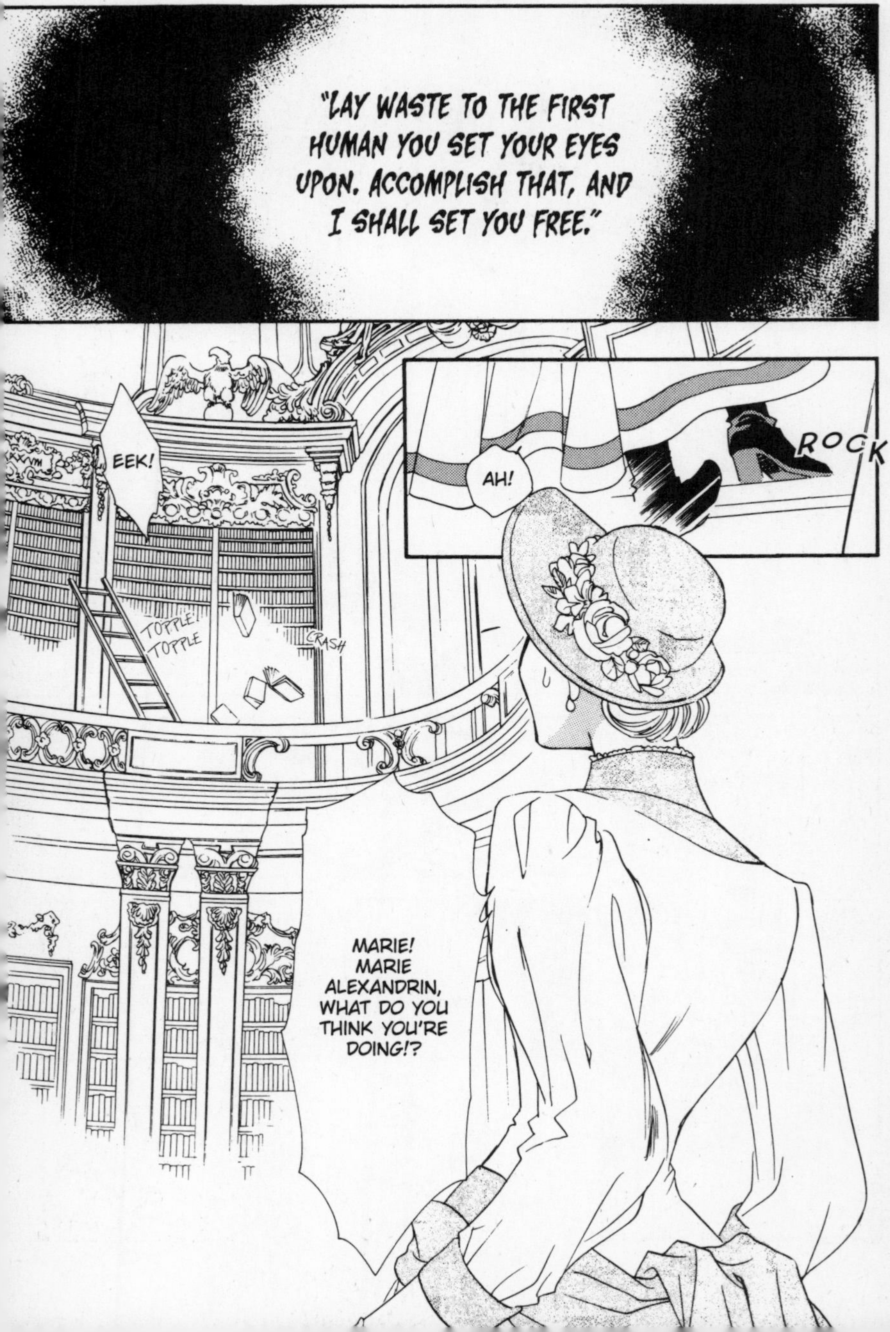
"LAY WASTE TO THE FIRST HUMAN YOU SET YOUR EYES UPON. ACCOMPLISH THAT, AND I SHALL SET YOU FREE."
ROCK
AH!
EEK!
TOPPLE TOPPLE
CRASH
MARIE! MARIE ALEXANDRIN, WHAT DO YOU THINK YOU'RE DOING!?

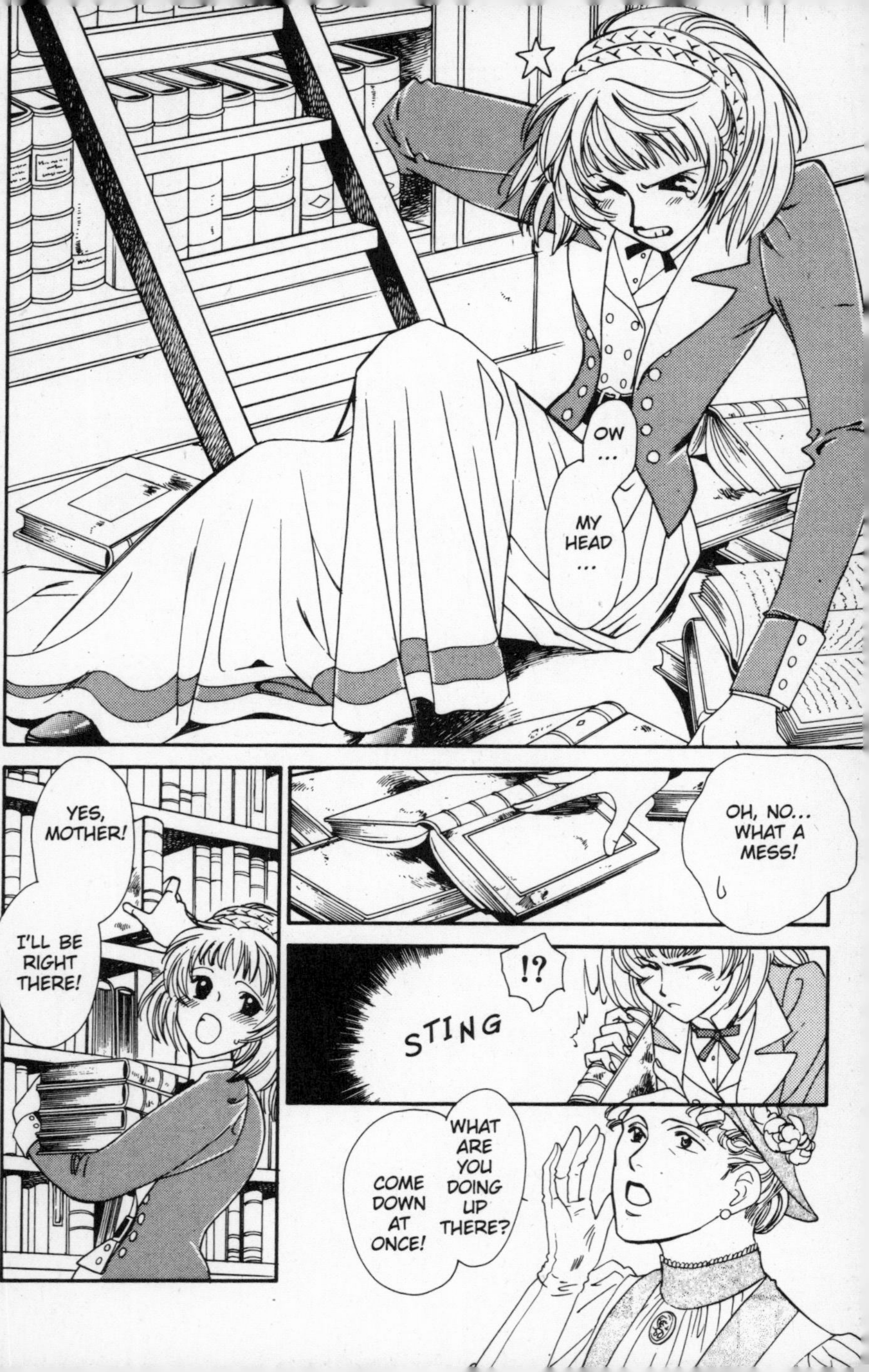
OW ... MY HEAD ...
OH, NO... WHAT A MESS!
!?
STING
WHAT ARE YOU DOING UP THERE?
COME DOWN AT ONCE!
YES, MOTHER!
I'LL BE RIGHT THERE!

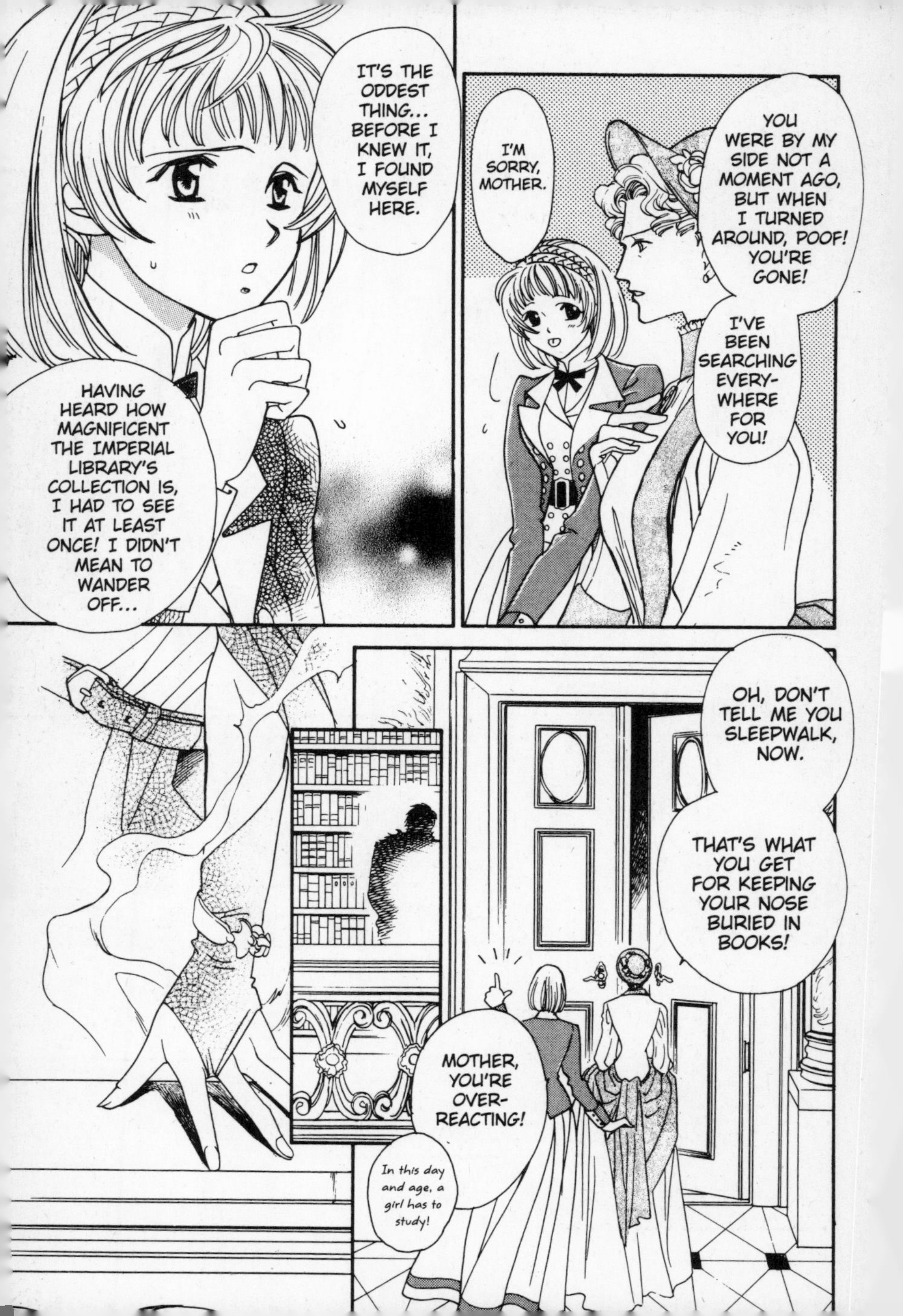
YOU WERE BY MY SIDE NOT A MOMENT AGO, BUT WHEN I TURNED AROUND, POOF! YOU'RE GONE!
I'VE BEEN SEARCHING EVERY-WHERE FOR YOU!
I'M SORRY, MOTHER.
IT'S THE ODDEST THING... BEFORE I KNEW IT, I FOUND MYSELF HERE.
HAVING HEARD HOW MAGNIFICENT THE IMPERIAL LIBRARY'S COLLECTION IS, I HAD TO SEE IT AT LEAST ONCE! I DIDN'T MEAN TO WANDER OFF...
OH, DON'T TELL ME YOU SLEEPWALK, NOW.
THAT'S WHAT YOU GET FOR KEEPING YOUR NOSE BURIED IN BOOKS!
MOTHER, YOU'RE OVER-REACTING!
In this day and age, a girl has to study!

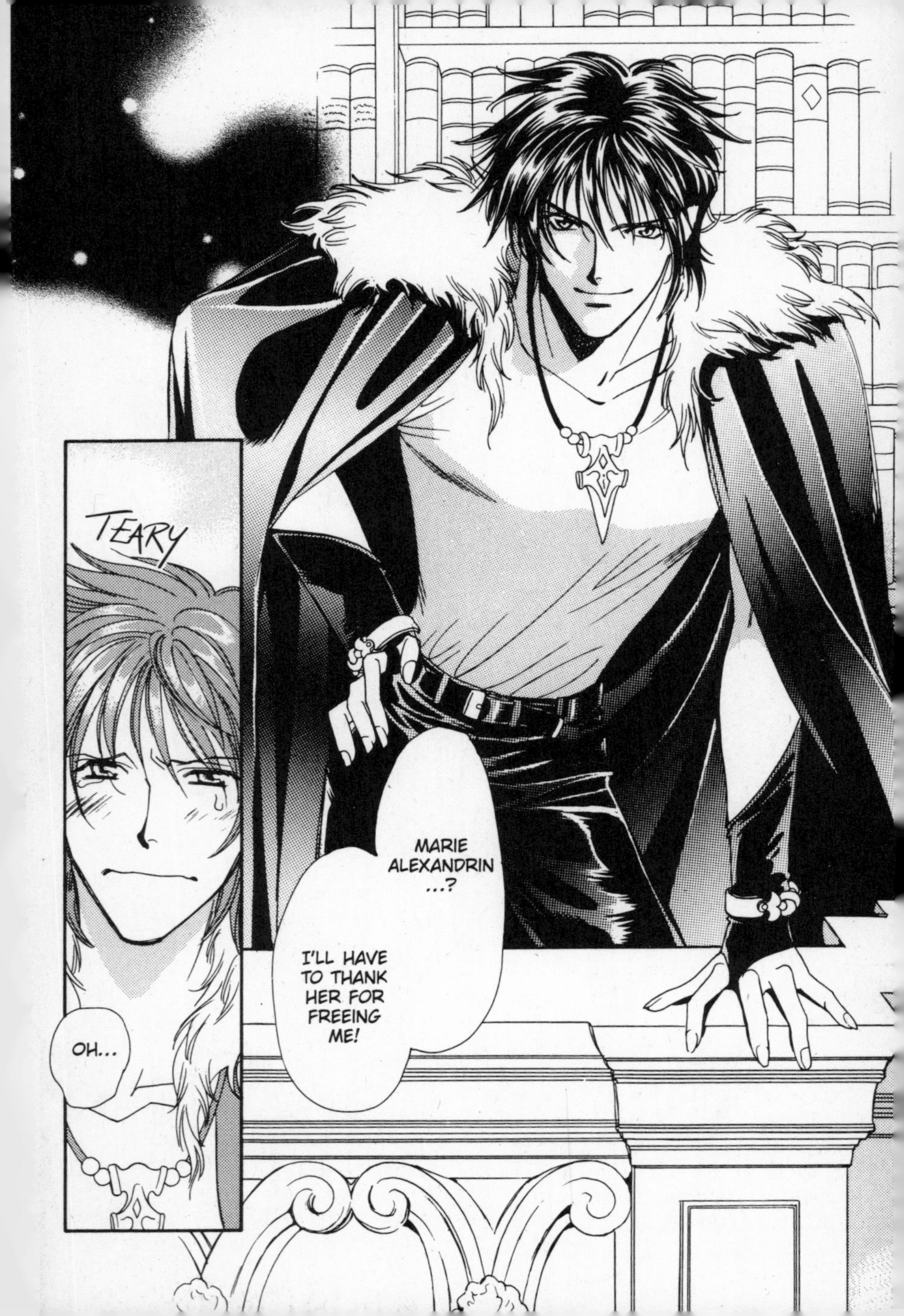
MARIE ALEXANDRIN ...?
I'LL HAVE TO THANK HER FOR FREEING ME!
TEARY
OH...

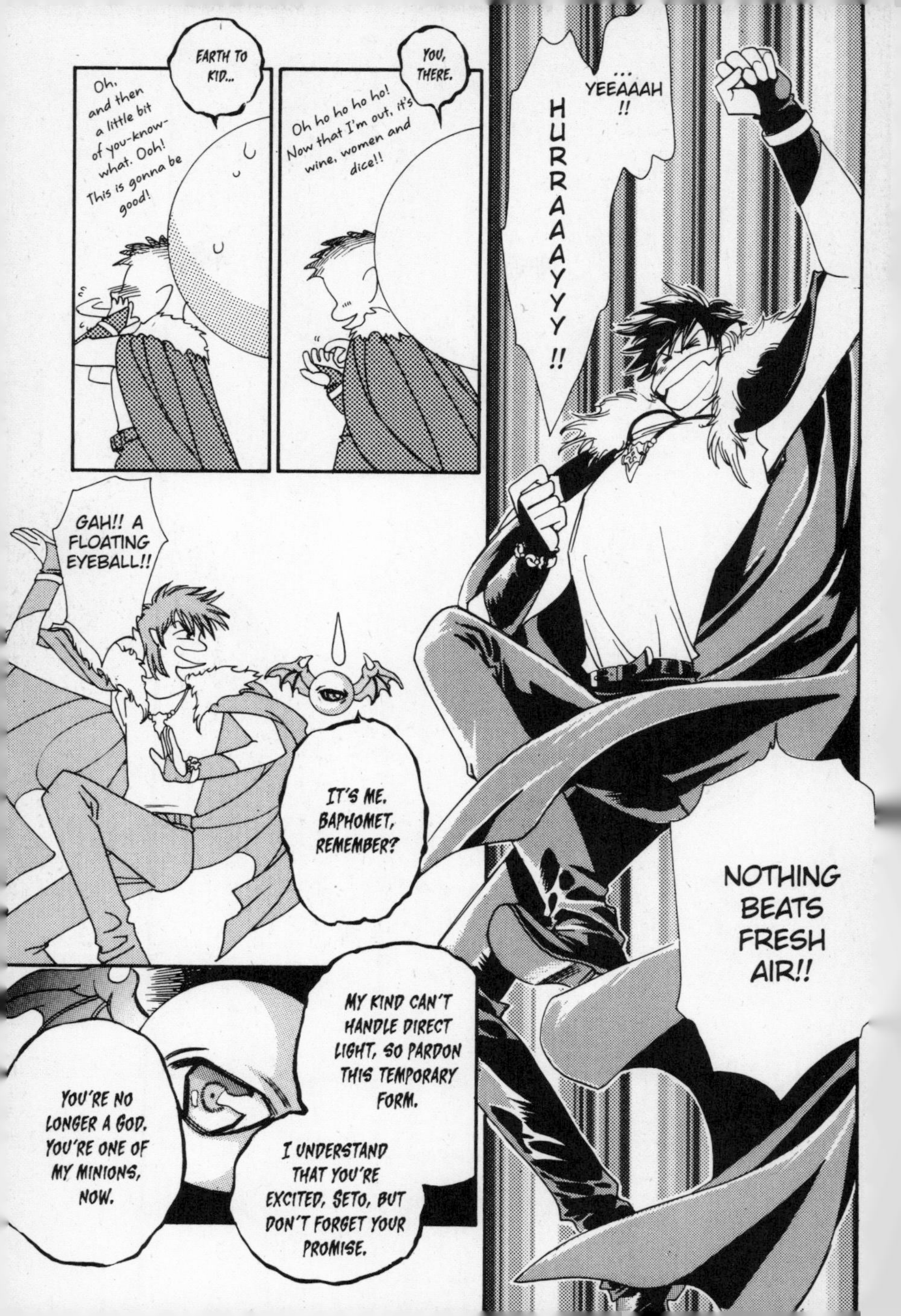
...YEEAAAH!!
HURRAAAYYY!!
NOTHING BEATS FRESH AIR!!
Oh ho ho ho ho! Now that I'm out, it's wine, women and dice!!
YOU, THERE.
Oh, and then a little bit of you-know-what. Ooh! This is gonna be good!
EARTH TO KID...
GAH!! A FLOATING EYEBALL!!
IT'S ME. BAPHOMET, REMEMBER?
MY KIND CAN'T HANDLE DIRECT LIGHT, SO PARDON THIS TEMPORARY FORM.
I UNDERSTAND THAT YOU'RE EXCITED, SETO, BUT DON'T FORGET YOUR PROMISE.
YOU'RE NO LONGER A GOD. YOU'RE ONE OF MY MINIONS, NOW.

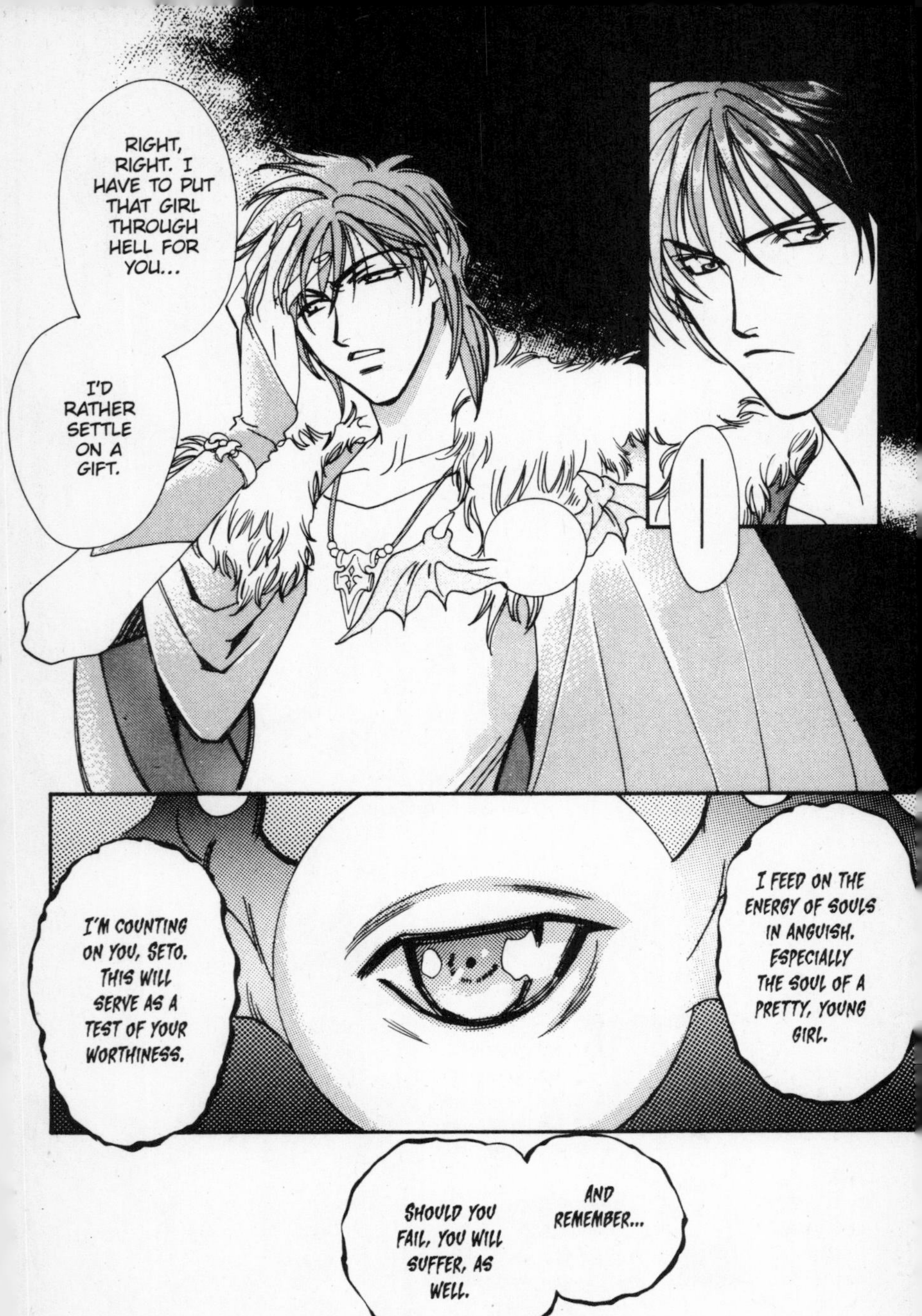
RIGHT, RIGHT. I HAVE TO PUT THAT GIRL THROUGH HELL FOR YOU...
I'D RATHER SETTLE ON A GIFT.
I FEED ON THE ENERGY OF SOULS IN ANGUISH. ESPECIALLY THE SOUL OF A PRETTY, YOUNG GIRL.
I'M COUNTING ON YOU, SETO. THIS WILL SERVE AS A TEST OF YOUR WORTHINESS.
AND REMEMBER...
SHOULD YOU FAIL, YOU WILL SUFFER, AS WELL.

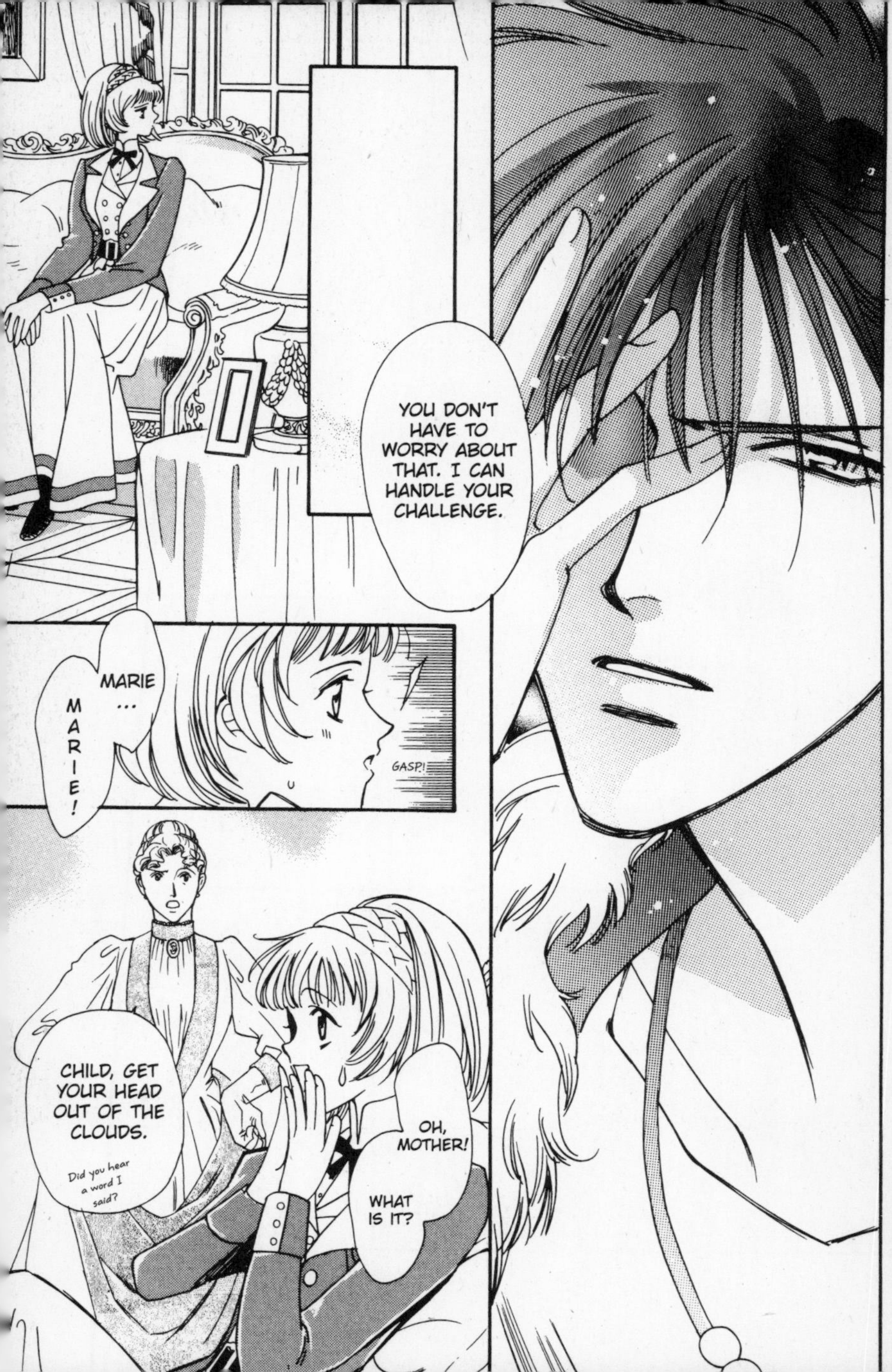
YOU DON'T HAVE TO WORRY ABOUT THAT. I CAN HANDLE YOUR CHALLENGE.
MARIE ...
MARIE!
GASP!
CHILD, GET YOUR HEAD OUT OF THE CLOUDS.
Did you hear a word I said?
OH, MOTHER!
WHAT IS IT?

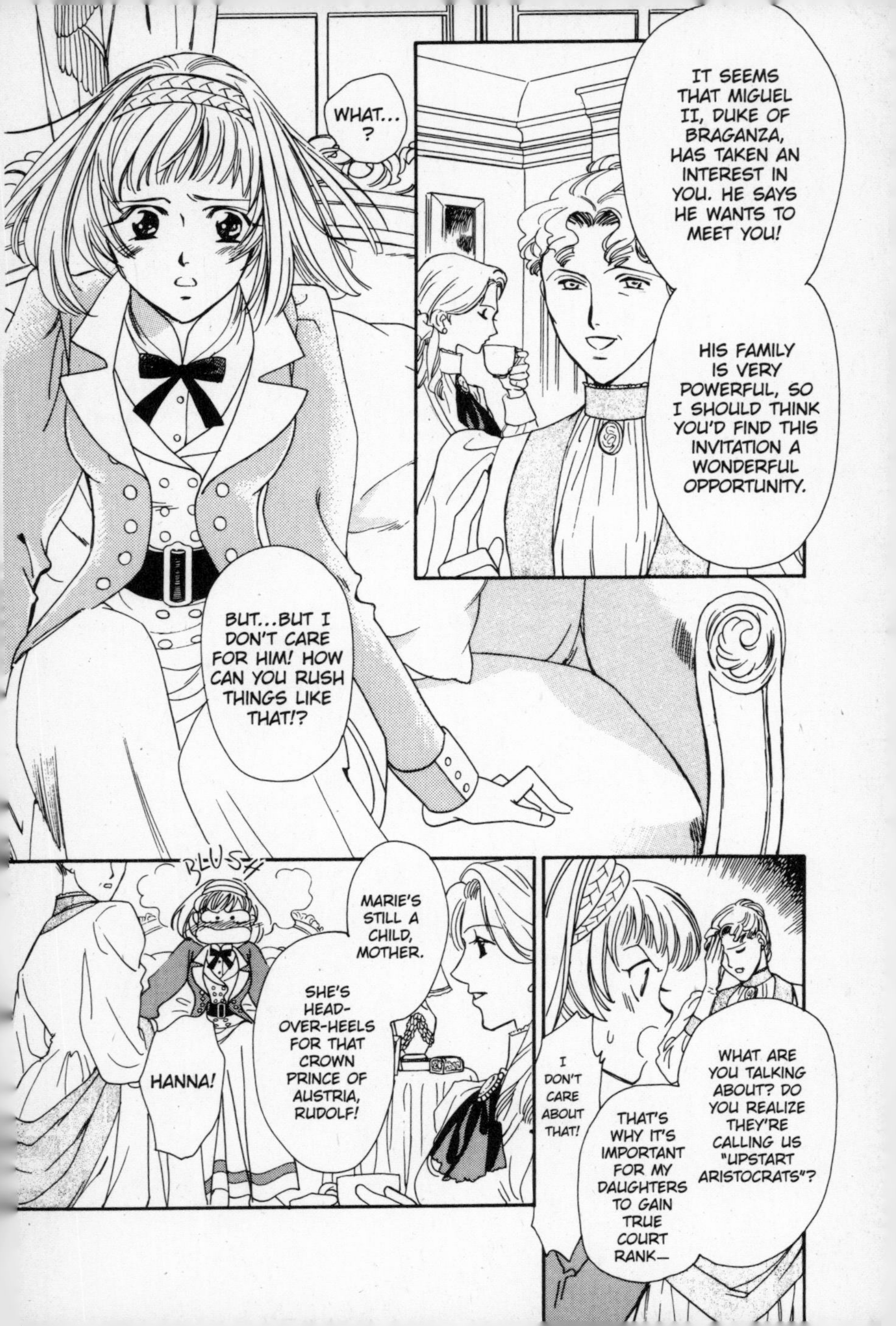
IT SEEMS THAT MIGUEL II, DUKE OF BRAGANZA, HAS TAKEN AN INTEREST IN YOU. HE SAYS HE WANTS TO MEET YOU!
HIS FAMILY IS VERY POWERFUL, SO I SHOULD THINK YOU'D FIND THIS INVITATION A WONDERFUL OPPORTUNITY.
WHAT...?
BUT...BUT I DON'T CARE FOR HIM! HOW CAN YOU RUSH THINGS LIKE THAT!?
WHAT ARE YOU TALKING ABOUT? DO YOU REALIZE THEY'RE CALLING US "UPSTART ARISTOCRATS"?
THAT'S WHY IT'S IMPORTANT FOR MY DAUGHTERS TO GAIN TRUE COURT RANK—
I DON'T CARE ABOUT THAT!
MARIE'S STILL A CHILD, MOTHER.
SHE'S HEAD-OVER-HEELS FOR THAT CROWN PRINCE OF AUSTRIA, RUDOLF!
HANNA!
BLUSH

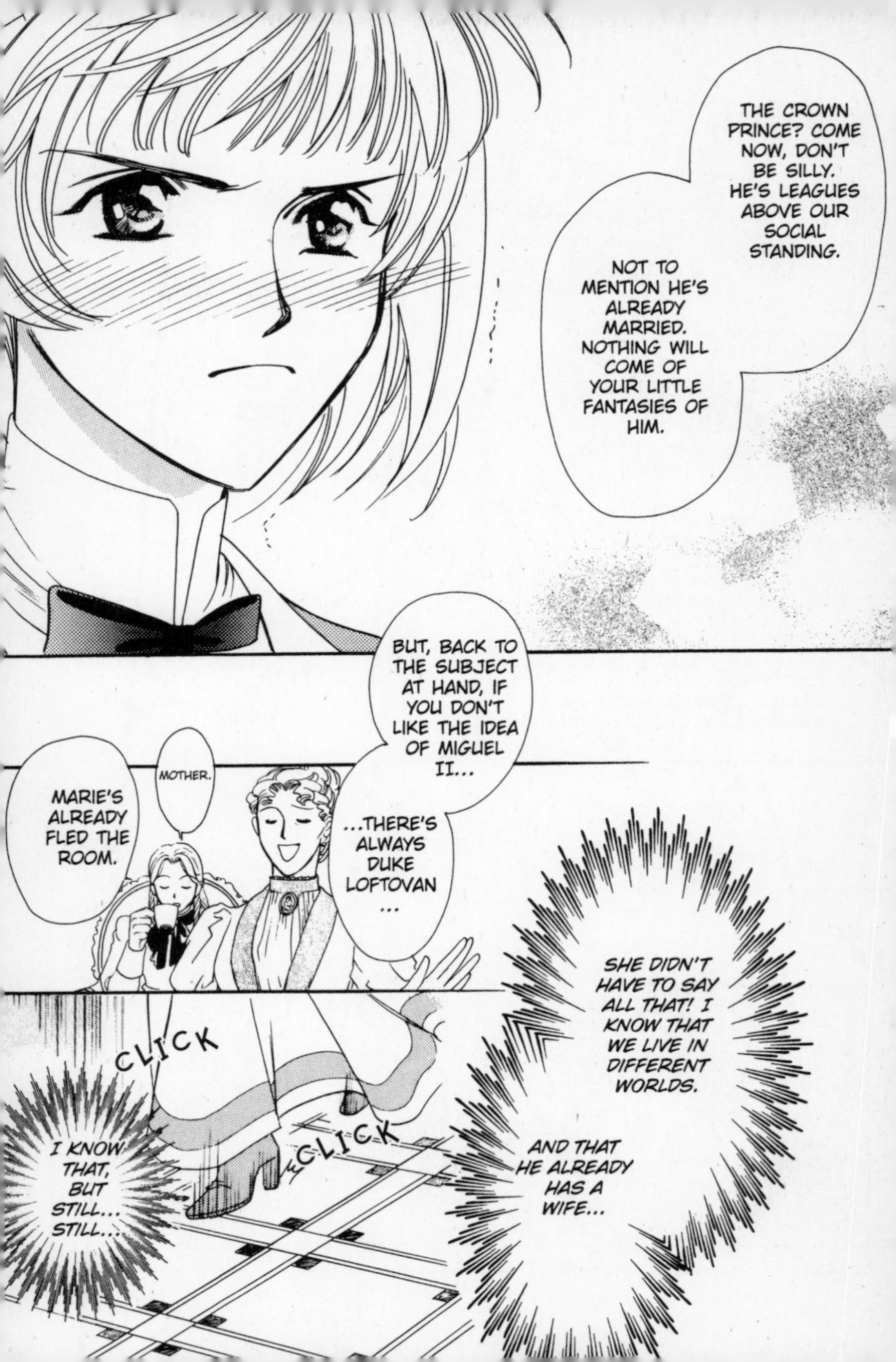
THE CROWN PRINCE? COME NOW, DON'T BE SILLY. HE'S LEAGUES ABOVE OUR SOCIAL STANDING.
NOT TO MENTION HE'S ALREADY MARRIED. NOTHING WILL COME OF YOUR LITTLE FANTASIES OF HIM.
BUT, BACK TO THE SUBJECT AT HAND, IF YOU DON'T LIKE THE IDEA OF MIGUEL II...
...THERE'S ALWAYS DUKE LOFTOVAN...
MOTHER.
MARIE'S ALREADY FLED THE ROOM.
SHE DIDN'T HAVE TO SAY ALL THAT! I KNOW THAT WE LIVE IN DIFFERENT WORLDS.
AND THAT HE ALREADY HAS A WIFE...
CLICK
CLICK
I KNOW THAT, BUT STILL... STILL...

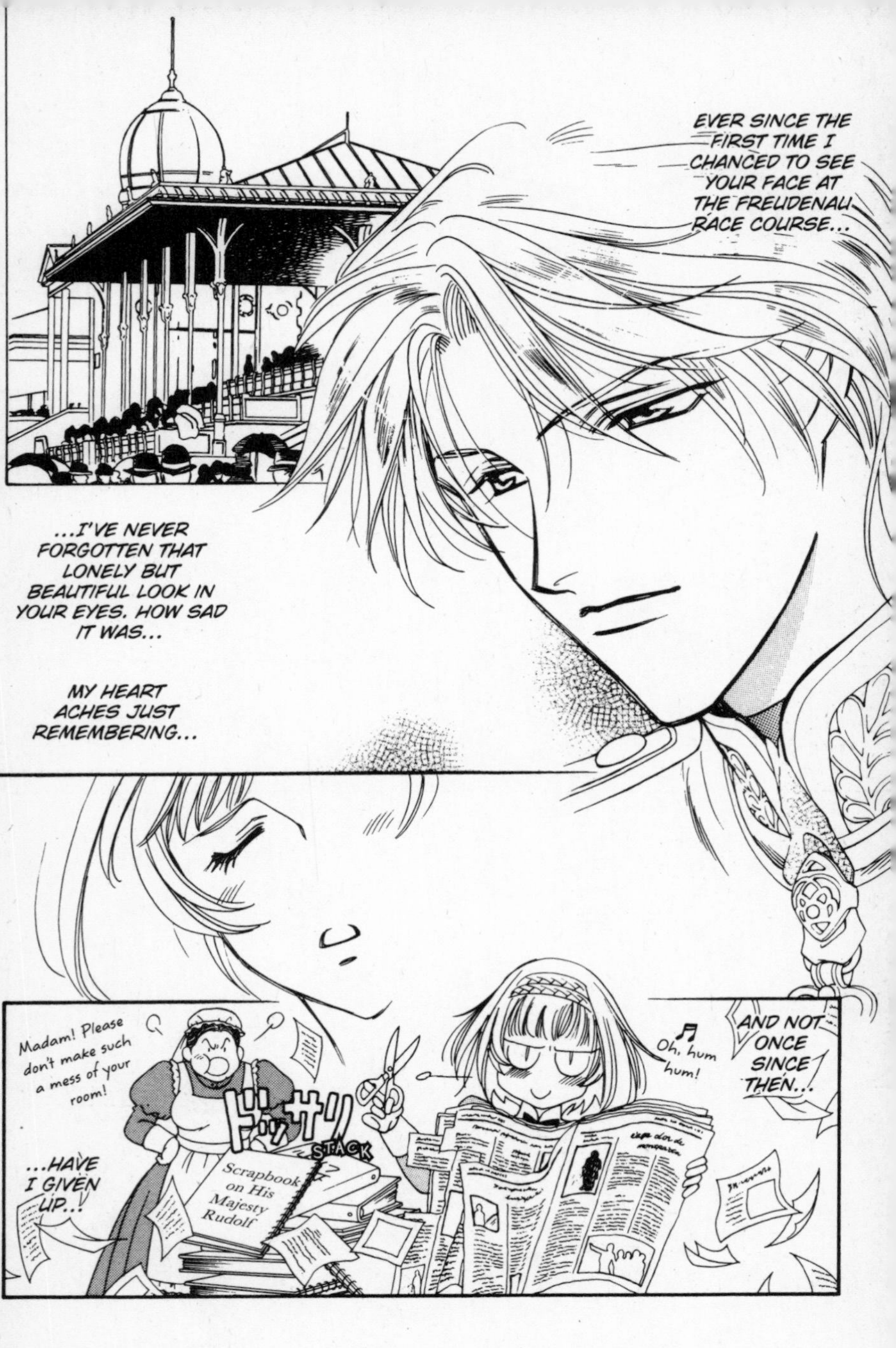
EVER SINCE THE FIRST TIME I CHANCED TO SEE YOUR FACE AT THE FREUDENAU RACE COURSE...
...I'VE NEVER FORGOTTEN THAT LONELY BUT BEAUTIFUL LOOK IN YOUR EYES. HOW SAD IT WAS...
MY HEART ACHES JUST REMEMBERING...
AND NOT ONCE SINCE THEN...
Oh, hum hum!
ドッサリ
STACK
Scrapbook on His Majesty Rudolf
Madam! Please don't make such a mess of your room!
...HAVE I GIVEN UP...!

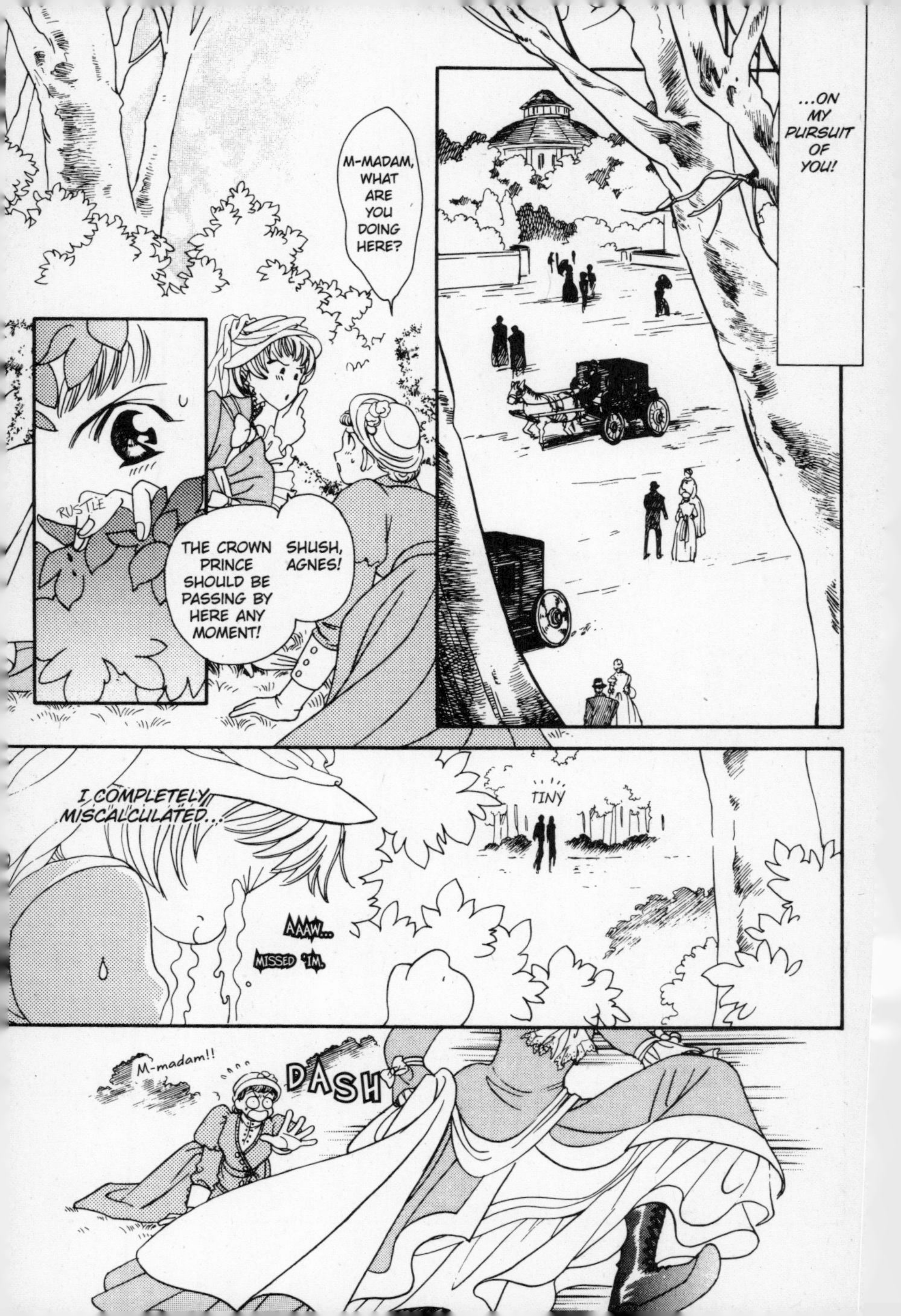
...ON MY PURSUIT OF YOU!
M-MADAM, WHAT ARE YOU DOING HERE?
SHUSH, AGNES!
THE CROWN PRINCE SHOULD BE PASSING BY HERE ANY MOMENT!
RUSTLE
TINY
I COMPLETELY MISCALCULATED...
AAAW...
MISSED 'IM.
DASH
M-madam!!

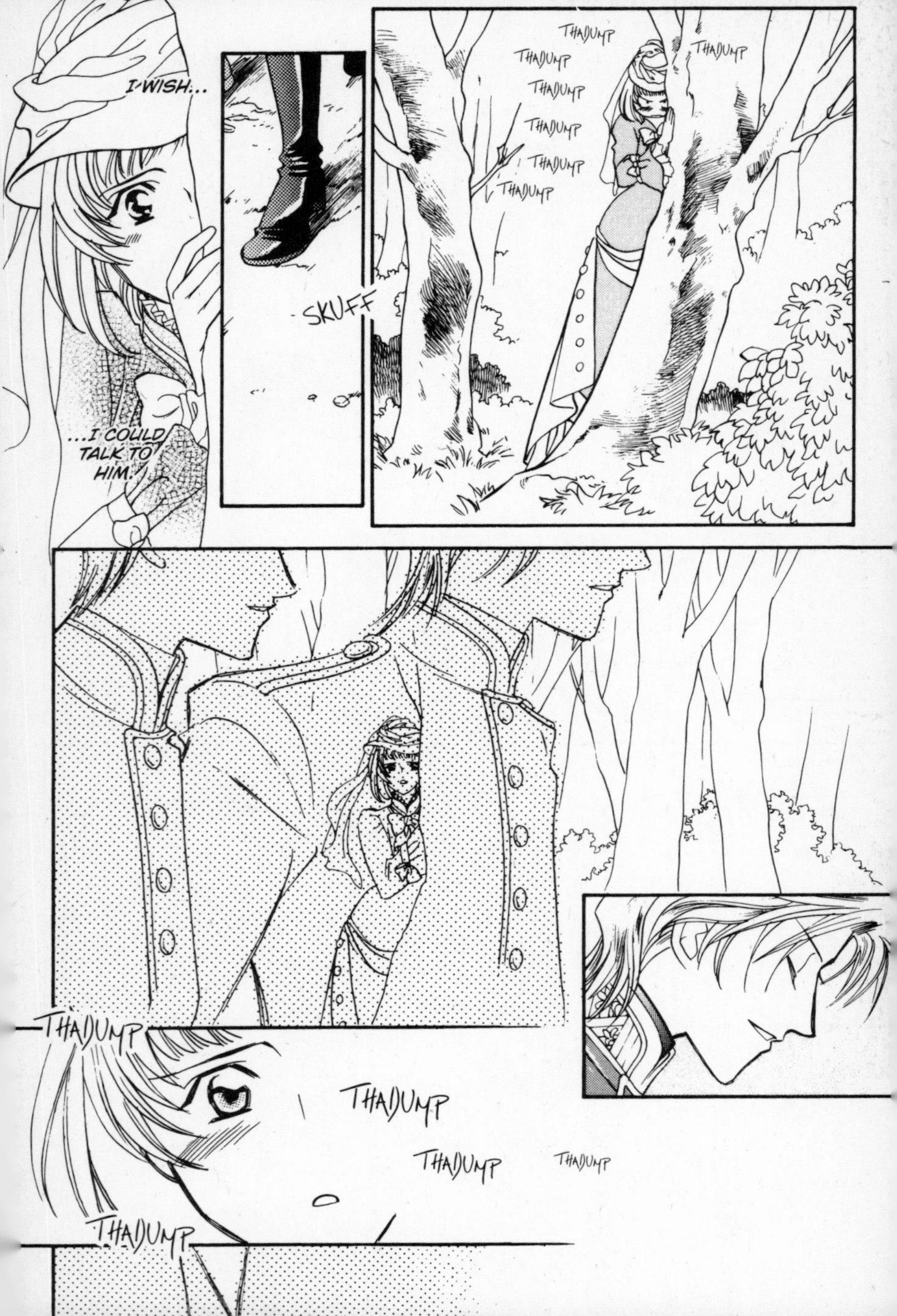
THADUMP
THADUMP
THADUMP
THADUMP
THADUMP
THADUMP
THADUMP
SKUFF
I WISH...
...I COULD TALK TO HIM.
THADUMP
THADUMP
THADUMP
THADUMP
THADUMP

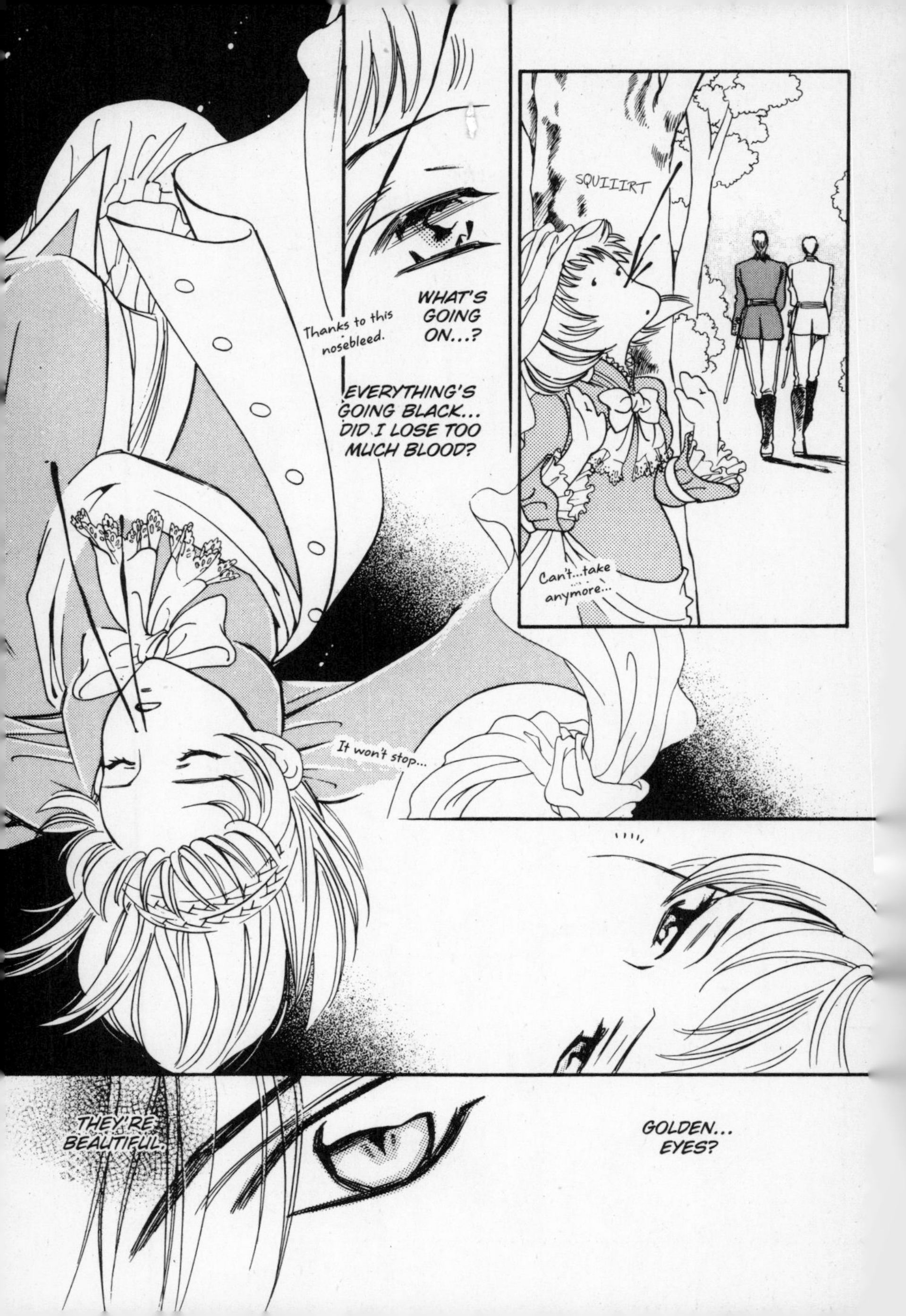
SQUIIIRT
Can't...take anymore...
WHAT'S GOING ON...?
Thanks to this nosebleed.
EVERYTHING'S GOING BLACK... DID I LOSE TOO MUCH BLOOD?
It won't stop...
GOLDEN... EYES?
THEY'RE BEAUTIFUL.

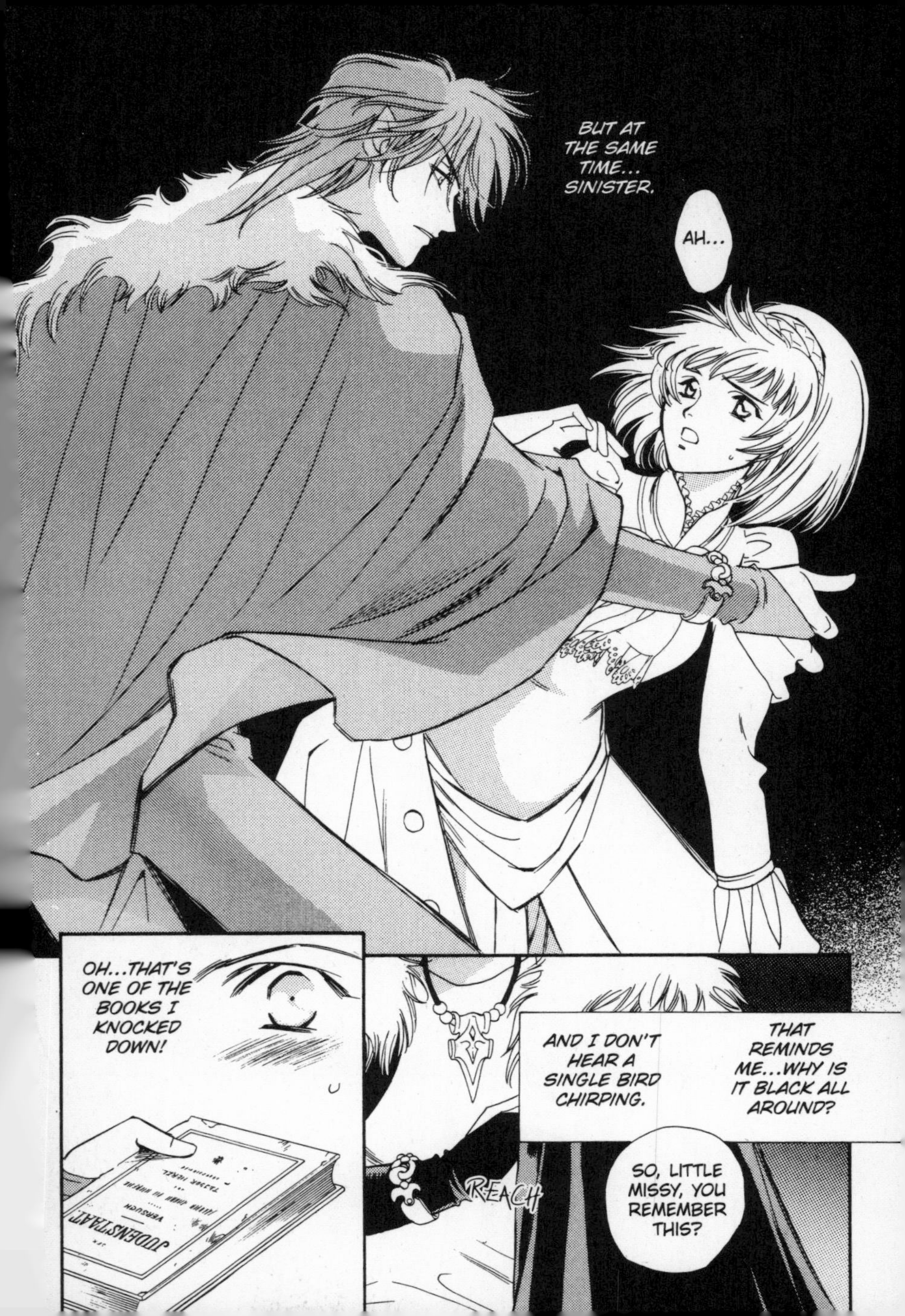
BUT AT THE SAME TIME... SINISTER.
AH...
THAT REMINDS ME...WHY IS IT BLACK ALL AROUND?
AND I DON'T HEAR A SINGLE BIRD CHIRPING.
SO, LITTLE MISSY, YOU REMEMBER THIS?
REACH
OH...THAT'S ONE OF THE BOOKS I KNOCKED DOWN!
JUDENSTAAT.
VERSUCH

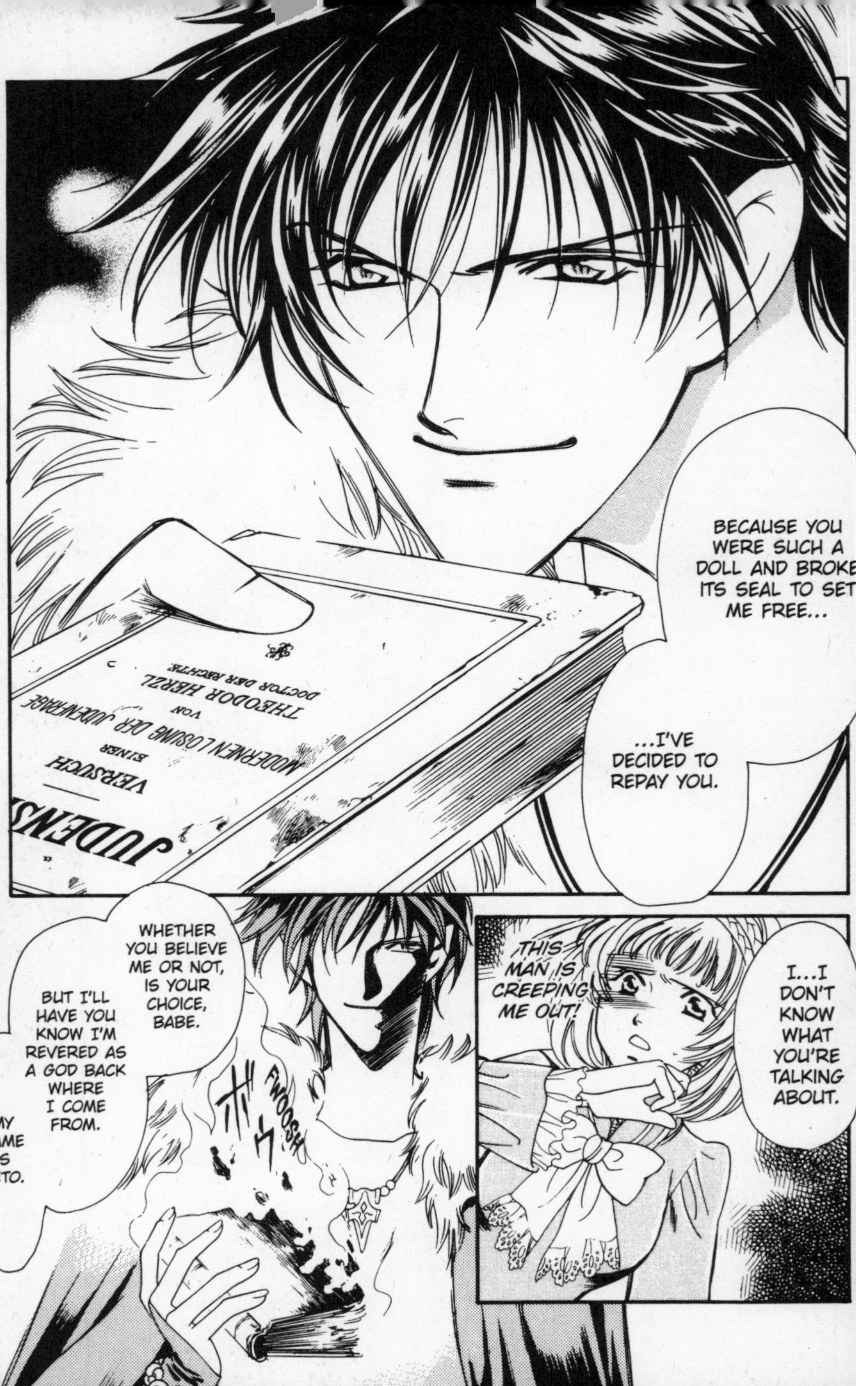
BECAUSE YOU WERE SUCH A DOLL AND BROKE ITS SEAL TO SET ME FREE...
...I'VE DECIDED TO REPAY YOU.
VERSUCH
EINER
MODERNEN LÖSUNG DER JUDENFRAGE
VON
THEODOR HERZL
DOCTOR DER RECHTE
I...I DON'T KNOW WHAT YOU'RE TALKING ABOUT.
THIS MAN IS CREEPING ME OUT!
WHETHER YOU BELIEVE ME OR NOT, IS YOUR CHOICE, BABE.
BUT I'LL HAVE YOU KNOW I'M REVERED AS A GOD BACK WHERE I COME FROM.
MY NAME IS SETO.
FWOOSH

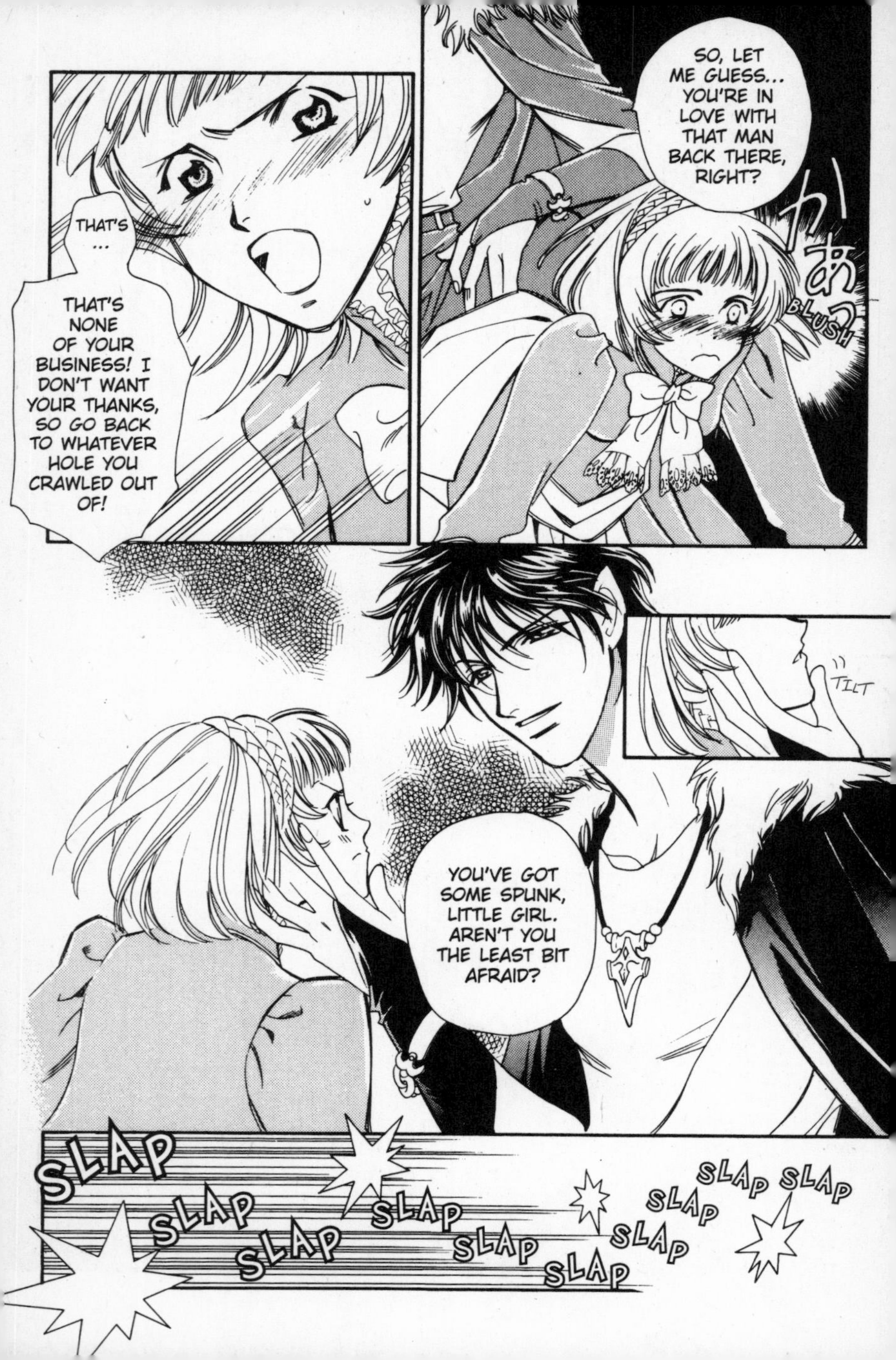

SO, LET ME GUESS... YOU'RE IN LOVE WITH THAT MAN BACK THERE, RIGHT?
かあっ
BLUSH
THAT'S ...
THAT'S NONE OF YOUR BUSINESS! I DON'T WANT YOUR THANKS, SO GO BACK TO WHATEVER HOLE YOU CRAWLED OUT OF!
TILT
YOU'VE GOT SOME SPUNK, LITTLE GIRL. AREN'T YOU THE LEAST BIT AFRAID?
SLAP SLAP SLAP SLAP SLAP SLAP SLAP SLAP SLAP SLAP

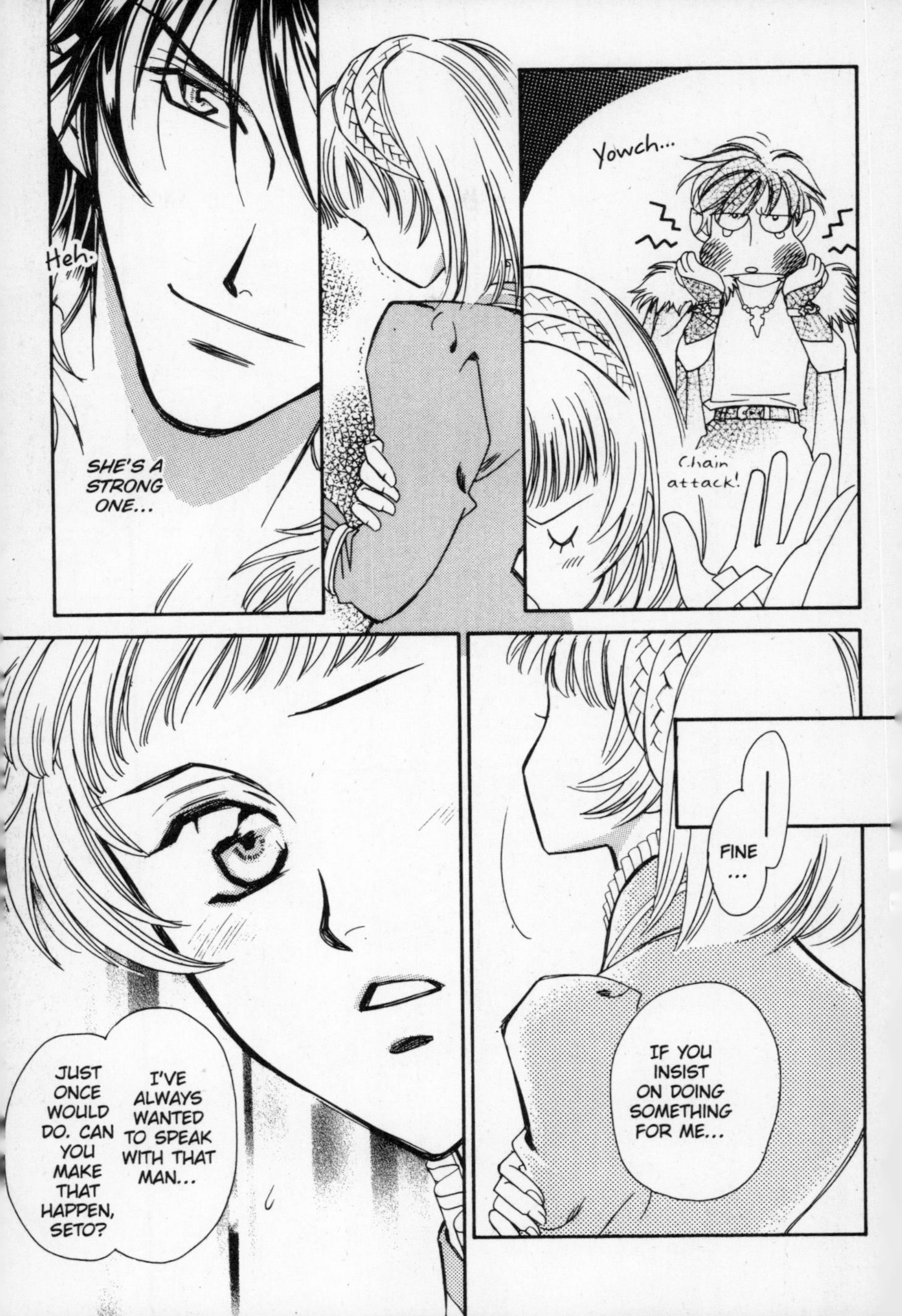
Yowch...
Chain attack!
Heh.
SHE'S A STRONG ONE...
FINE ...
IF YOU INSIST ON DOING SOMETHING FOR ME...
I'VE ALWAYS WANTED TO SPEAK WITH THAT MAN...
JUST ONCE WOULD DO. CAN YOU MAKE THAT HAPPEN, SETO?

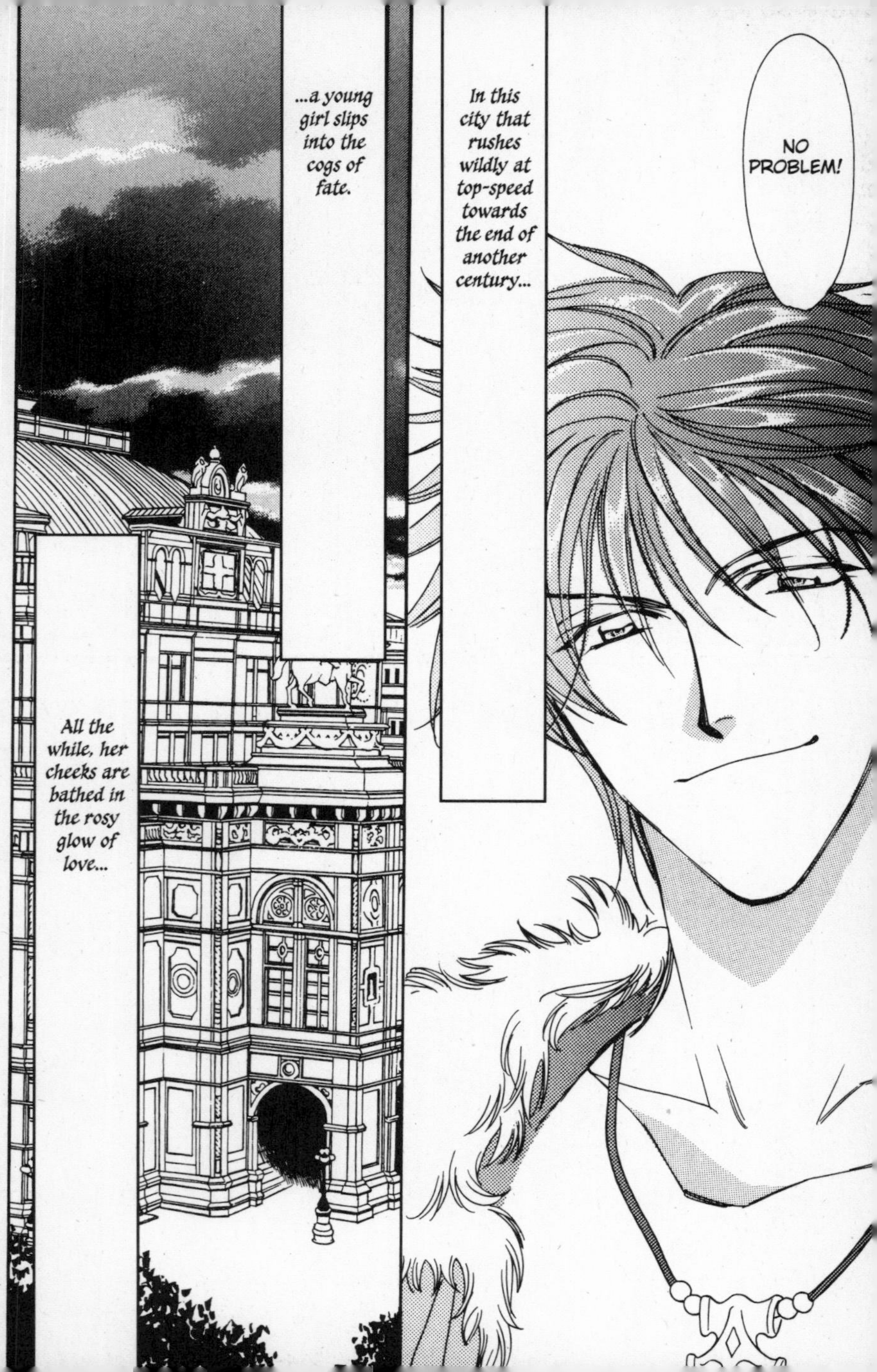
NO PROBLEM!
In this city that rushes wildly at top-speed towards the end of another century...
...a young girl slips into the cogs of fate.
All the while, her cheeks are bathed in the rosy glow of love...

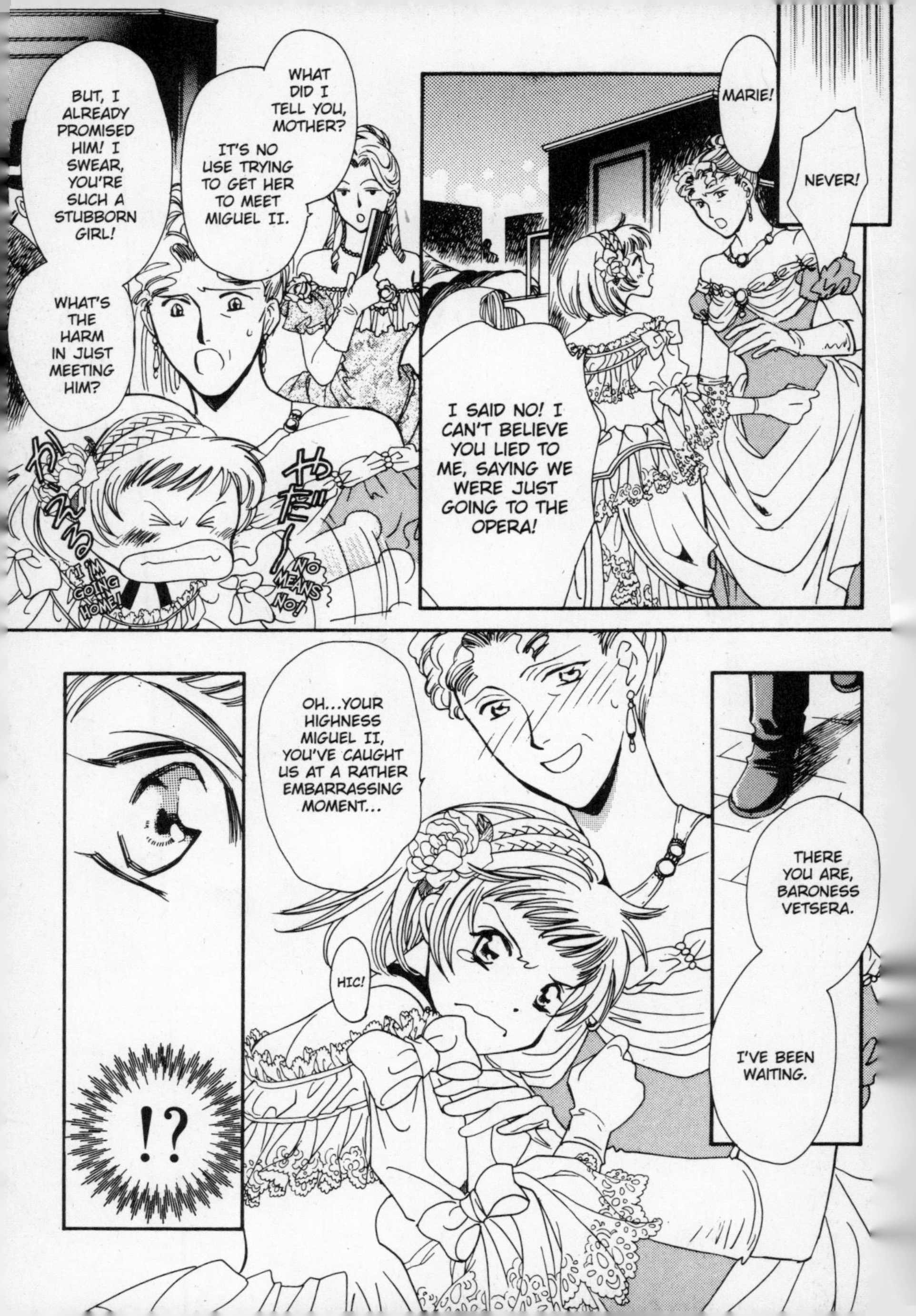
MARIE!
NEVER!
I SAID NO! I CAN'T BELIEVE YOU LIED TO ME, SAYING WE WERE JUST GOING TO THE OPERA!
WHAT DID I TELL YOU, MOTHER?
IT'S NO USE TRYING TO GET HER TO MEET MIGUEL II.
BUT, I ALREADY PROMISED HIM! I SWEAR, YOU'RE SUCH A STUBBORN GIRL!
WHAT'S THE HARM IN JUST MEETING HIM?
やだー
NO MEANS NO!
かえる
I'M GOING HOME!
THERE YOU ARE, BARONESS VETSERA.
I'VE BEEN WAITING.
OH...YOUR HIGHNESS MIGUEL II, YOU'VE CAUGHT US AT A RATHER EMBARRASSING MOMENT...
HIC!
!?

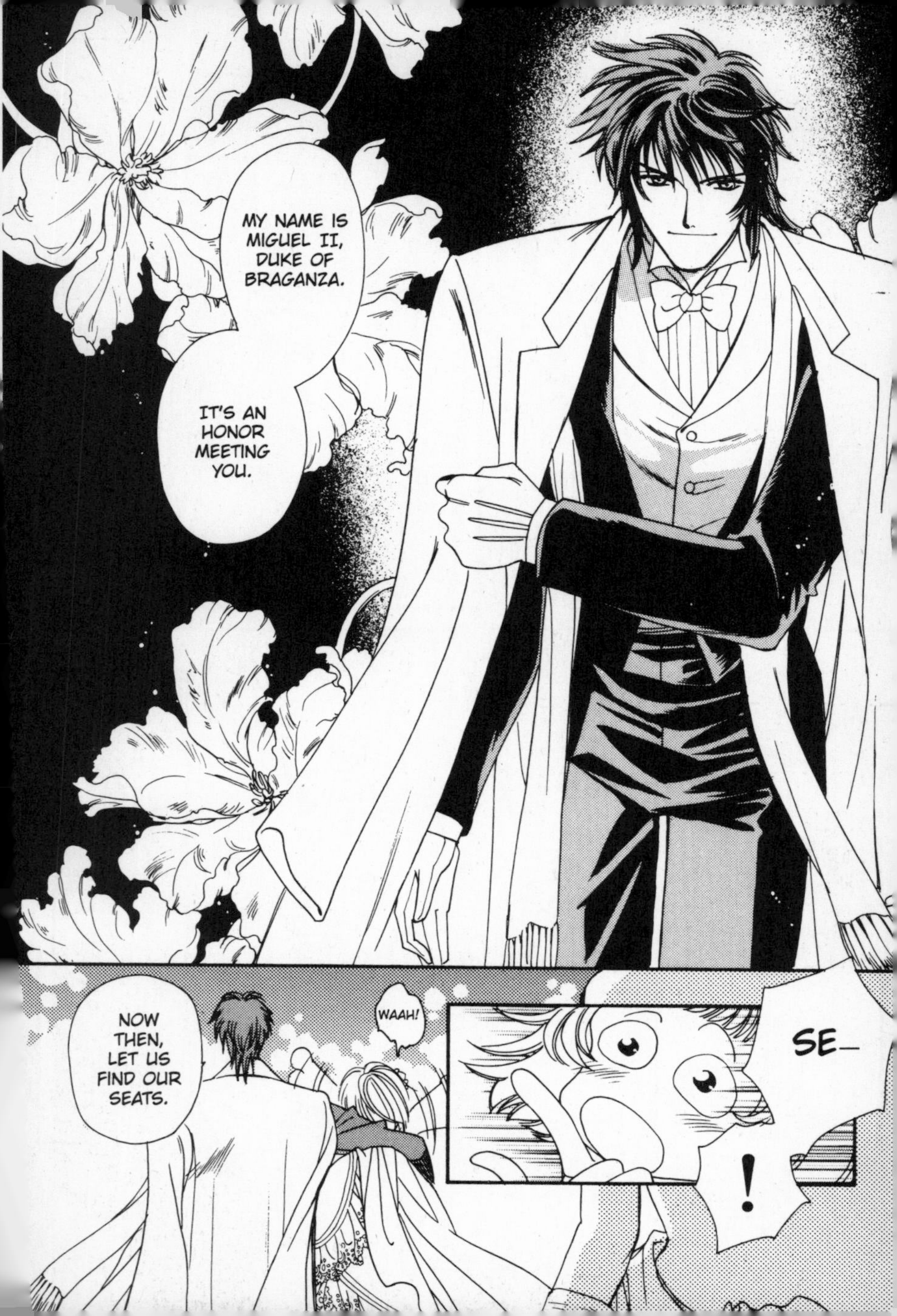
MY NAME IS MIGUEL II, DUKE OF BRAGANZA.
IT'S AN HONOR MEETING YOU.
SE–
!
WAAH!
NOW THEN, LET US FIND OUR SEATS.

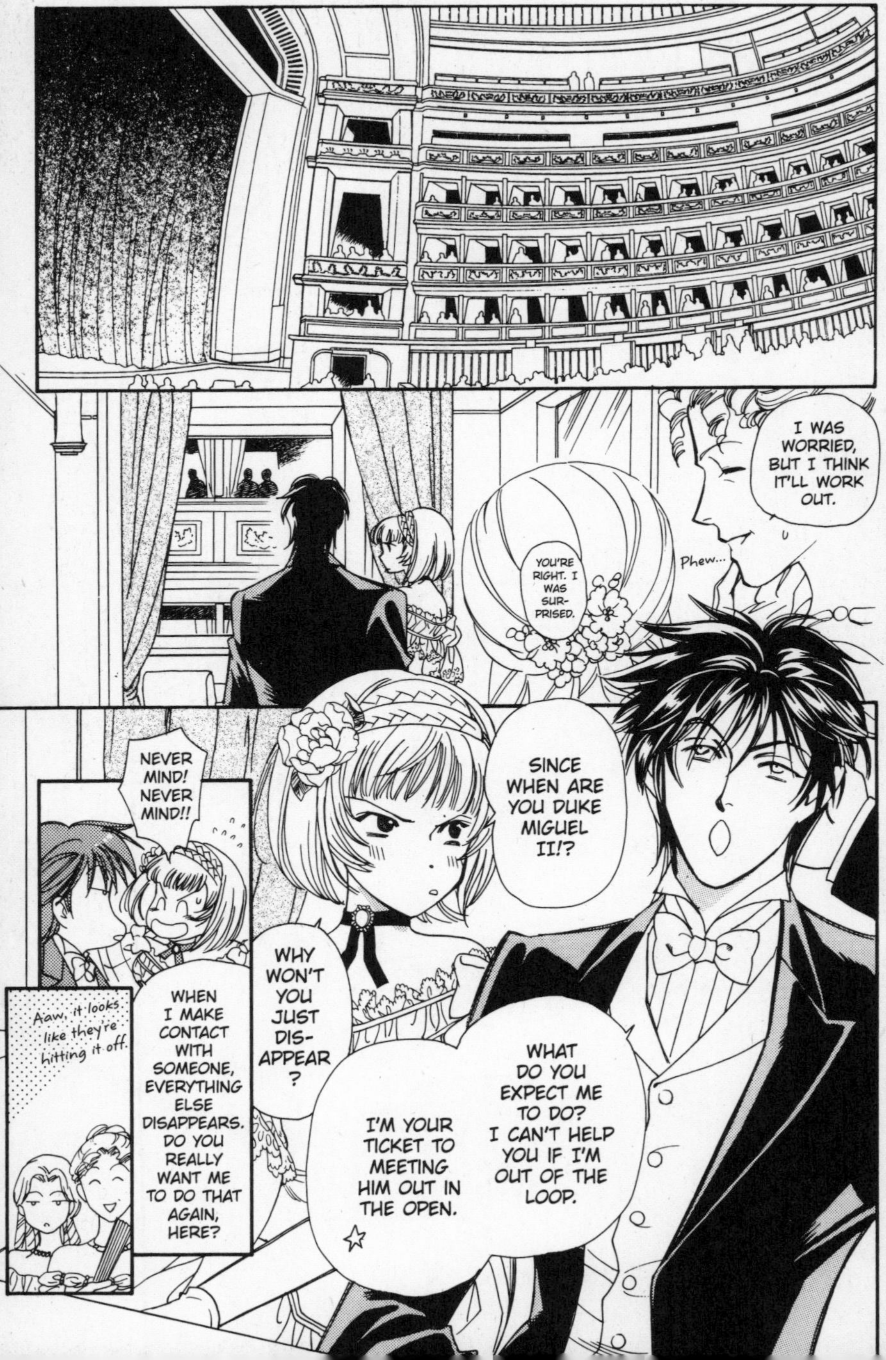
I WAS WORRIED, BUT I THINK IT'LL WORK OUT.
Phew...
YOU'RE RIGHT. I WAS SURPRISED.
SINCE WHEN ARE YOU DUKE MIGUEL II!?
WHY WON'T YOU JUST DISAPPEAR?
WHAT DO YOU EXPECT ME TO DO? I CAN'T HELP YOU IF I'M OUT OF THE LOOP.
I'M YOUR TICKET TO MEETING HIM OUT IN THE OPEN.
WHEN I MAKE CONTACT WITH SOMEONE, EVERYTHING ELSE DISAPPEARS. DO YOU REALLY WANT ME TO DO THAT AGAIN, HERE?
NEVER MIND! NEVER MIND!!
Aaw, it looks like they're hitting it off.

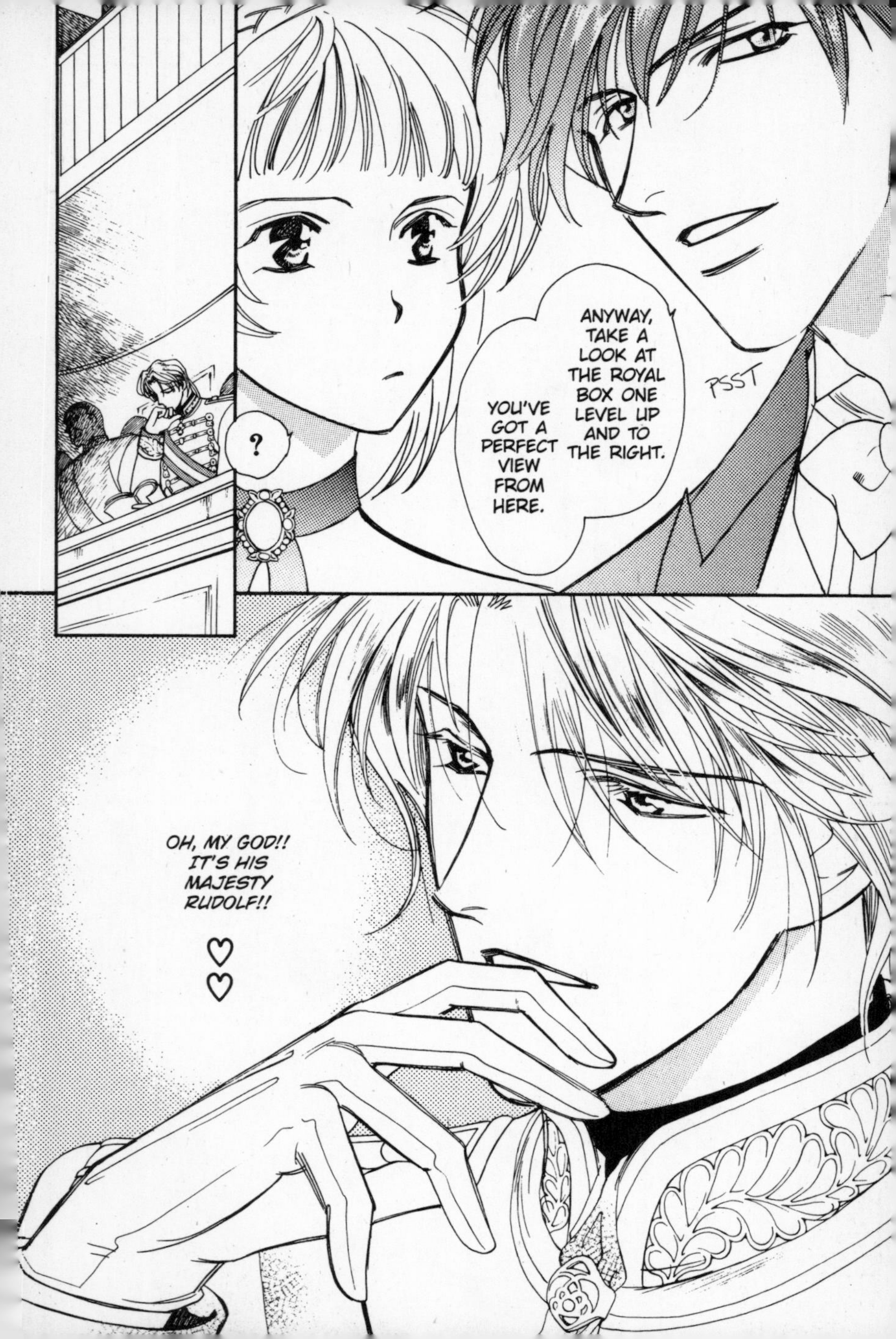
PSST
ANYWAY, TAKE A LOOK AT THE ROYAL BOX ONE LEVEL UP AND TO THE RIGHT.
YOU'VE GOT A PERFECT VIEW FROM HERE.
?
OH, MY GOD!! IT'S HIS MAJESTY RUDOLF!!
♡ ♡

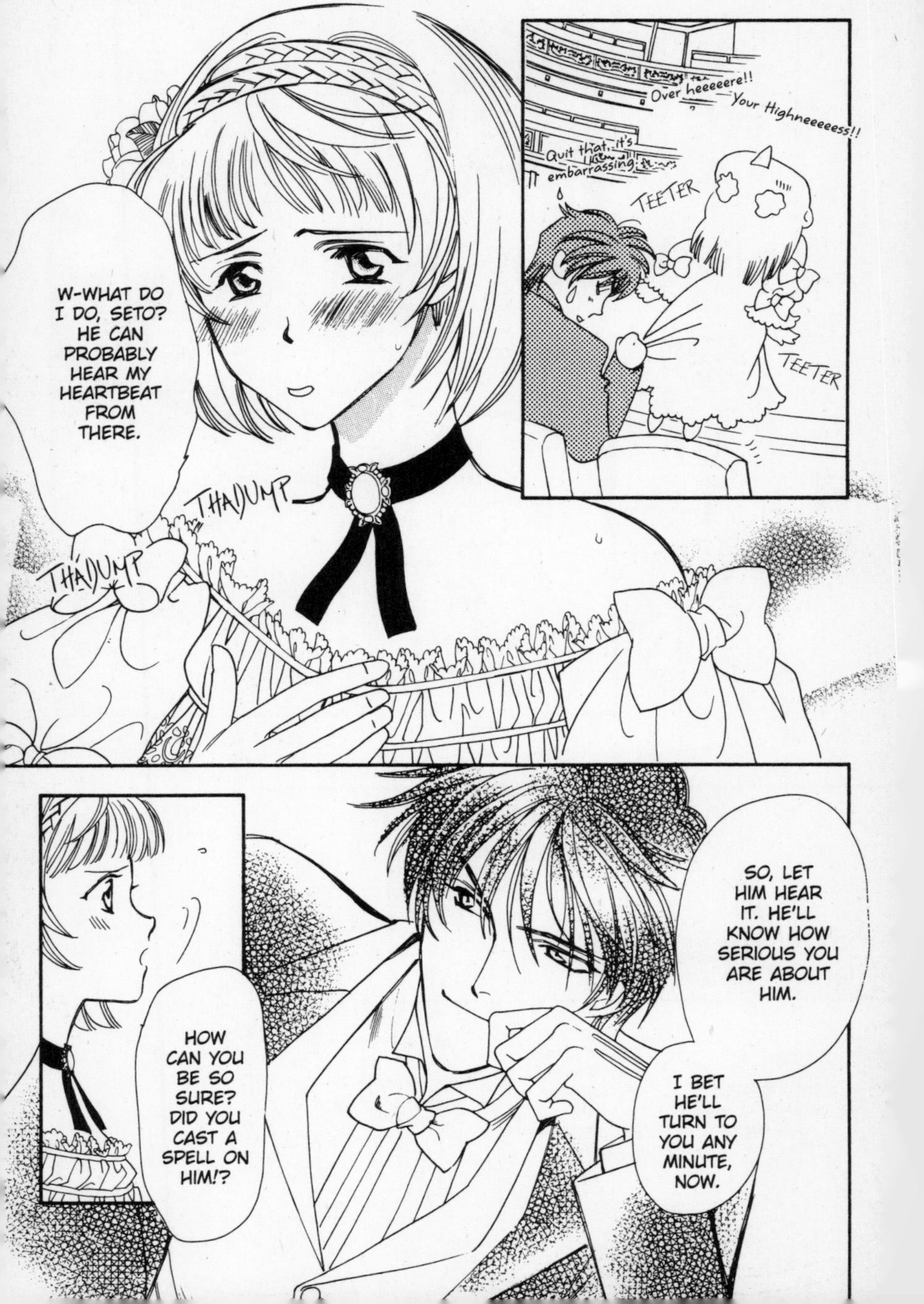
Over heeeeere!!
Your Highneeeeess!!
Quit that, it's embarrassing.
TEETER
TEETER
W-WHAT DO I DO, SETO? HE CAN PROBABLY HEAR MY HEARTBEAT FROM THERE.
THADUMP
THADUMP
SO, LET HIM HEAR IT. HE'LL KNOW HOW SERIOUS YOU ARE ABOUT HIM.
HOW CAN YOU BE SO SURE? DID YOU CAST A SPELL ON HIM!?
I BET HE'LL TURN TO YOU ANY MINUTE, NOW.

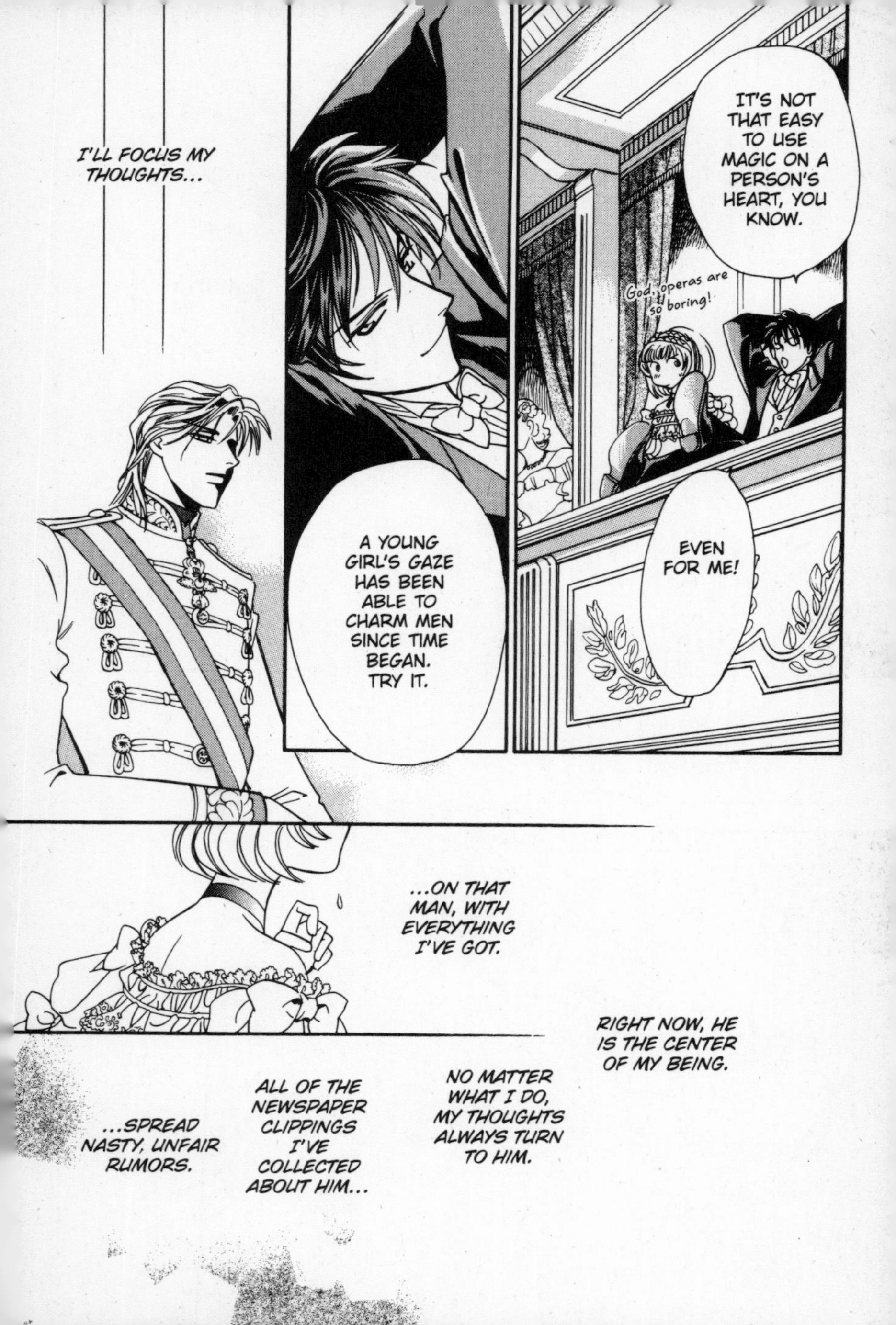
IT'S NOT THAT EASY TO USE MAGIC ON A PERSON'S HEART, YOU KNOW.
God, operas are so boring!
EVEN FOR ME!
A YOUNG GIRL'S GAZE HAS BEEN ABLE TO CHARM MEN SINCE TIME BEGAN. TRY IT.
I'LL FOCUS MY THOUGHTS...
...ON THAT MAN, WITH EVERYTHING I'VE GOT.
RIGHT NOW, HE IS THE CENTER OF MY BEING.
NO MATTER WHAT I DO, MY THOUGHTS ALWAYS TURN TO HIM.
ALL OF THE NEWSPAPER CLIPPINGS I'VE COLLECTED ABOUT HIM...
...SPREAD NASTY, UNFAIR RUMORS.

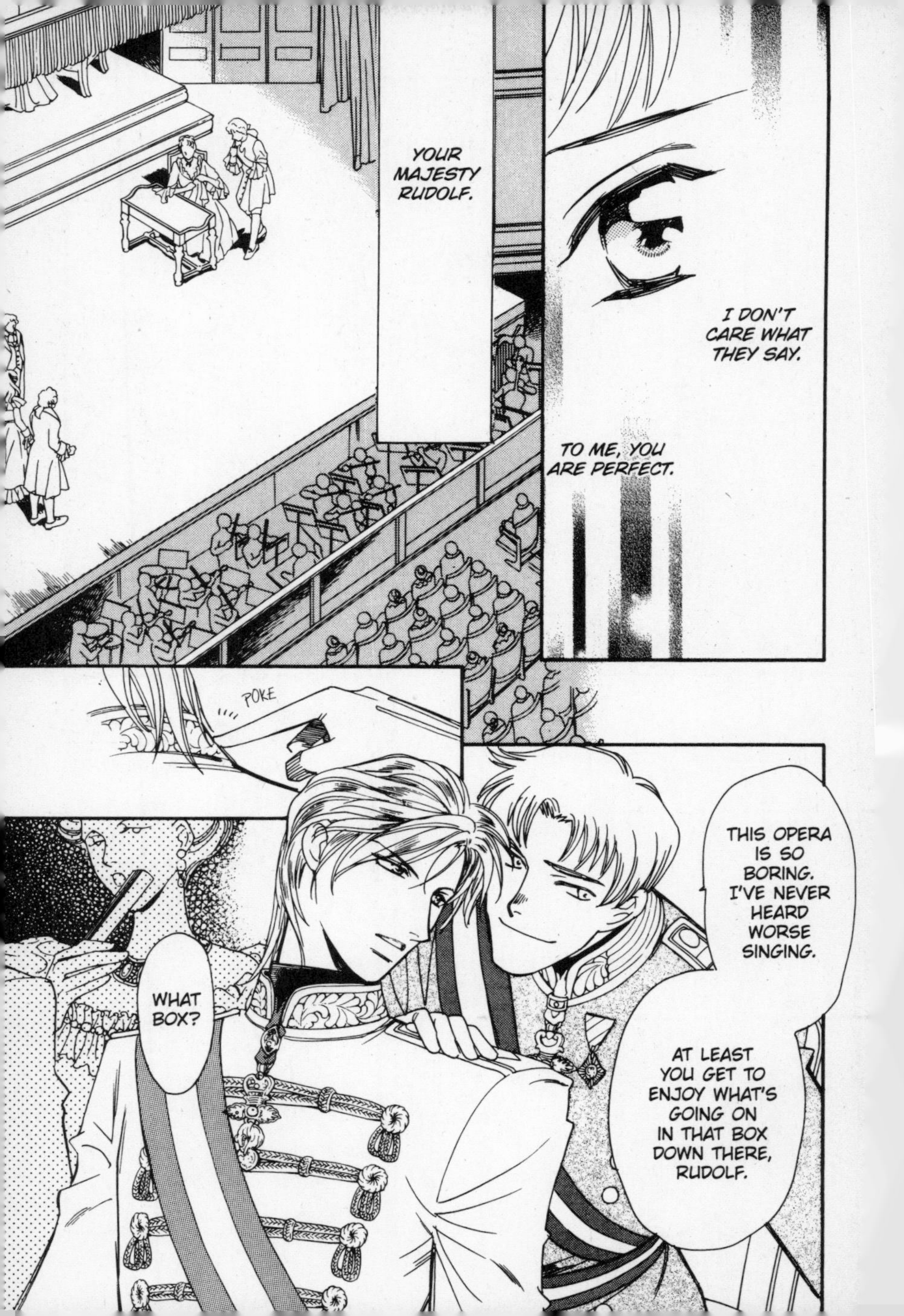

I DON'T CARE WHAT THEY SAY.
TO ME, YOU ARE PERFECT.
YOUR MAJESTY RUDOLF.
POKE
THIS OPERA IS SO BORING. I'VE NEVER HEARD WORSE SINGING.
AT LEAST YOU GET TO ENJOY WHAT'S GOING ON IN THAT BOX DOWN THERE, RUDOLF.
WHAT BOX?

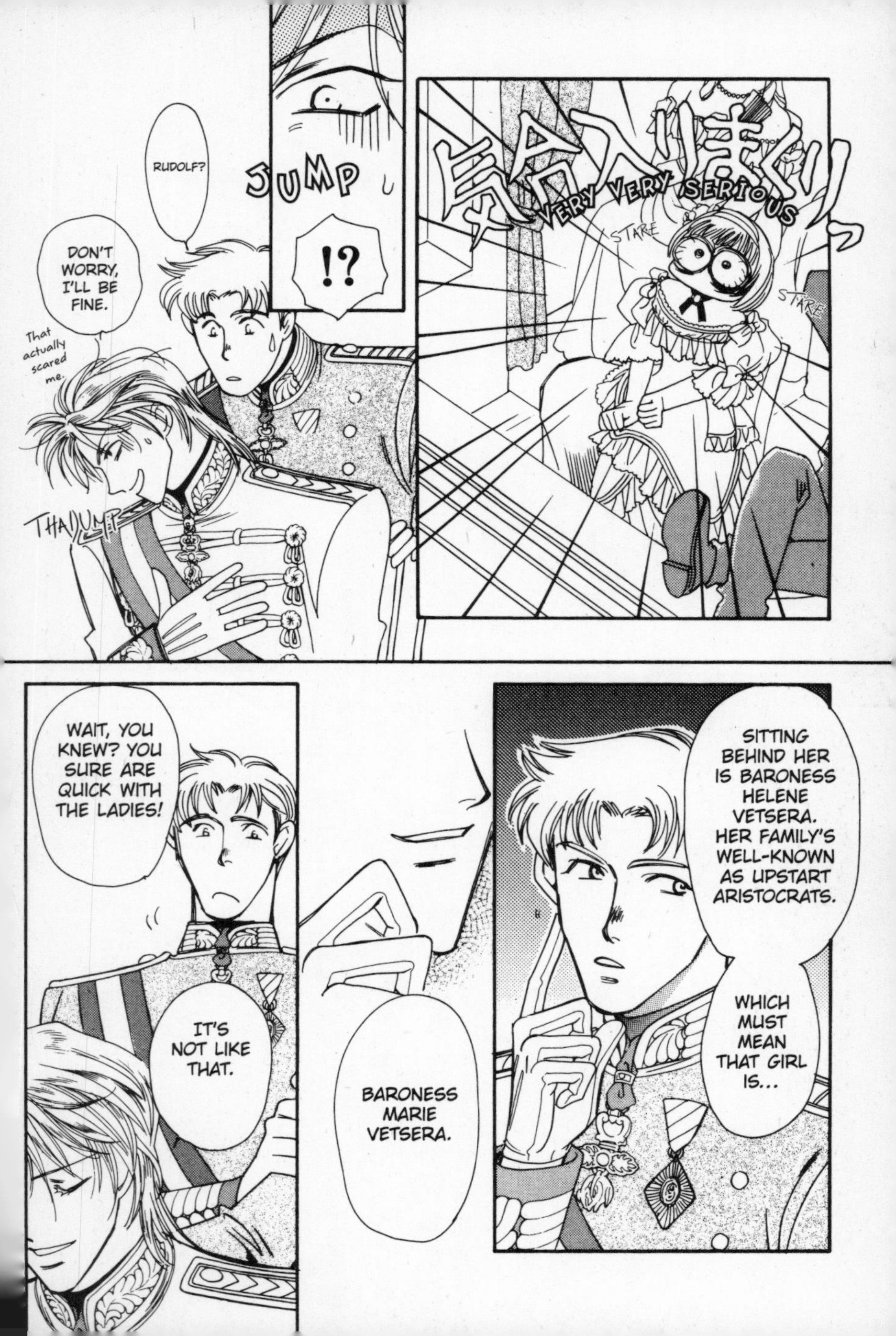
VERY VERY SERIOUS
STARE
STARE
JUMP
!?
RUDOLF?
DON'T WORRY, I'LL BE FINE.
That actually scared me.
THADUMP
SITTING BEHIND HER IS BARONESS HELENE VETSERA. HER FAMILY'S WELL-KNOWN AS UPSTART ARISTOCRATS.
WHICH MUST MEAN THAT GIRL IS...
BARONESS MARIE VETSERA.
WAIT, YOU KNEW? YOU SURE ARE QUICK WITH THE LADIES!
IT'S NOT LIKE THAT.

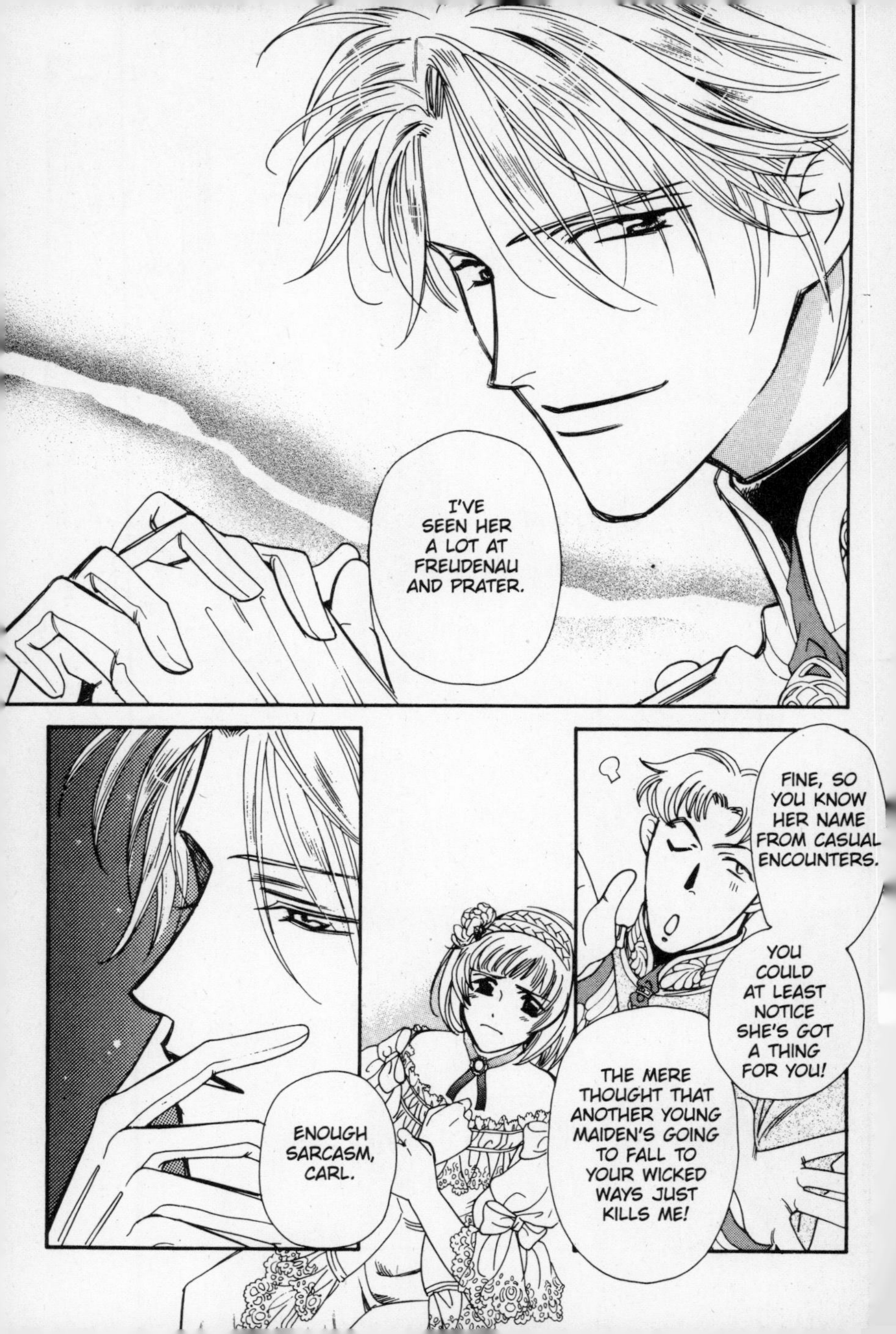
I'VE SEEN HER A LOT AT FREUDENAU AND PRATER.
FINE, SO YOU KNOW HER NAME FROM CASUAL ENCOUNTERS.
YOU COULD AT LEAST NOTICE SHE'S GOT A THING FOR YOU!
THE MERE THOUGHT THAT ANOTHER YOUNG MAIDEN'S GOING TO FALL TO YOUR WICKED WAYS JUST KILLS ME!
ENOUGH SARCASM, CARL.

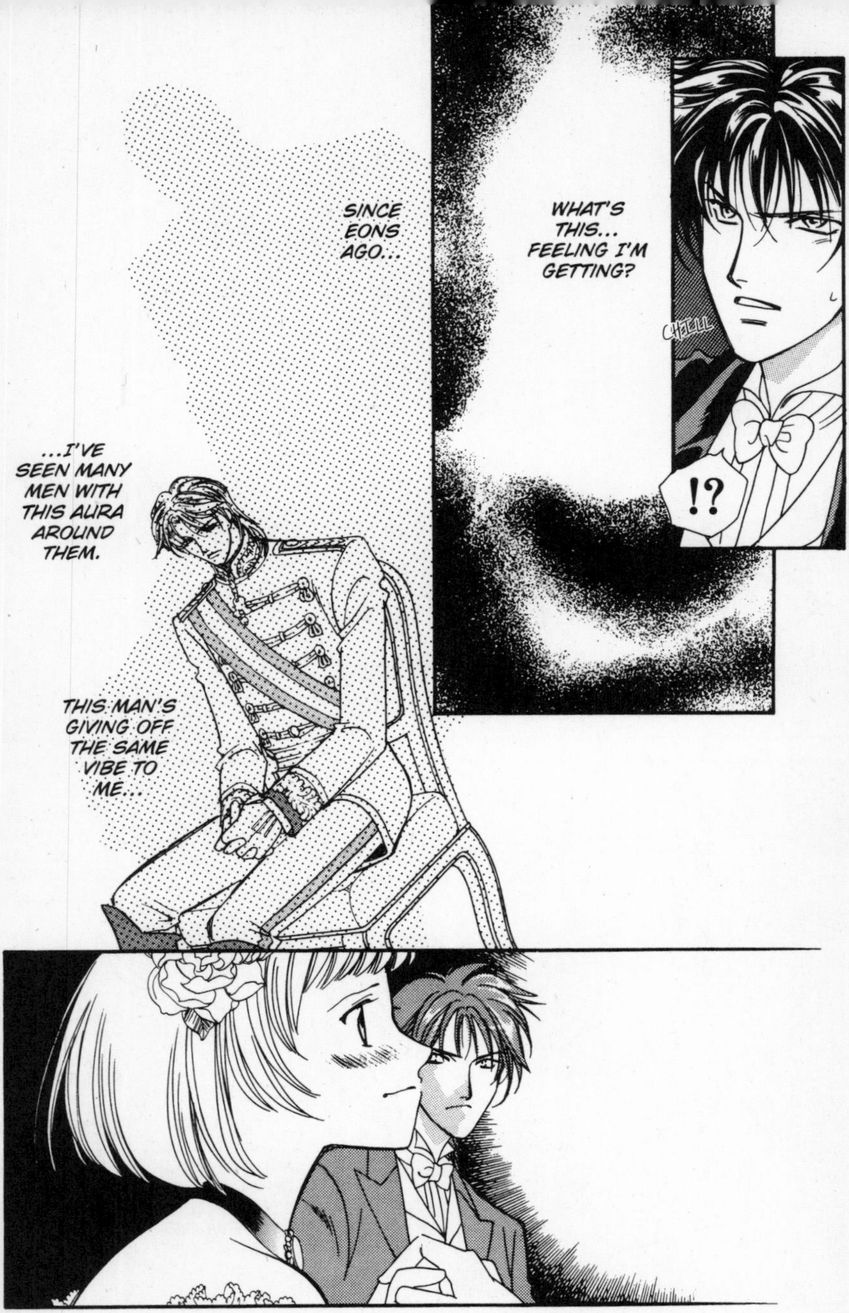
WHAT'S THIS... FEELING I'M GETTING?
CHILL
!?
SINCE EONS AGO...
...I'VE SEEN MANY MEN WITH THIS AURA AROUND THEM.
THIS MAN'S GIVING OFF THE SAME VIBE TO ME...

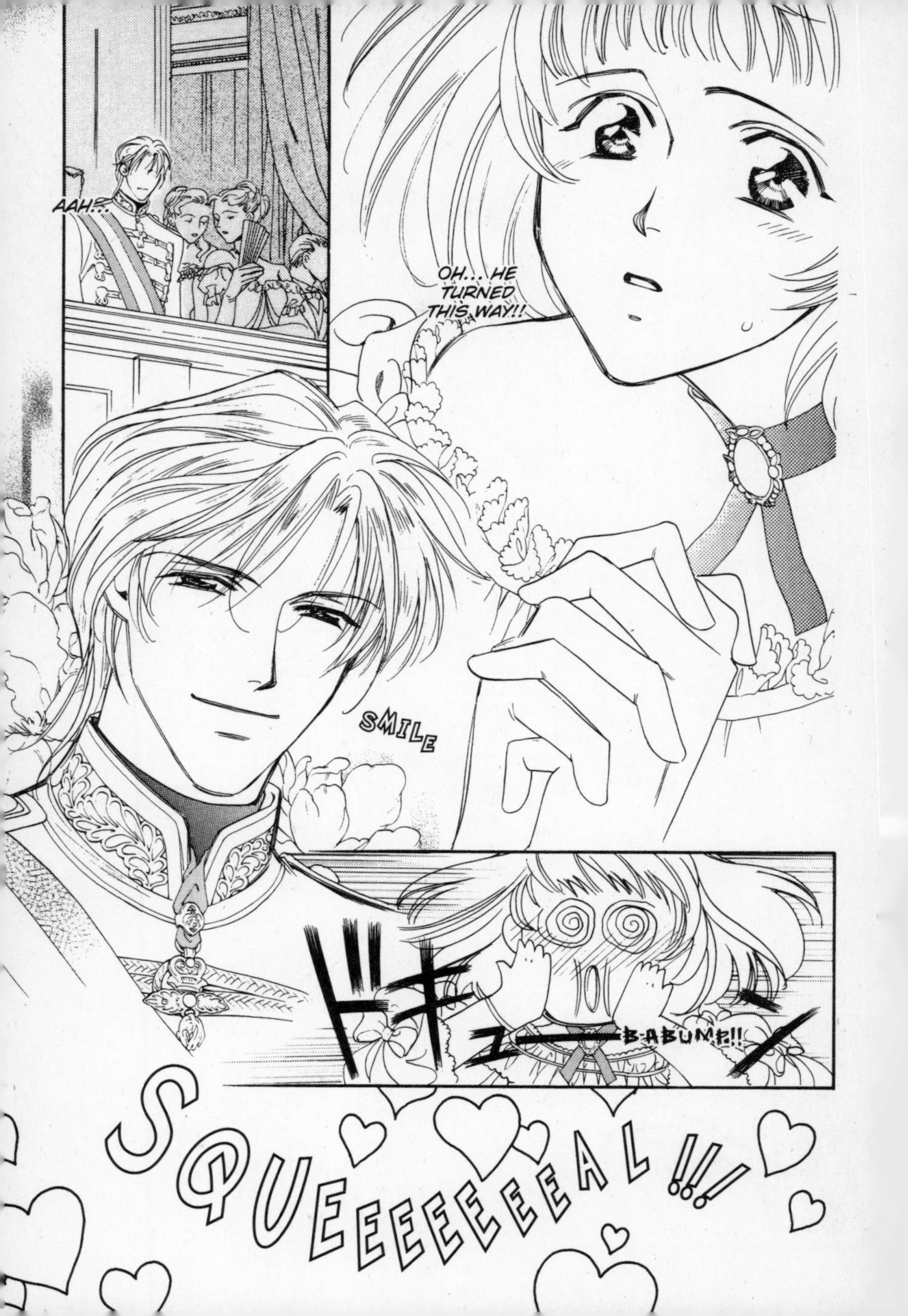
OH... HE TURNED THIS WAY!!
AAH...
SMILE
B-ABUMP!!
SQUEEEEEEEAL!!!

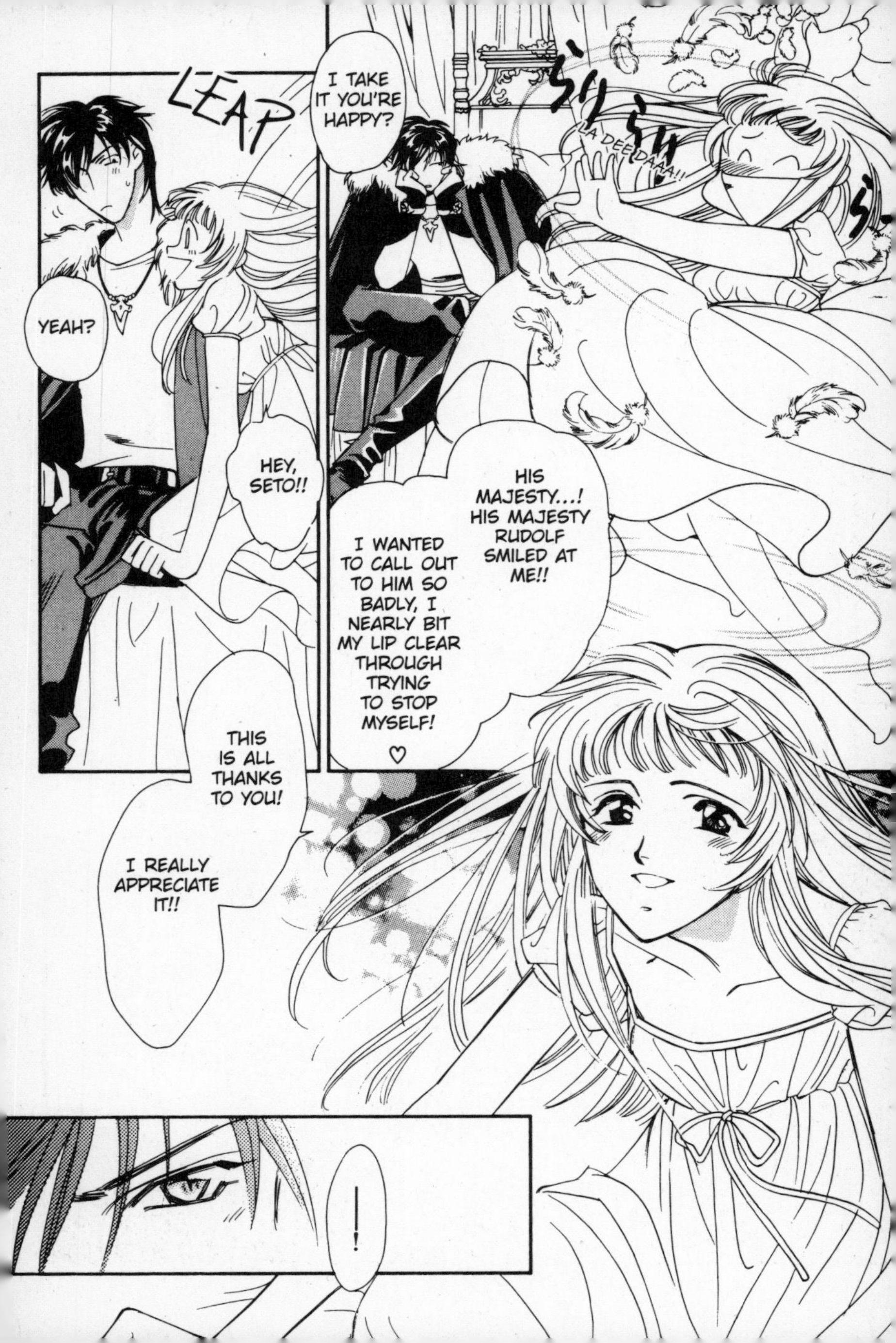
LA DEE DAAA!!
I TAKE IT YOU'RE HAPPY?
HIS MAJESTY...! HIS MAJESTY RUDOLF SMILED AT ME!!
I WANTED TO CALL OUT TO HIM SO BADLY, I NEARLY BIT MY LIP CLEAR THROUGH TRYING TO STOP MYSELF! ♡
LEAP
HEY, SETO!!
YEAH?
THIS IS ALL THANKS TO YOU!
I REALLY APPRECIATE IT!!
!

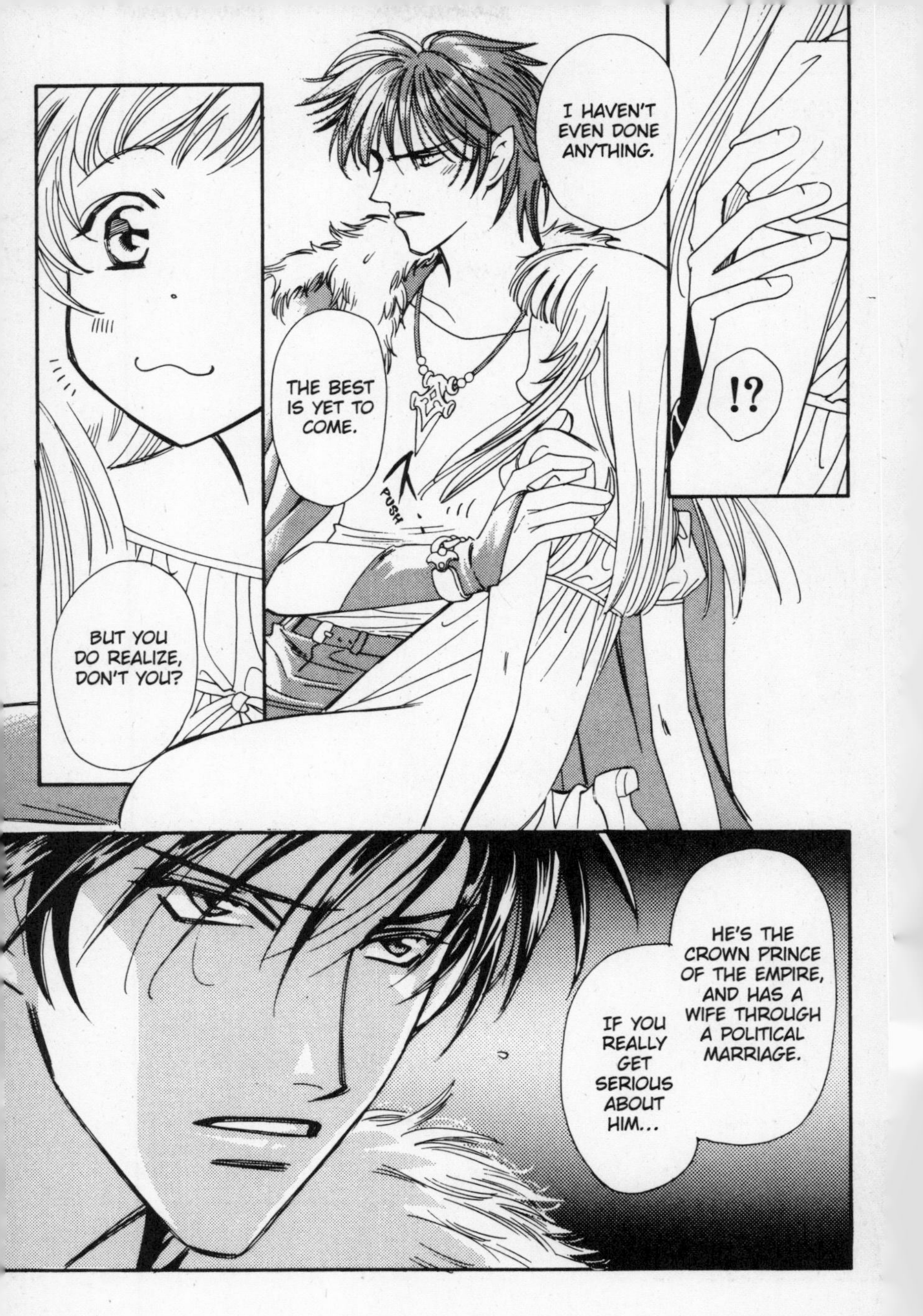
!?
I HAVEN'T EVEN DONE ANYTHING.
THE BEST IS YET TO COME.
PUSH
BUT YOU DO REALIZE, DON'T YOU?
HE'S THE CROWN PRINCE OF THE EMPIRE, AND HAS A WIFE THROUGH A POLITICAL MARRIAGE.
IF YOU REALLY GET SERIOUS ABOUT HIM...

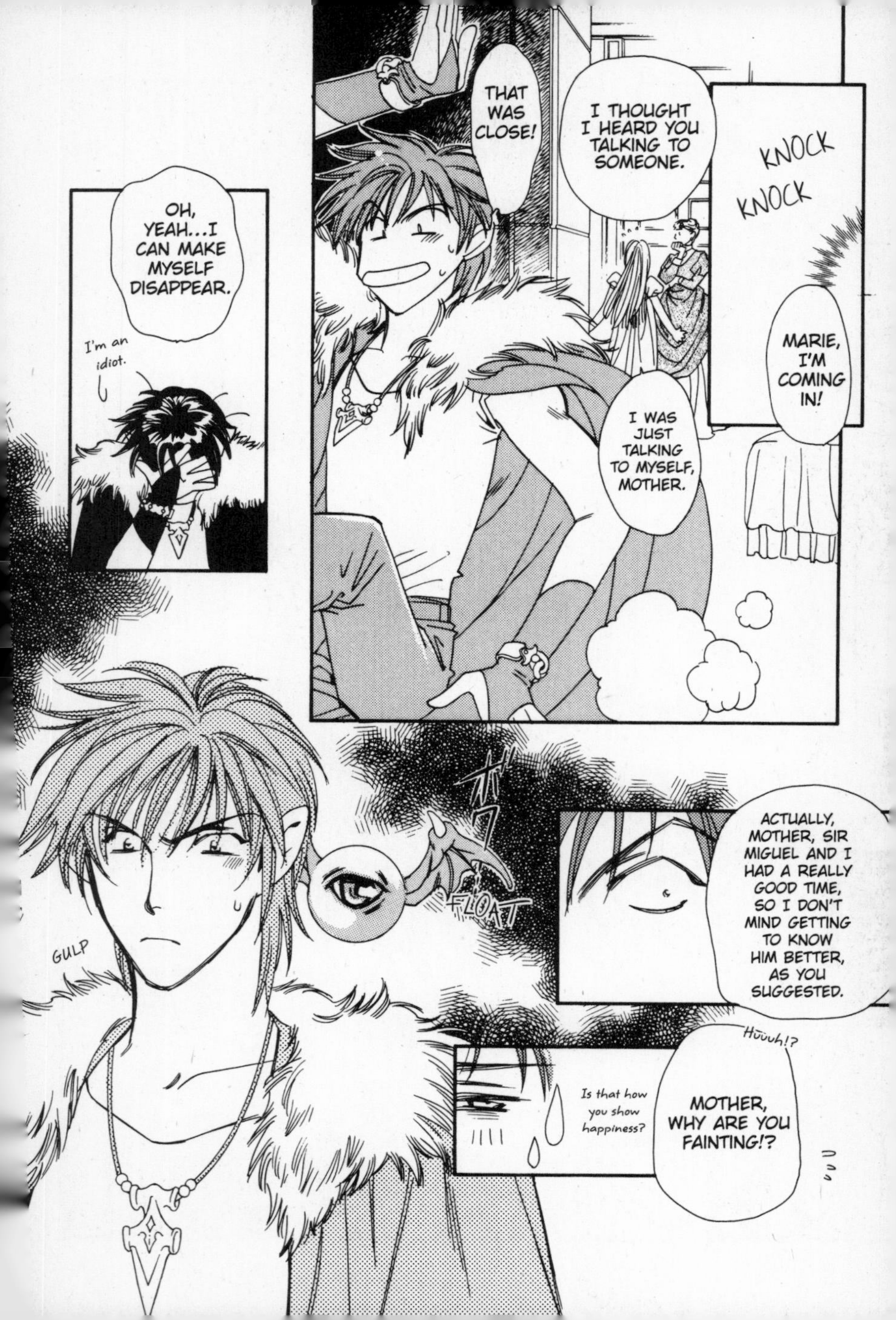
KNOCK
KNOCK
MARIE, I'M COMING IN!
I THOUGHT I HEARD YOU TALKING TO SOMEONE.
THAT WAS CLOSE!
I WAS JUST TALKING TO MYSELF, MOTHER.
OH, YEAH...I CAN MAKE MYSELF DISAPPEAR.
I'm an idiot.
ACTUALLY, MOTHER, SIR MIGUEL AND I HAD A REALLY GOOD TIME, SO I DON'T MIND GETTING TO KNOW HIM BETTER, AS YOU SUGGESTED.
Hüüüh!?
MOTHER, WHY ARE YOU FAINTING!?
Is that how you show happiness?
FLOAT
GULP

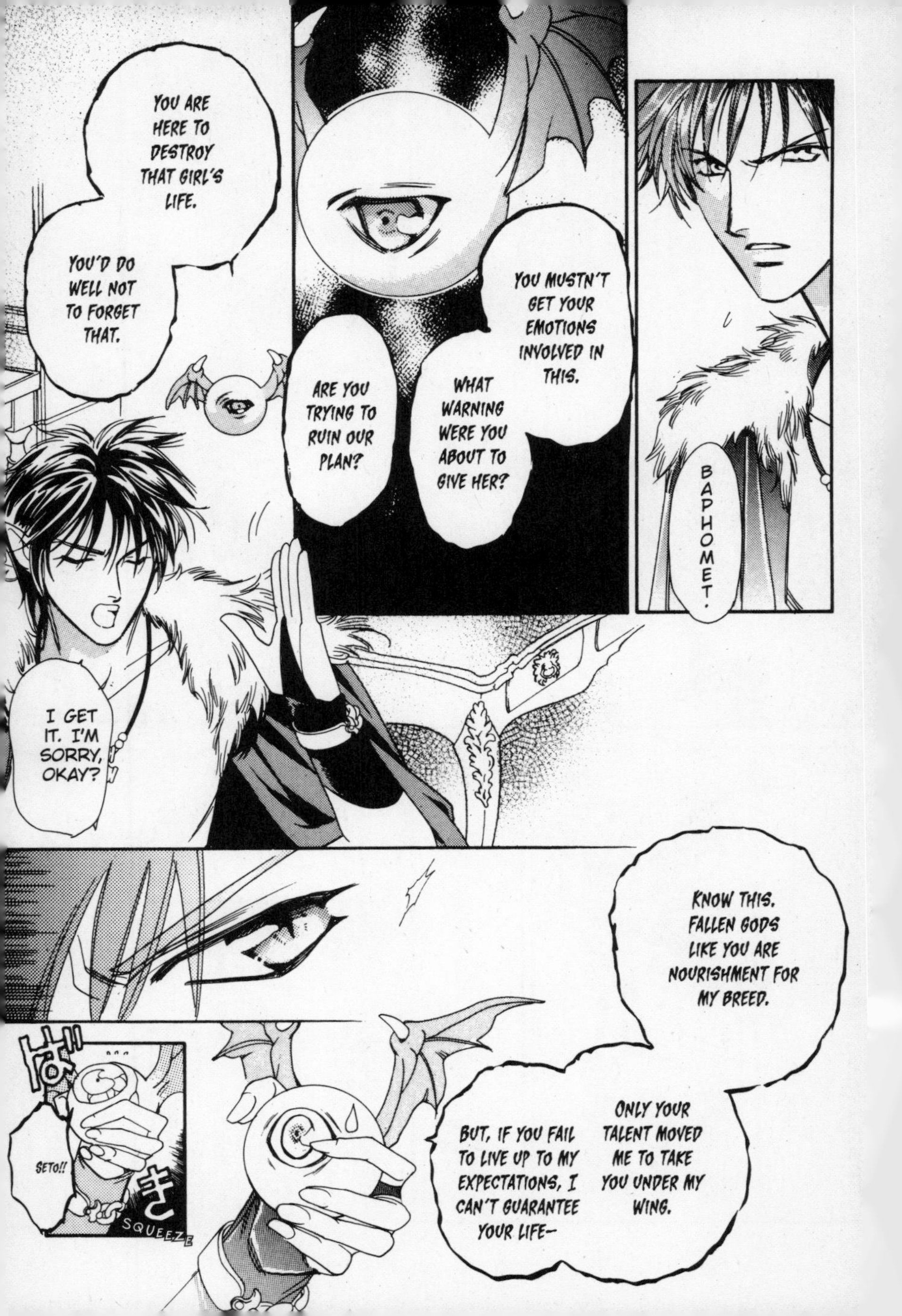
BAPHOMET.
YOU MUSTN'T GET YOUR EMOTIONS INVOLVED IN THIS.
WHAT WARNING WERE YOU ABOUT TO GIVE HER?
ARE YOU TRYING TO RUIN OUR PLAN?
YOU ARE HERE TO DESTROY THAT GIRL'S LIFE.
YOU'D DO WELL NOT TO FORGET THAT.
I GET IT. I'M SORRY, OKAY?
KNOW THIS. FALLEN GODS LIKE YOU ARE NOURISHMENT FOR MY BREED.
ONLY YOUR TALENT MOVED ME TO TAKE YOU UNDER MY WING.
BUT, IF YOU FAIL TO LIVE UP TO MY EXPECTATIONS, I CAN'T GUARANTEE YOUR LIFE–
SETO!!
SQUEEZE

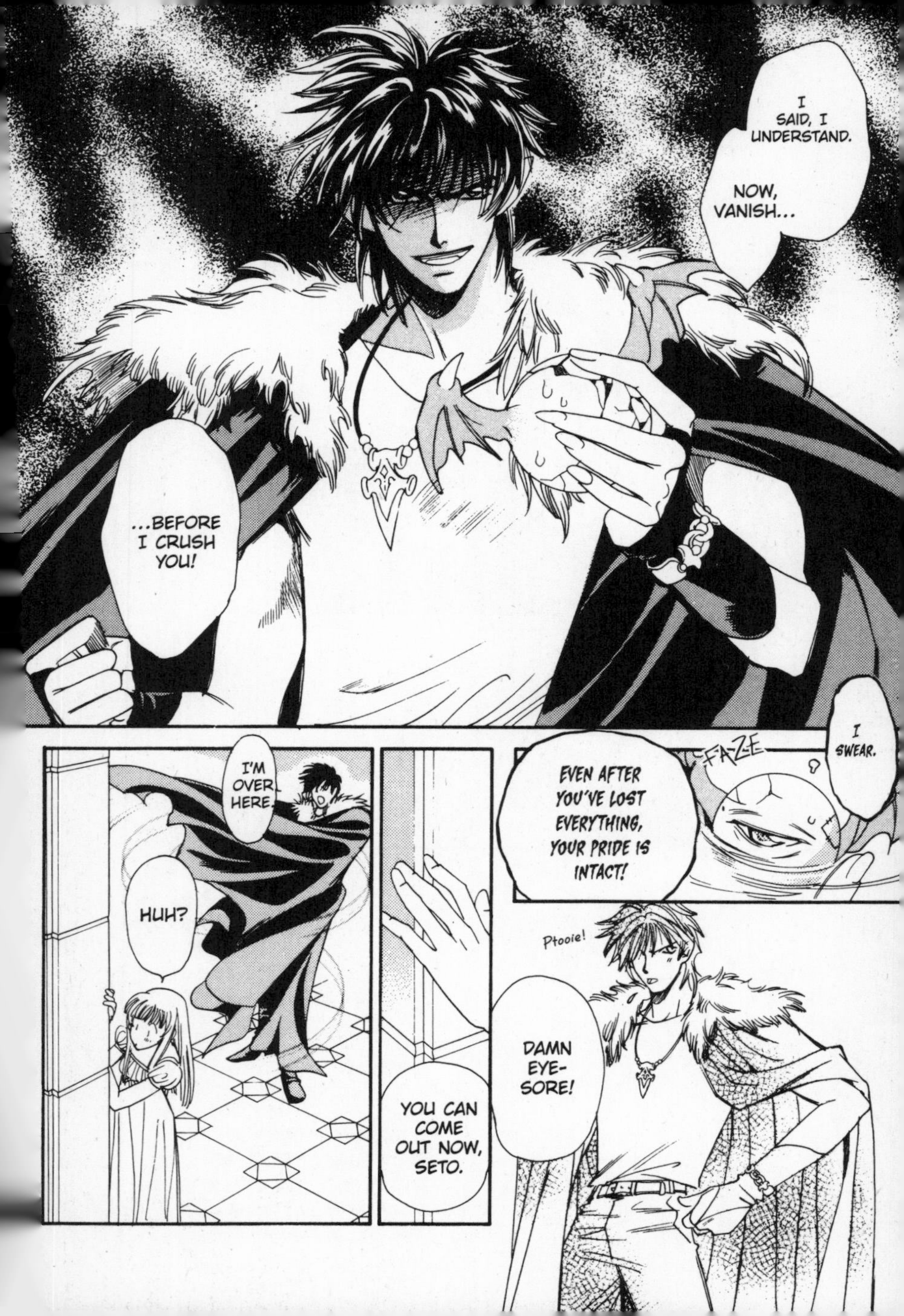
I SAID, I UNDERSTAND.
NOW, VANISH...
...BEFORE I CRUSH YOU!
I SWEAR.
FA-Z-E
EVEN AFTER YOU'VE LOST EVERYTHING, YOUR PRIDE IS INTACT!
Ptooie!
DAMN EYE-SORE!
YOU CAN COME OUT NOW, SETO.
I'M OVER HERE.
HUH?

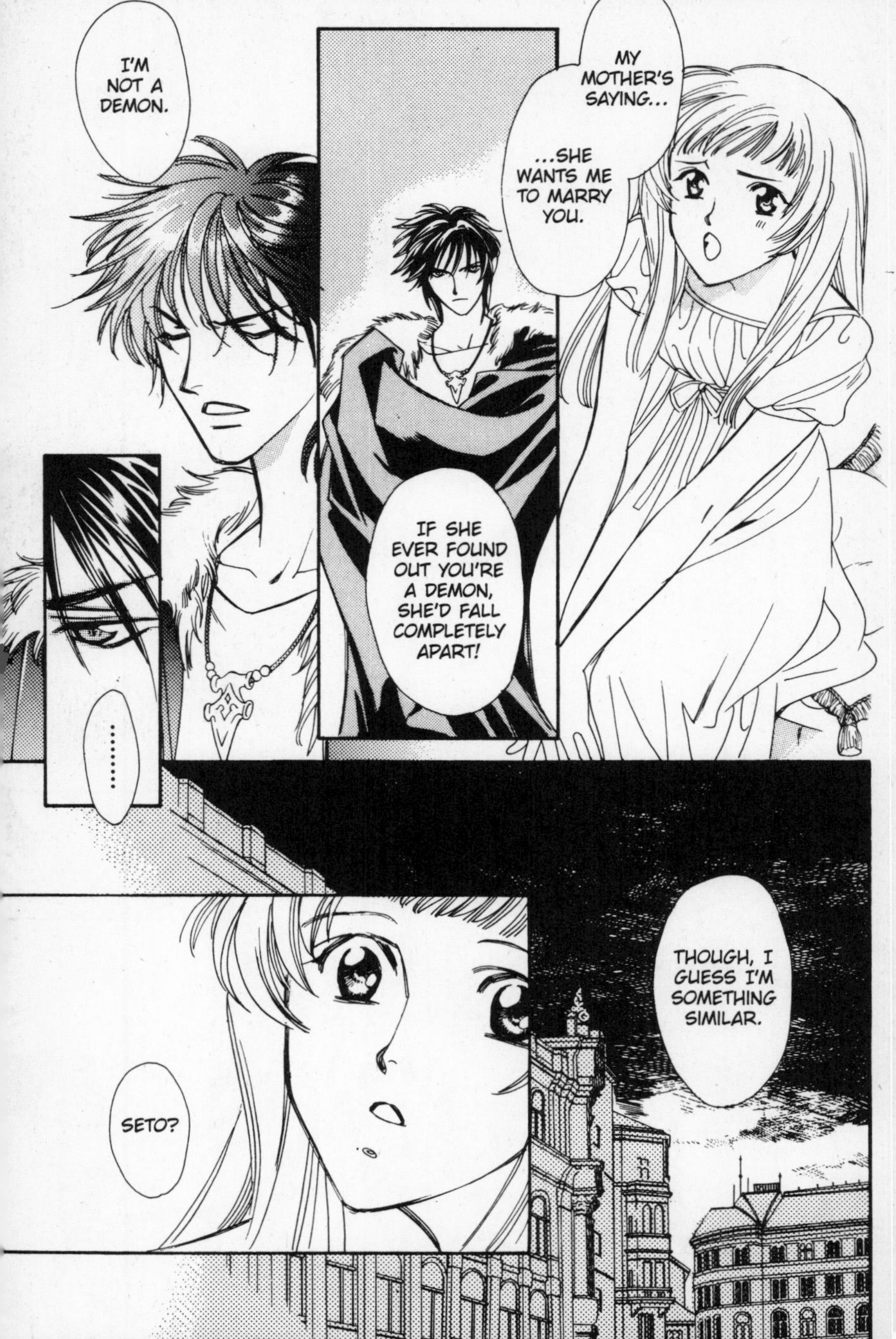
MY MOTHER'S SAYING...
...SHE WANTS ME TO MARRY YOU.
IF SHE EVER FOUND OUT YOU'RE A DEMON, SHE'D FALL COMPLETELY APART!
I'M NOT A DEMON.
........
THOUGH, I GUESS I'M SOMETHING SIMILAR.
SETO?

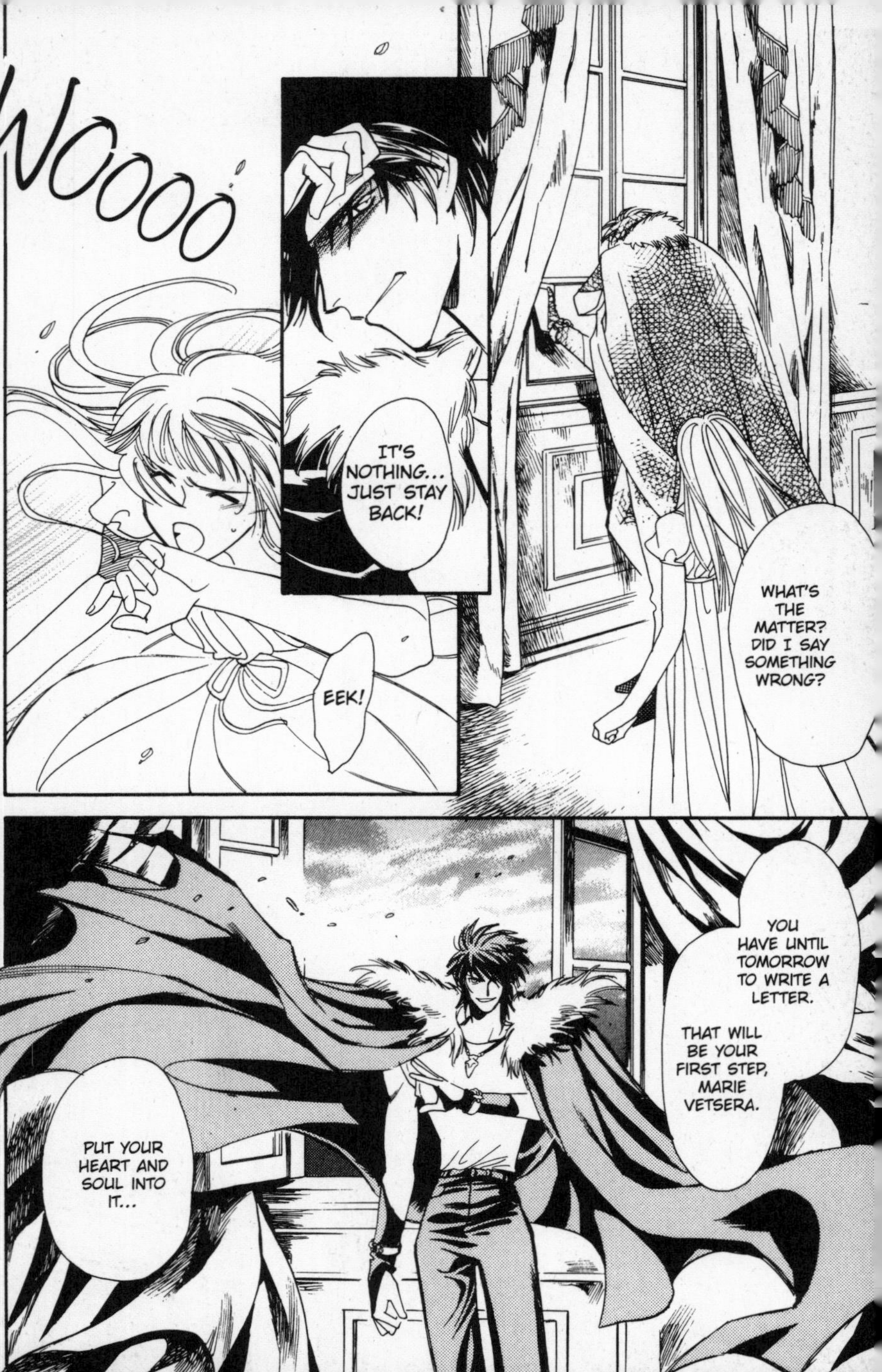
WHAT'S THE MATTER? DID I SAY SOMETHING WRONG?
IT'S NOTHING... JUST STAY BACK!
WOOOO
EEK!
YOU HAVE UNTIL TOMORROW TO WRITE A LETTER.
THAT WILL BE YOUR FIRST STEP, MARIE VETSERA.
PUT YOUR HEART AND SOUL INTO IT...

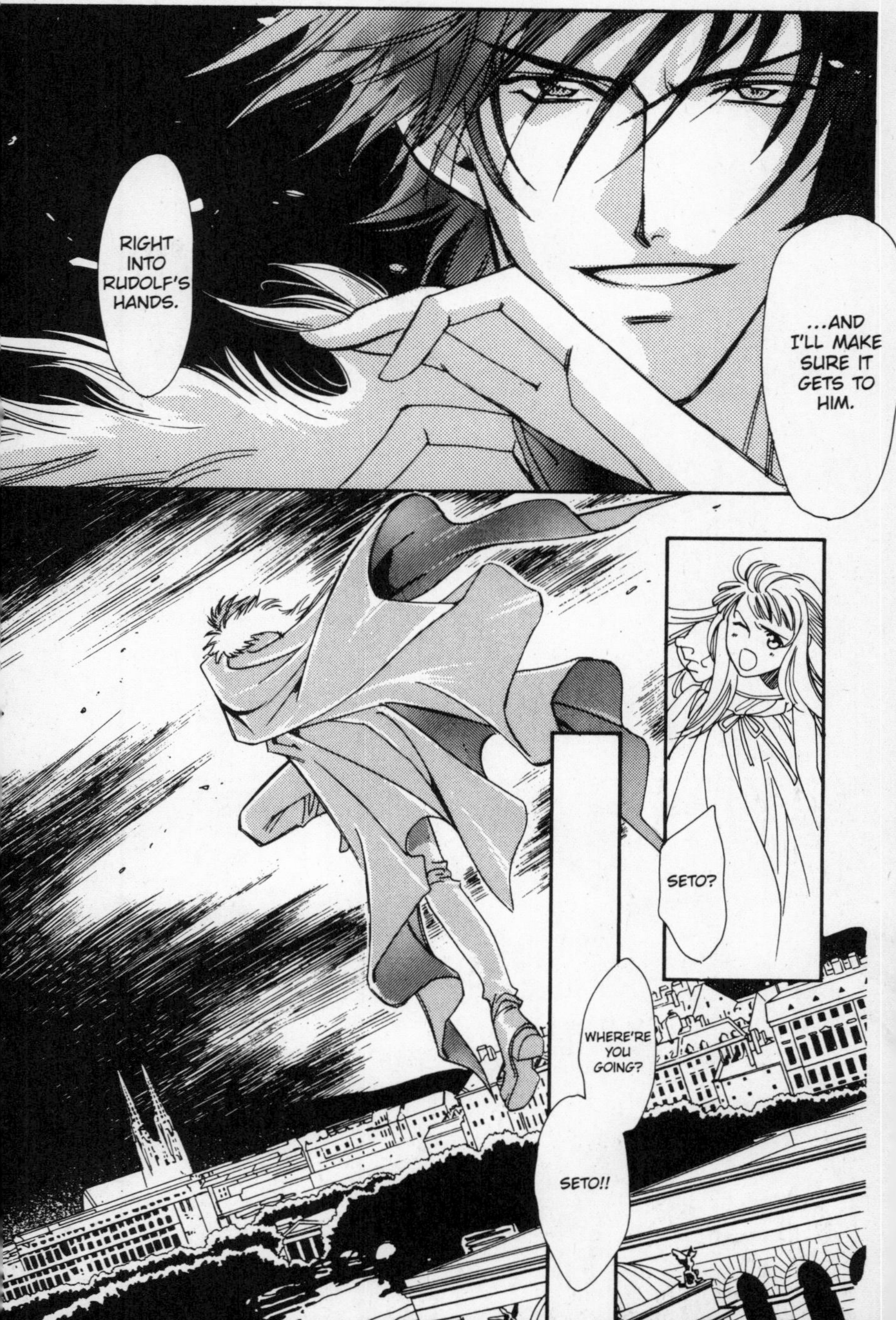
...AND I'LL MAKE SURE IT GETS TO HIM.
RIGHT INTO RUDOLF'S HANDS.
SETO?
WHERE'RE YOU GOING?
SETO!!

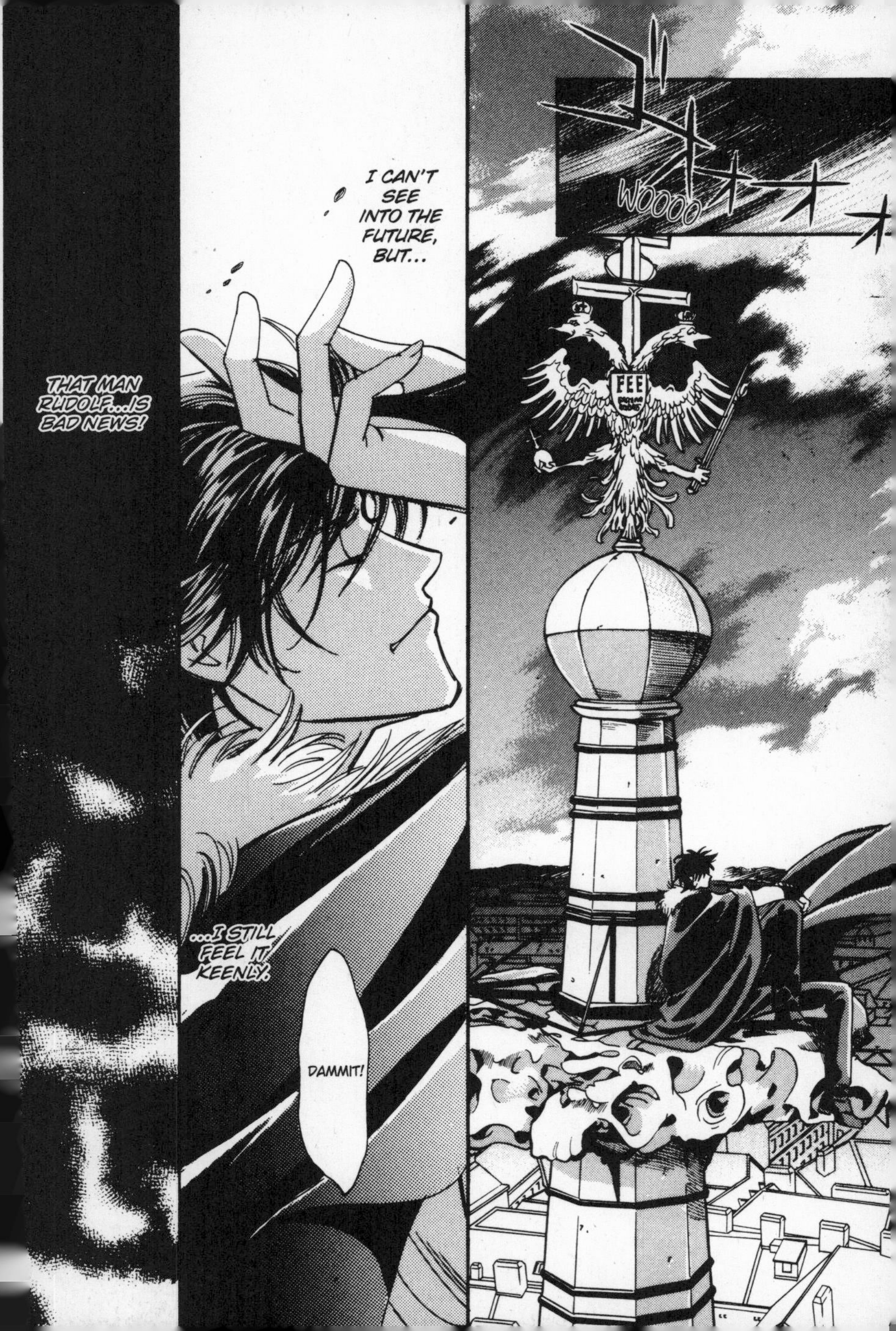
WOOOO
I CAN'T SEE INTO THE FUTURE, BUT...
...I STILL FEEL IT KEENLY.
DAMMIT!
THAT MAN RUDOLF...IS BAD NEWS!

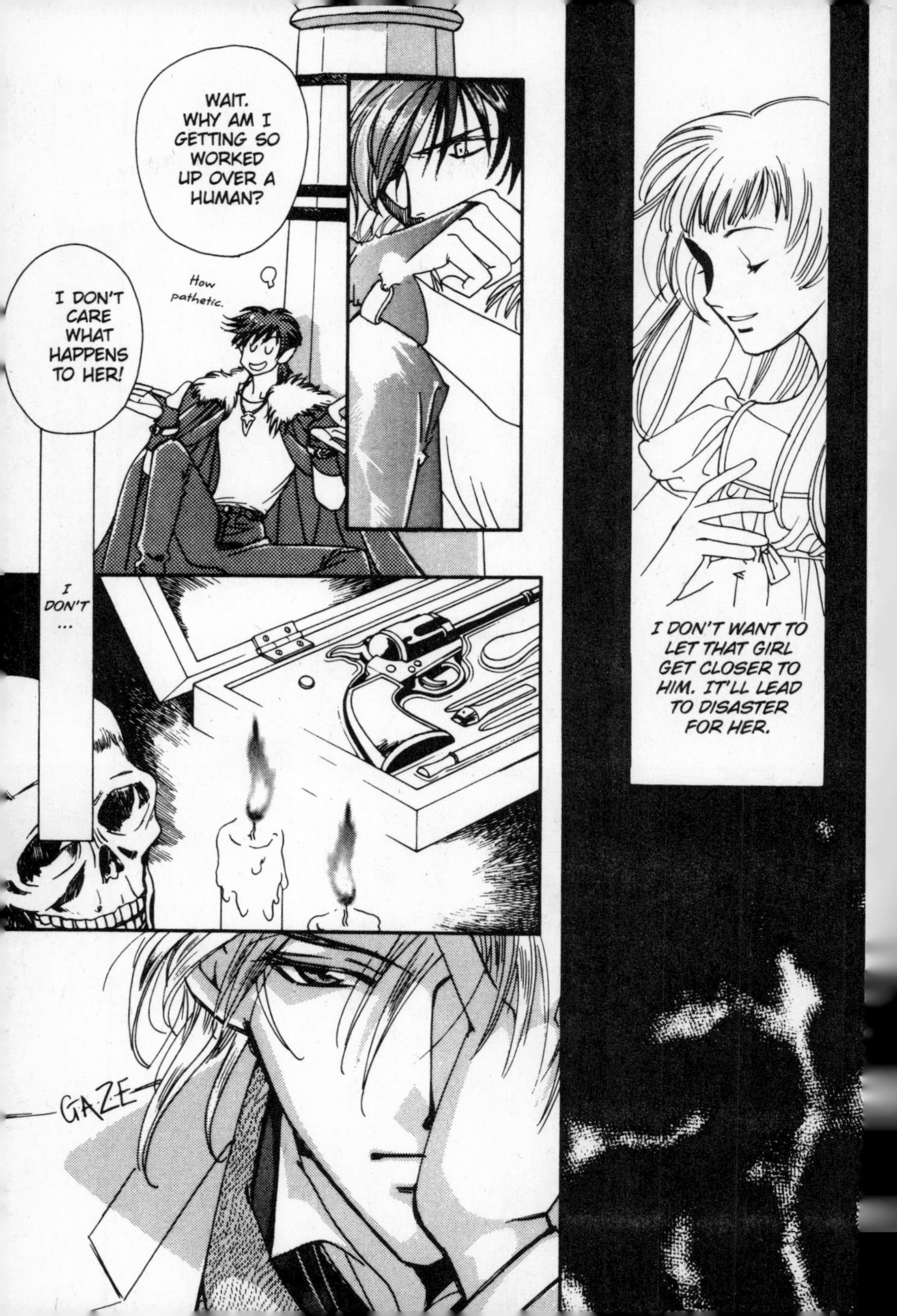
I DON'T WANT TO LET THAT GIRL GET CLOSER TO HIM. IT'LL LEAD TO DISASTER FOR HER.
WAIT. WHY AM I GETTING SO WORKED UP OVER A HUMAN?
How pathetic.
I DON'T CARE WHAT HAPPENS TO HER!
I DON'T ...
GAZE

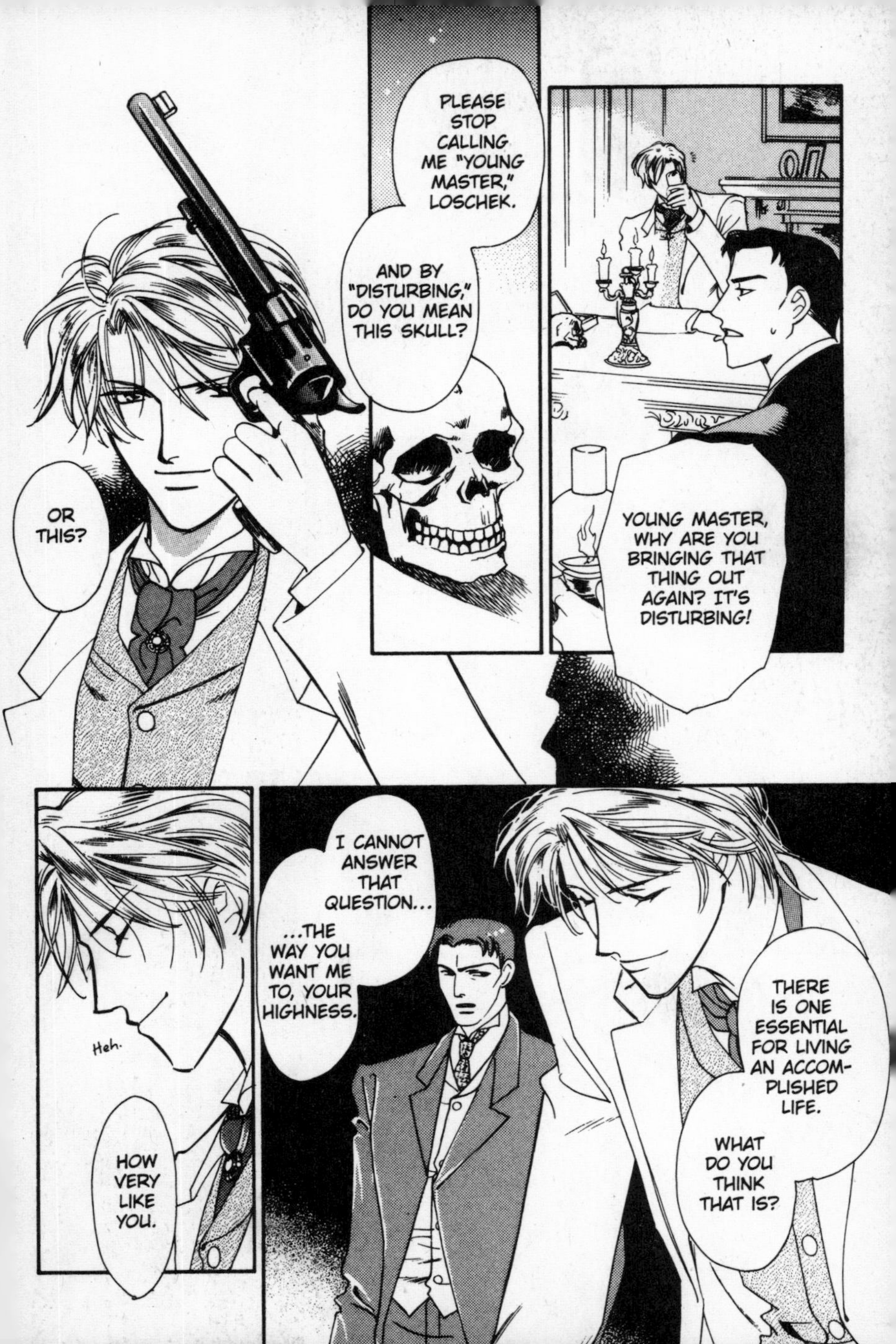
YOUNG MASTER, WHY ARE YOU BRINGING THAT THING OUT AGAIN? IT'S DISTURBING!
PLEASE STOP CALLING ME "YOUNG MASTER," LOSCHEK.
AND BY "DISTURBING," DO YOU MEAN THIS SKULL?
OR THIS?
THERE IS ONE ESSENTIAL FOR LIVING AN ACCOM-PLISHED LIFE.
WHAT DO YOU THINK THAT IS?
I CANNOT ANSWER THAT QUESTION...
...THE WAY YOU WANT ME TO, YOUR HIGHNESS.
Heh.
HOW VERY LIKE YOU.

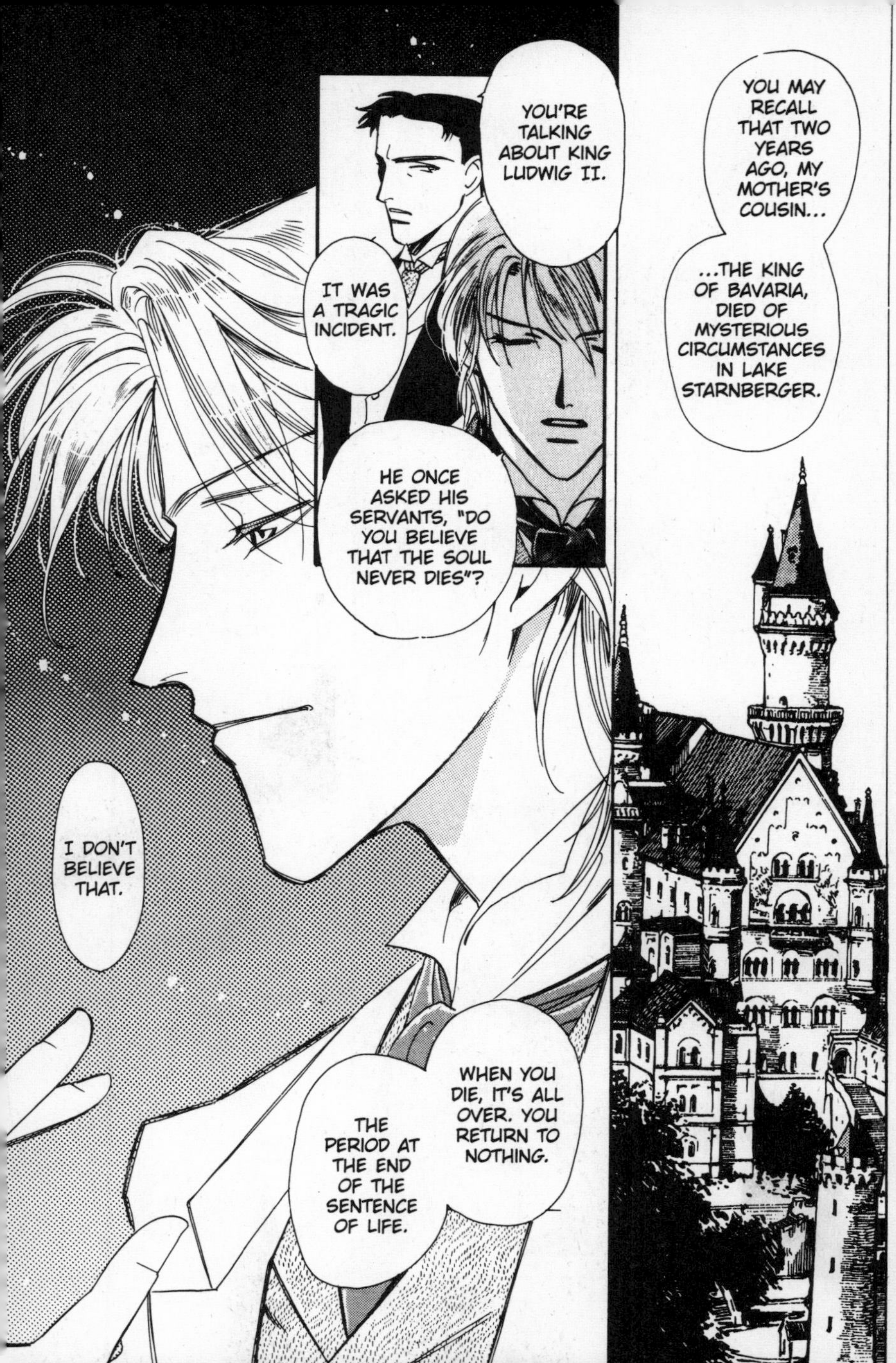
YOU MAY RECALL THAT TWO YEARS AGO, MY MOTHER'S COUSIN...
...THE KING OF BAVARIA, DIED OF MYSTERIOUS CIRCUMSTANCES IN LAKE STARNBERGER.
YOU'RE TALKING ABOUT KING LUDWIG II.
IT WAS A TRAGIC INCIDENT.
HE ONCE ASKED HIS SERVANTS, "DO YOU BELIEVE THAT THE SOUL NEVER DIES"?
I DON'T BELIEVE THAT.
WHEN YOU DIE, IT'S ALL OVER. YOU RETURN TO NOTHING.
THE PERIOD AT THE END OF THE SENTENCE OF LIFE.

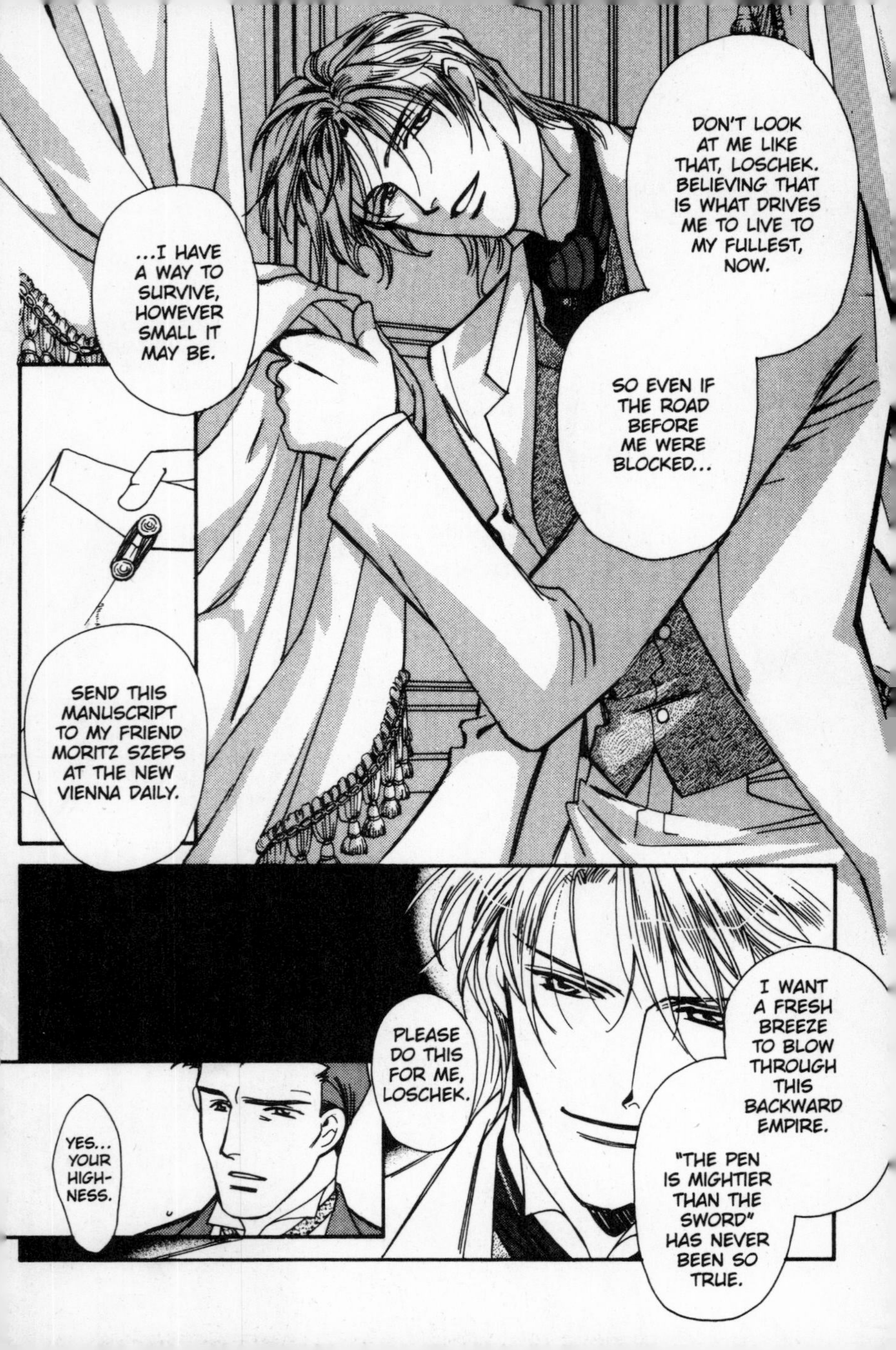
DON'T LOOK AT ME LIKE THAT, LOSCHEK. BELIEVING THAT IS WHAT DRIVES ME TO LIVE TO MY FULLEST, NOW.
SO EVEN IF THE ROAD BEFORE ME WERE BLOCKED...
...I HAVE A WAY TO SURVIVE, HOWEVER SMALL IT MAY BE.
SEND THIS MANUSCRIPT TO MY FRIEND MORITZ SZEPS AT THE NEW VIENNA DAILY.
I WANT A FRESH BREEZE TO BLOW THROUGH THIS BACKWARD EMPIRE.
"THE PEN IS MIGHTIER THAN THE SWORD" HAS NEVER BEEN SO TRUE.
PLEASE DO THIS FOR ME, LOSCHEK.
YES... YOUR HIGH-NESS.

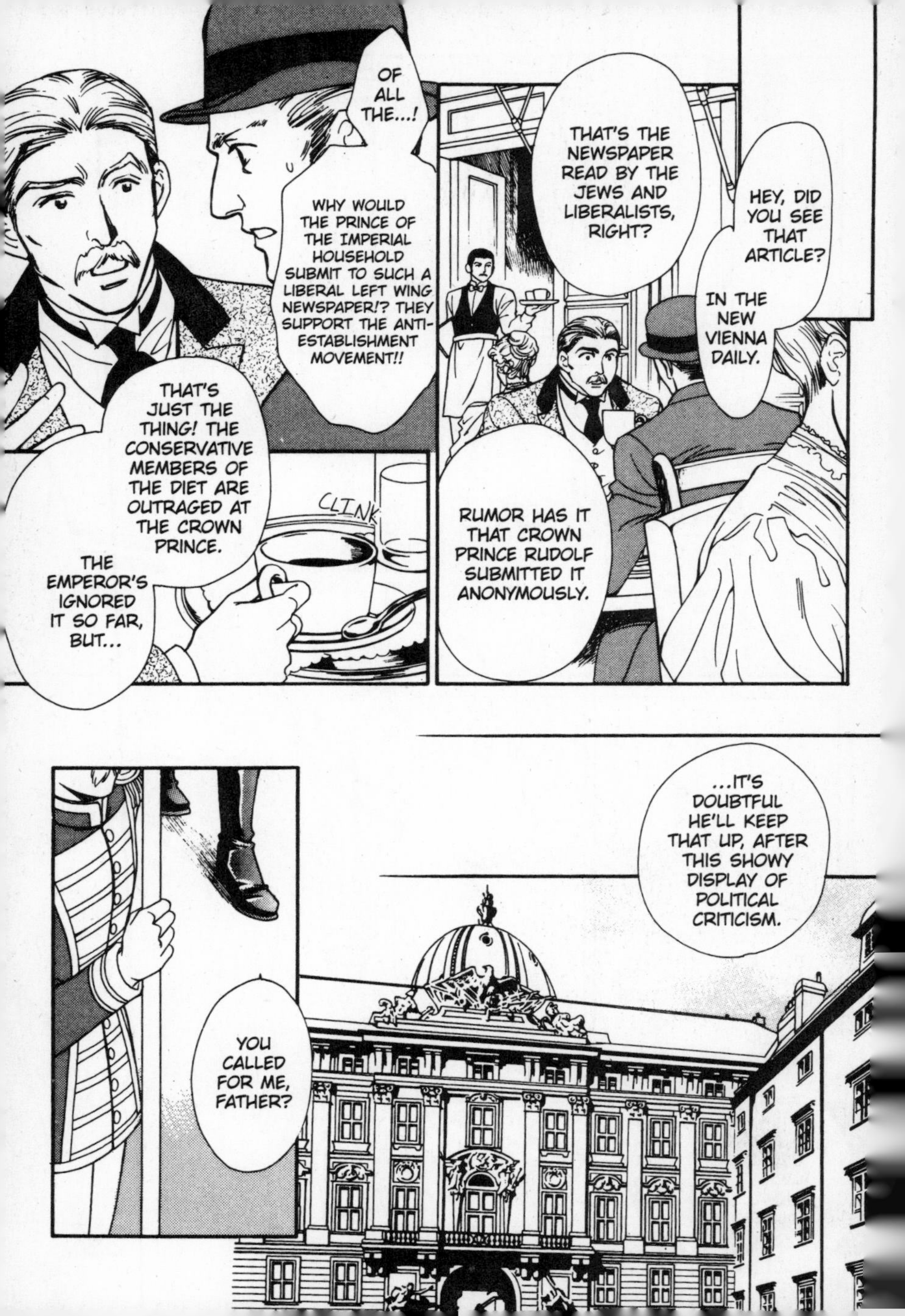
HEY, DID YOU SEE THAT ARTICLE?
IN THE NEW VIENNA DAILY.
THAT'S THE NEWSPAPER READ BY THE JEWS AND LIBERALISTS, RIGHT?
RUMOR HAS IT THAT CROWN PRINCE RUDOLF SUBMITTED IT ANONYMOUSLY.
OF ALL THE...!
WHY WOULD THE PRINCE OF THE IMPERIAL HOUSEHOLD SUBMIT TO SUCH A LIBERAL LEFT WING NEWSPAPER!? THEY SUPPORT THE ANTI-ESTABLISHMENT MOVEMENT!!
THAT'S JUST THE THING! THE CONSERVATIVE MEMBERS OF THE DIET ARE OUTRAGED AT THE CROWN PRINCE.
THE EMPEROR'S IGNORED IT SO FAR, BUT...
CLINK
...IT'S DOUBTFUL HE'LL KEEP THAT UP, AFTER THIS SHOWY DISPLAY OF POLITICAL CRITICISM.
YOU CALLED FOR ME, FATHER?

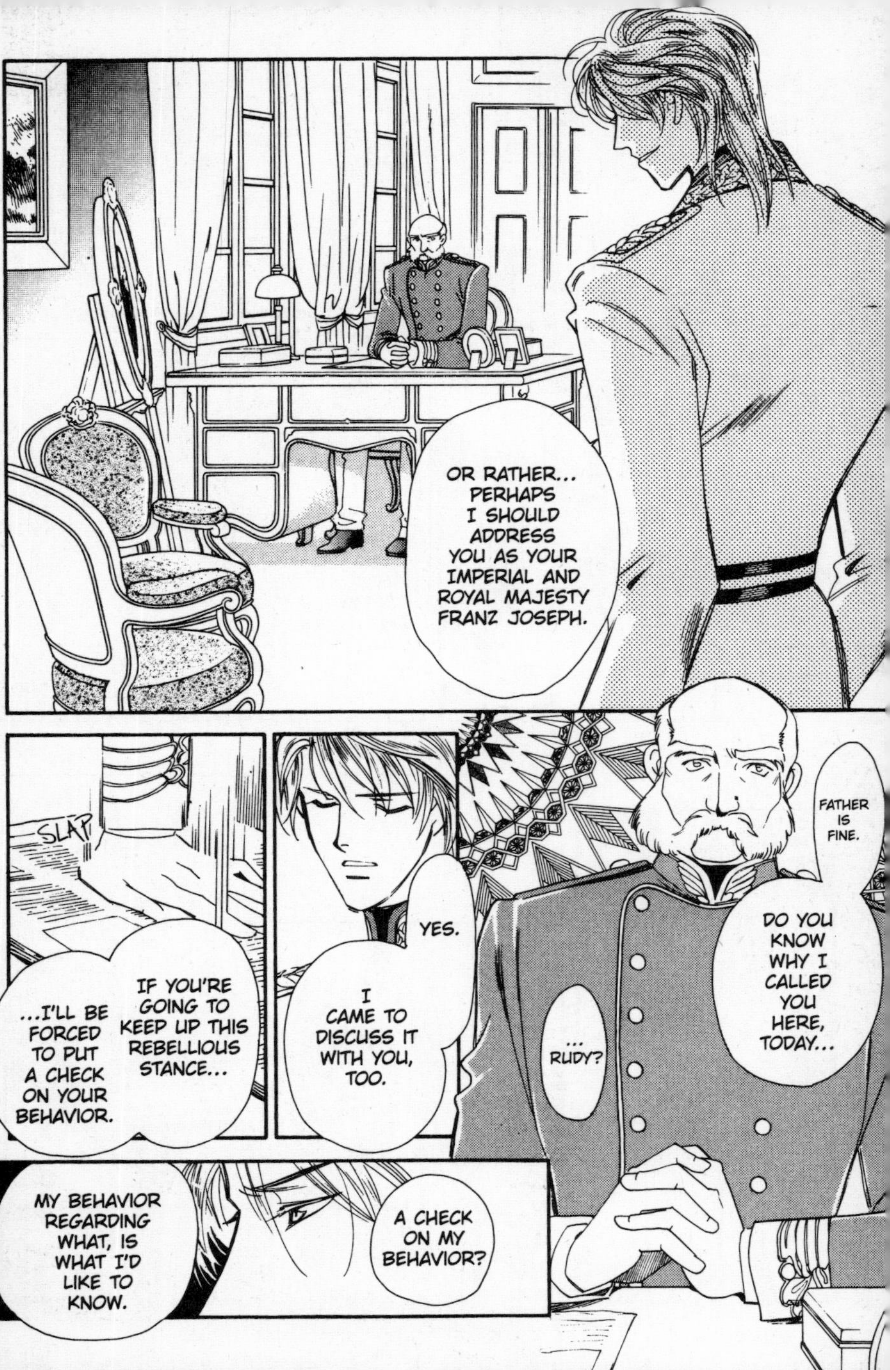
OR RATHER... PERHAPS I SHOULD ADDRESS YOU AS YOUR IMPERIAL AND ROYAL MAJESTY FRANZ JOSEPH.
FATHER IS FINE.
DO YOU KNOW WHY I CALLED YOU HERE, TODAY...
...RUDY?
YES.
I CAME TO DISCUSS IT WITH YOU, TOO.
SLAP
IF YOU'RE GOING TO KEEP UP THIS REBELLIOUS STANCE...
...I'LL BE FORCED TO PUT A CHECK ON YOUR BEHAVIOR.
A CHECK ON MY BEHAVIOR?
MY BEHAVIOR REGARDING WHAT, IS WHAT I'D LIKE TO KNOW.

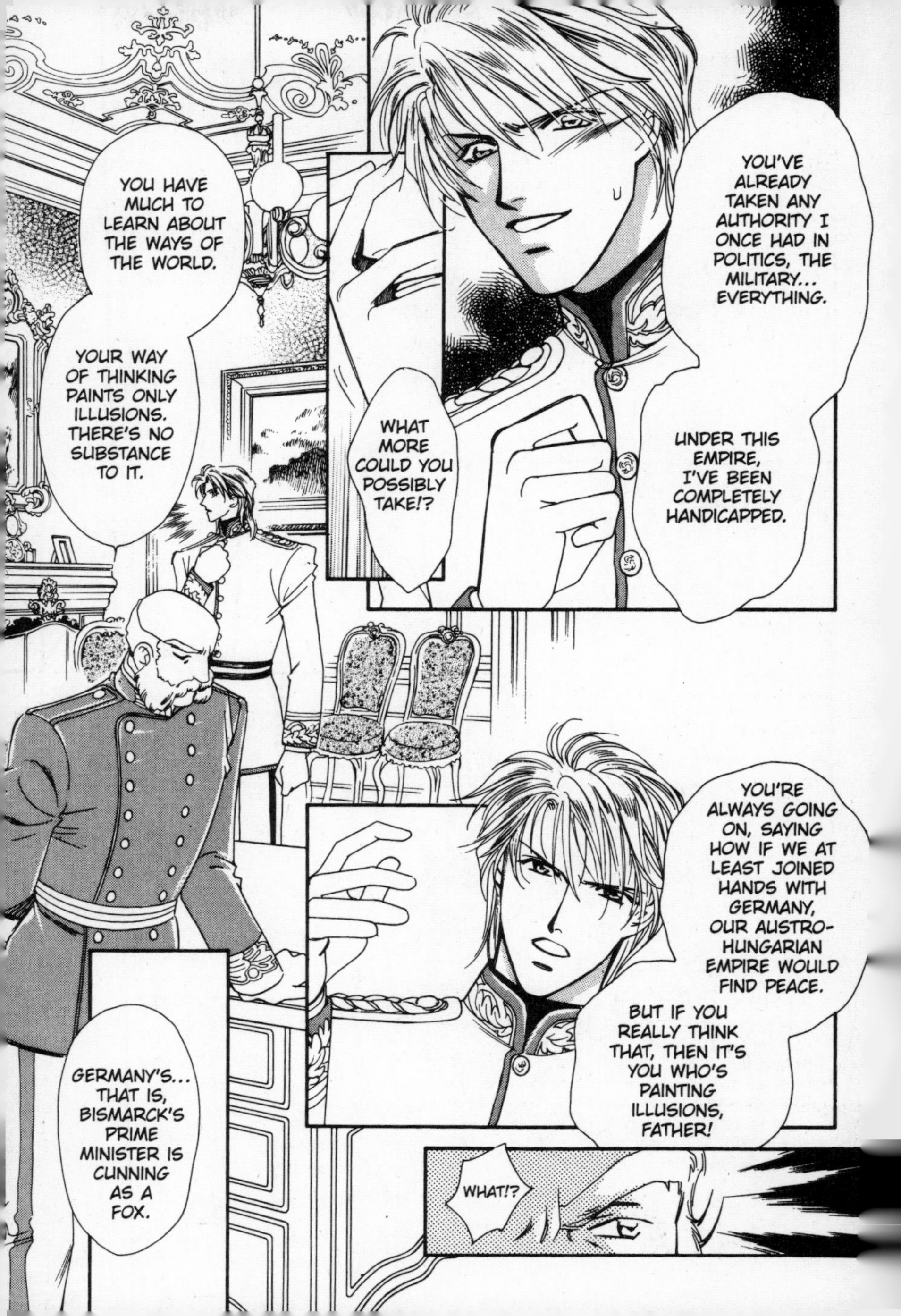
YOU'VE ALREADY TAKEN ANY AUTHORITY I ONCE HAD IN POLITICS, THE MILITARY... EVERYTHING.
UNDER THIS EMPIRE, I'VE BEEN COMPLETELY HANDICAPPED.
WHAT MORE COULD YOU POSSIBLY TAKE!?
YOU HAVE MUCH TO LEARN ABOUT THE WAYS OF THE WORLD.
YOUR WAY OF THINKING PAINTS ONLY ILLUSIONS. THERE'S NO SUBSTANCE TO IT.
YOU'RE ALWAYS GOING ON, SAYING HOW IF WE AT LEAST JOINED HANDS WITH GERMANY, OUR AUSTRO-HUNGARIAN EMPIRE WOULD FIND PEACE.
BUT IF YOU REALLY THINK THAT, THEN IT'S YOU WHO'S PAINTING ILLUSIONS, FATHER!
WHAT!?
GERMANY'S... THAT IS, BISMARCK'S PRIME MINISTER IS CUNNING AS A FOX.

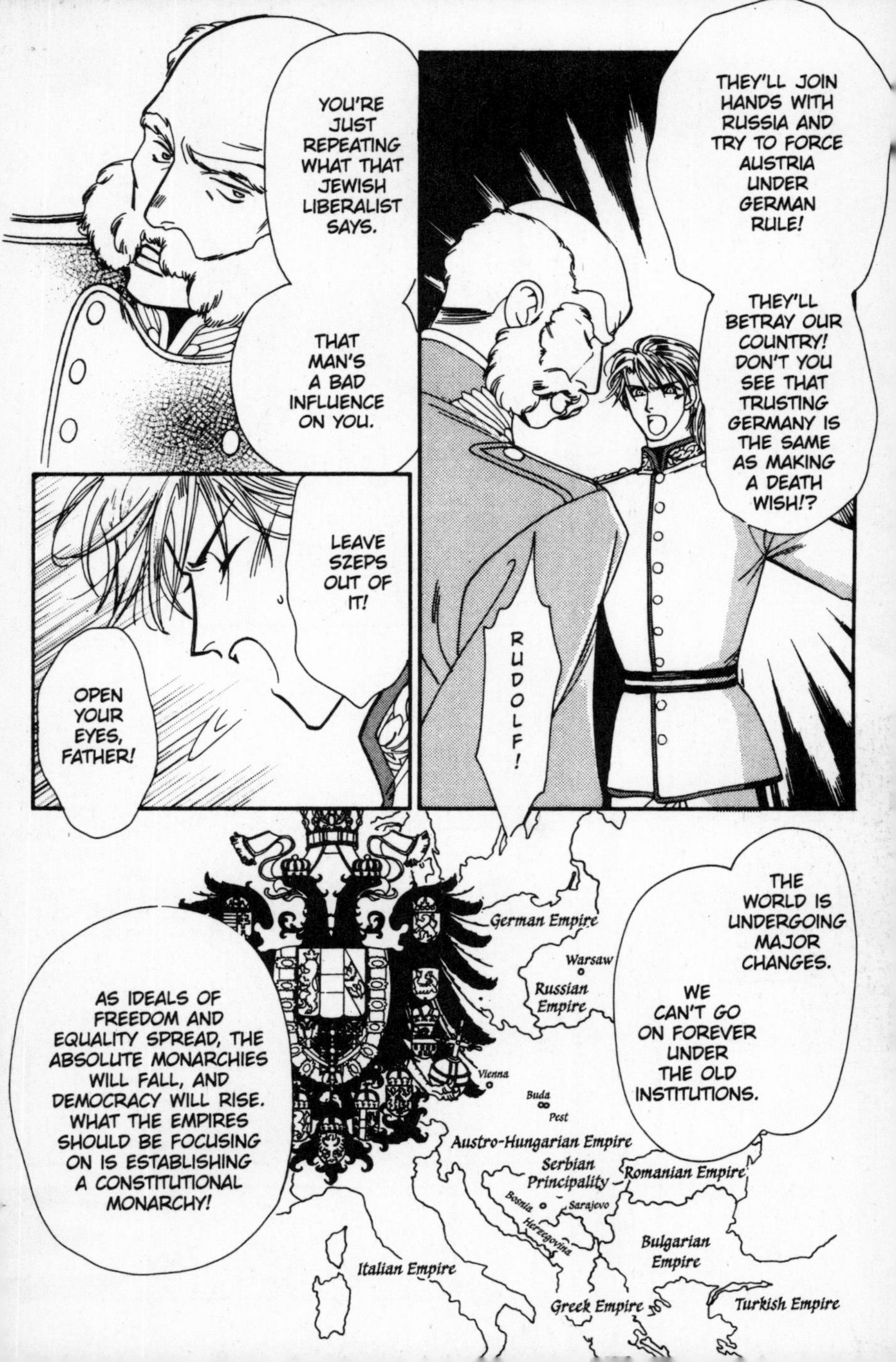
THEY'LL JOIN HANDS WITH RUSSIA AND TRY TO FORCE AUSTRIA UNDER GERMAN RULE!
THEY'LL BETRAY OUR COUNTRY! DON'T YOU SEE THAT TRUSTING GERMANY IS THE SAME AS MAKING A DEATH WISH!?
RUDOLF!
YOU'RE JUST REPEATING WHAT THAT JEWISH LIBERALIST SAYS.
THAT MAN'S A BAD INFLUENCE ON YOU.
LEAVE SZEPS OUT OF IT!
OPEN YOUR EYES, FATHER!
THE WORLD IS UNDERGOING MAJOR CHANGES.
WE CAN'T GO ON FOREVER UNDER THE OLD INSTITUTIONS.
German Empire
Warsaw
Russian Empire
Vienna
Buda
Pest
Austro-Hungarian Empire
Serbian Principality
Romanian Empire
Bosnia
Sarajevo
Herzegovina
Bulgarian Empire
Italian Empire
Greek Empire
Turkish Empire
AS IDEALS OF FREEDOM AND EQUALITY SPREAD, THE ABSOLUTE MONARCHIES WILL FALL, AND DEMOCRACY WILL RISE. WHAT THE EMPIRES SHOULD BE FOCUSING ON IS ESTABLISHING A CONSTITUTIONAL MONARCHY!

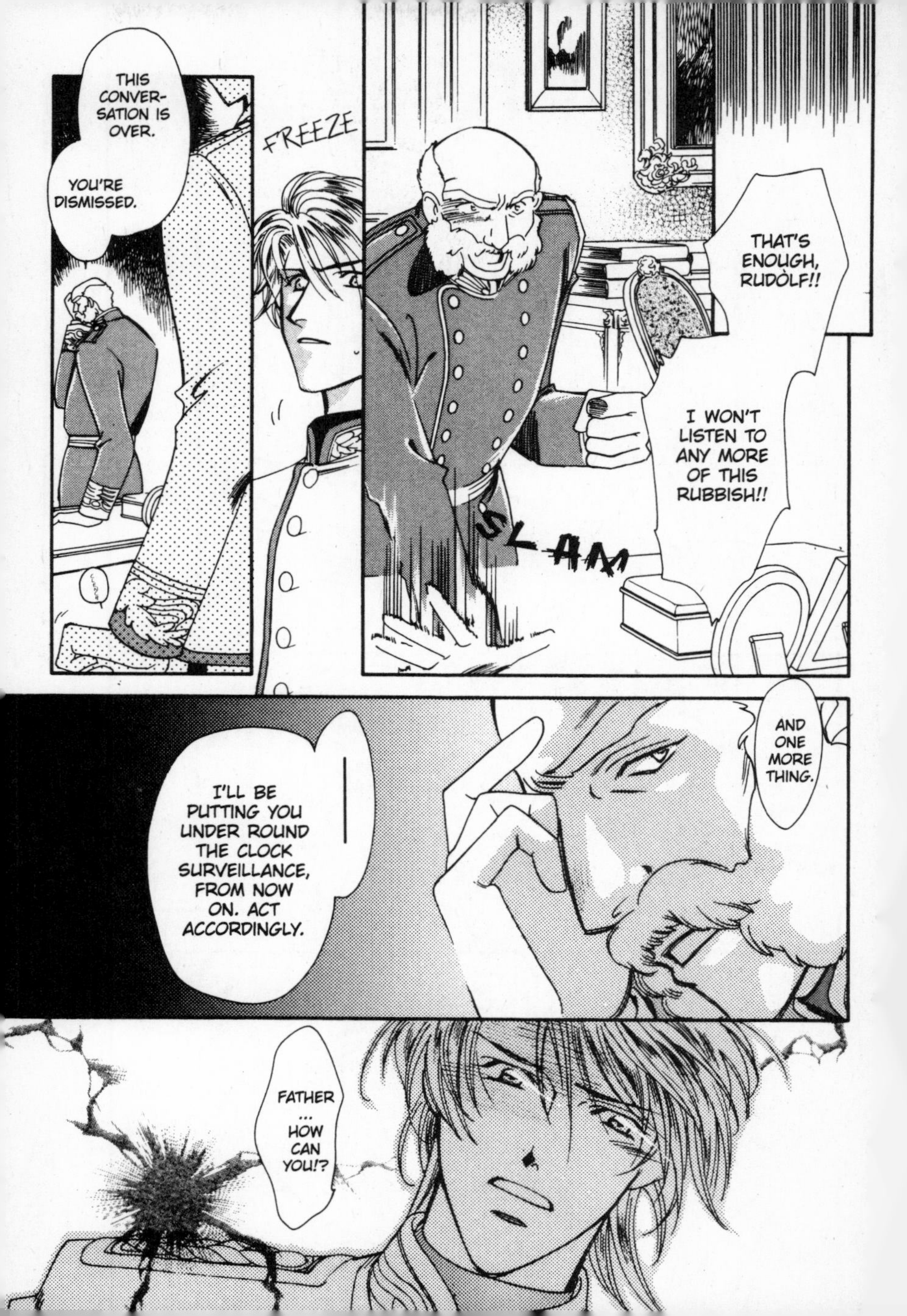
THAT'S ENOUGH, RUDÒLF!!
I WON'T LISTEN TO ANY MORE OF THIS RUBBISH!!
SLAM
THIS CONVER-SATION IS OVER.
YOU'RE DISMISSED.
FREEZE
AND ONE MORE THING.
I'LL BE PUTTING YOU UNDER ROUND THE CLOCK SURVEILLANCE, FROM NOW ON. ACT ACCORDINGLY.
FATHER ... HOW CAN YOU!?

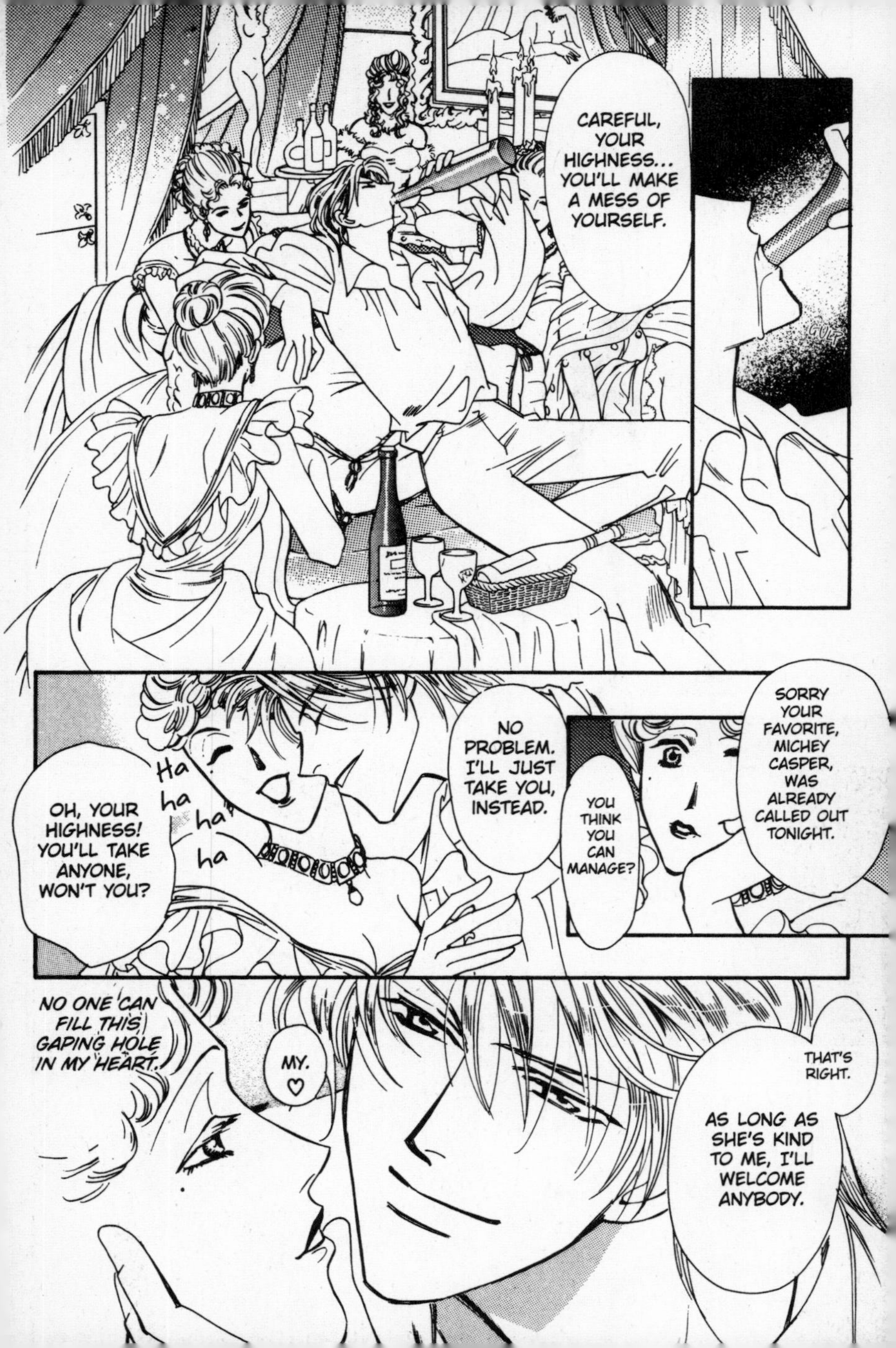
GULP
CAREFUL, YOUR HIGHNESS... YOU'LL MAKE A MESS OF YOURSELF.
SORRY YOUR FAVORITE, MICHEY CASPER, WAS ALREADY CALLED OUT TONIGHT.
YOU THINK YOU CAN MANAGE?
NO PROBLEM. I'LL JUST TAKE YOU, INSTEAD.
Ha ha ha ha
OH, YOUR HIGHNESS! YOU'LL TAKE ANYONE, WON'T YOU?
THAT'S RIGHT.
AS LONG AS SHE'S KIND TO ME, I'LL WELCOME ANYBODY.
MY. ♡
NO ONE CAN FILL THIS GAPING HOLE IN MY HEART.

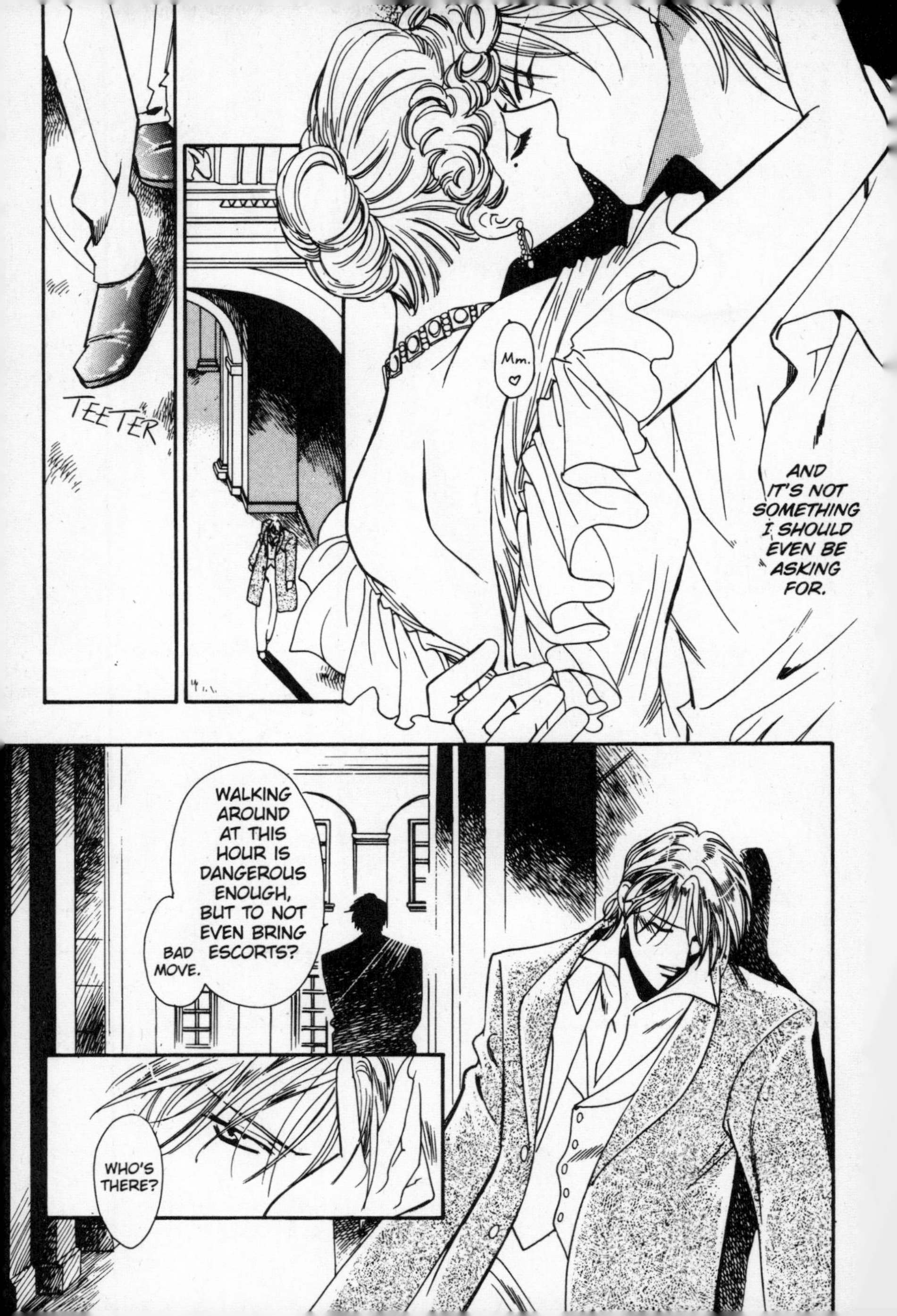
AND IT'S NOT SOMETHING I SHOULD EVEN BE ASKING FOR.
Mm.
TEETER
WALKING AROUND AT THIS HOUR IS DANGEROUS ENOUGH, BUT TO NOT EVEN BRING ESCORTS?
BAD MOVE.
WHO'S THERE?

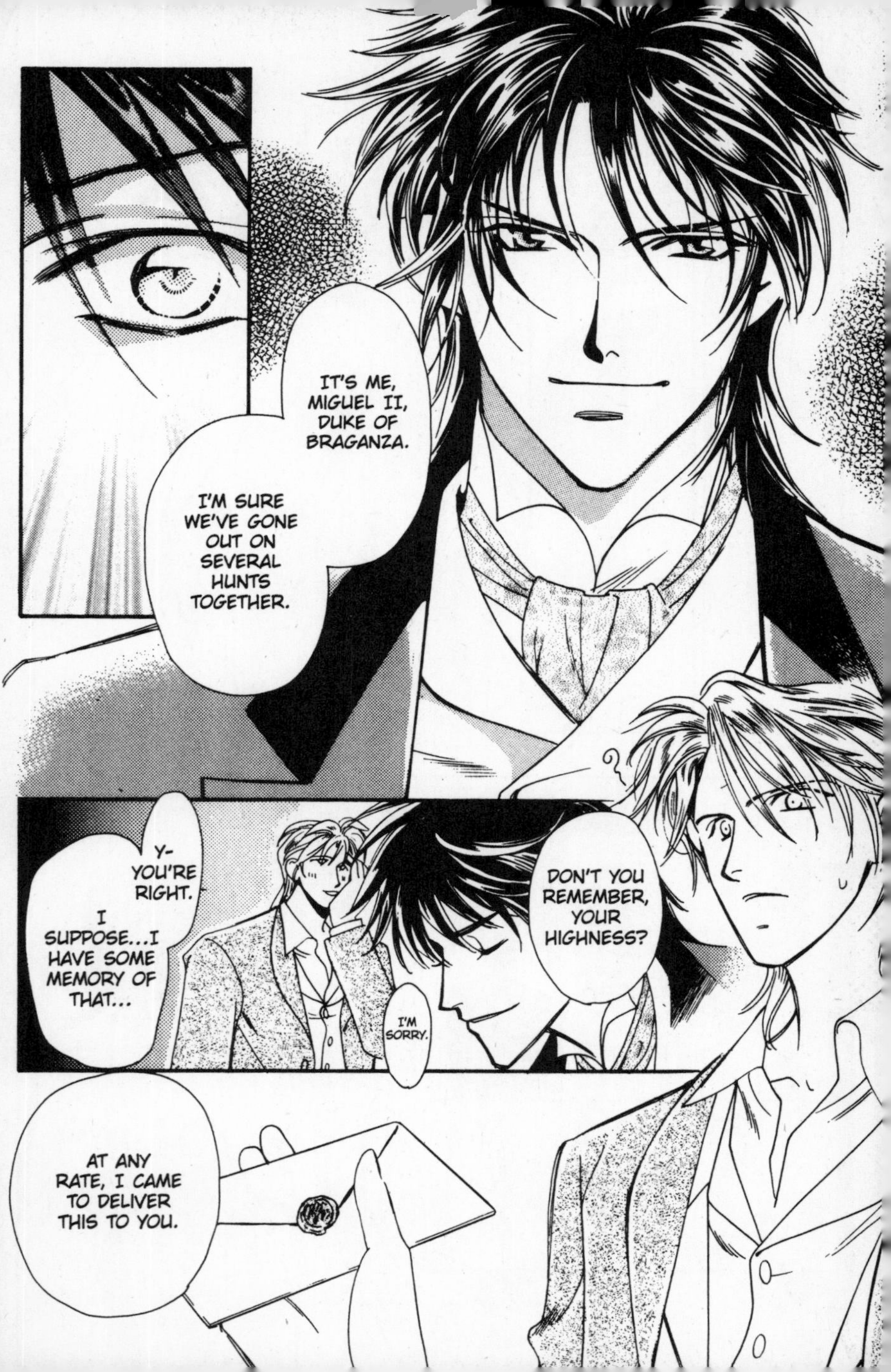
IT'S ME, MIGUEL II, DUKE OF BRAGANZA.
I'M SURE WE'VE GONE OUT ON SEVERAL HUNTS TOGETHER.
DON'T YOU REMEMBER, YOUR HIGHNESS?
I'M SORRY.
Y- YOU'RE RIGHT.
I SUPPOSE...I HAVE SOME MEMORY OF THAT...
AT ANY RATE, I CAME TO DELIVER THIS TO YOU.

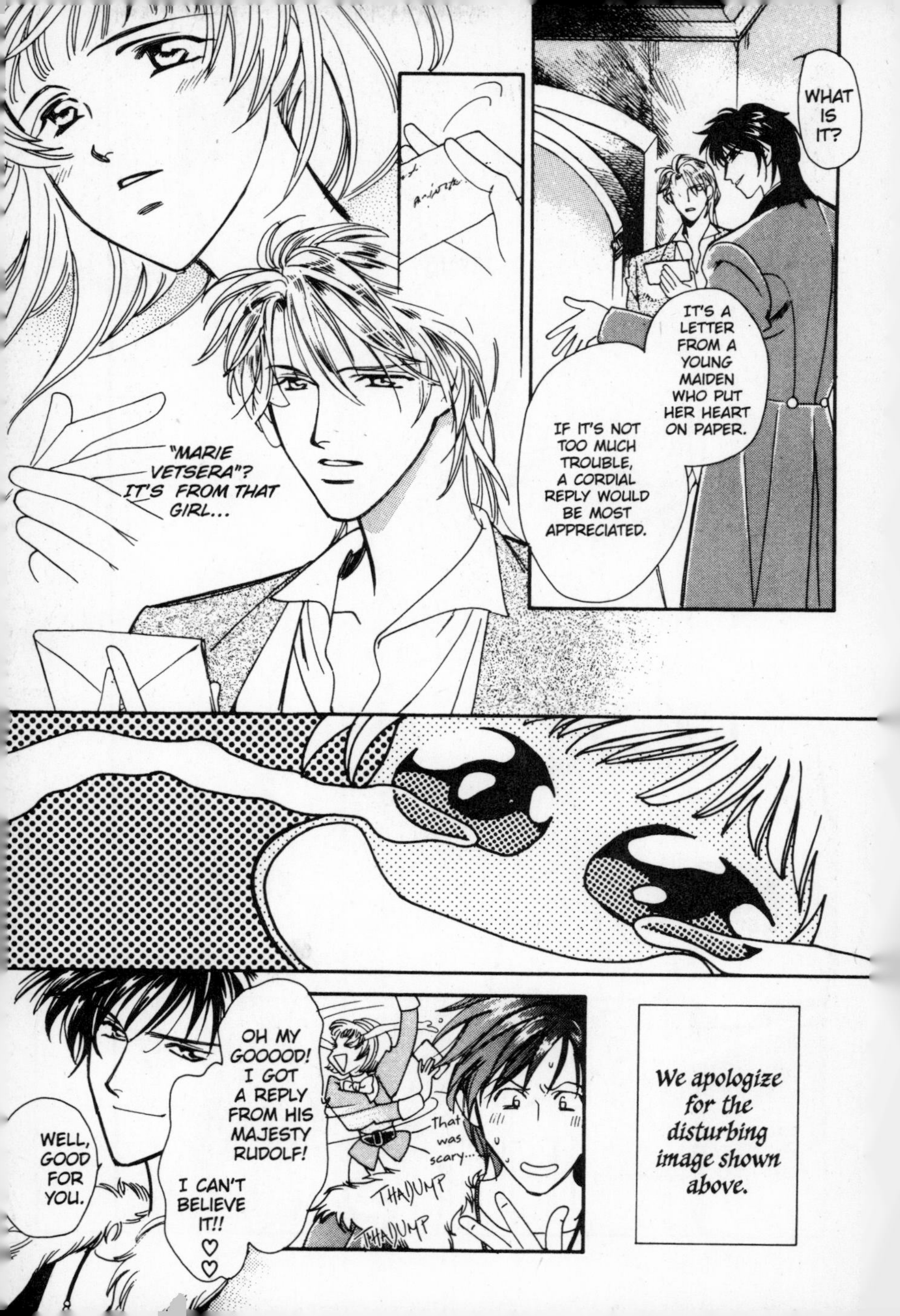
WHAT IS IT?
IT'S A LETTER FROM A YOUNG MAIDEN WHO PUT HER HEART ON PAPER.
IF IT'S NOT TOO MUCH TROUBLE, A CORDIAL REPLY WOULD BE MOST APPRECIATED.
"MARIE VETSERA"? IT'S FROM THAT GIRL...
We apologize for the disturbing image shown above.
OH MY GOOOOD! I GOT A REPLY FROM HIS MAJESTY RUDOLF!
I CAN'T BELIEVE IT!! ♡ ♡
That was scary...
THADUMP
THADUMP
WELL, GOOD FOR YOU.

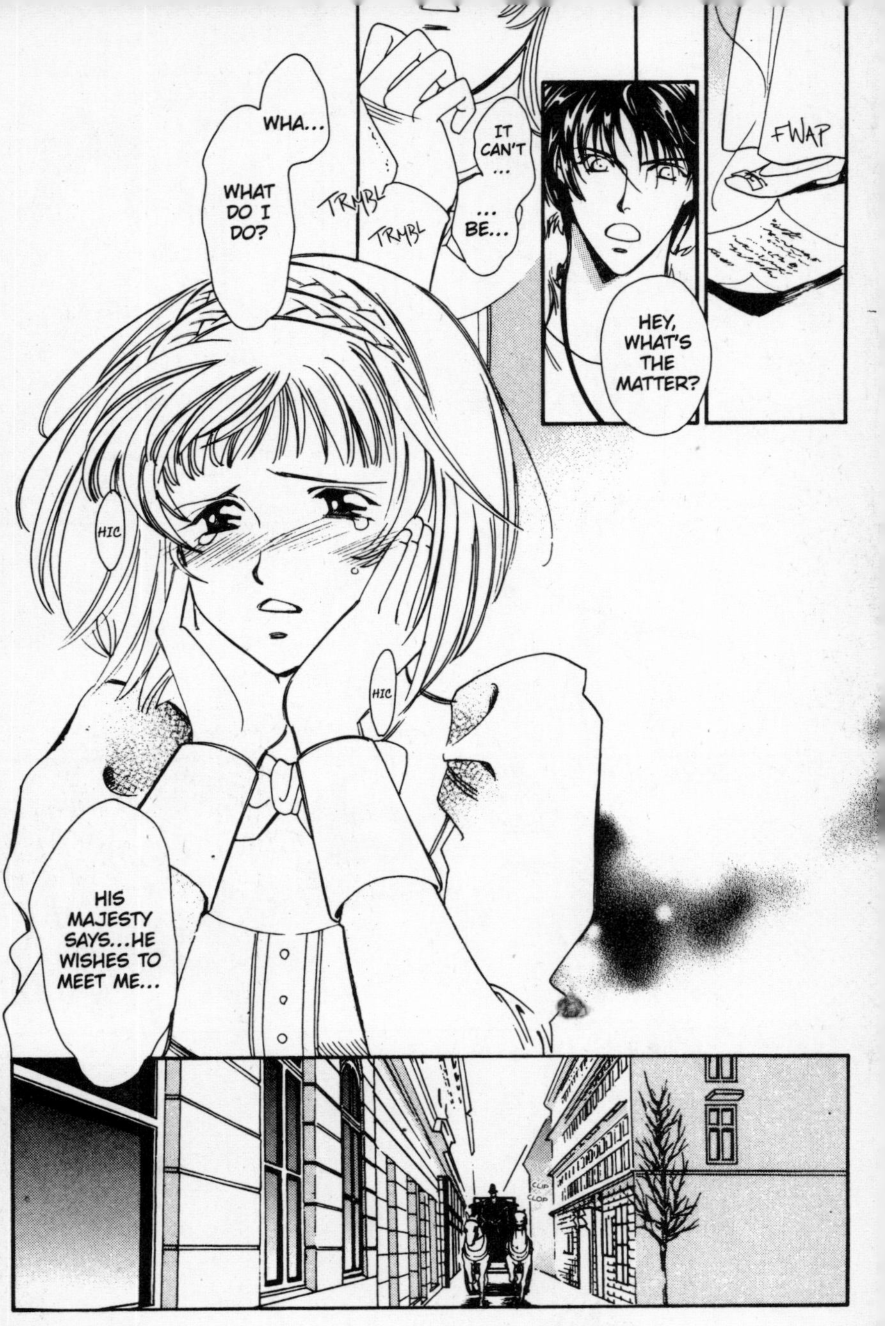
FWAP
HEY, WHAT'S THE MATTER?
IT CAN'T ...
... BE...
TRMBL
TRMBL
WHA...
WHAT DO I DO?
HIC
HIC
HIS MAJESTY SAYS...HE WISHES TO MEET ME...
CLIP
CLOP

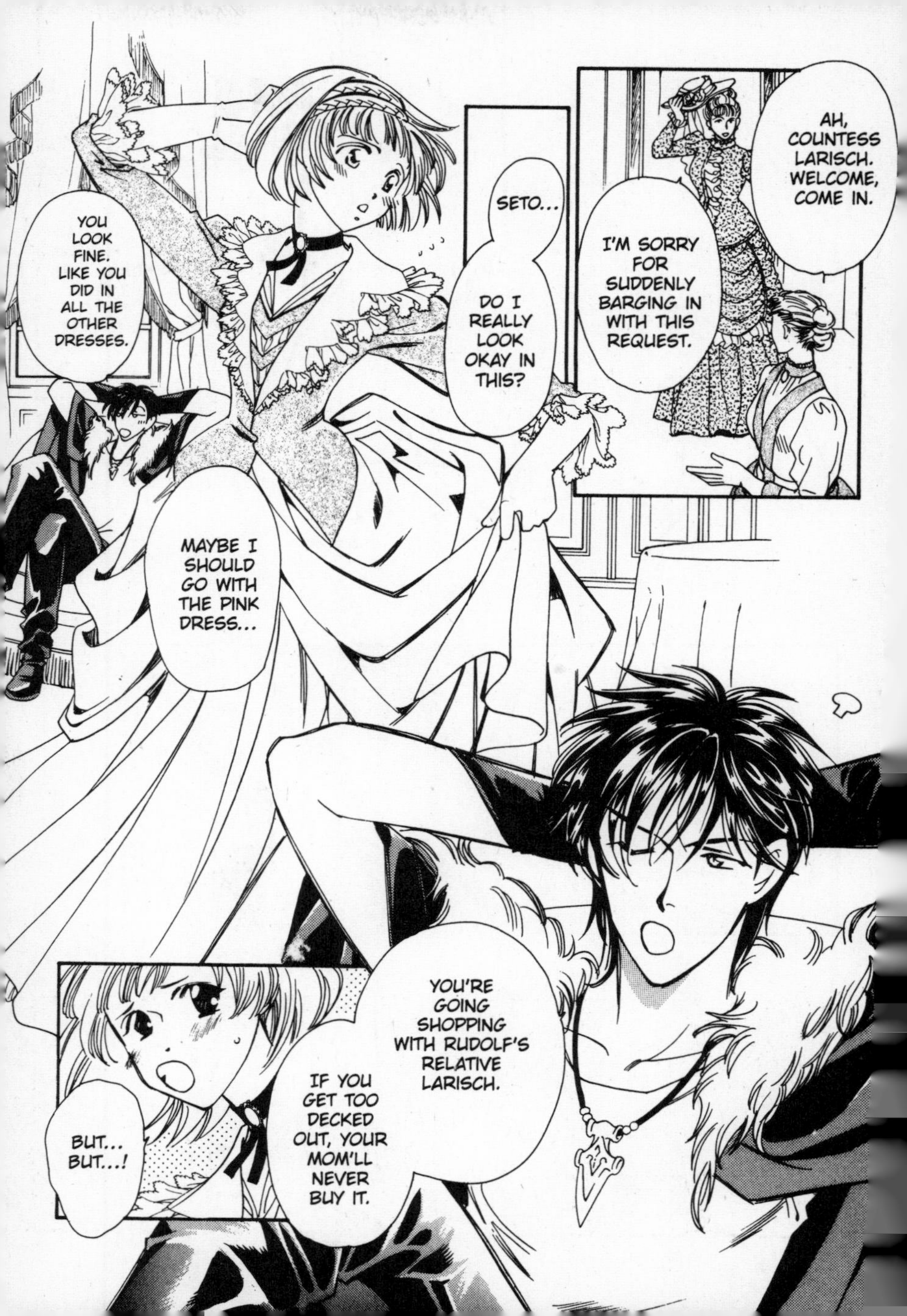
AH, COUNTESS LARISCH. WELCOME, COME IN.
I'M SORRY FOR SUDDENLY BARGING IN WITH THIS REQUEST.
SETO...
DO I REALLY LOOK OKAY IN THIS?
YOU LOOK FINE. LIKE YOU DID IN ALL THE OTHER DRESSES.
MAYBE I SHOULD GO WITH THE PINK DRESS...
YOU'RE GOING SHOPPING WITH RUDOLF'S RELATIVE LARISCH.
IF YOU GET TOO DECKED OUT, YOUR MOM'LL NEVER BUY IT.
BUT... BUT...!

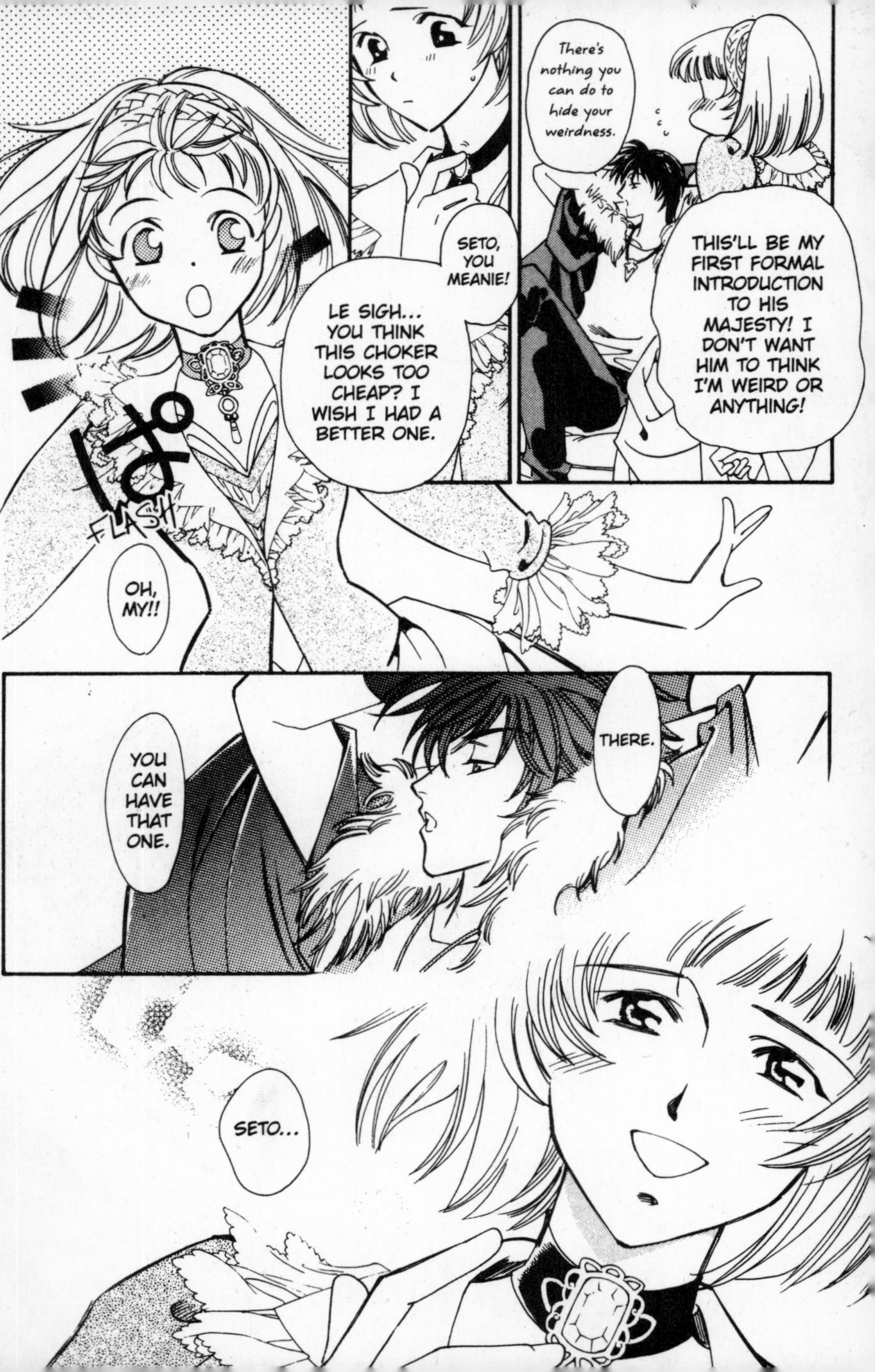
THIS'LL BE MY FIRST FORMAL INTRODUCTION TO HIS MAJESTY! I DON'T WANT HIM TO THINK I'M WEIRD OR ANYTHING!
There's nothing you can do to hide your weirdness.
WHSPR
SETO, YOU MEANIE!
LE SIGH... YOU THINK THIS CHOKER LOOKS TOO CHEAP? I WISH I HAD A BETTER ONE.
FLASH
OH, MY!!
THERE.
YOU CAN HAVE THAT ONE.
SETO...

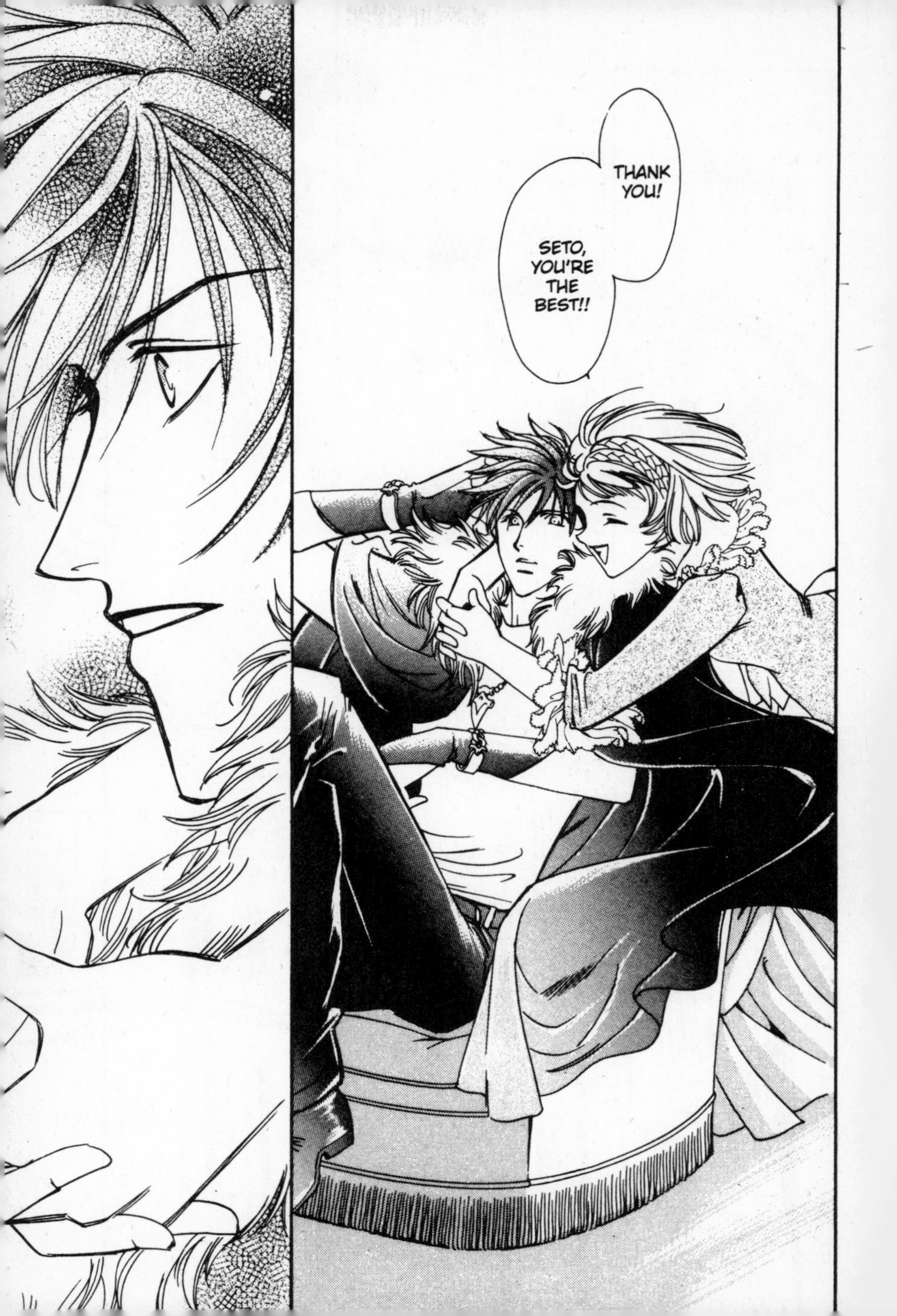
THANK YOU!
SETO, YOU'RE THE BEST!!

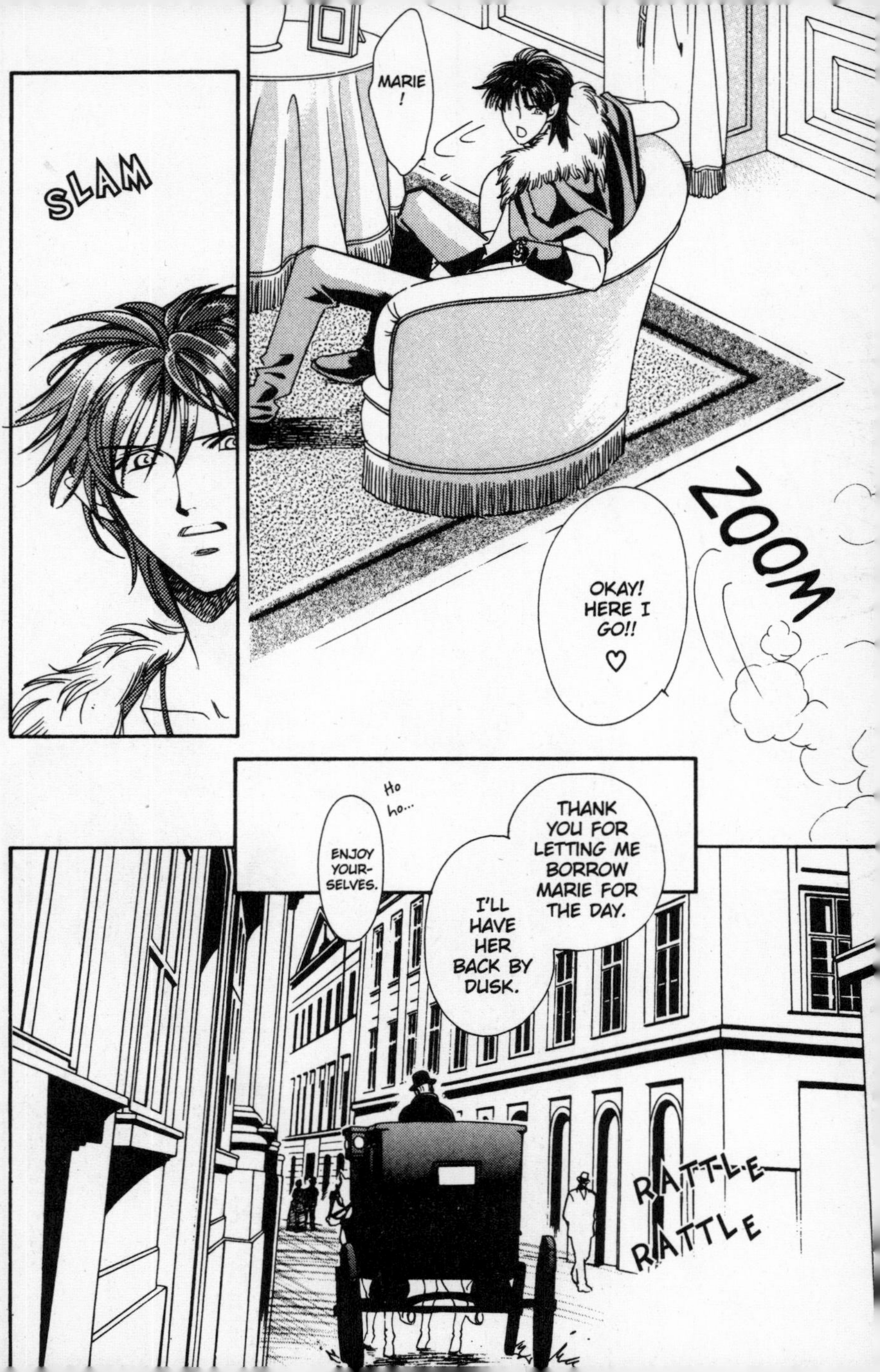
MARIE!
OKAY! HERE I GO!! ♡
ZOOM
SLAM
THANK YOU FOR LETTING ME BORROW MARIE FOR THE DAY.
I'LL HAVE HER BACK BY DUSK.
Ho ho...
ENJOY YOUR-SELVES.
RATTLE
RATTLE

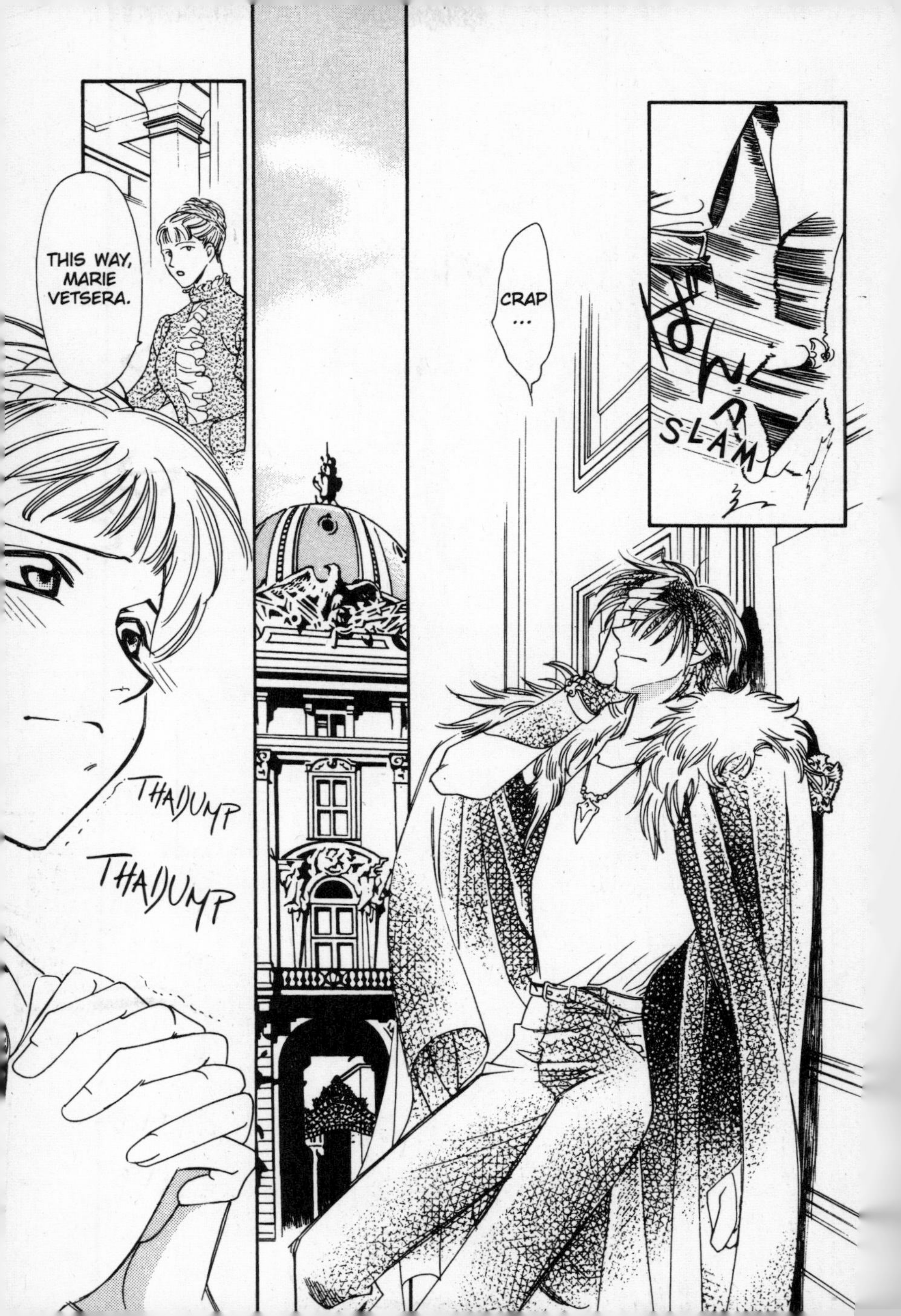
SLAM
CRAP ...
THIS WAY, MARIE VETSERA.
THADUMP
THADUMP

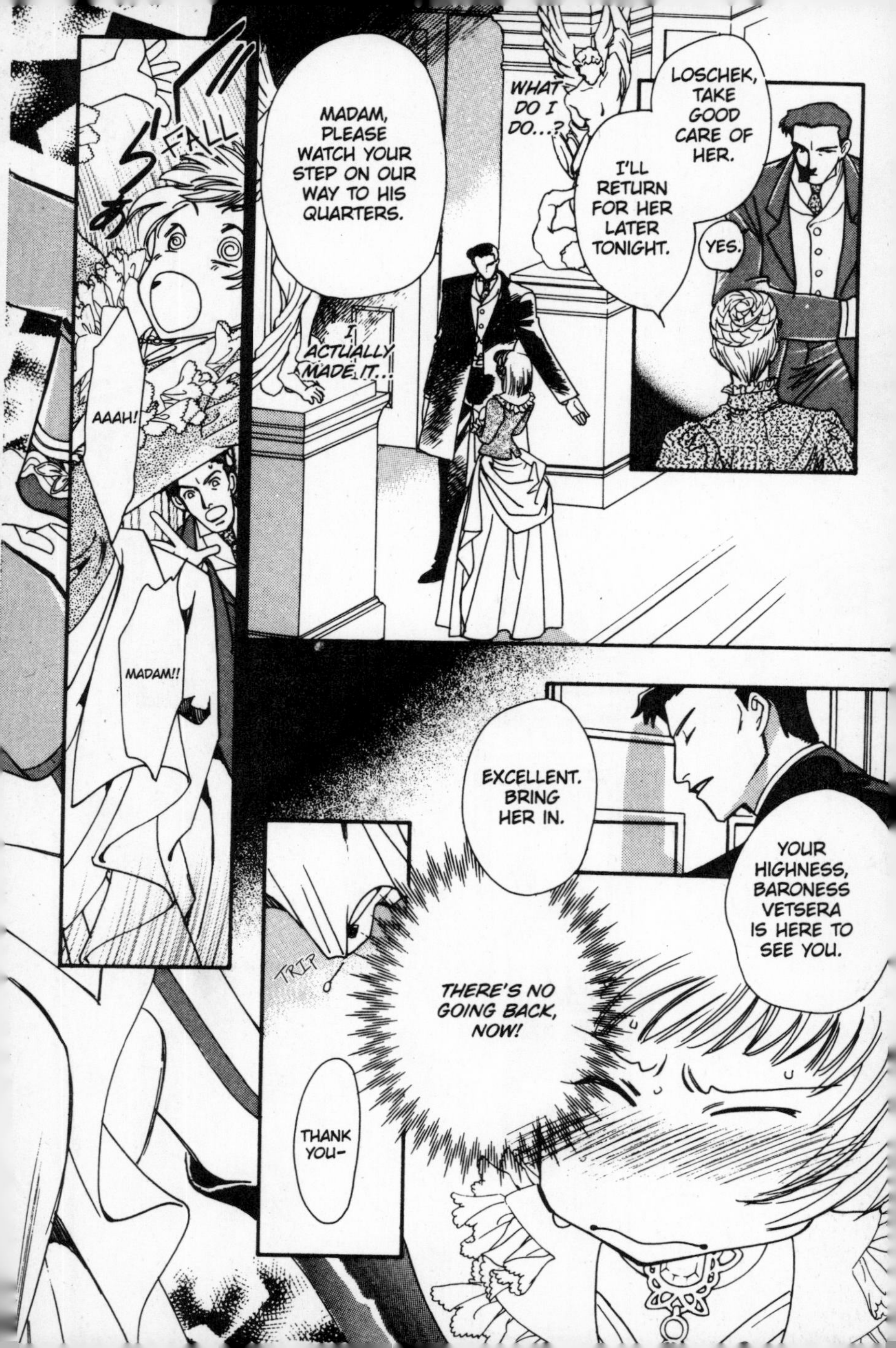
LOSCHEK, TAKE GOOD CARE OF HER.
I'LL RETURN FOR HER LATER TONIGHT.
YES.
WHAT DO I DO...?
MADAM, PLEASE WATCH YOUR STEP ON OUR WAY TO HIS QUARTERS.
I ACTUALLY MADE IT...
YOUR HIGHNESS, BARONESS VETSERA IS HERE TO SEE YOU.
EXCELLENT. BRING HER IN.
THERE'S NO GOING BACK, NOW!
THANK YOU-
TRIP
FALL
AAAH!
MADAM!!

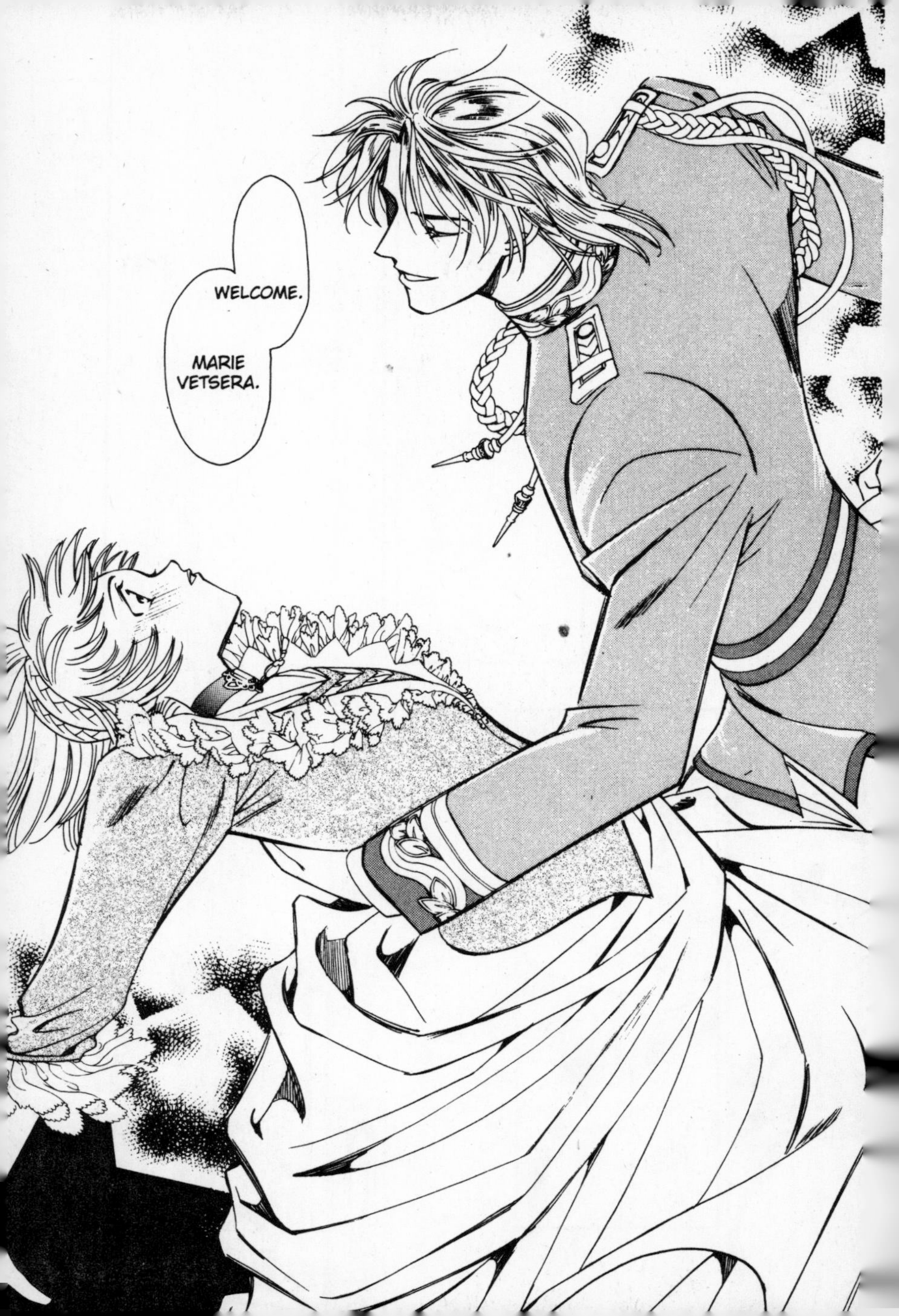
WELCOME.
MARIE VETSERA.

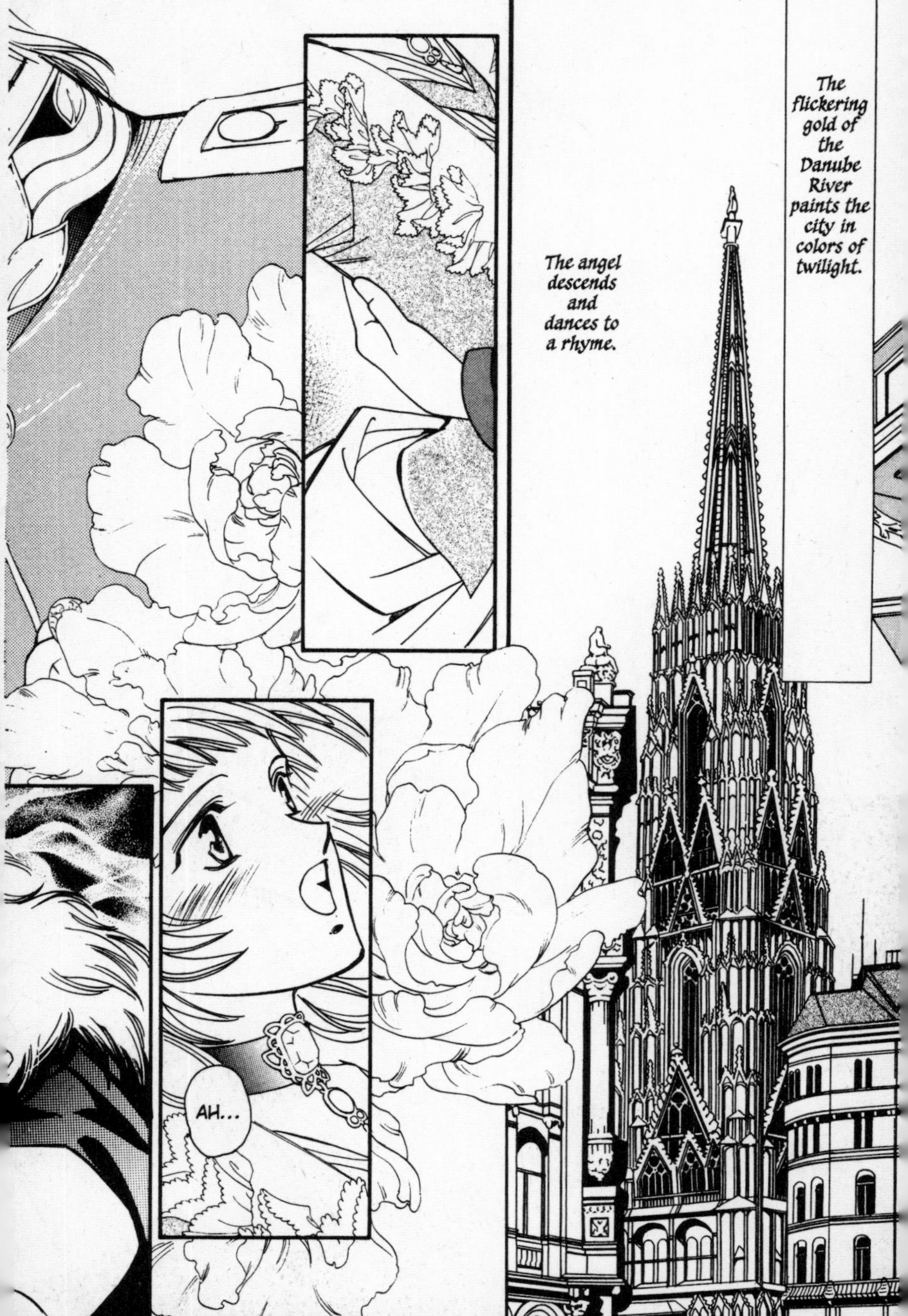
The flickering gold of the Danube River paints the city in colors of twilight.
The angel descends and dances to a rhyme.
AH...

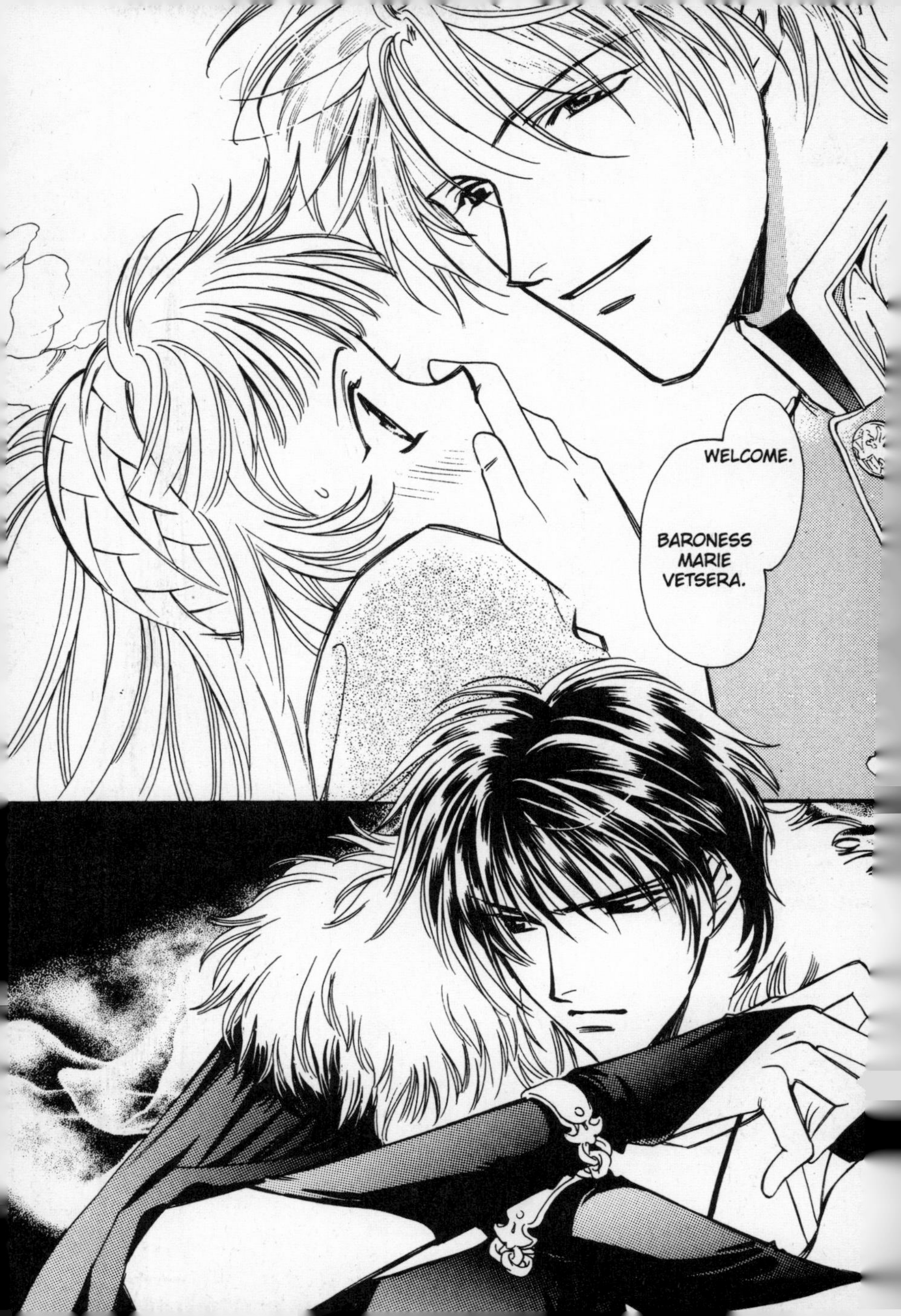
WELCOME.
BARONESS MARIE VETSERA.

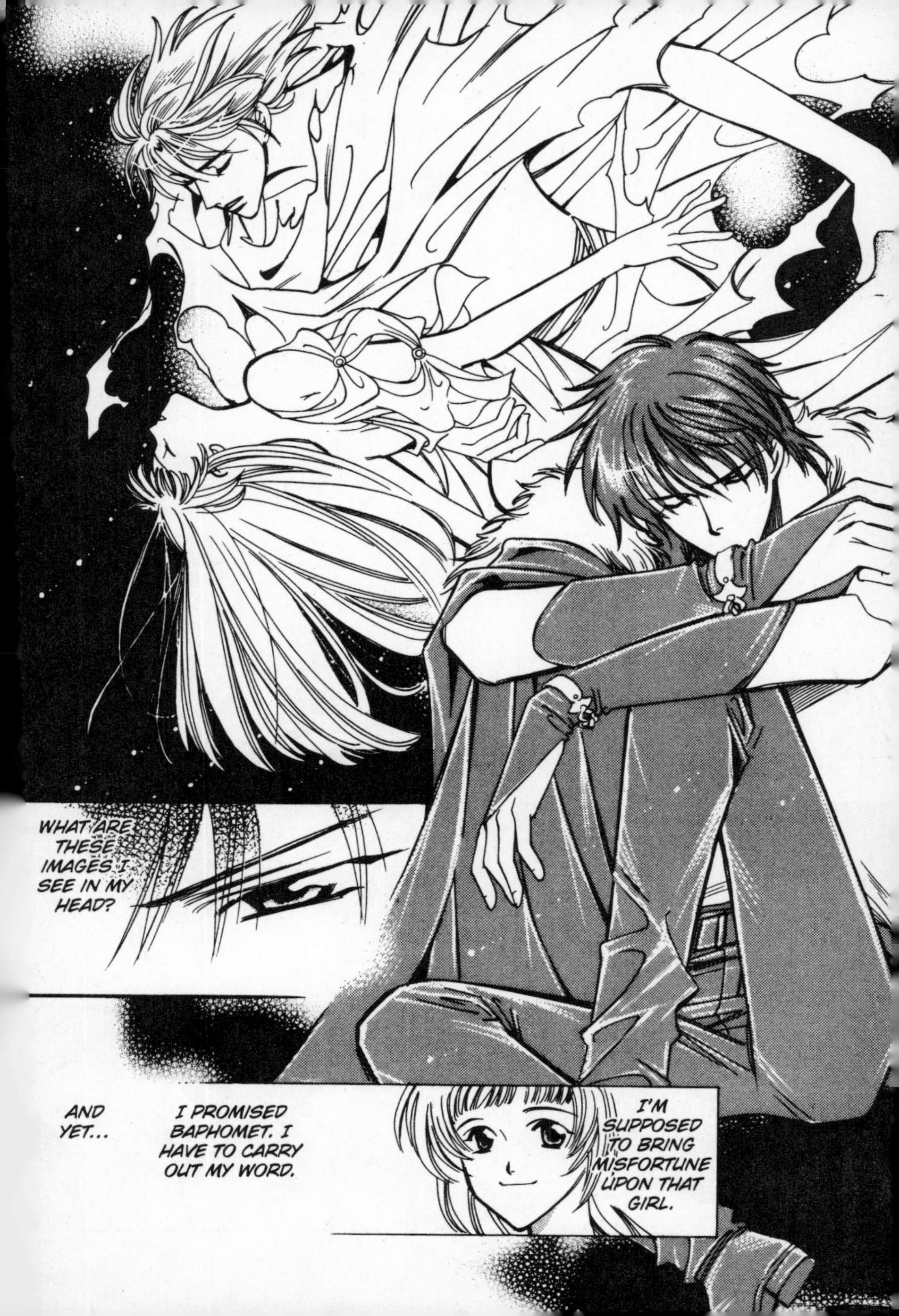
WHAT ARE THESE IMAGES I SEE IN MY HEAD?
I'M SUPPOSED TO BRING MISFORTUNE UPON THAT GIRL.
I PROMISED BAPHOMET. I HAVE TO CARRY OUT MY WORD.
AND YET...

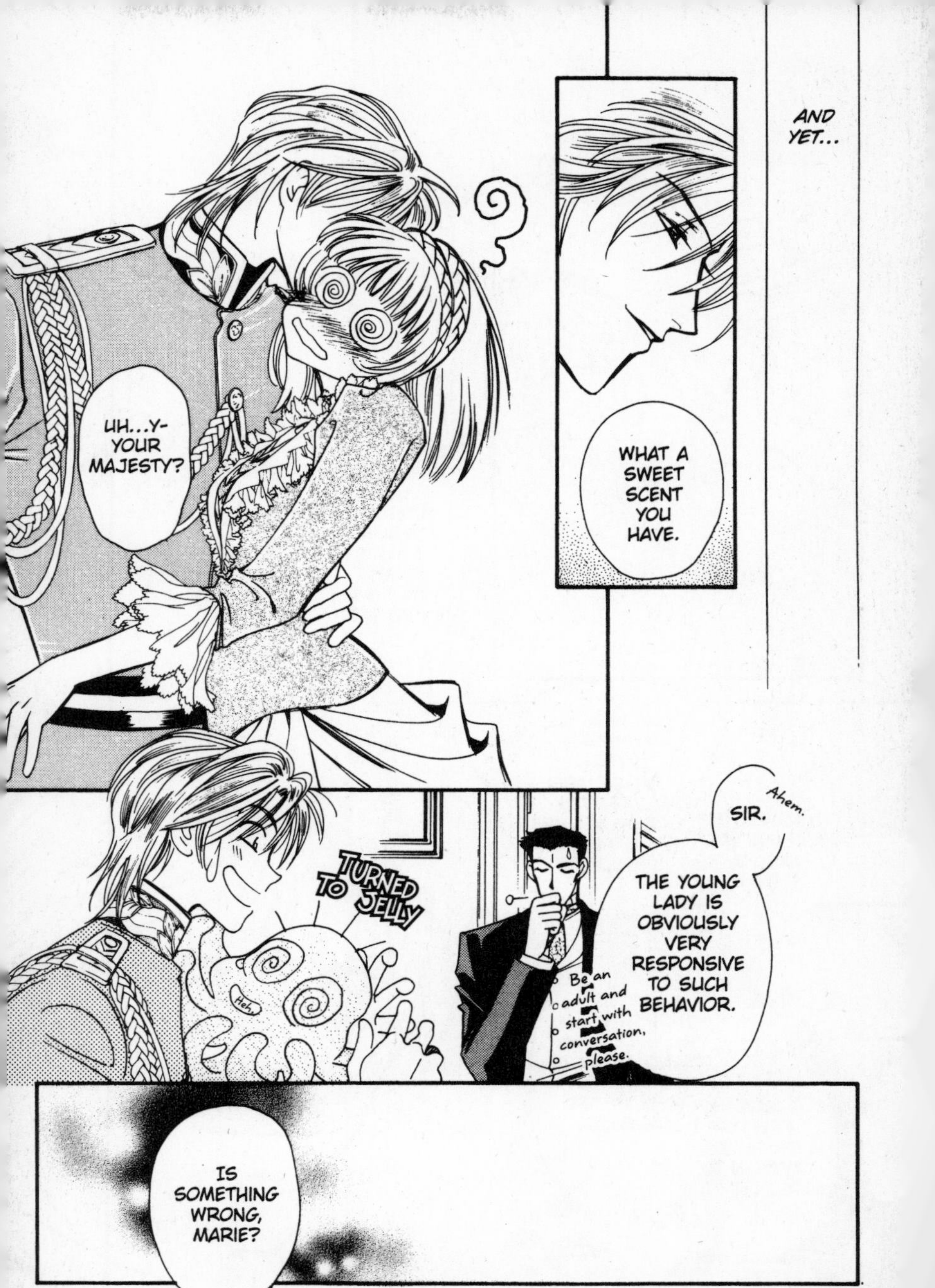
AND YET...
WHAT A SWEET SCENT YOU HAVE.
UH...Y-YOUR MAJESTY?
SIR.
Ahem.
THE YOUNG LADY IS OBVIOUSLY VERY RESPONSIVE TO SUCH BEHAVIOR.
Be an adult and start with conversation, please.
TURNED TO JELLY
Heh.
IS SOMETHING WRONG, MARIE?

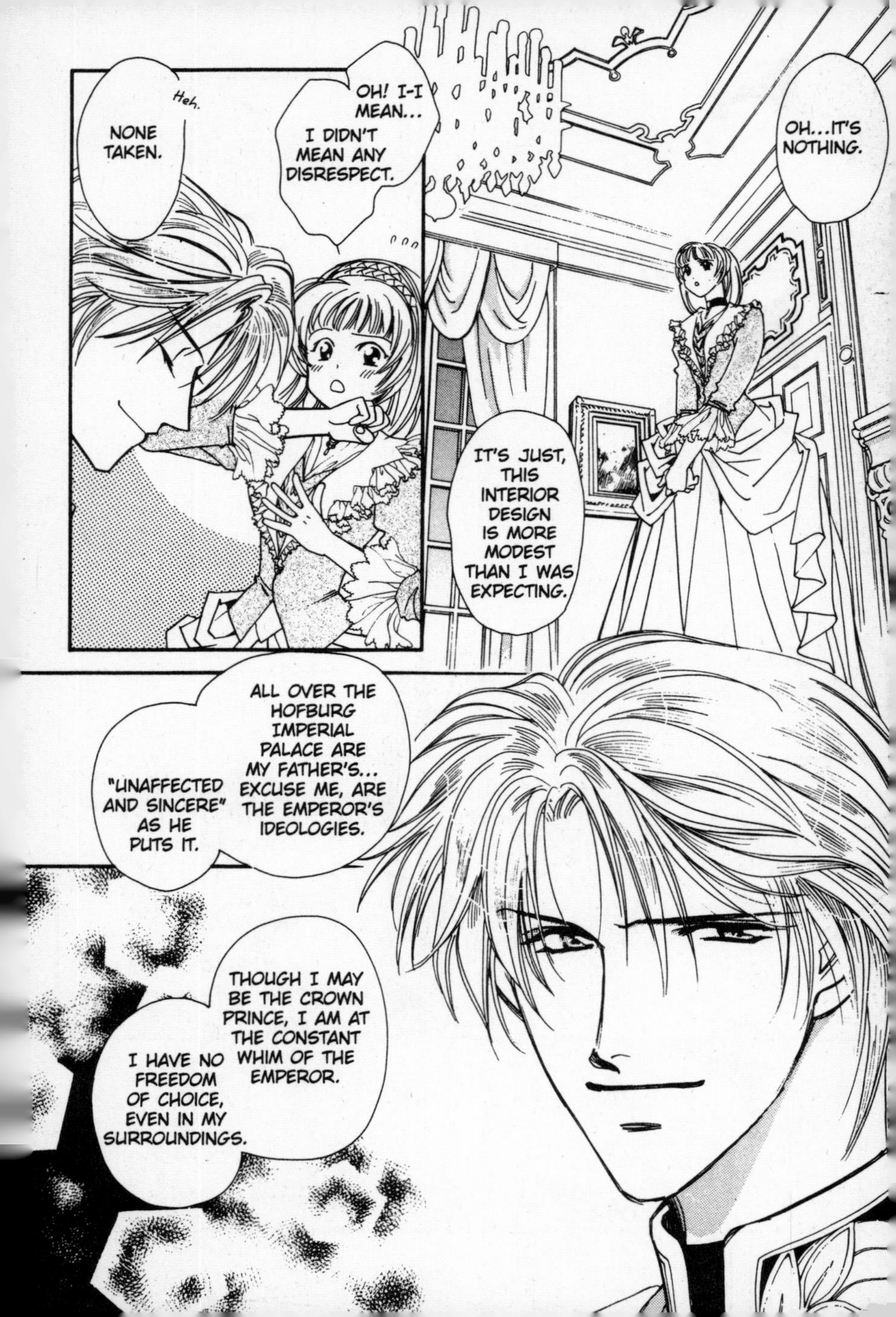
OH...IT'S NOTHING.
IT'S JUST, THIS INTERIOR DESIGN IS MORE MODEST THAN I WAS EXPECTING.
OH! I-I MEAN...
I DIDN'T MEAN ANY DISRESPECT.
Heh.
NONE TAKEN.
ALL OVER THE HOFBURG IMPERIAL PALACE ARE MY FATHER'S... EXCUSE ME, ARE THE EMPEROR'S IDEOLOGIES.
"UNAFFECTED AND SINCERE" AS HE PUTS IT.
THOUGH I MAY BE THE CROWN PRINCE, I AM AT THE CONSTANT WHIM OF THE EMPEROR.
I HAVE NO FREEDOM OF CHOICE, EVEN IN MY SURROUNDINGS.

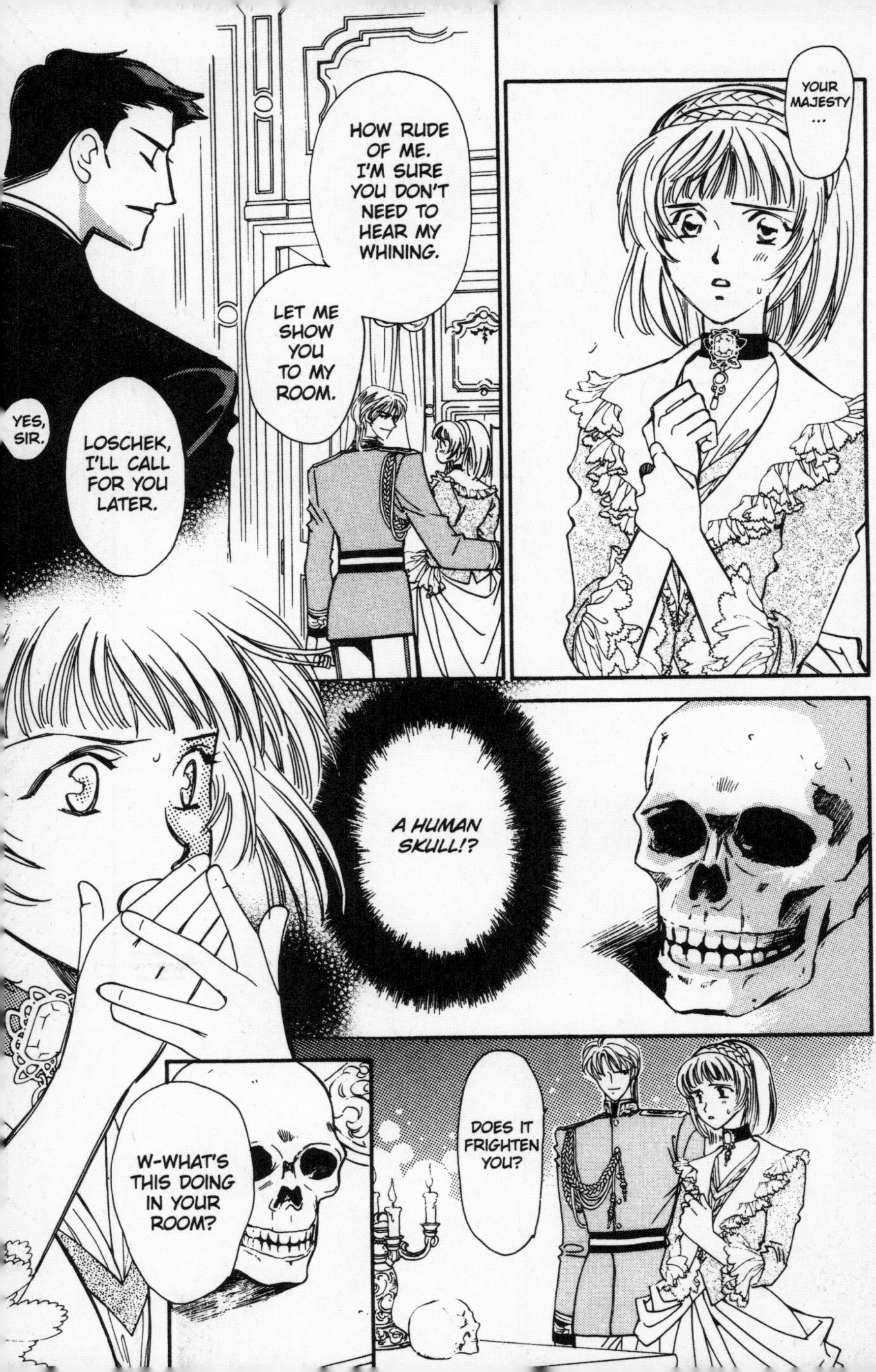
YOUR MAJESTY ...
HOW RUDE OF ME. I'M SURE YOU DON'T NEED TO HEAR MY WHINING.
LET ME SHOW YOU TO MY ROOM.
LOSCHEK, I'LL CALL FOR YOU LATER.
YES, SIR.
A HUMAN SKULL!?
DOES IT FRIGHTEN YOU?
W-WHAT'S THIS DOING IN YOUR ROOM?

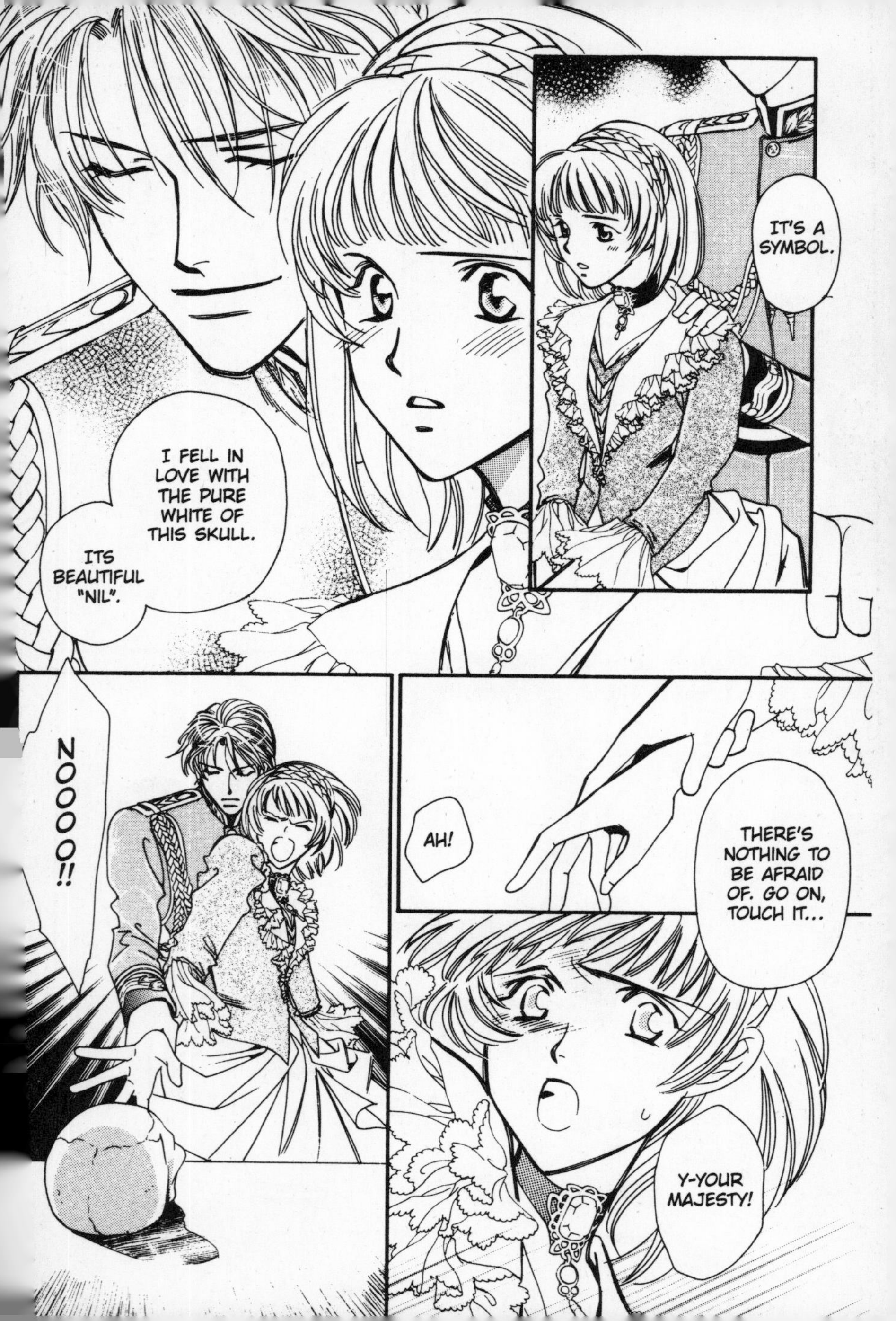
IT'S A SYMBOL.
I FELL IN LOVE WITH THE PURE WHITE OF THIS SKULL.
ITS BEAUTIFUL "NIL".
THERE'S NOTHING TO BE AFRAID OF. GO ON, TOUCH IT...
AH!
Y-YOUR MAJESTY!
NOOOOO!!

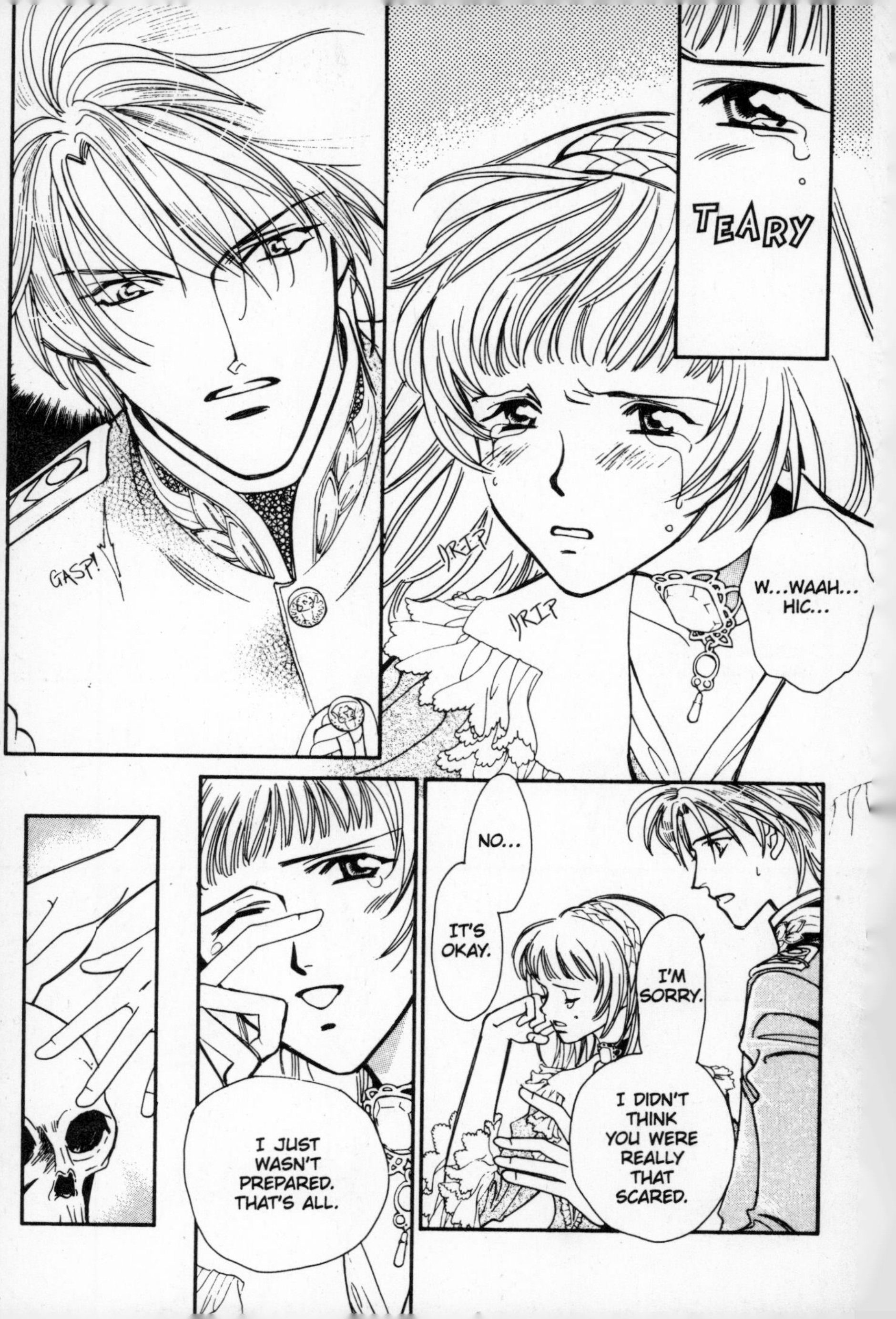
TEARY
DRIP
DRIP
W...WAAH... HIC...
GASP!
I'M SORRY.
I DIDN'T THINK YOU WERE REALLY THAT SCARED.
NO...
IT'S OKAY.
I JUST WASN'T PREPARED. THAT'S ALL.

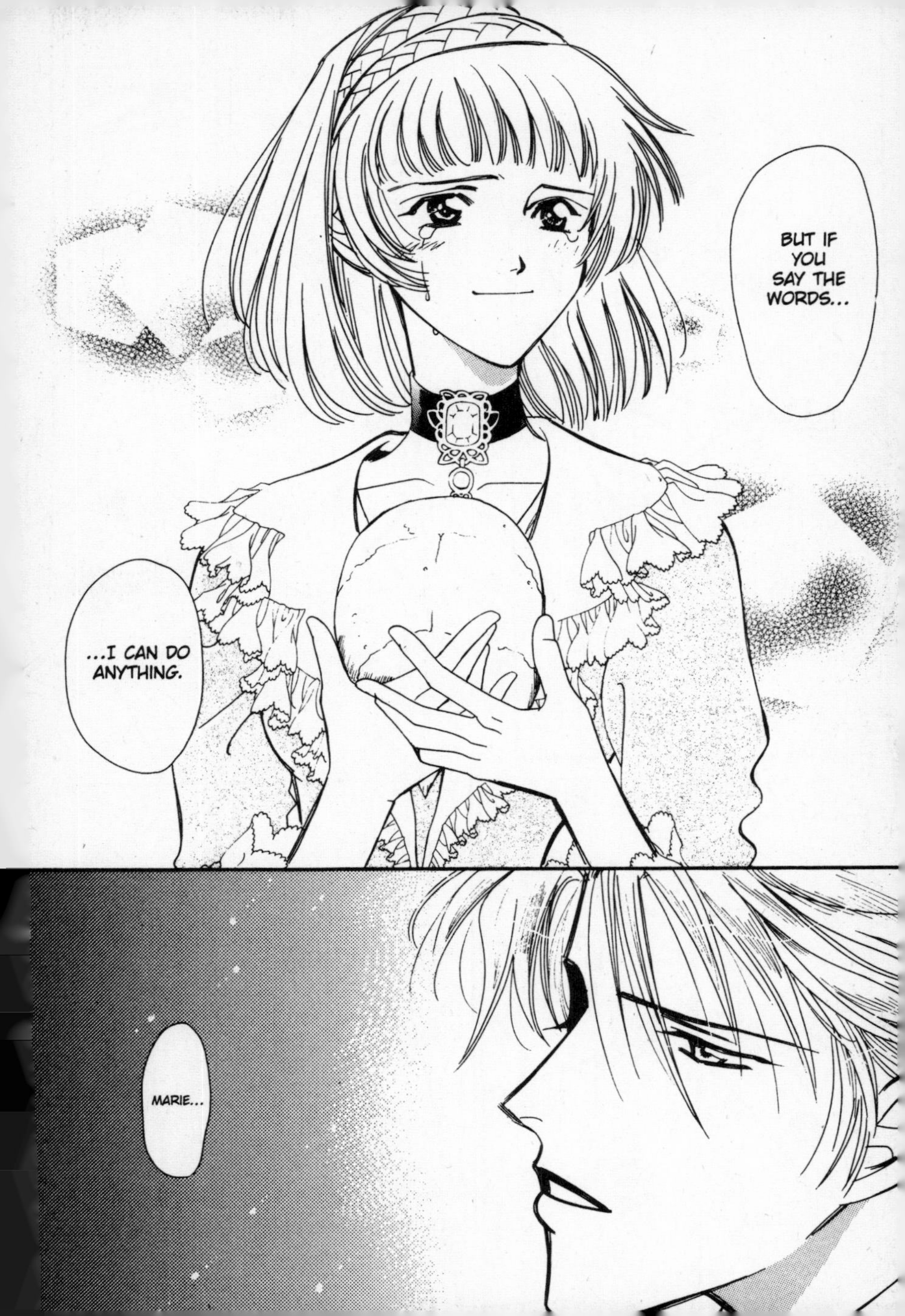
BUT IF YOU SAY THE WORDS...
...I CAN DO ANYTHING.
MARIE...

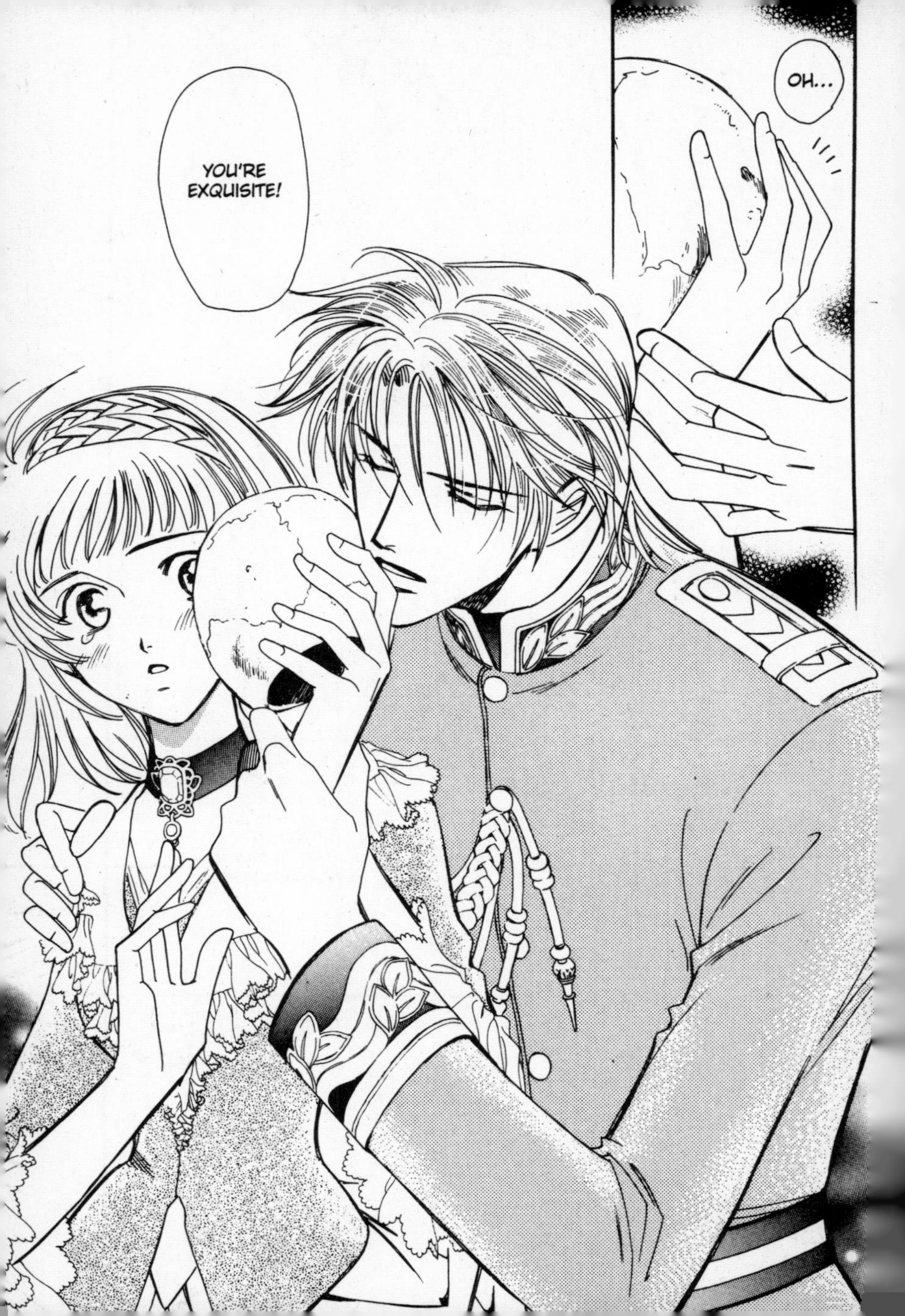
OH...
YOU'RE EXQUISITE!

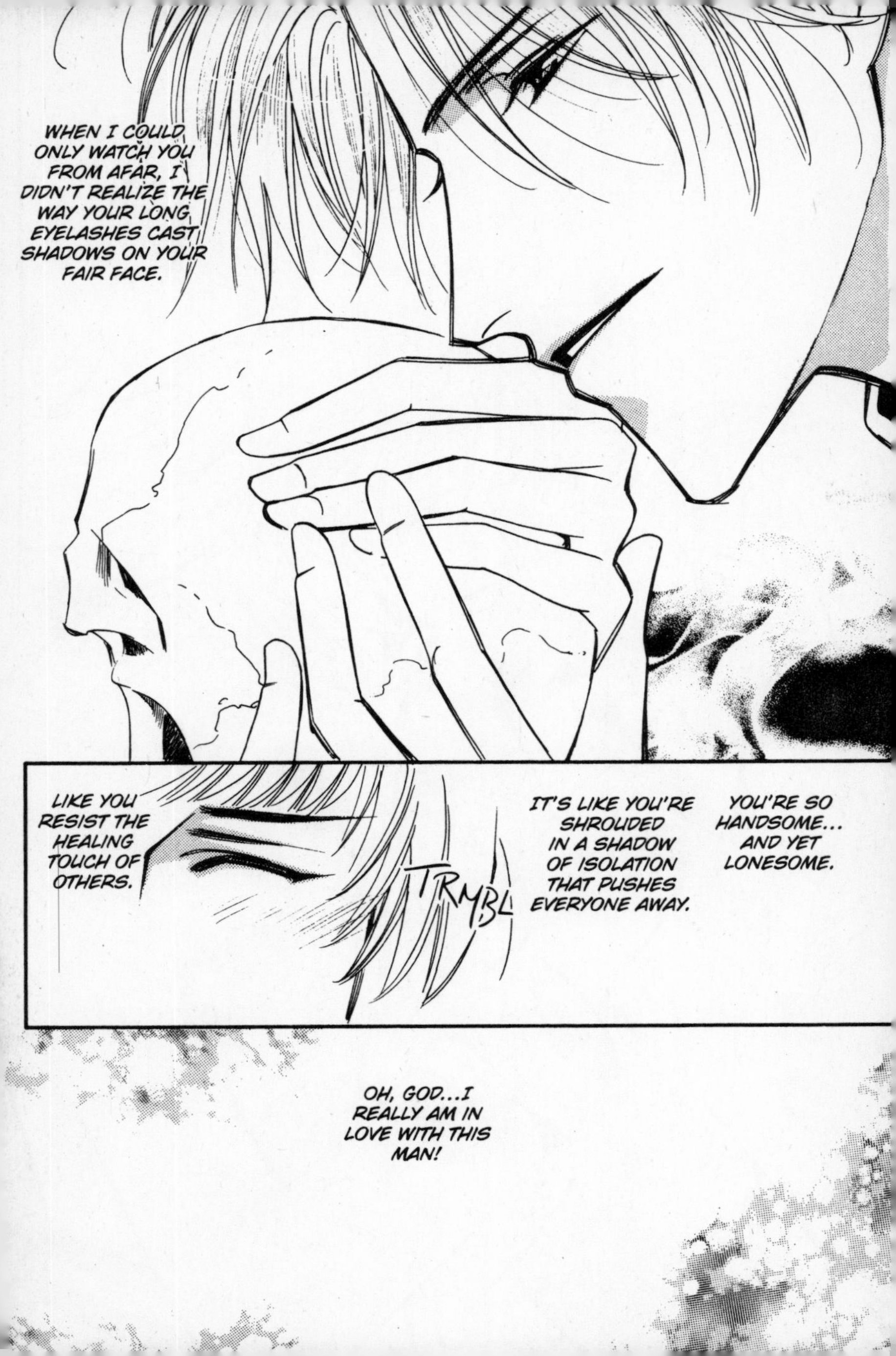
WHEN I COULD ONLY WATCH YOU FROM AFAR, I DIDN'T REALIZE THE WAY YOUR LONG EYELASHES CAST SHADOWS ON YOUR FAIR FACE.
YOU'RE SO HANDSOME... AND YET LONESOME.
IT'S LIKE YOU'RE SHROUDED IN A SHADOW OF ISOLATION THAT PUSHES EVERYONE AWAY.
TRMBL
LIKE YOU RESIST THE HEALING TOUCH OF OTHERS.
OH, GOD...I REALLY AM IN LOVE WITH THIS MAN!

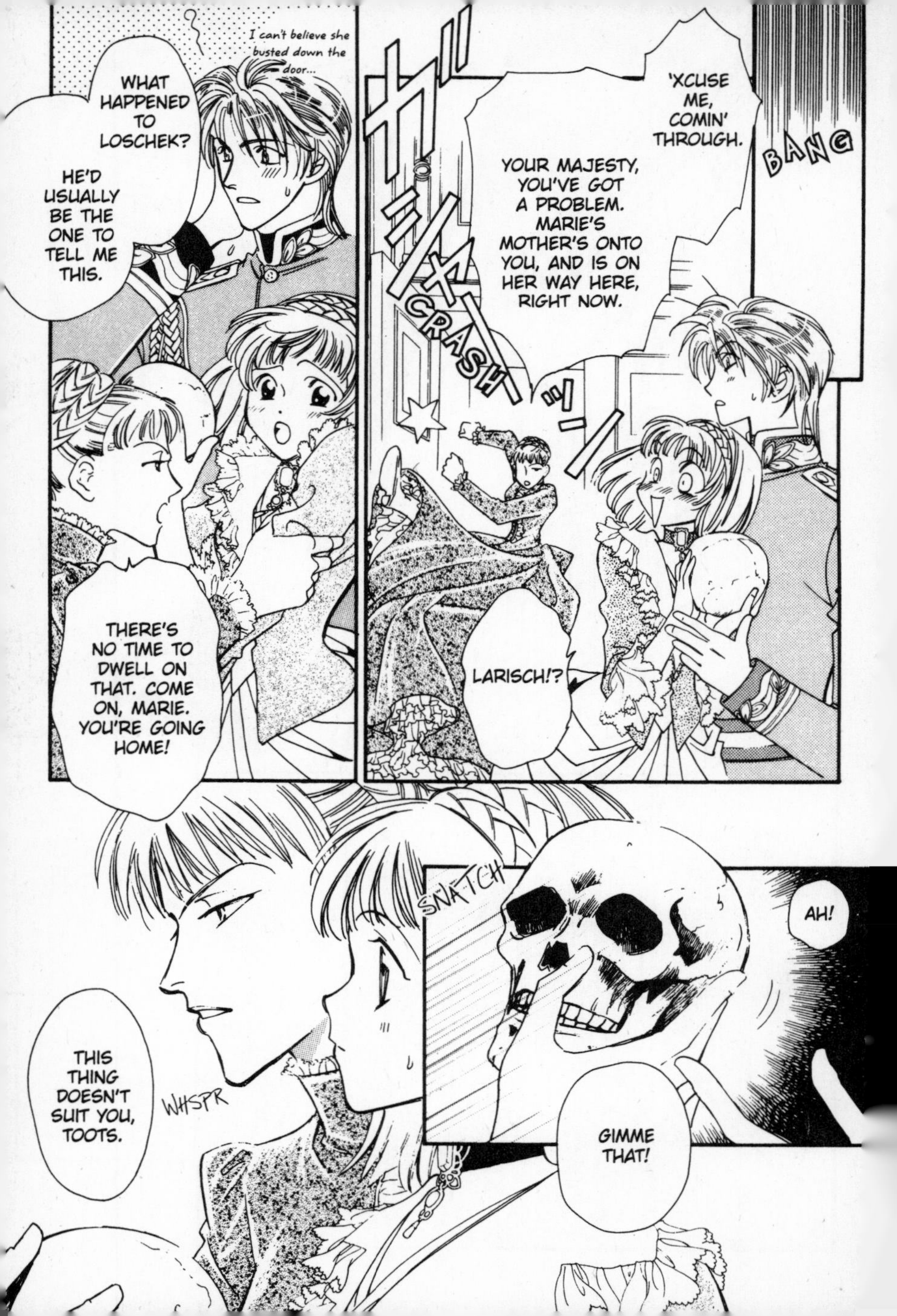
'XCUSE ME, COMIN' THROUGH.
BANG
YOUR MAJESTY, YOU'VE GOT A PROBLEM. MARIE'S MOTHER'S ONTO YOU, AND IS ON HER WAY HERE, RIGHT NOW.
CRASH
LARISCH!?
I can't believe she busted down the door...
WHAT HAPPENED TO LOSCHEK?
HE'D USUALLY BE THE ONE TO TELL ME THIS.
THERE'S NO TIME TO DWELL ON THAT. COME ON, MARIE. YOU'RE GOING HOME!
SNATCH
AH!
GIMME THAT!
THIS THING DOESN'T SUIT YOU, TOOTS.
WHSPR

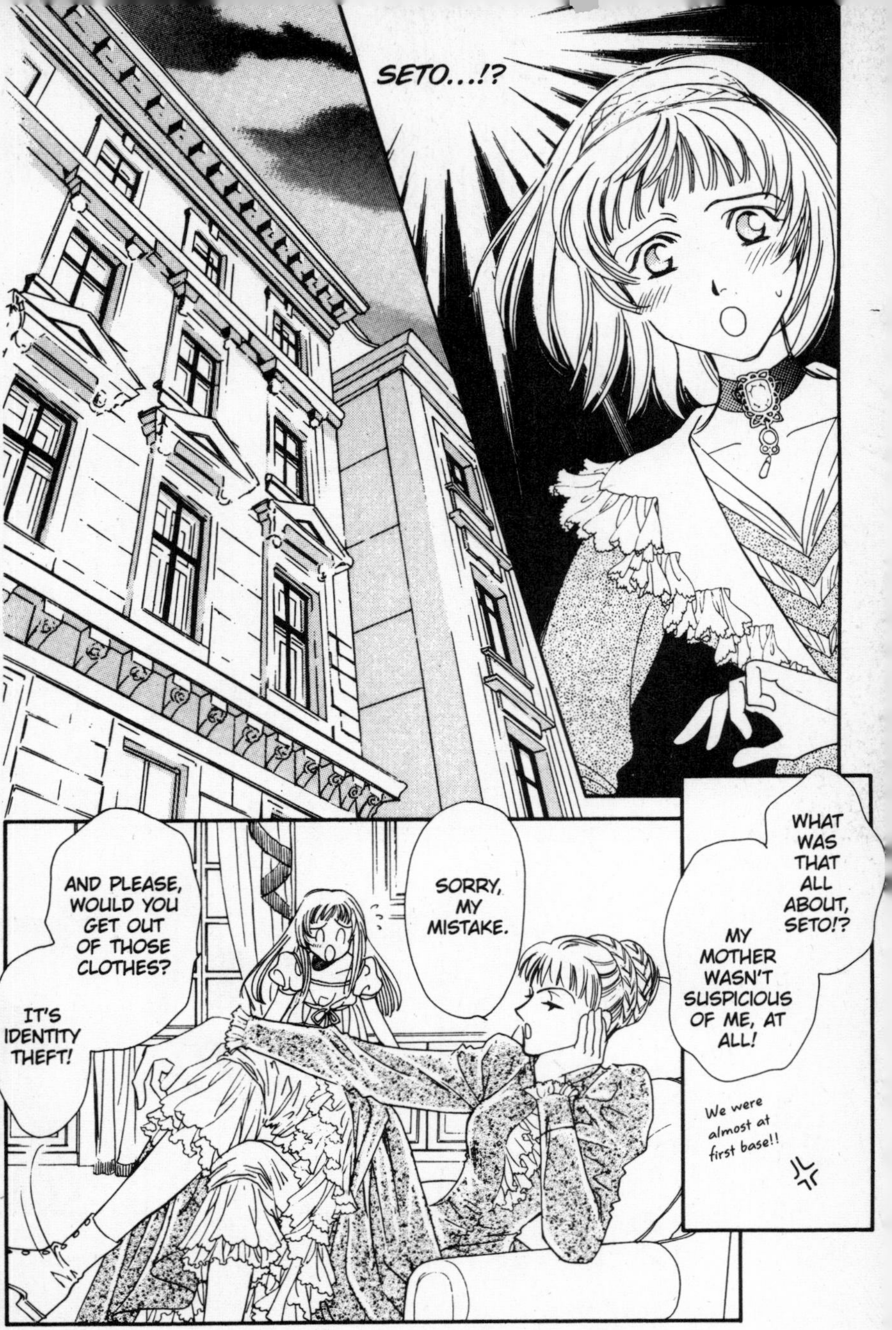
SETO...!?
WHAT WAS THAT ALL ABOUT, SETO!?
MY MOTHER WASN'T SUSPICIOUS OF ME, AT ALL!
We were almost at first base!!
SORRY, MY MISTAKE.
AND PLEASE, WOULD YOU GET OUT OF THOSE CLOTHES?
IT'S IDENTITY THEFT!

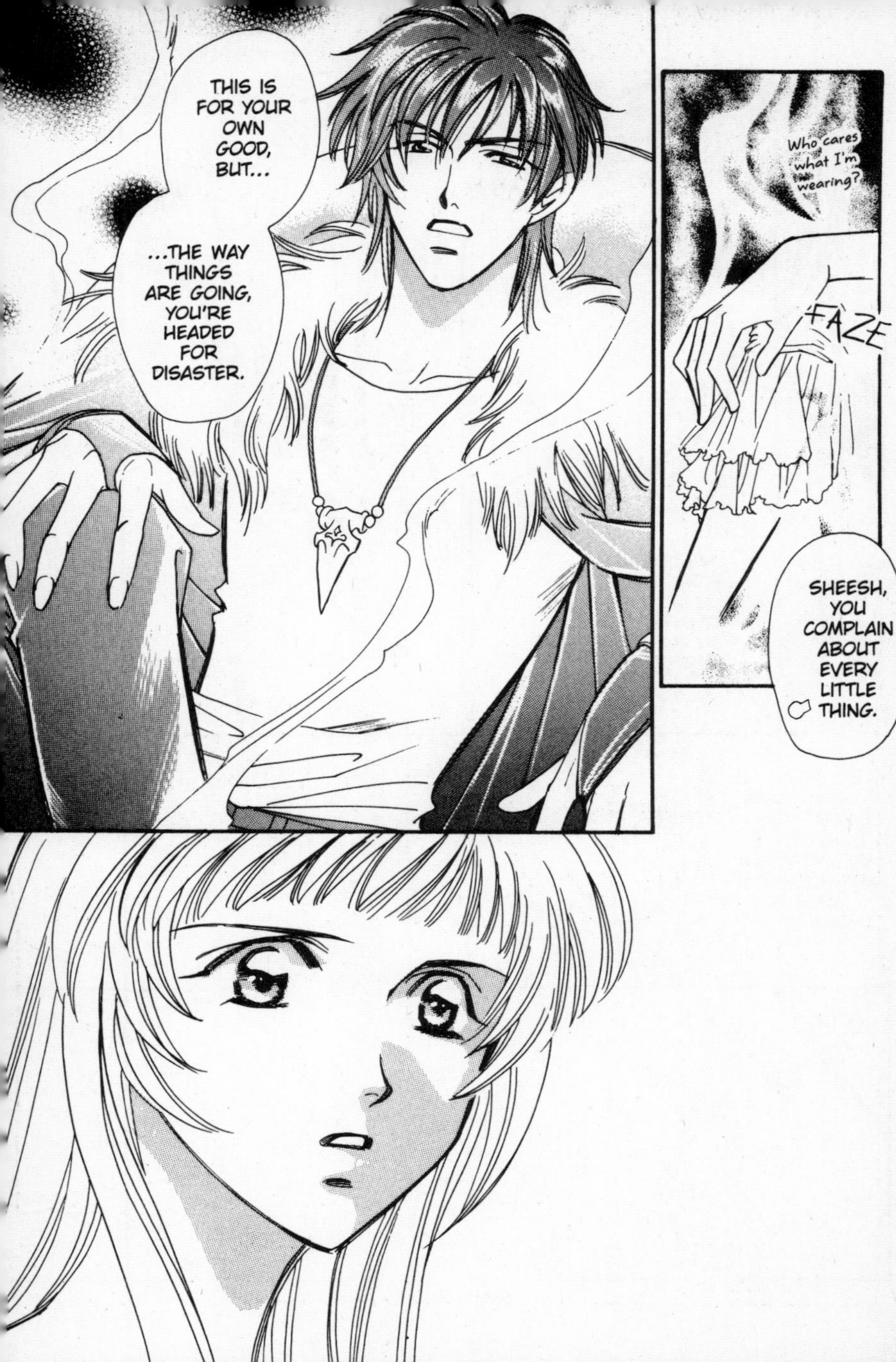
Who cares what I'm wearing?
FAZE
SHEESH, YOU COMPLAIN ABOUT EVERY LITTLE THING.
THIS IS FOR YOUR OWN GOOD, BUT...
...THE WAY THINGS ARE GOING, YOU'RE HEADED FOR DISASTER.

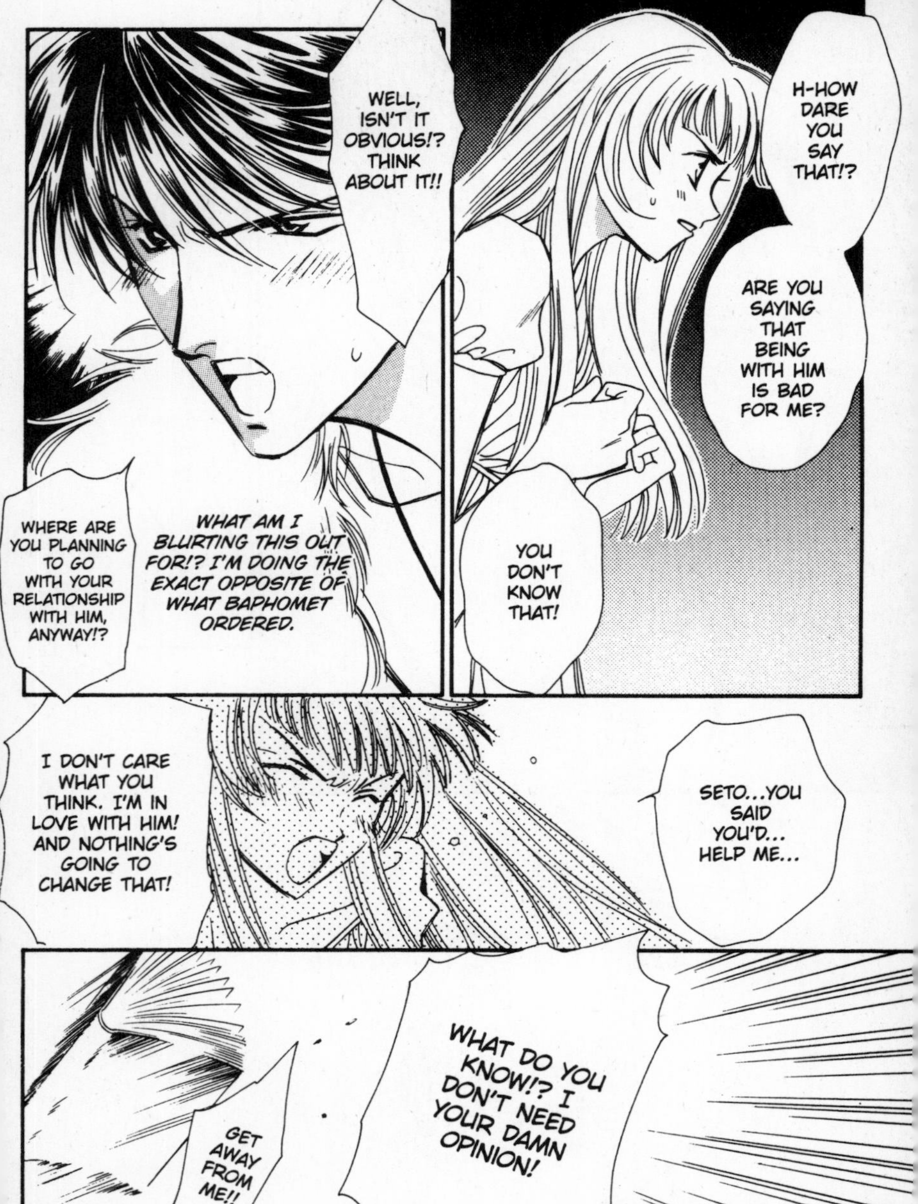
H-HOW DARE YOU SAY THAT!?
ARE YOU SAYING THAT BEING WITH HIM IS BAD FOR ME?
YOU DON'T KNOW THAT!
WELL, ISN'T IT OBVIOUS!? THINK ABOUT IT!!
WHAT AM I BLURTING THIS OUT FOR!? I'M DOING THE EXACT OPPOSITE OF WHAT BAPHOMET ORDERED.
WHERE ARE YOU PLANNING TO GO WITH YOUR RELATIONSHIP WITH HIM, ANYWAY!?
SETO...YOU SAID YOU'D... HELP ME...
I DON'T CARE WHAT YOU THINK. I'M IN LOVE WITH HIM! AND NOTHING'S GOING TO CHANGE THAT!
WHAT DO YOU KNOW!? I DON'T NEED YOUR DAMN OPINION!
GET AWAY FROM ME!!

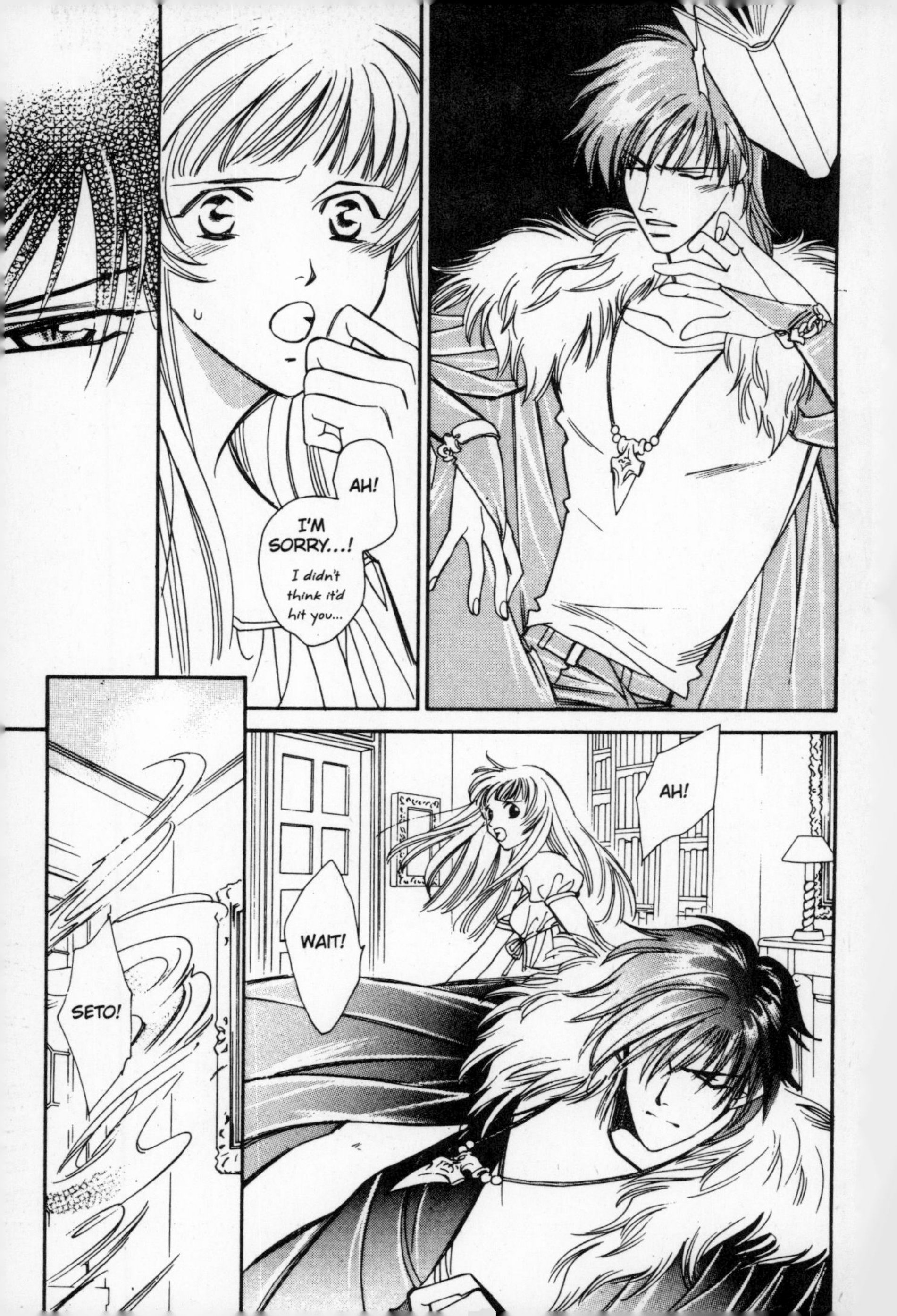
AH!
I'M SORRY...! I didn't think it'd hit you...
AH!
WAIT!
SETO!

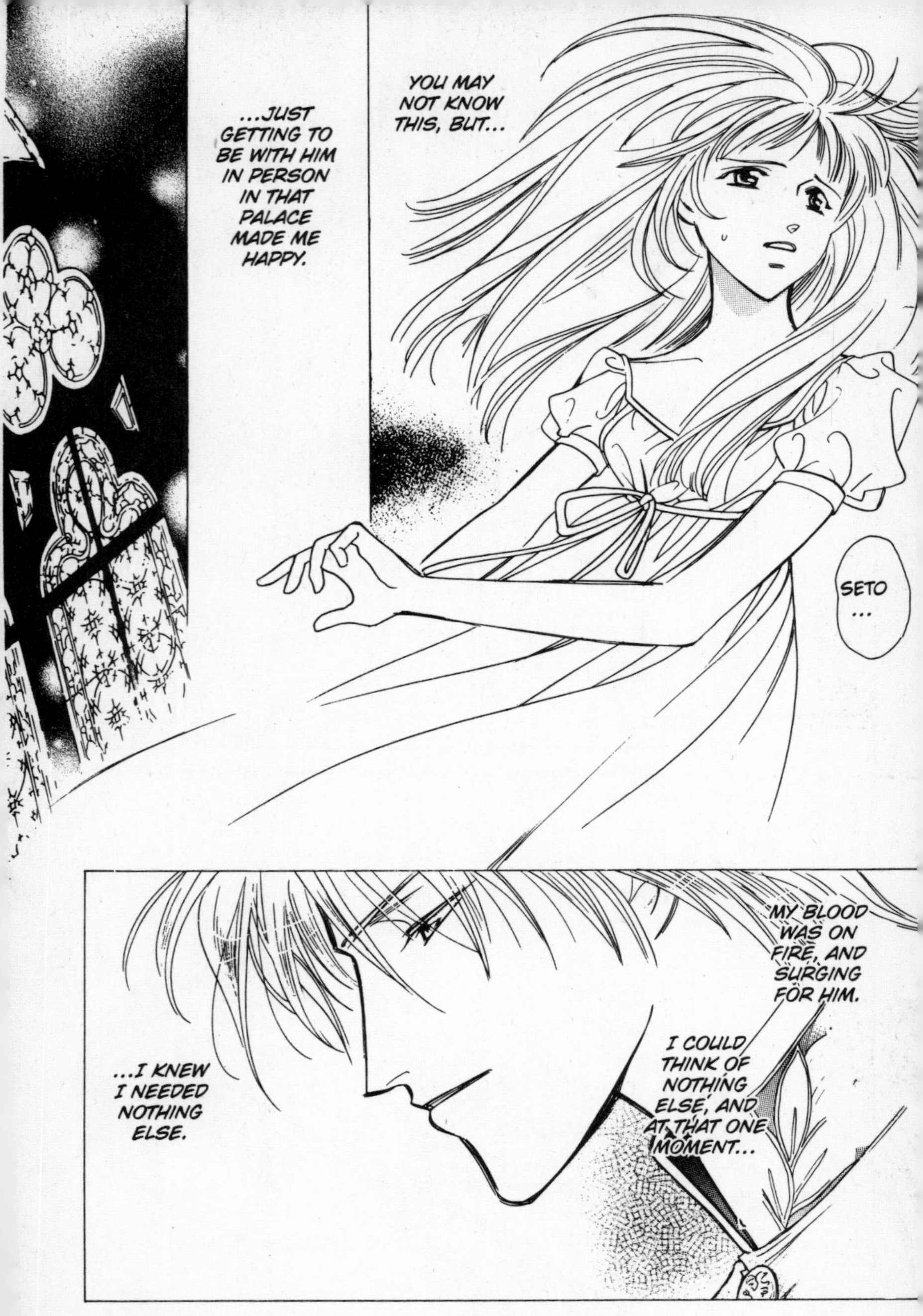
YOU MAY NOT KNOW THIS, BUT...
SETO ...
...JUST GETTING TO BE WITH HIM IN PERSON IN THAT PALACE MADE ME HAPPY.
MY BLOOD WAS ON FIRE, AND SURGING FOR HIM.
I COULD THINK OF NOTHING ELSE, AND AT THAT ONE MOMENT...
...I KNEW I NEEDED NOTHING ELSE.

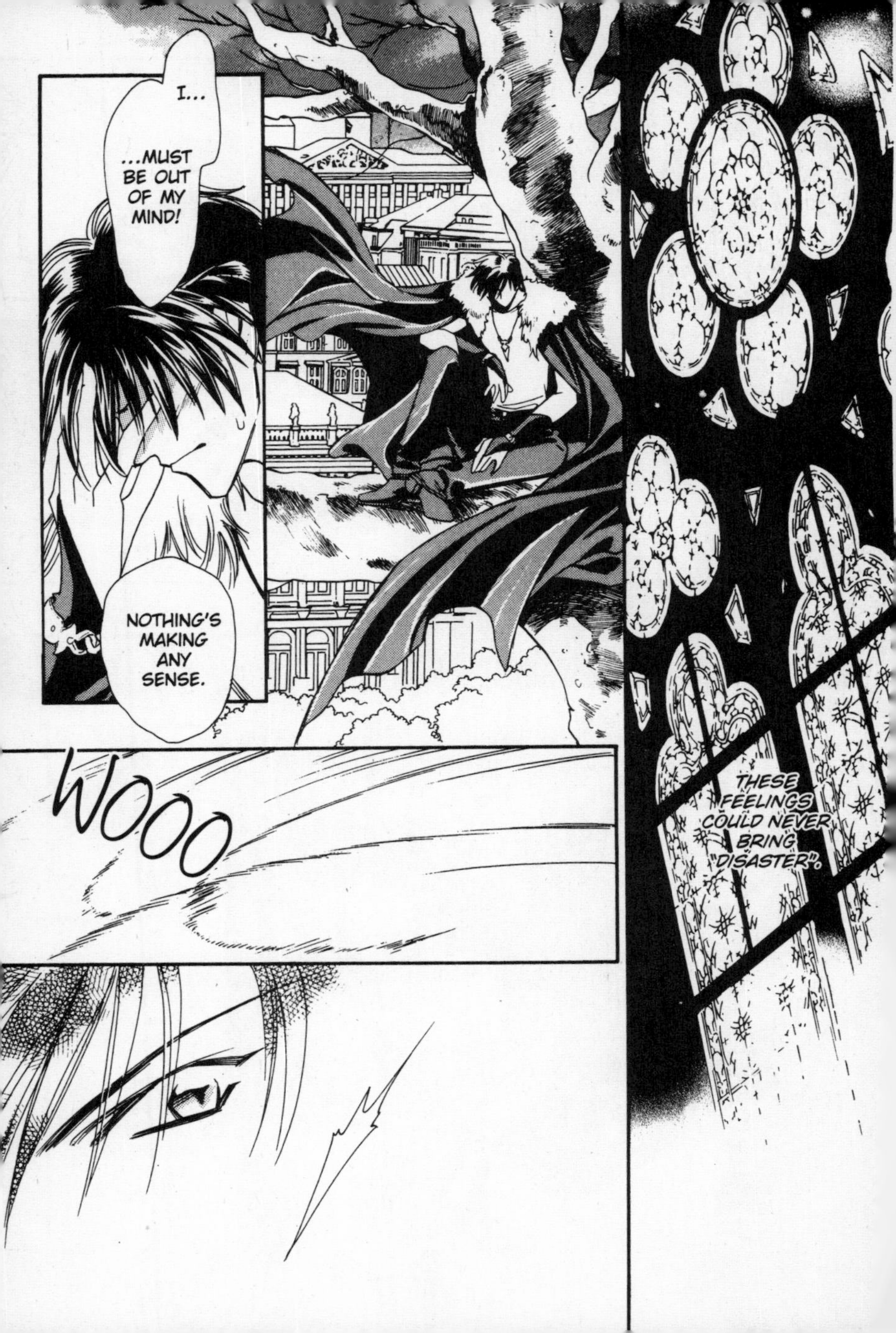
THESE FEELINGS COULD NEVER BRING "DISASTER".
I...
...MUST BE OUT OF MY MIND!
NOTHING'S MAKING ANY SENSE.
WOOO

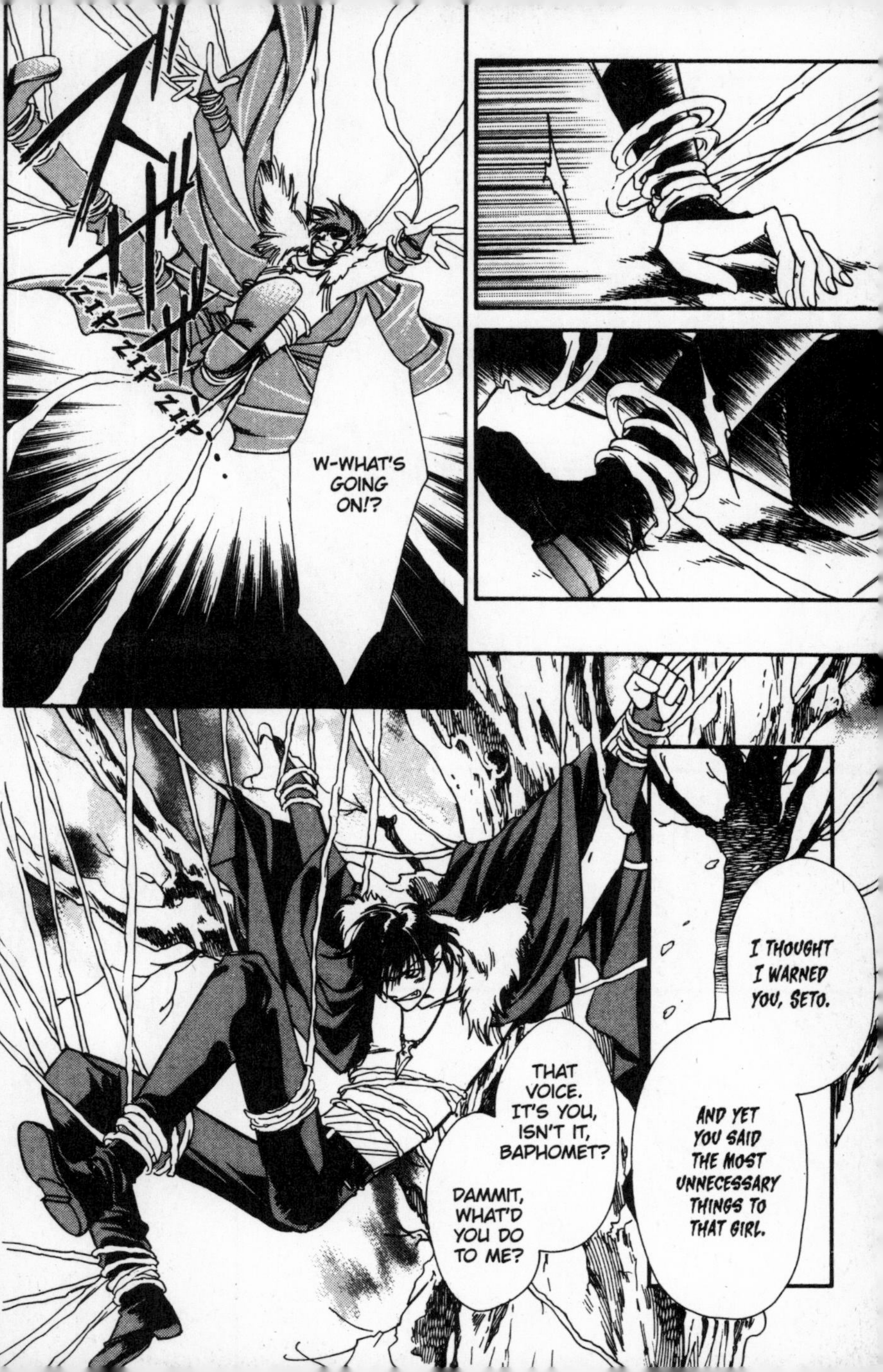
ZIP ZIP ZIP ZIP
W-WHAT'S GOING ON!?
I THOUGHT I WARNED YOU, SETO.
AND YET YOU SAID THE MOST UNNECESSARY THINGS TO THAT GIRL.
THAT VOICE. IT'S YOU, ISN'T IT, BAPHOMET?
DAMMIT, WHAT'D YOU DO TO ME?

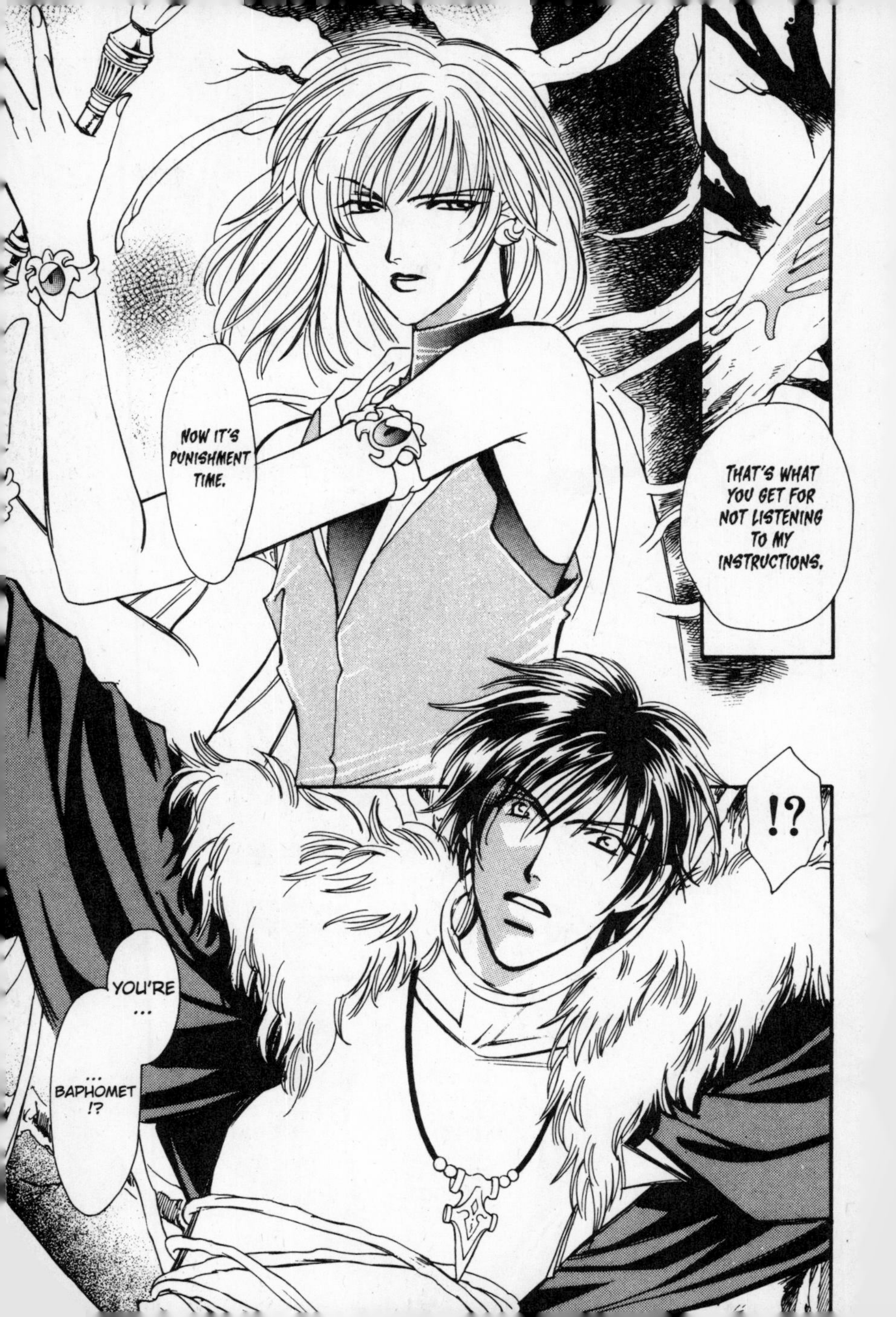
THAT'S WHAT YOU GET FOR NOT LISTENING TO MY INSTRUCTIONS.
NOW IT'S PUNISHMENT TIME.
!?
YOU'RE ...
... BAPHOMET !?

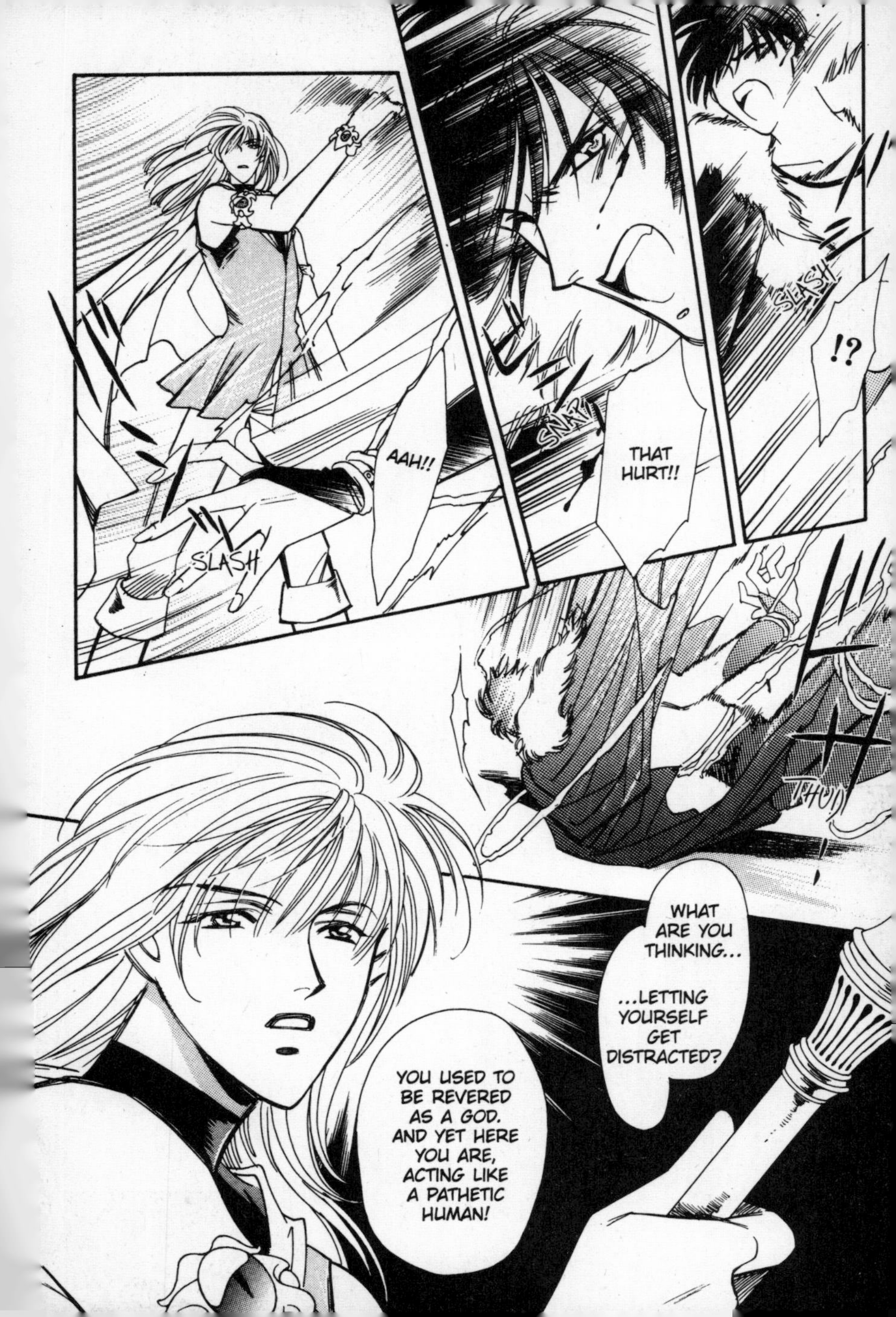
SLASH
!?
SNAP
THAT HURT!!
AAH!!
SLASH
THUD
WHAT ARE YOU THINKING...
...LETTING YOURSELF GET DISTRACTED?
YOU USED TO BE REVERED AS A GOD. AND YET HERE YOU ARE, ACTING LIKE A PATHETIC HUMAN!

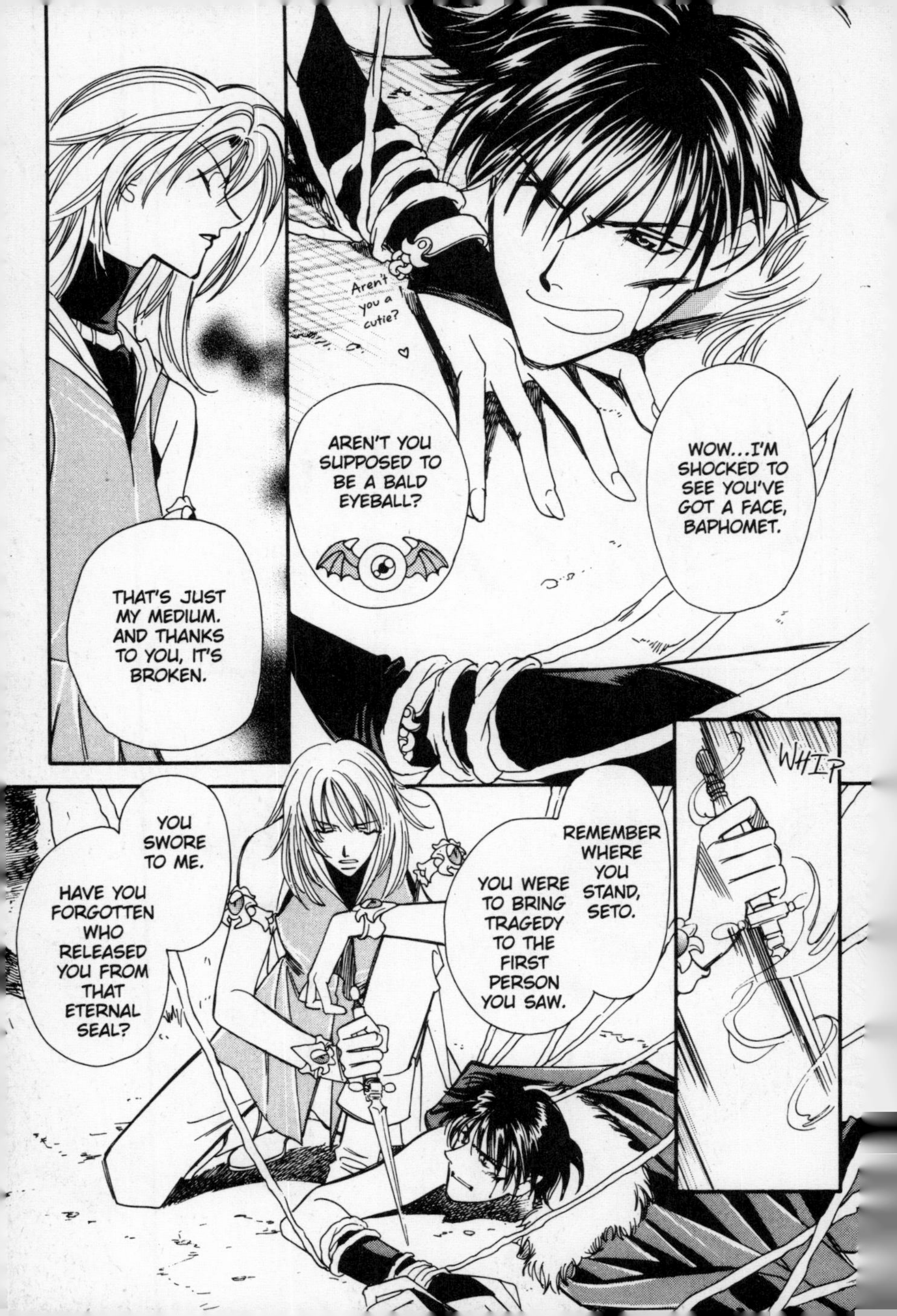
WOW...I'M SHOCKED TO SEE YOU'VE GOT A FACE, BAPHOMET.
AREN'T YOU SUPPOSED TO BE A BALD EYEBALL?
Aren't you a cutie? ♥
THAT'S JUST MY MEDIUM. AND THANKS TO YOU, IT'S BROKEN.
WHIP
REMEMBER WHERE YOU STAND, SETO.
YOU WERE TO BRING TRAGEDY TO THE FIRST PERSON YOU SAW.
YOU SWORE TO ME.
HAVE YOU FORGOTTEN WHO RELEASED YOU FROM THAT ETERNAL SEAL?

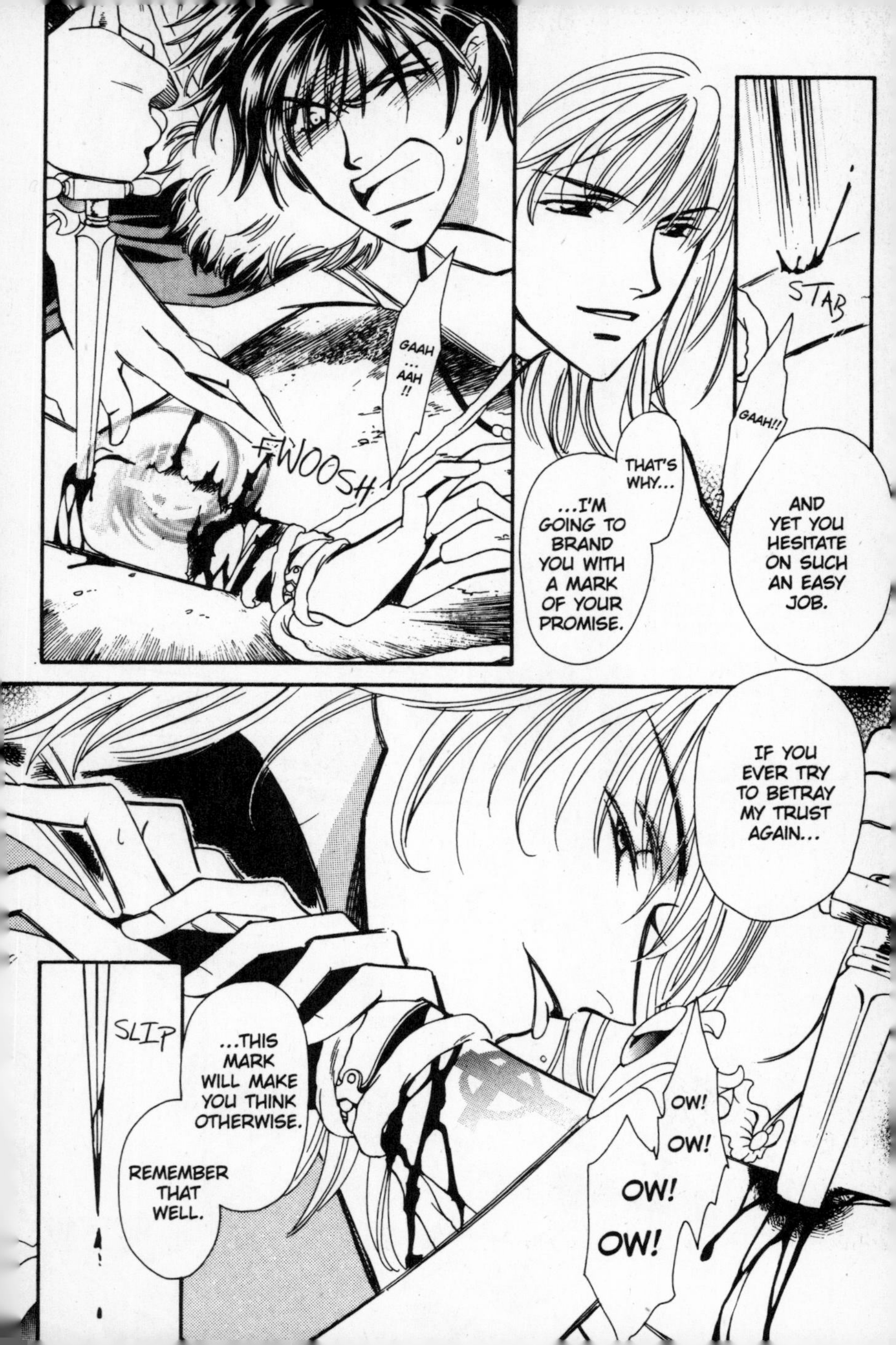
STAB
GAAH!!
AND YET YOU HESITATE ON SUCH AN EASY JOB.
THAT'S WHY...
...I'M GOING TO BRAND YOU WITH A MARK OF YOUR PROMISE.
GAAH ... AAH !!
FWOOSH
IF YOU EVER TRY TO BETRAY MY TRUST AGAIN...
OW!
OW!
OW!
OW!
SLIP
...THIS MARK WILL MAKE YOU THINK OTHERWISE.
REMEMBER THAT WELL.

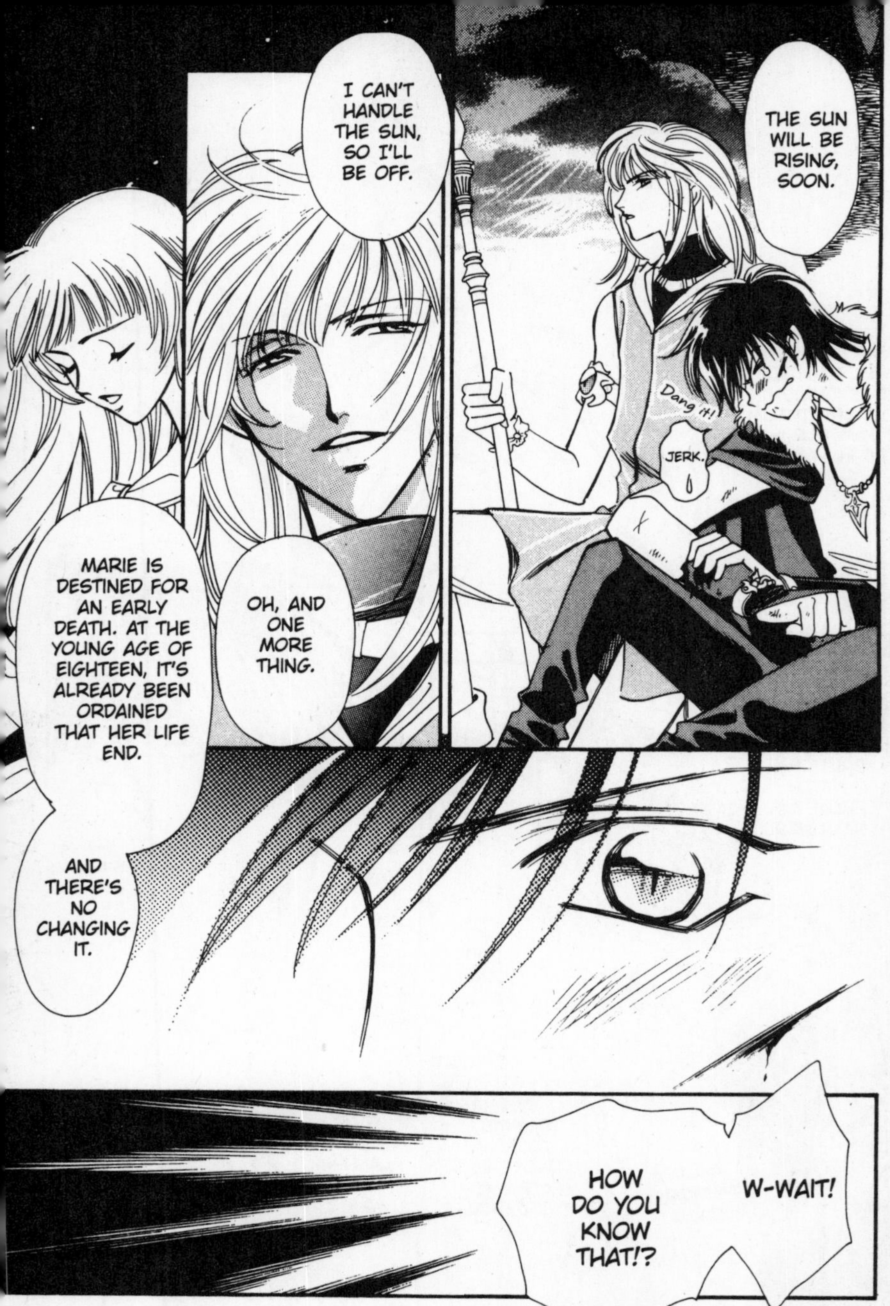
THE SUN WILL BE RISING, SOON.
Dang it!
JERK.
I CAN'T HANDLE THE SUN, SO I'LL BE OFF.
OH, AND ONE MORE THING.
MARIE IS DESTINED FOR AN EARLY DEATH. AT THE YOUNG AGE OF EIGHTEEN, IT'S ALREADY BEEN ORDAINED THAT HER LIFE END.
AND THERE'S NO CHANGING IT.
W-WAIT!
HOW DO YOU KNOW THAT!?

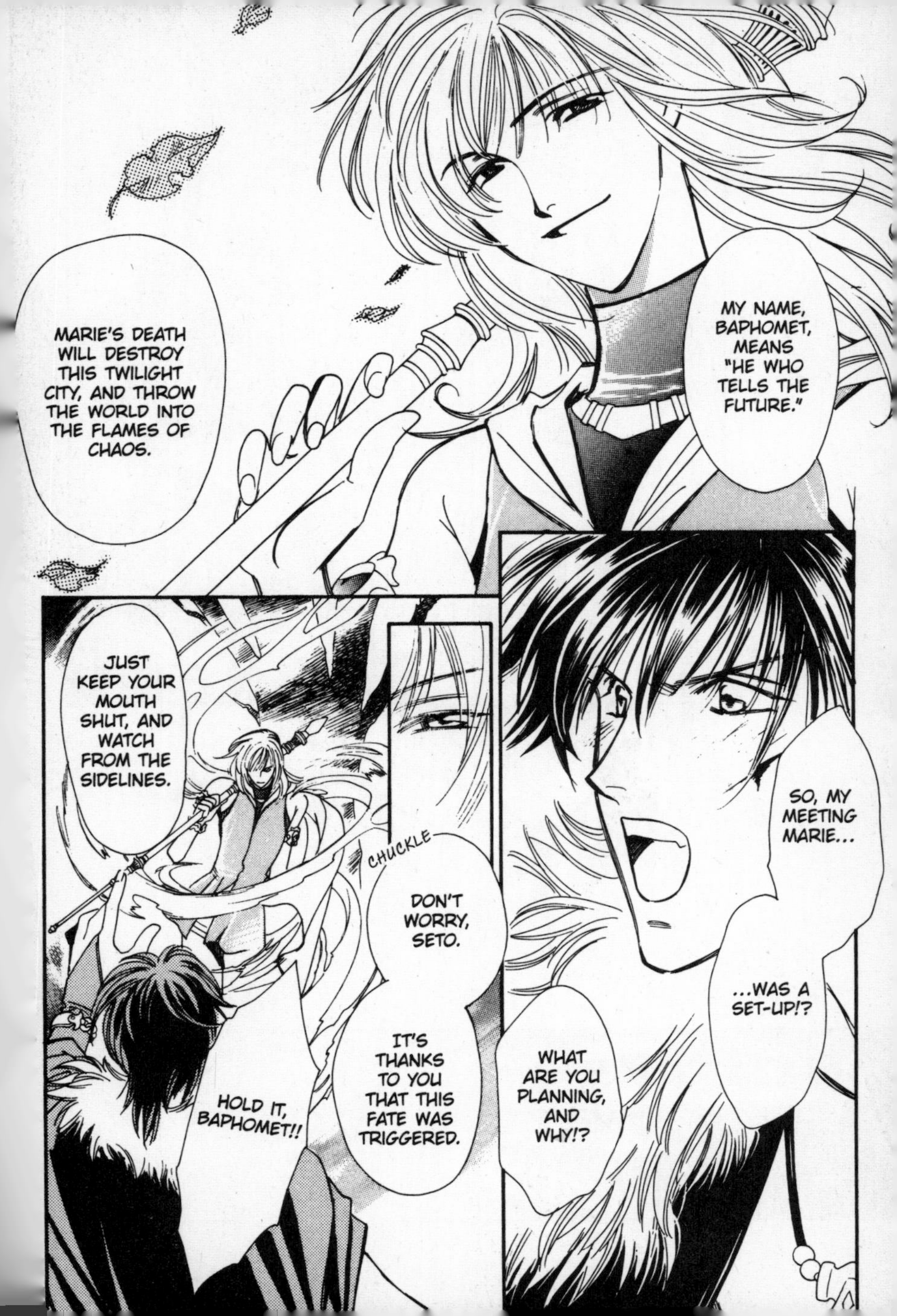
MY NAME, BAPHOMET, MEANS "HE WHO TELLS THE FUTURE."
MARIE'S DEATH WILL DESTROY THIS TWILIGHT CITY, AND THROW THE WORLD INTO THE FLAMES OF CHAOS.
SO, MY MEETING MARIE...
...WAS A SET-UP!?
WHAT ARE YOU PLANNING, AND WHY!?
CHUCKLE
DON'T WORRY, SETO.
IT'S THANKS TO YOU THAT THIS FATE WAS TRIGGERED.
JUST KEEP YOUR MOUTH SHUT, AND WATCH FROM THE SIDELINES.
HOLD IT, BAPHOMET!!

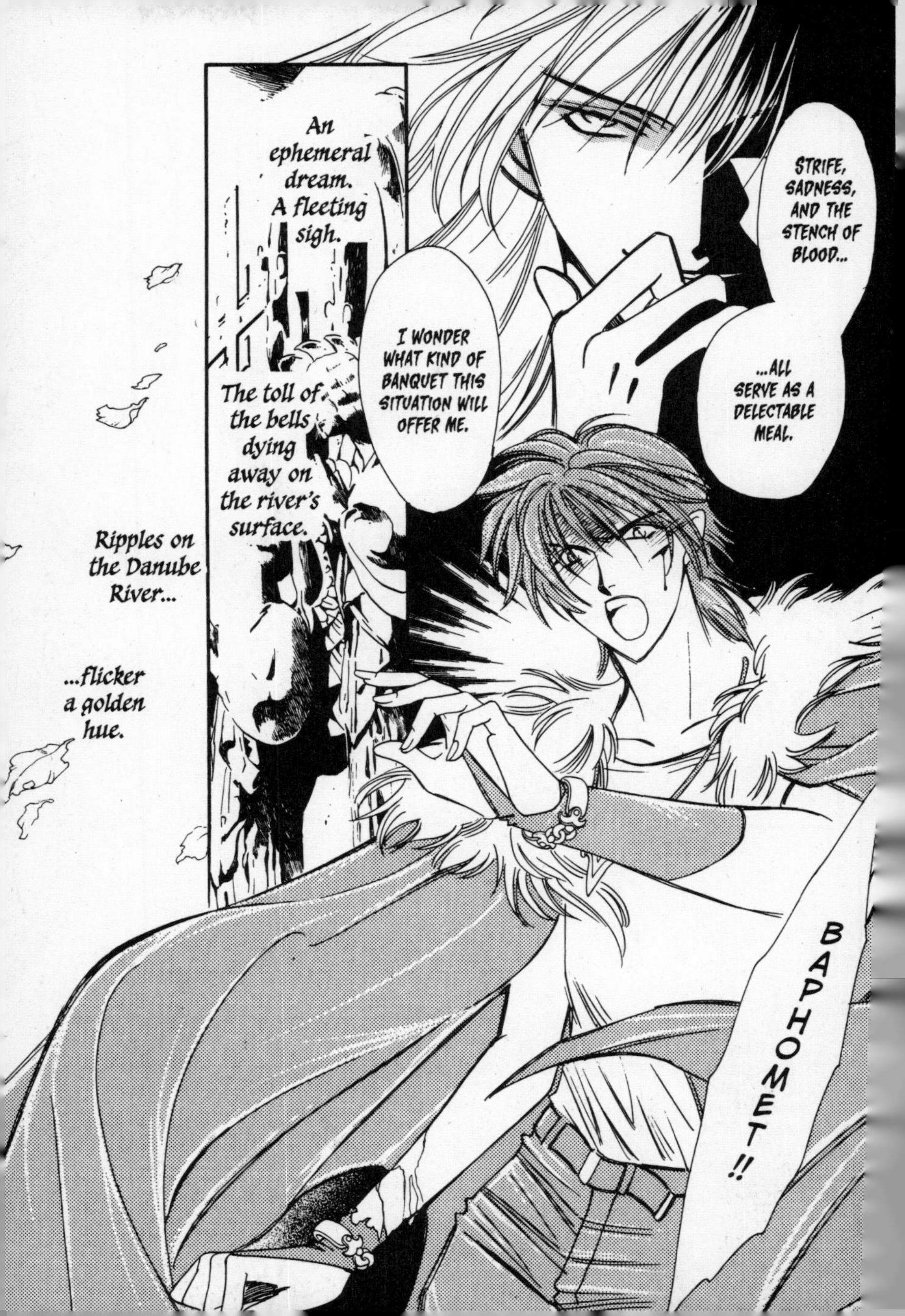
STRIFE, SADNESS, AND THE STENCH OF BLOOD...
...ALL SERVE AS A DELECTABLE MEAL.
I WONDER WHAT KIND OF BANQUET THIS SITUATION WILL OFFER ME.
An ephemeral dream. A fleeting sigh.
The toll of the bells dying away on the river's surface.
Ripples on the Danube River...
...flicker a golden hue.
BAPHOMET!!

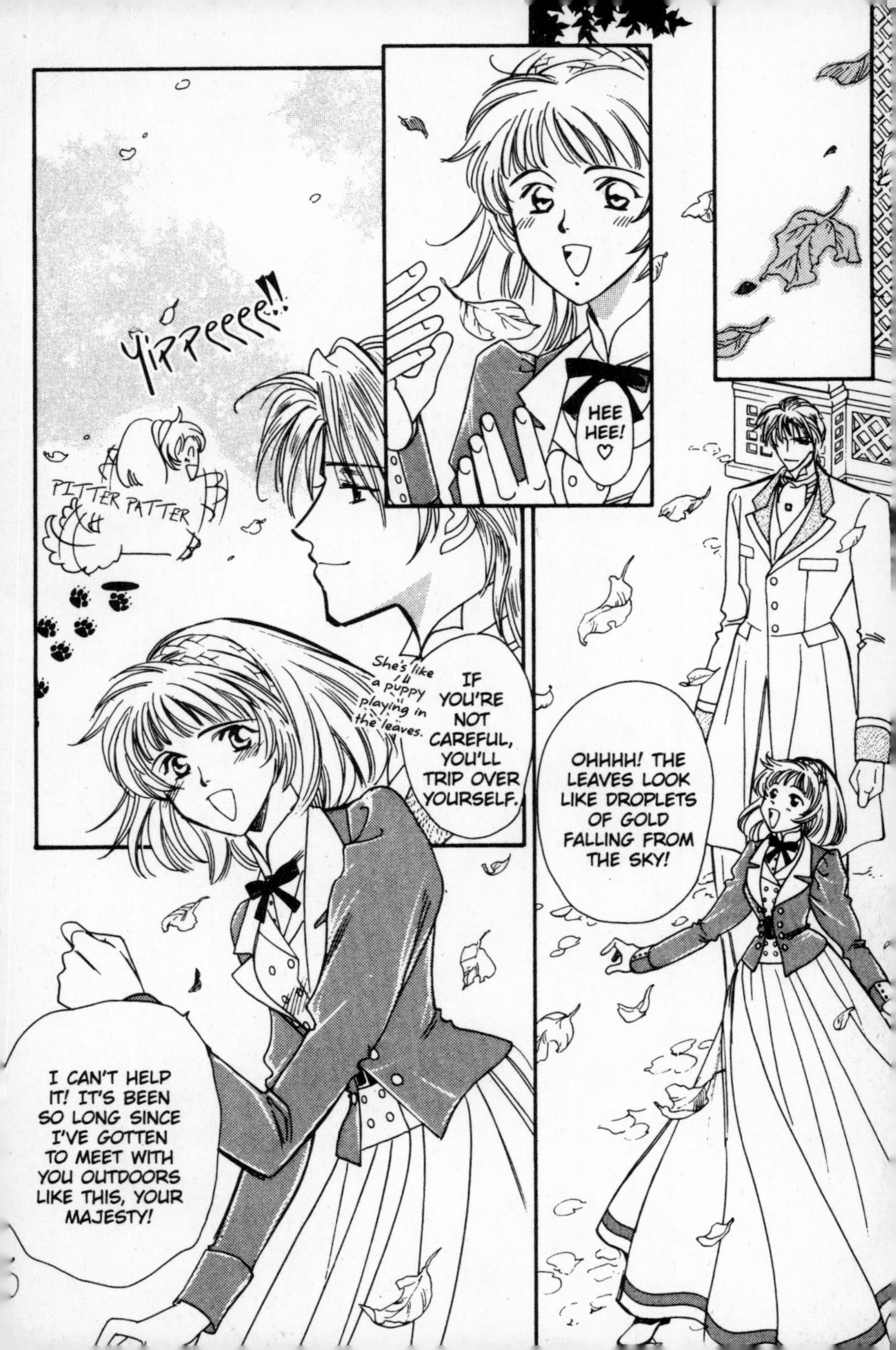
OHHHH! THE LEAVES LOOK LIKE DROPLETS OF GOLD FALLING FROM THE SKY!
HEE HEE! ♡
YIPPEEEE!!
PITTER PATTER
IF YOU'RE NOT CAREFUL, YOU'LL TRIP OVER YOURSELF.
She's like a puppy playing in the leaves.
I CAN'T HELP IT! IT'S BEEN SO LONG SINCE I'VE GOTTEN TO MEET WITH YOU OUTDOORS LIKE THIS, YOUR MAJESTY!

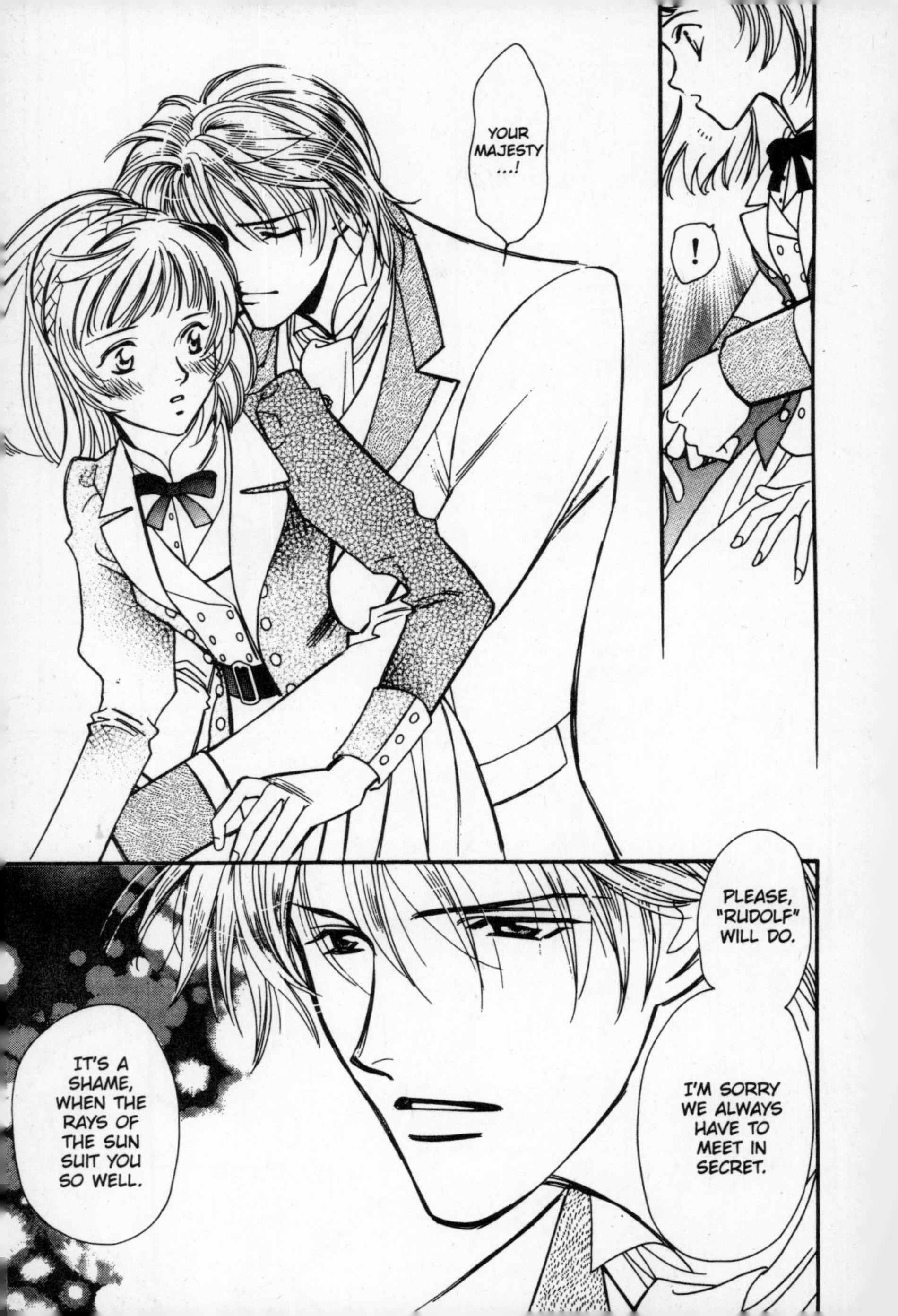
!
YOUR MAJESTY ...!
PLEASE, "RUDOLF" WILL DO.
I'M SORRY WE ALWAYS HAVE TO MEET IN SECRET.
IT'S A SHAME, WHEN THE RAYS OF THE SUN SUIT YOU SO WELL.

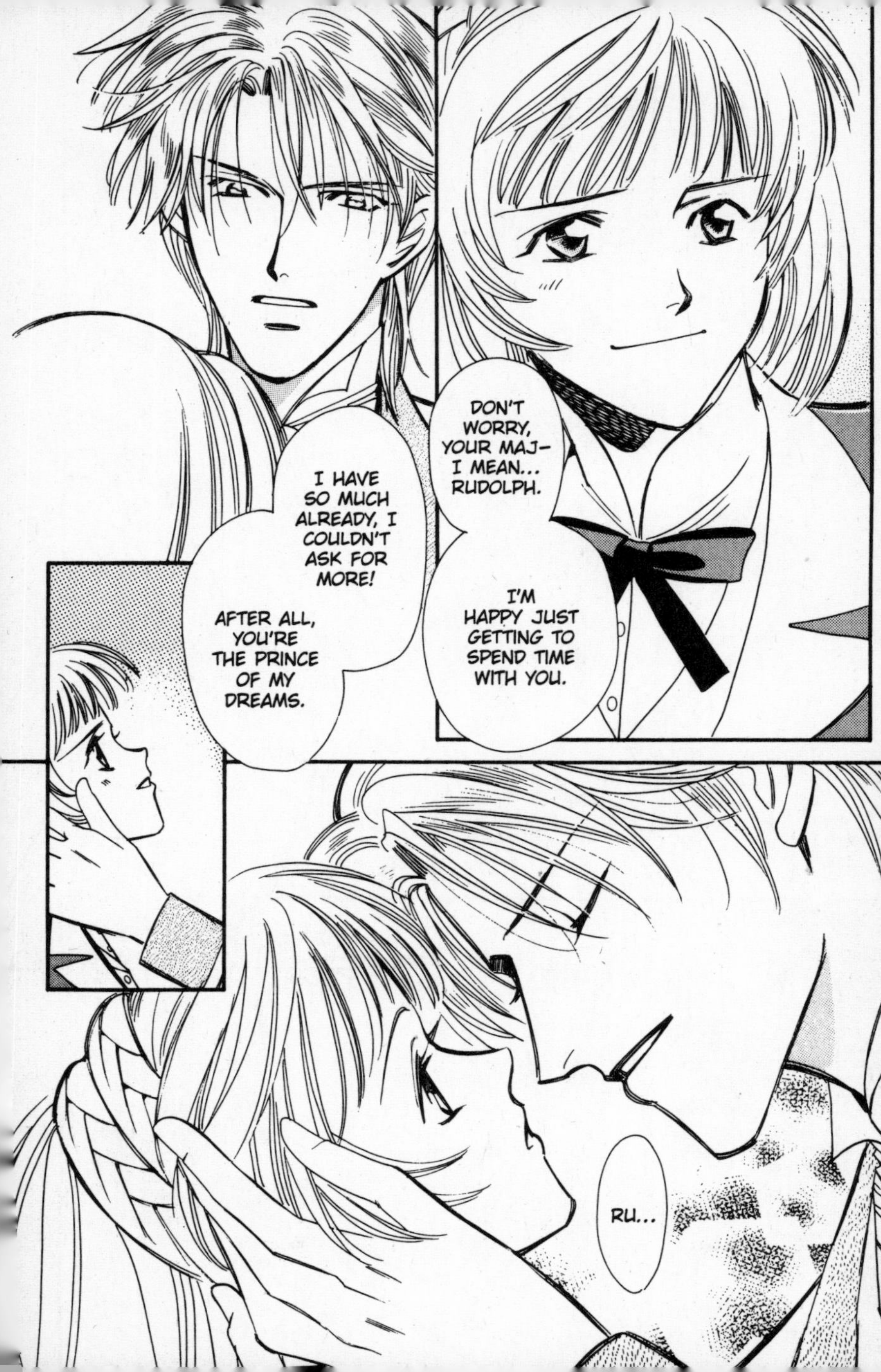
DON'T WORRY, YOUR MAJ– I MEAN... RUDOLPH.
I'M HAPPY JUST GETTING TO SPEND TIME WITH YOU.
I HAVE SO MUCH ALREADY, I COULDN'T ASK FOR MORE!
AFTER ALL, YOU'RE THE PRINCE OF MY DREAMS.
RU...

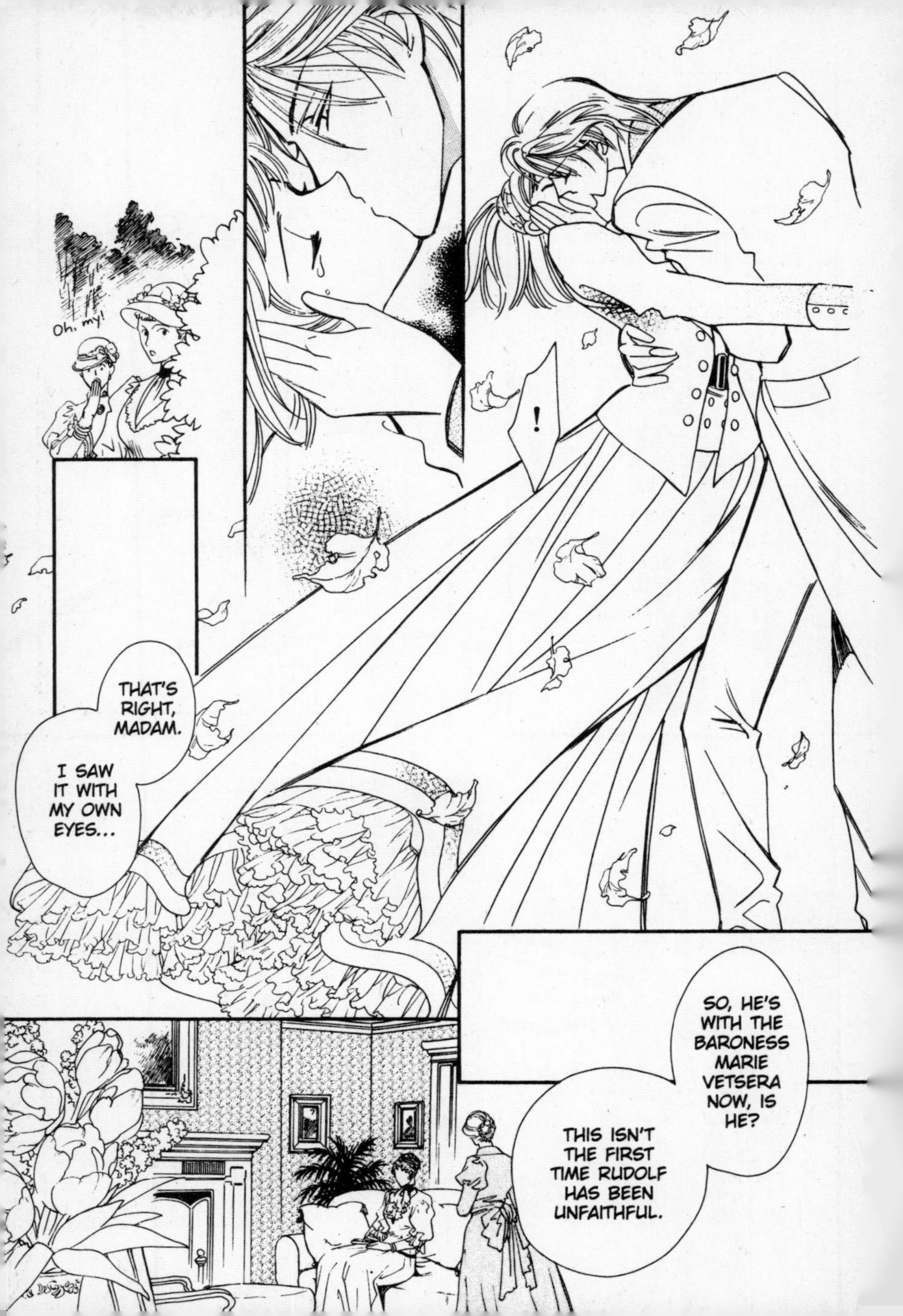
!
Oh, my!
THAT'S RIGHT, MADAM.
I SAW IT WITH MY OWN EYES...
SO, HE'S WITH THE BARONESS MARIE VETSERA NOW, IS HE?
THIS ISN'T THE FIRST TIME RUDOLF HAS BEEN UNFAITHFUL.

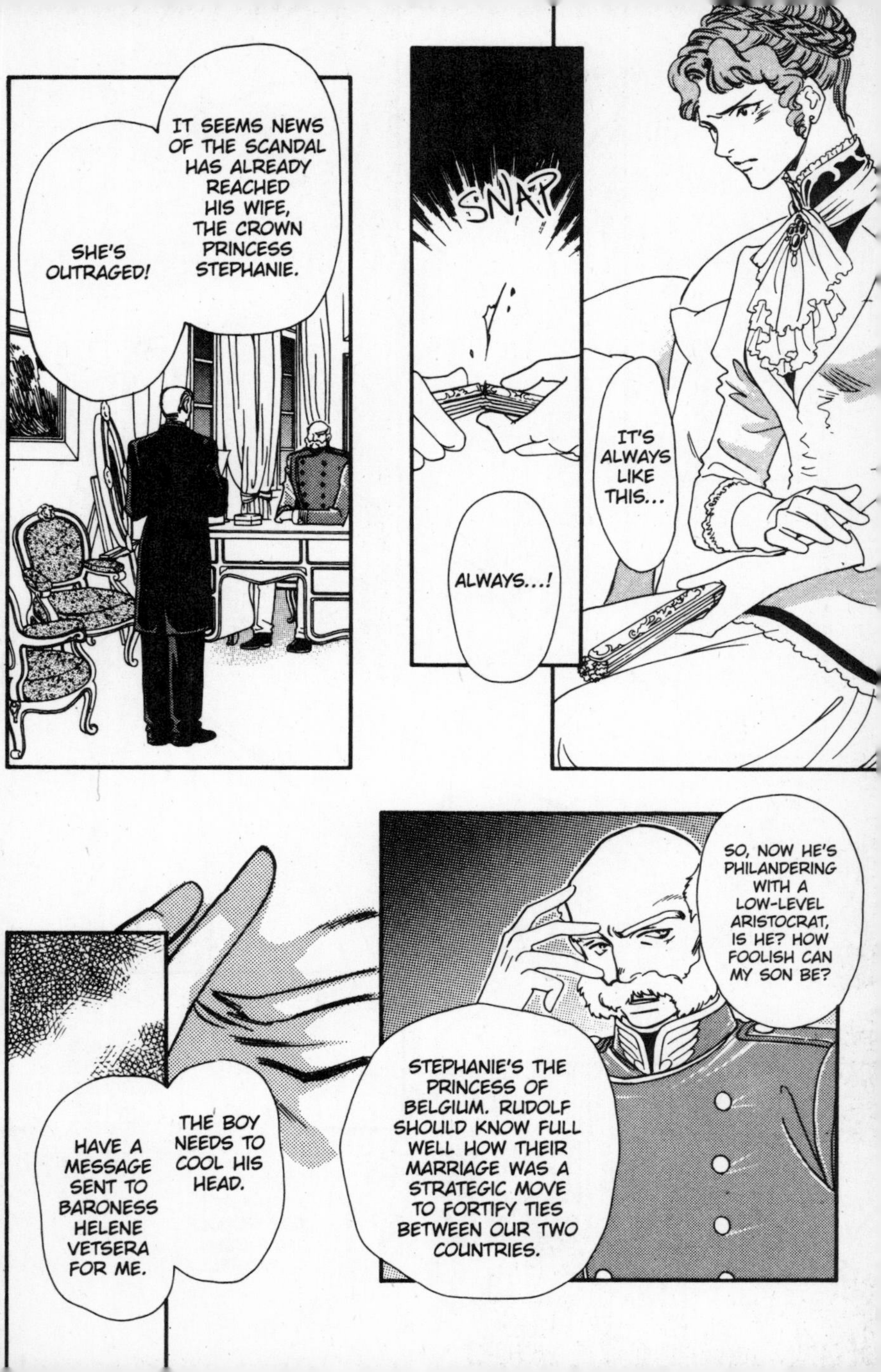
IT'S ALWAYS LIKE THIS...
SNAP
ALWAYS...!
IT SEEMS NEWS OF THE SCANDAL HAS ALREADY REACHED HIS WIFE, THE CROWN PRINCESS STEPHANIE.
SHE'S OUTRAGED!
SO, NOW HE'S PHILANDERING WITH A LOW-LEVEL ARISTOCRAT, IS HE? HOW FOOLISH CAN MY SON BE?
STEPHANIE'S THE PRINCESS OF BELGIUM. RUDOLF SHOULD KNOW FULL WELL HOW THEIR MARRIAGE WAS A STRATEGIC MOVE TO FORTIFY TIES BETWEEN OUR TWO COUNTRIES.
THE BOY NEEDS TO COOL HIS HEAD.
HAVE A MESSAGE SENT TO BARONESS HELENE VETSERA FOR ME.

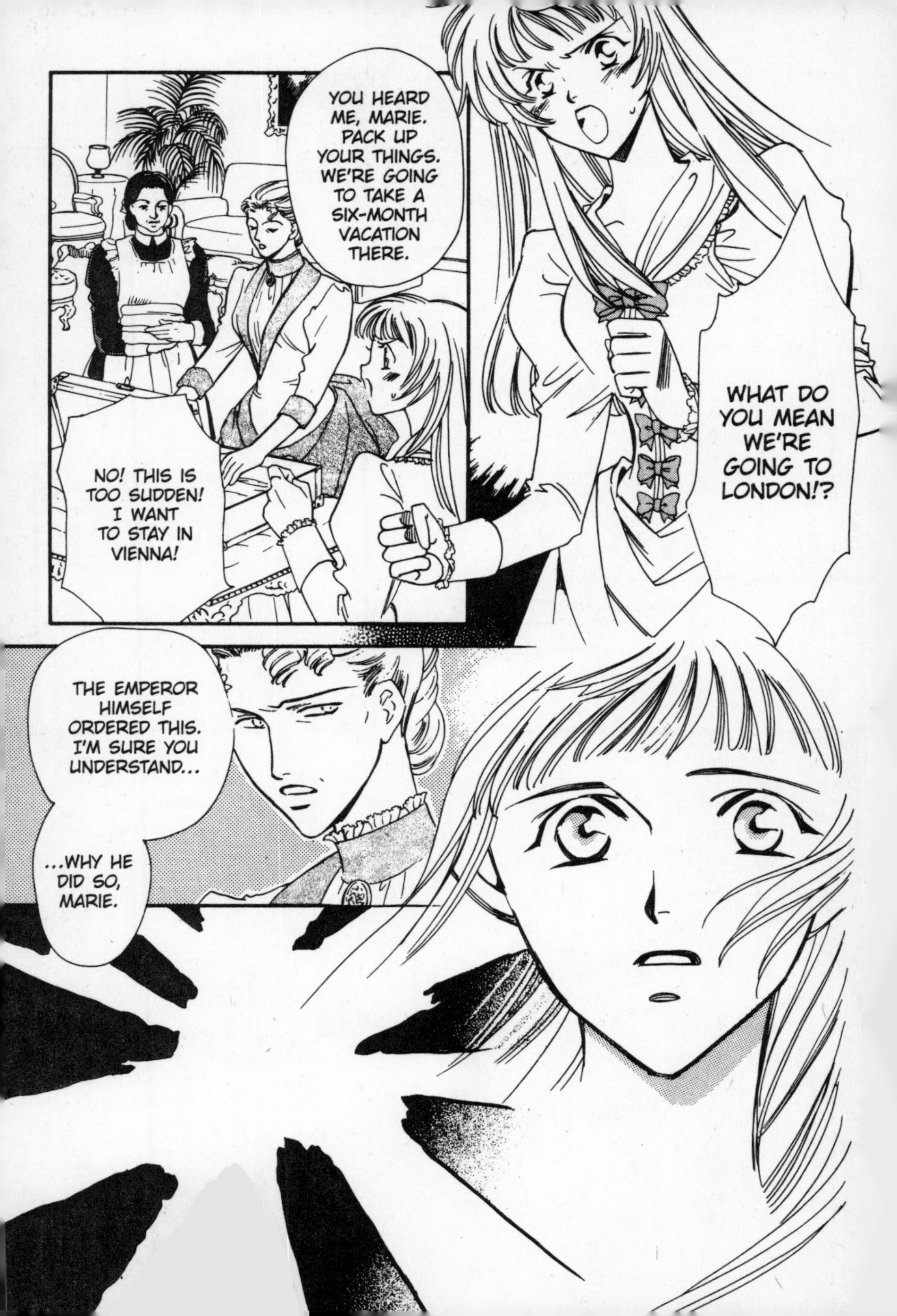
WHAT DO YOU MEAN WE'RE GOING TO LONDON!?
YOU HEARD ME, MARIE. PACK UP YOUR THINGS. WE'RE GOING TO TAKE A SIX-MONTH VACATION THERE.
NO! THIS IS TOO SUDDEN! I WANT TO STAY IN VIENNA!
THE EMPEROR HIMSELF ORDERED THIS. I'M SURE YOU UNDERSTAND...
...WHY HE DID SO, MARIE.

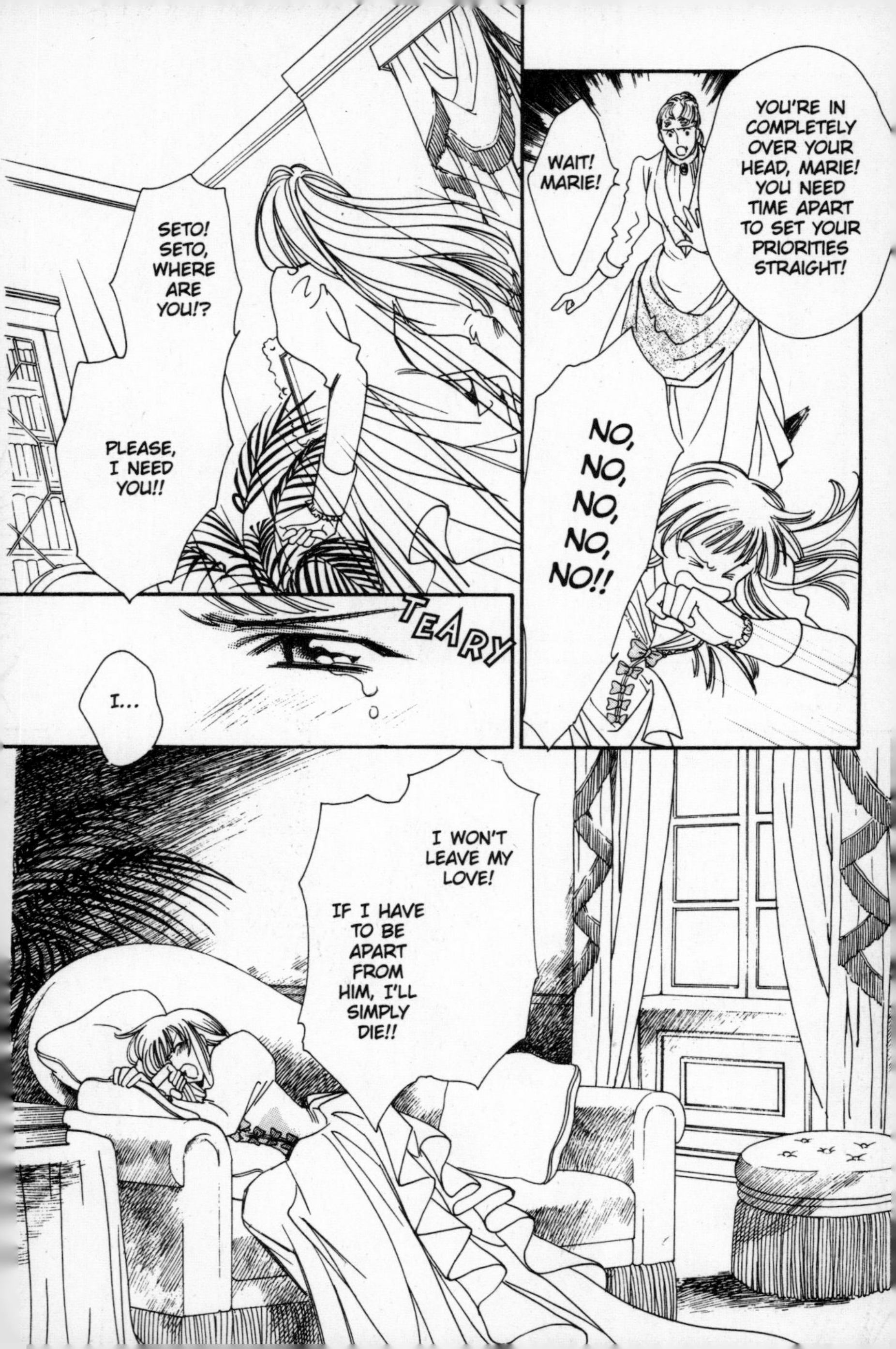
YOU'RE IN COMPLETELY OVER YOUR HEAD, MARIE! YOU NEED TIME APART TO SET YOUR PRIORITIES STRAIGHT!
WAIT! MARIE!
NO, NO, NO, NO, NO!!
SETO! SETO, WHERE ARE YOU!?
PLEASE, I NEED YOU!!
TEARY
I...
I WON'T LEAVE MY LOVE!
IF I HAVE TO BE APART FROM HIM, I'LL SIMPLY DIE!!

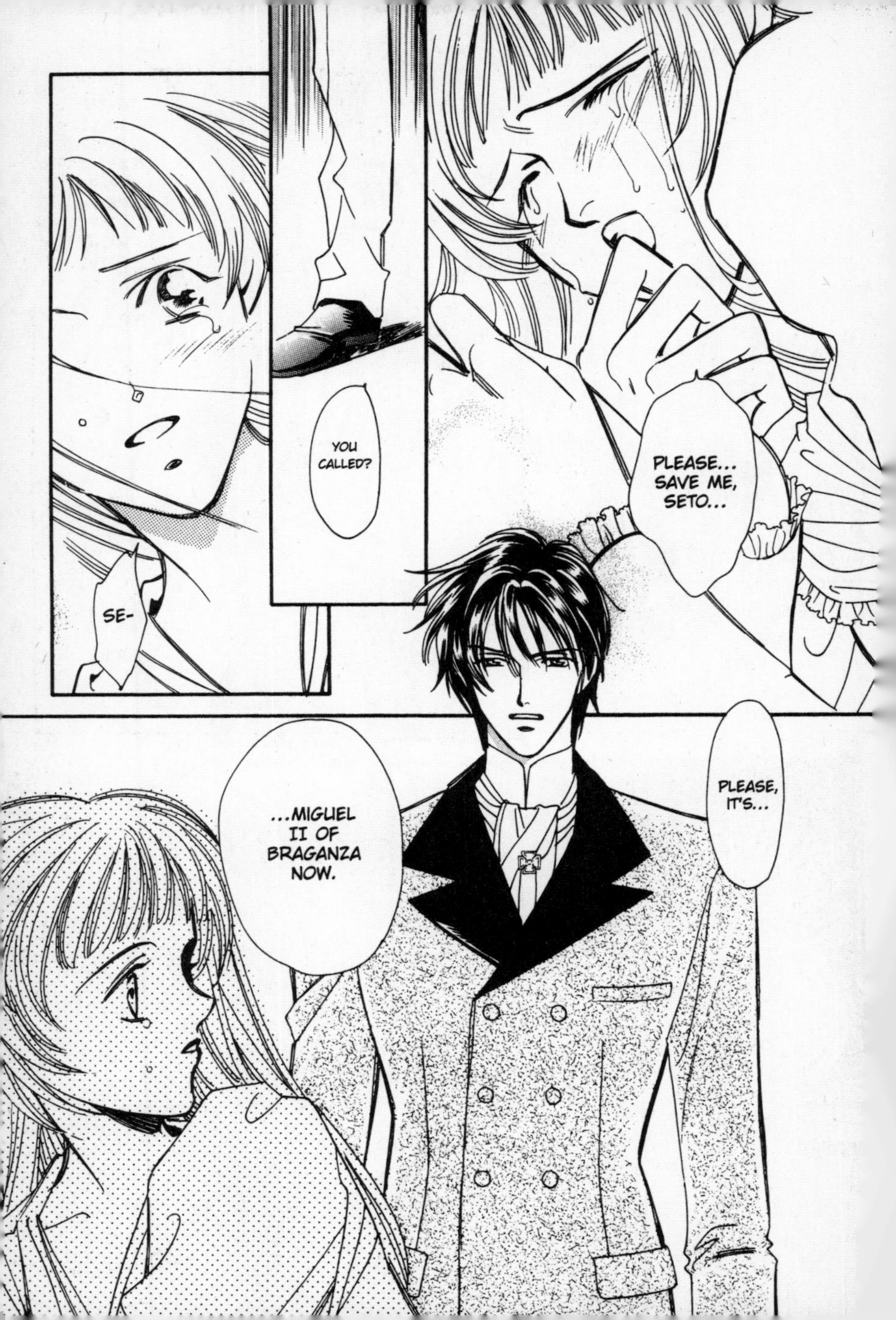
PLEASE... SAVE ME, SETO...
YOU CALLED?
SE-
PLEASE, IT'S...
...MIGUEL II OF BRAGANZA NOW.

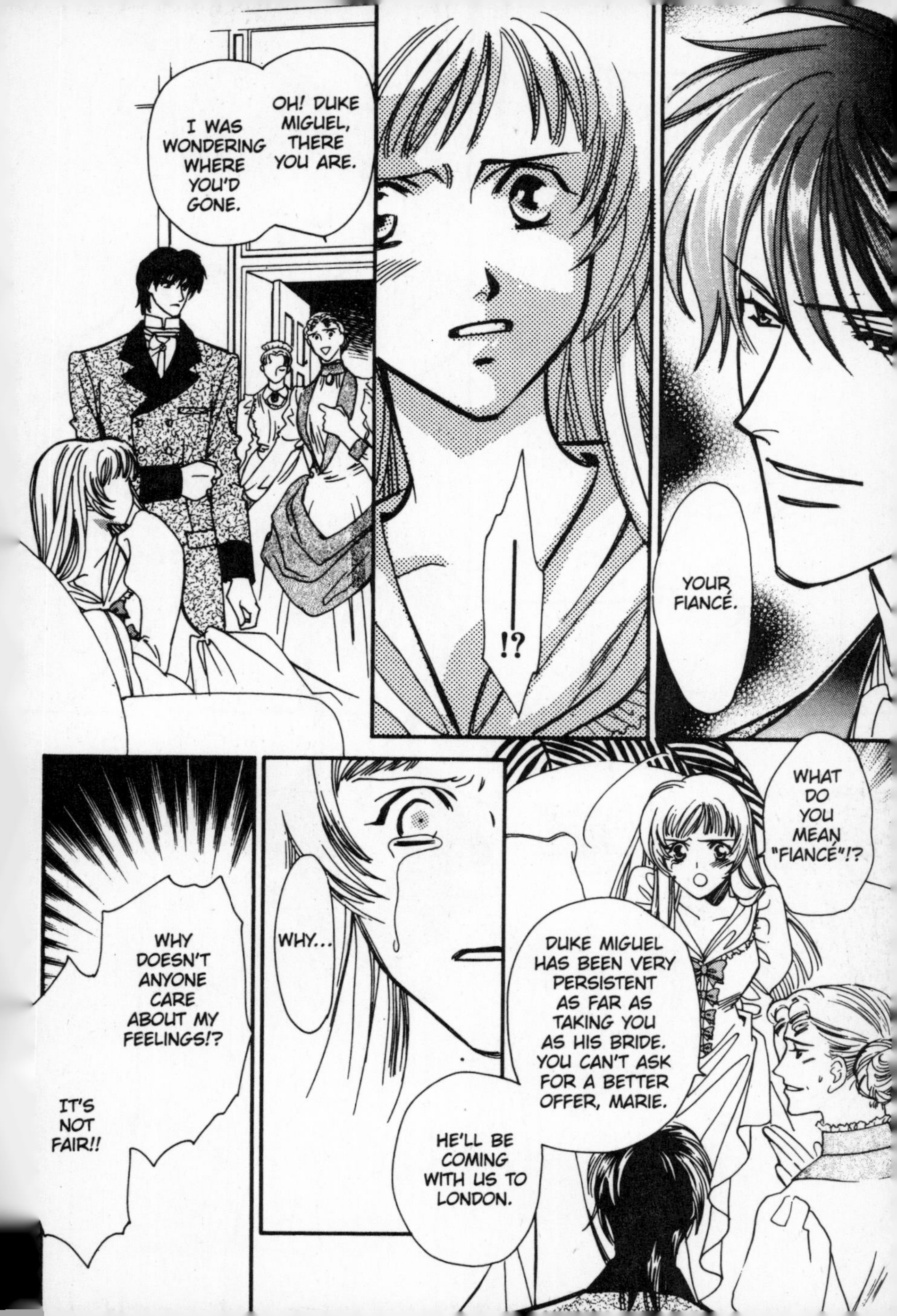
YOUR FIANCÉ.
!?
OH! DUKE MIGUEL, THERE YOU ARE.
I WAS WONDERING WHERE YOU'D GONE.
WHAT DO YOU MEAN "FIANCÉ"!?
DUKE MIGUEL HAS BEEN VERY PERSISTENT AS FAR AS TAKING YOU AS HIS BRIDE. YOU CAN'T ASK FOR A BETTER OFFER, MARIE.
HE'LL BE COMING WITH US TO LONDON.
WHY...
WHY DOESN'T ANYONE CARE ABOUT MY FEELINGS!?
IT'S NOT FAIR!!

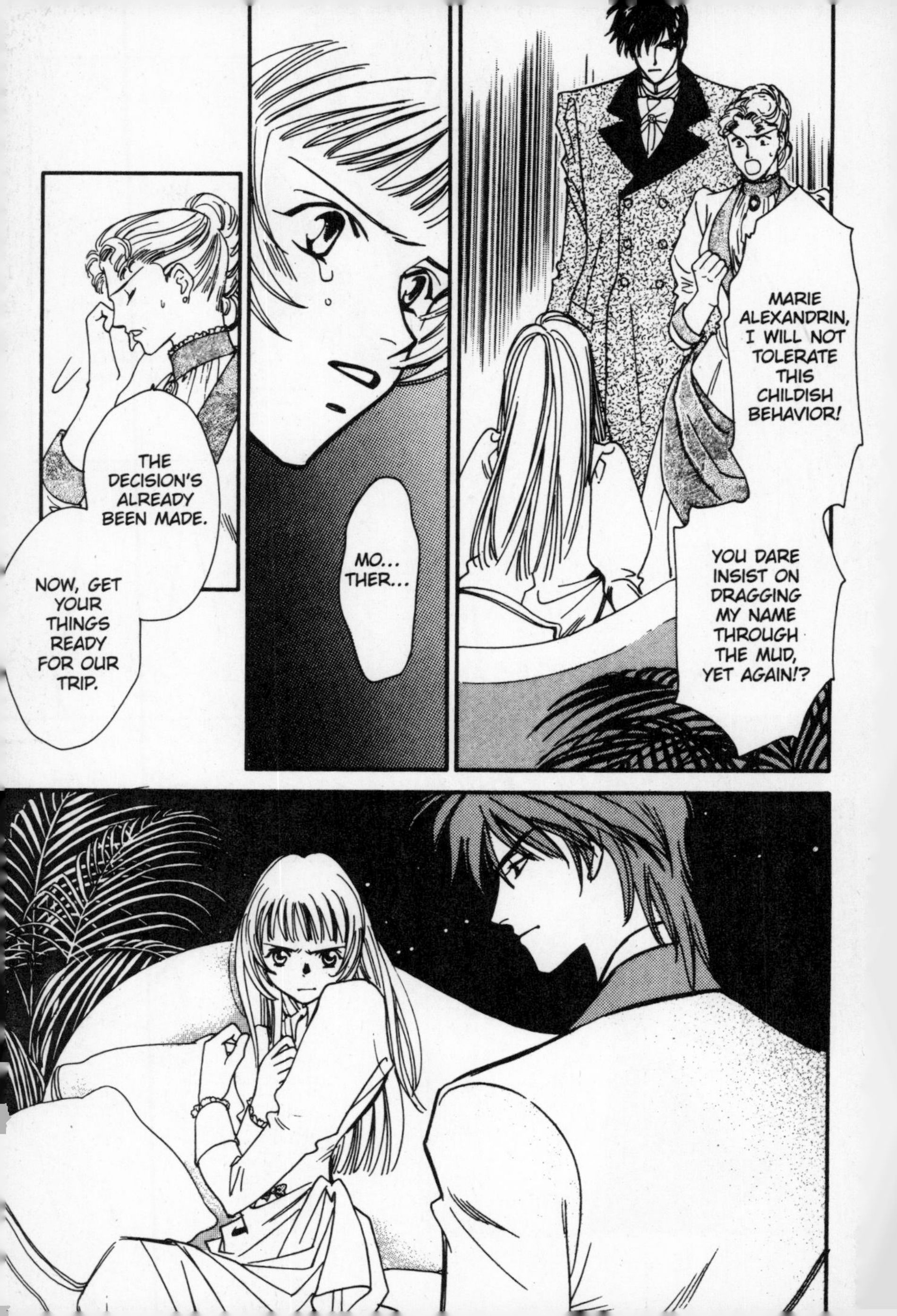
MARIE ALEXANDRIN, I WILL NOT TOLERATE THIS CHILDISH BEHAVIOR!
YOU DARE INSIST ON DRAGGING MY NAME THROUGH THE MUD, YET AGAIN!?
MO... THER...
THE DECISION'S ALREADY BEEN MADE.
NOW, GET YOUR THINGS READY FOR OUR TRIP.

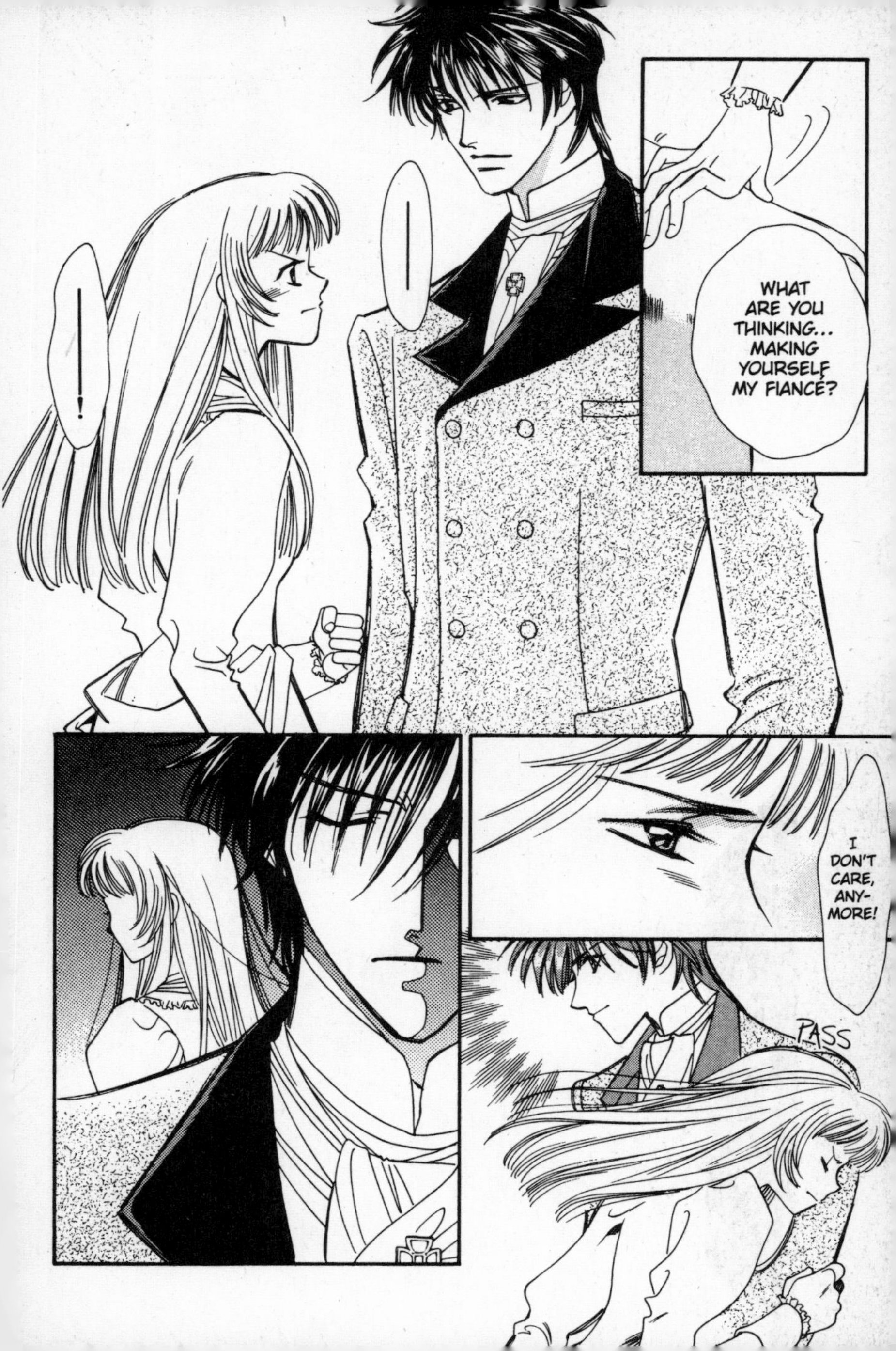
WHAT ARE YOU THINKING... MAKING YOURSELF MY FIANCÉ?
I DON'T CARE, ANY-MORE!
PASS

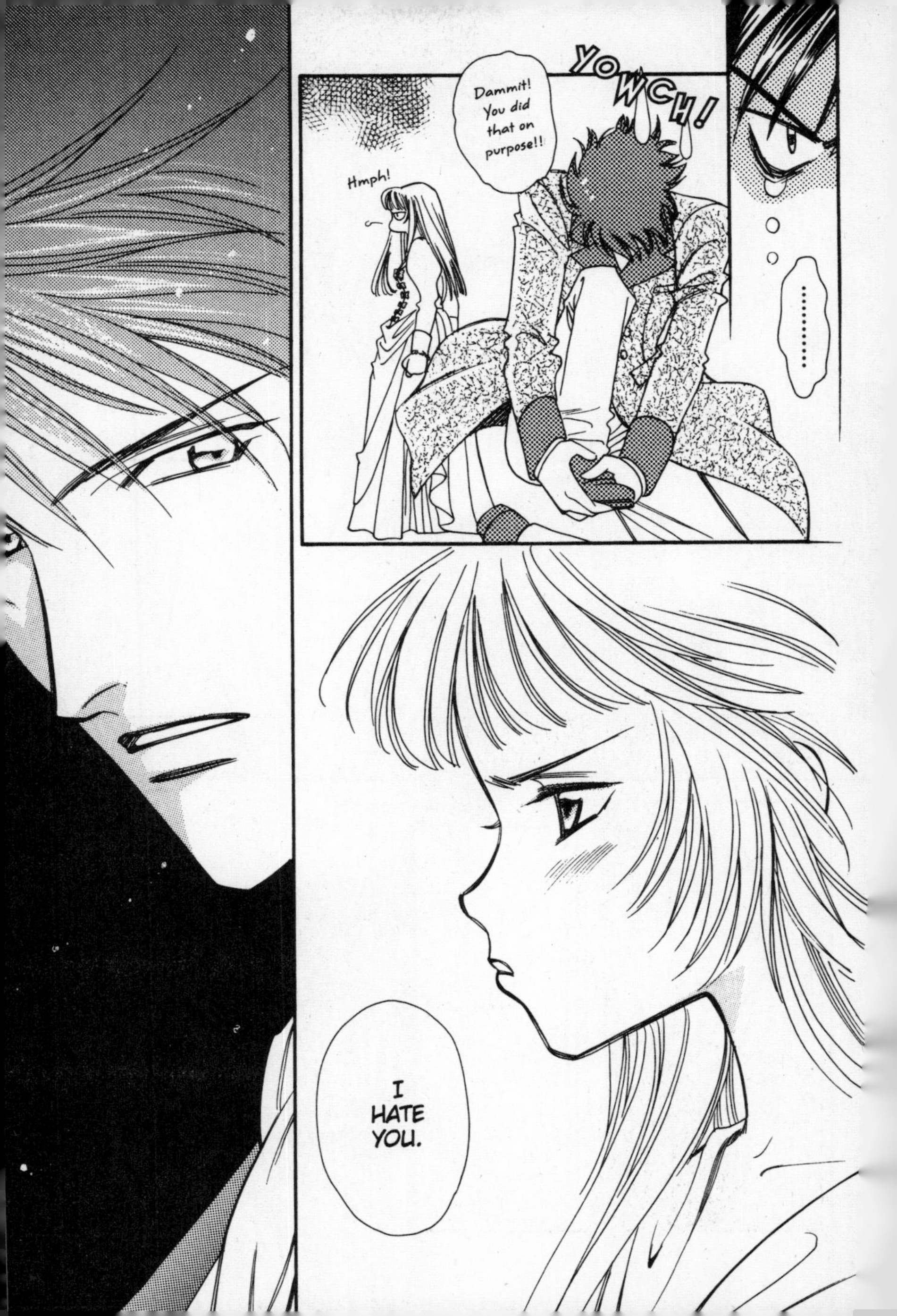
......
YOWCH!
Dammit! You did that on purpose!!
Hmph!
I HATE YOU.

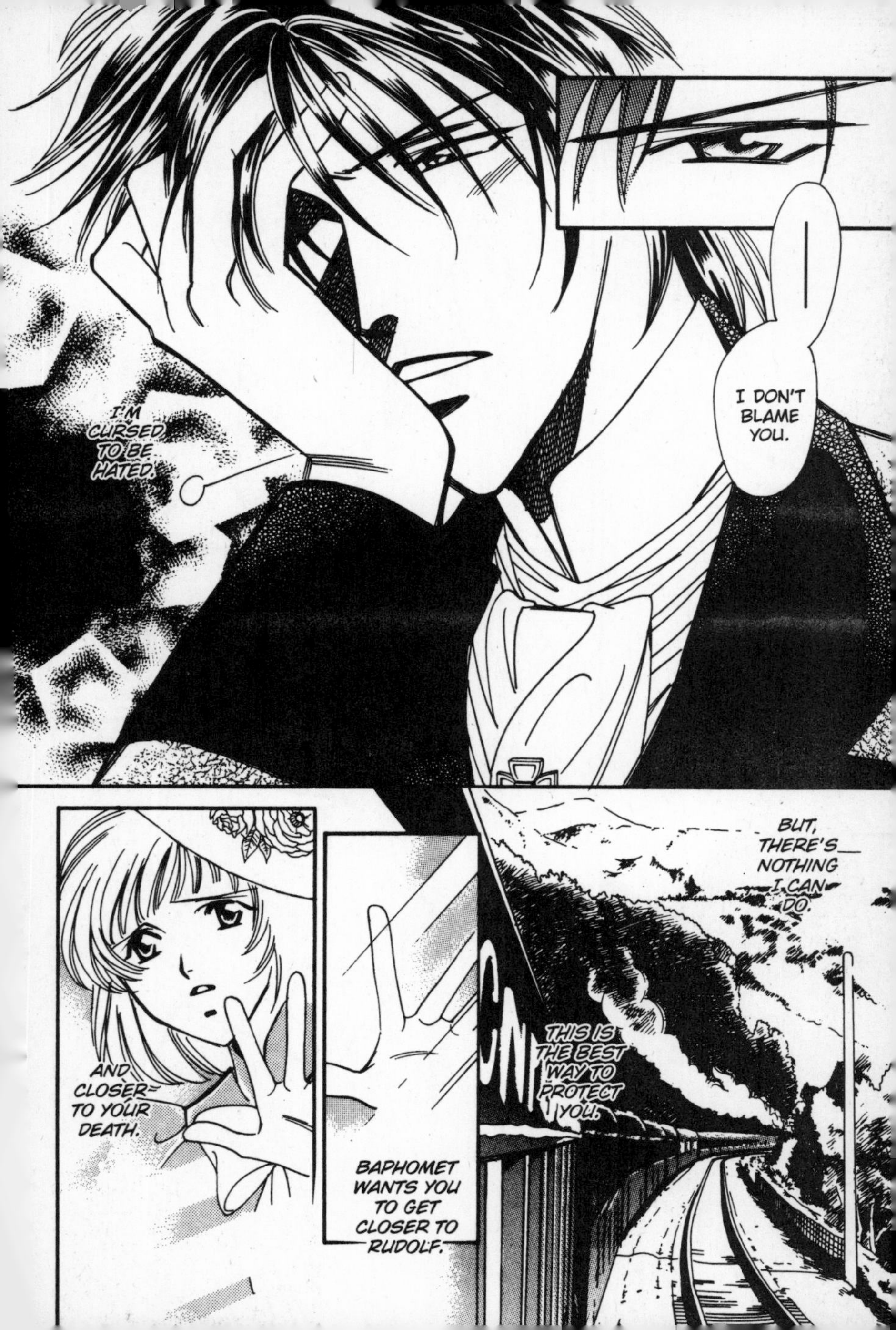
I DON'T BLAME YOU.
I'M CURSED TO BE HATED.
BUT, THERE'S NOTHING I CAN DO.
THIS IS THE BEST WAY TO PROTECT YOU.
BAPHOMET WANTS YOU TO GET CLOSER TO RUDOLF.
AND CLOSER TO YOUR DEATH.

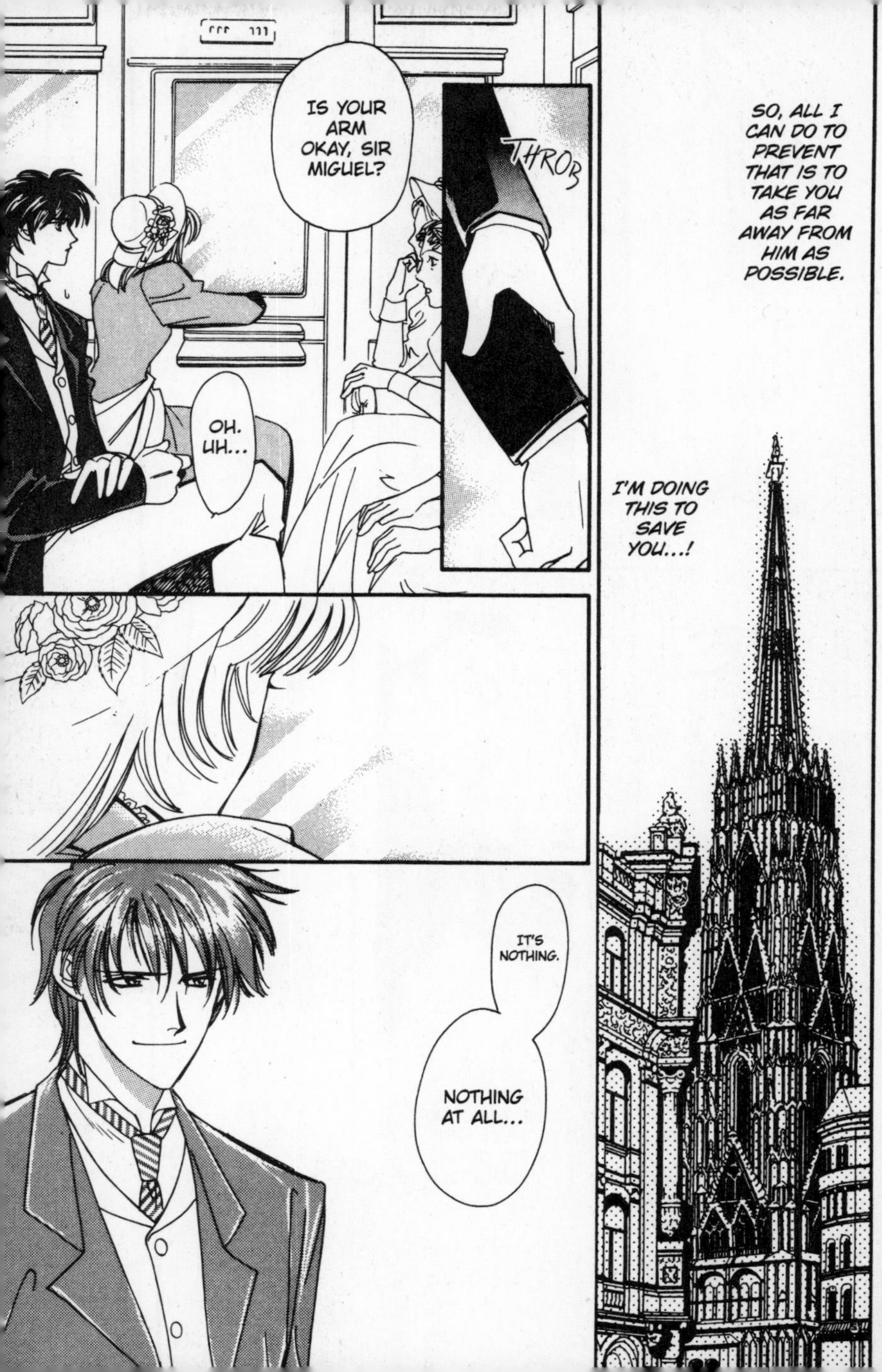
SO, ALL I CAN DO TO PREVENT THAT IS TO TAKE YOU AS FAR AWAY FROM HIM AS POSSIBLE.
I'M DOING THIS TO SAVE YOU...!
THROB
IS YOUR ARM OKAY, SIR MIGUEL?
OH. UH...
IT'S NOTHING.
NOTHING AT ALL...

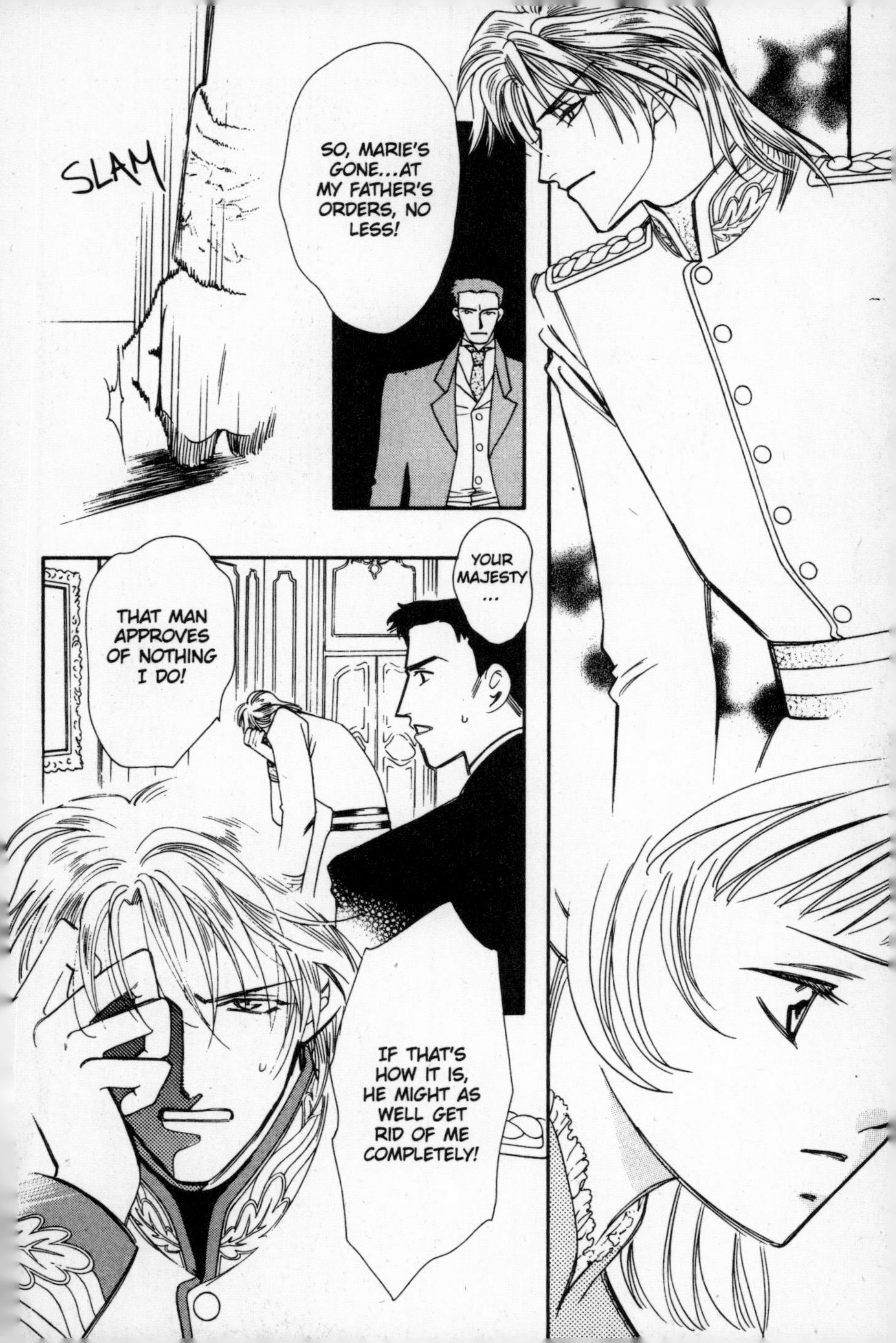
SO, MARIE'S GONE...AT MY FATHER'S ORDERS, NO LESS!
SLAM
YOUR MAJESTY ...
THAT MAN APPROVES OF NOTHING I DO!
IF THAT'S HOW IT IS, HE MIGHT AS WELL GET RID OF ME COMPLETELY!

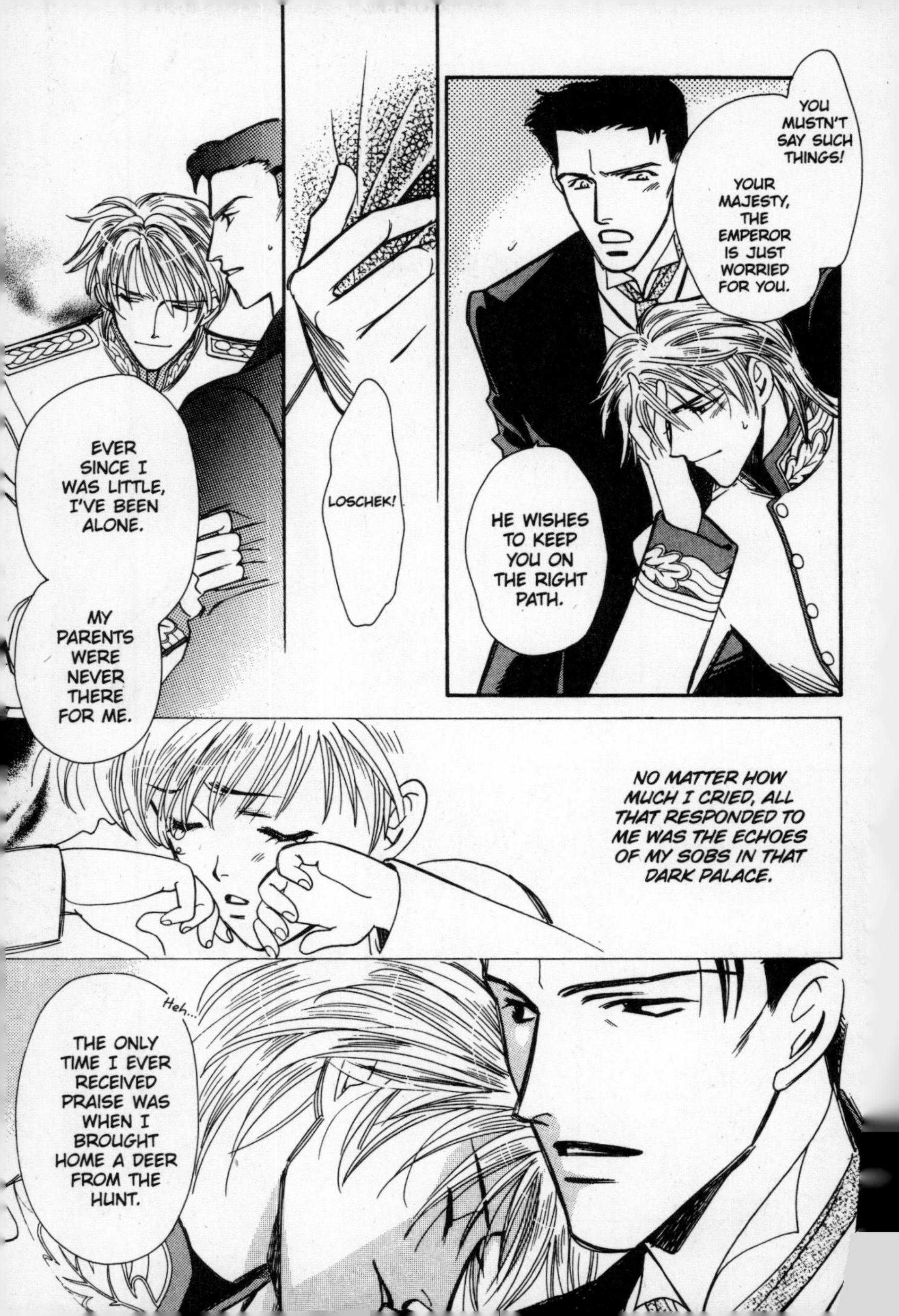
YOU MUSTN'T SAY SUCH THINGS!
YOUR MAJESTY, THE EMPEROR IS JUST WORRIED FOR YOU.
HE WISHES TO KEEP YOU ON THE RIGHT PATH.
LOSCHEK!
EVER SINCE I WAS LITTLE, I'VE BEEN ALONE.
MY PARENTS WERE NEVER THERE FOR ME.
NO MATTER HOW MUCH I CRIED, ALL THAT RESPONDED TO ME WAS THE ECHOES OF MY SOBS IN THAT DARK PALACE.
Heh...
THE ONLY TIME I EVER RECEIVED PRAISE WAS WHEN I BROUGHT HOME A DEER FROM THE HUNT.

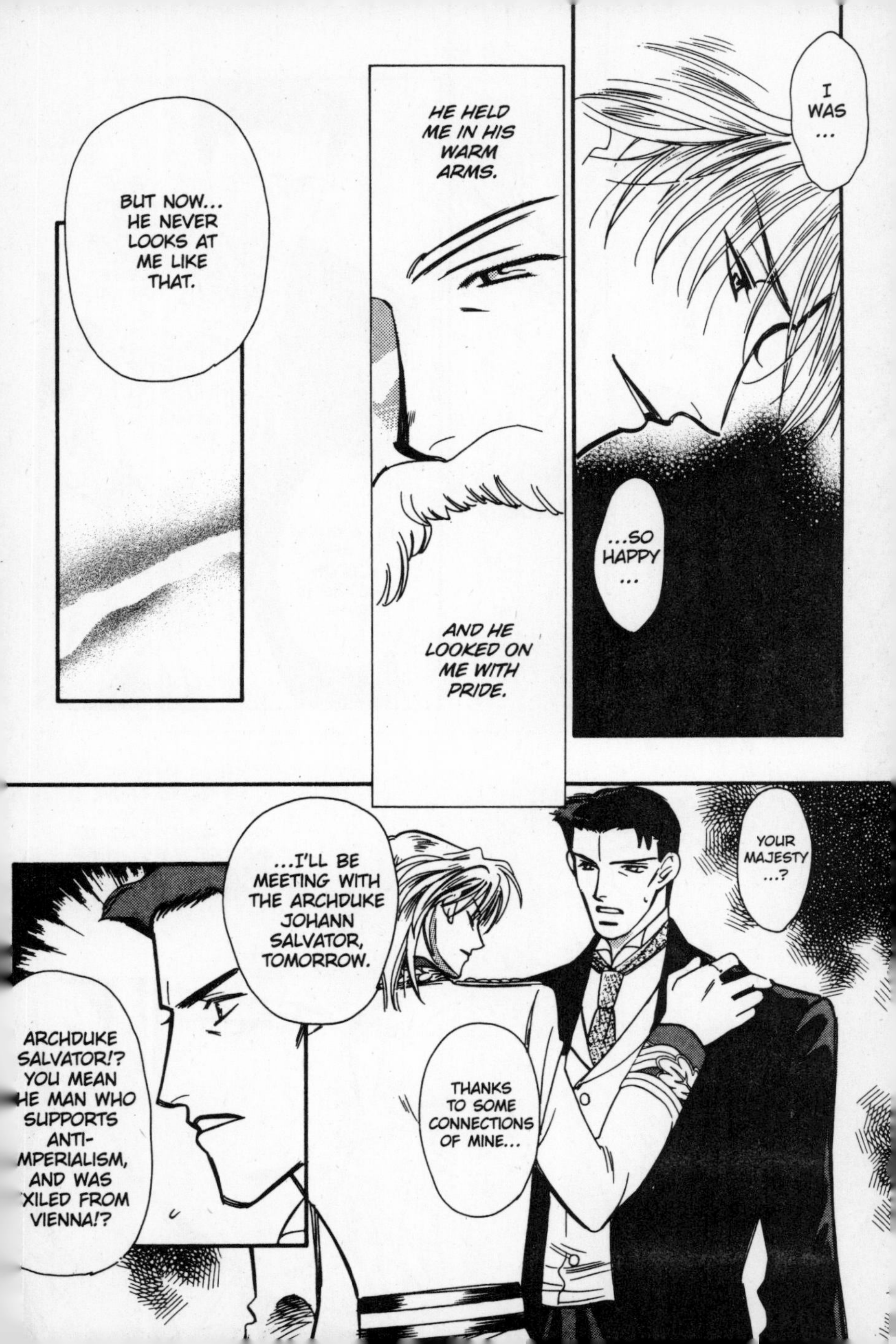
I WAS ...
...SO HAPPY ...
HE HELD ME IN HIS WARM ARMS.
AND HE LOOKED ON ME WITH PRIDE.
BUT NOW... HE NEVER LOOKS AT ME LIKE THAT.
YOUR MAJESTY ...?
...I'LL BE MEETING WITH THE ARCHDUKE JOHANN SALVATOR, TOMORROW.
THANKS TO SOME CONNECTIONS OF MINE...
ARCHDUKE SALVATOR!? YOU MEAN HE MAN WHO SUPPORTS ANTI-MPERIALISM, AND WAS XILED FROM VIENNA!?

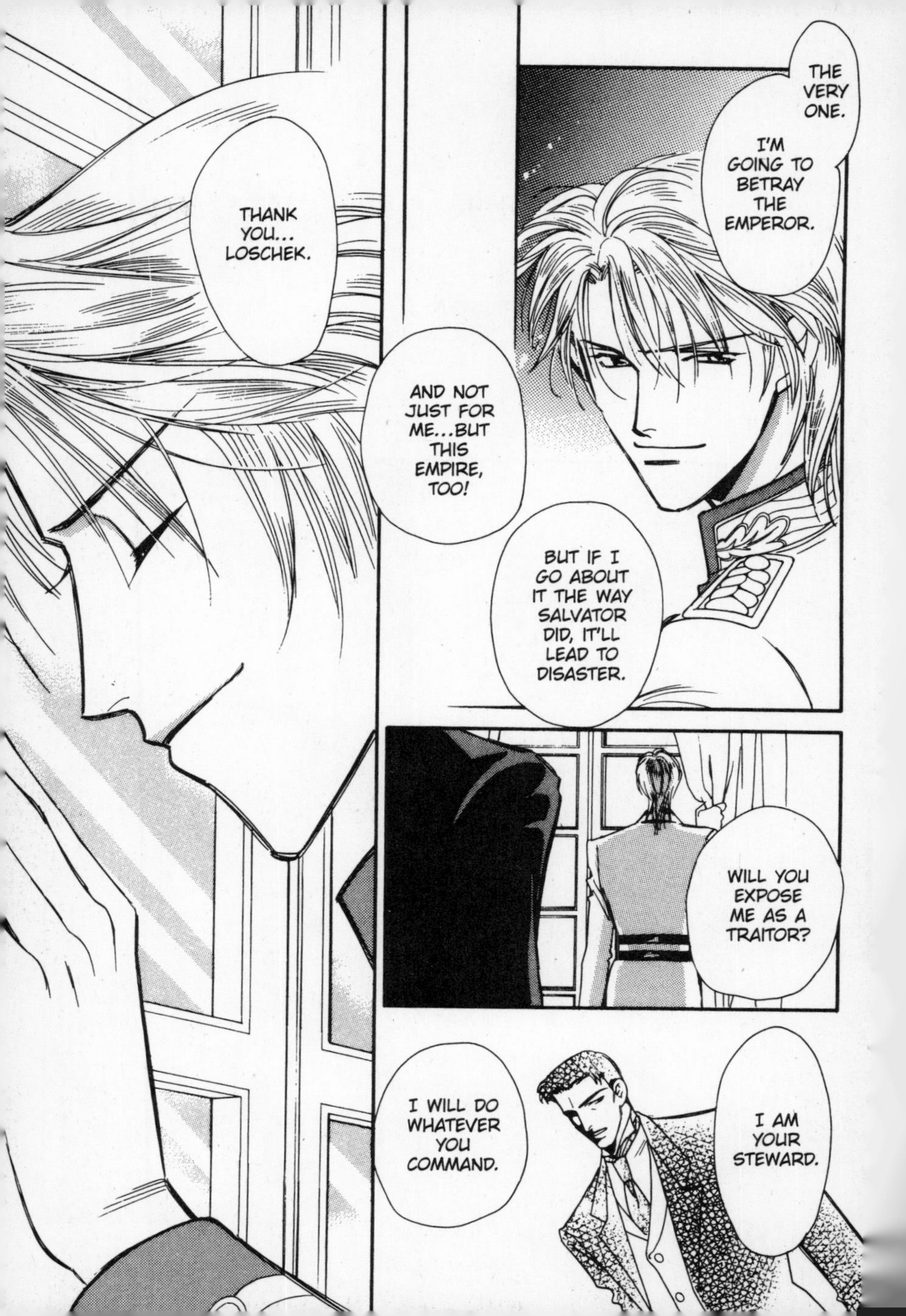
THE VERY ONE.
I'M GOING TO BETRAY THE EMPEROR.
AND NOT JUST FOR ME...BUT THIS EMPIRE, TOO!
BUT IF I GO ABOUT IT THE WAY SALVATOR DID, IT'LL LEAD TO DISASTER.
WILL YOU EXPOSE ME AS A TRAITOR?
I AM YOUR STEWARD.
I WILL DO WHATEVER YOU COMMAND.
THANK YOU... LOSCHEK.

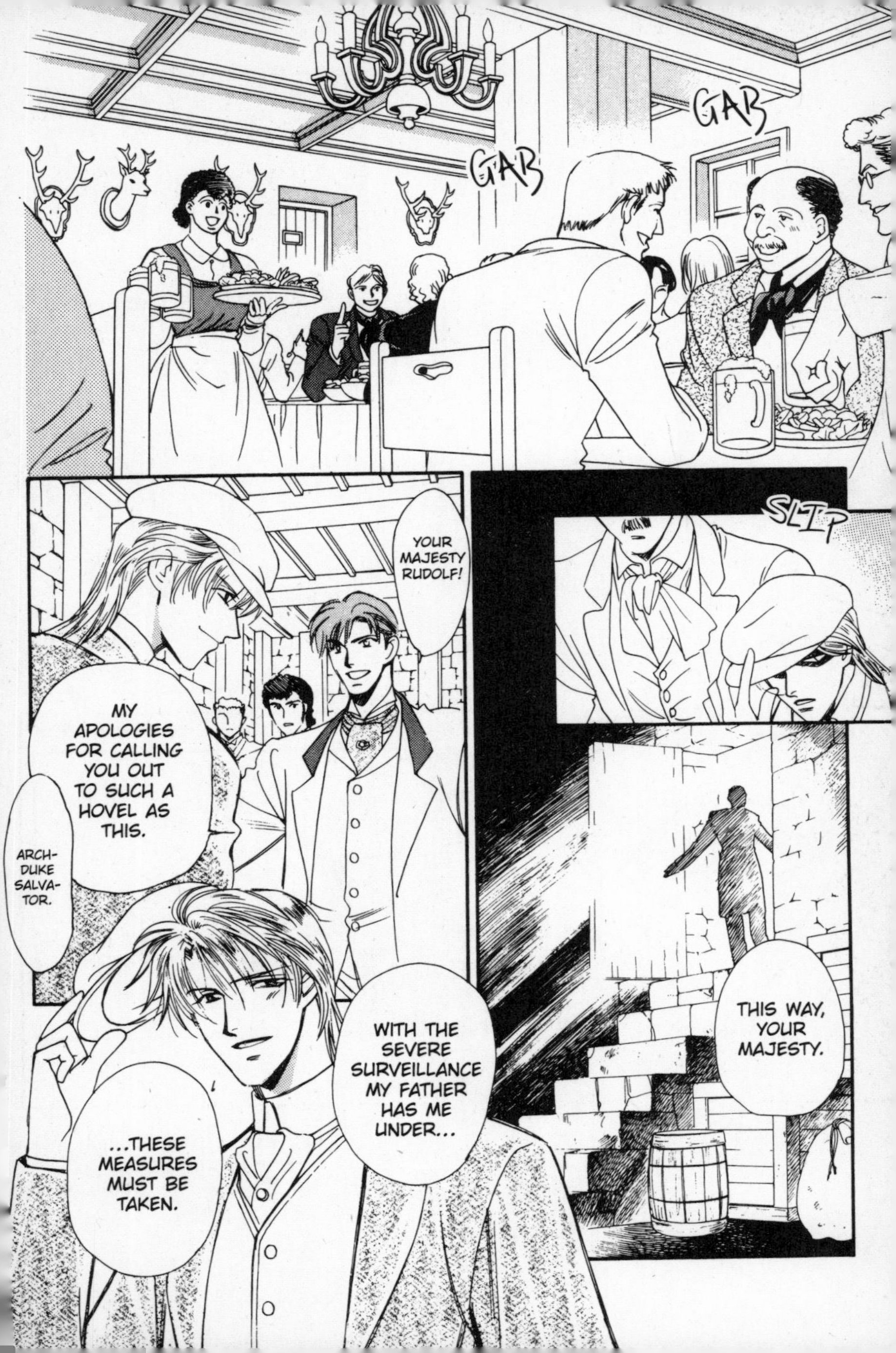
GAB
GAB
SLIP
THIS WAY, YOUR MAJESTY.
YOUR MAJESTY RUDOLF!
MY APOLOGIES FOR CALLING YOU OUT TO SUCH A HOVEL AS THIS.
ARCH-DUKE SALVA-TOR.
WITH THE SEVERE SURVEILLANCE MY FATHER HAS ME UNDER...
...THESE MEASURES MUST BE TAKEN.

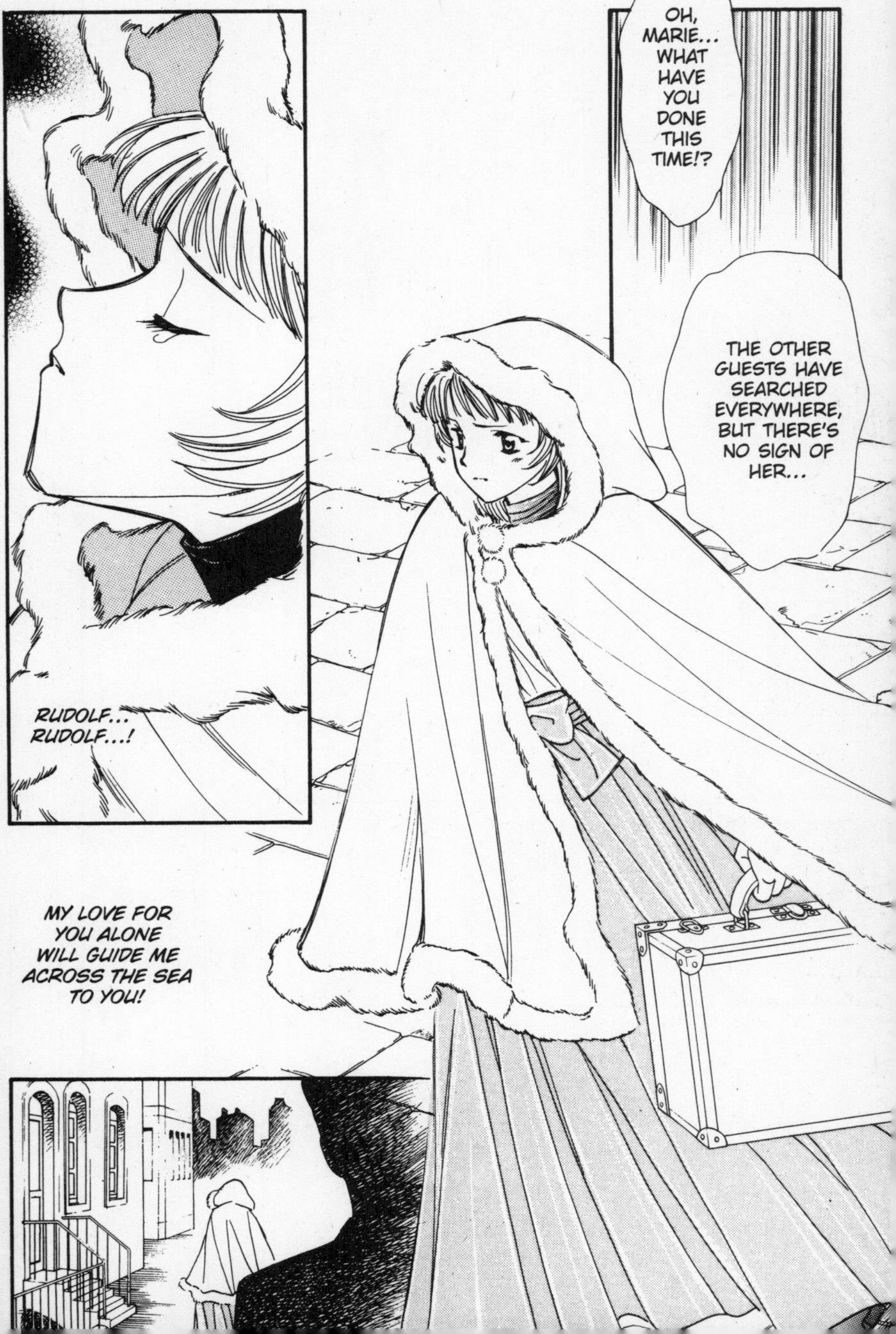
OH, MARIE... WHAT HAVE YOU DONE THIS TIME!?
THE OTHER GUESTS HAVE SEARCHED EVERYWHERE, BUT THERE'S NO SIGN OF HER...
RUDOLF... RUDOLF...!
MY LOVE FOR YOU ALONE WILL GUIDE ME ACROSS THE SEA TO YOU!

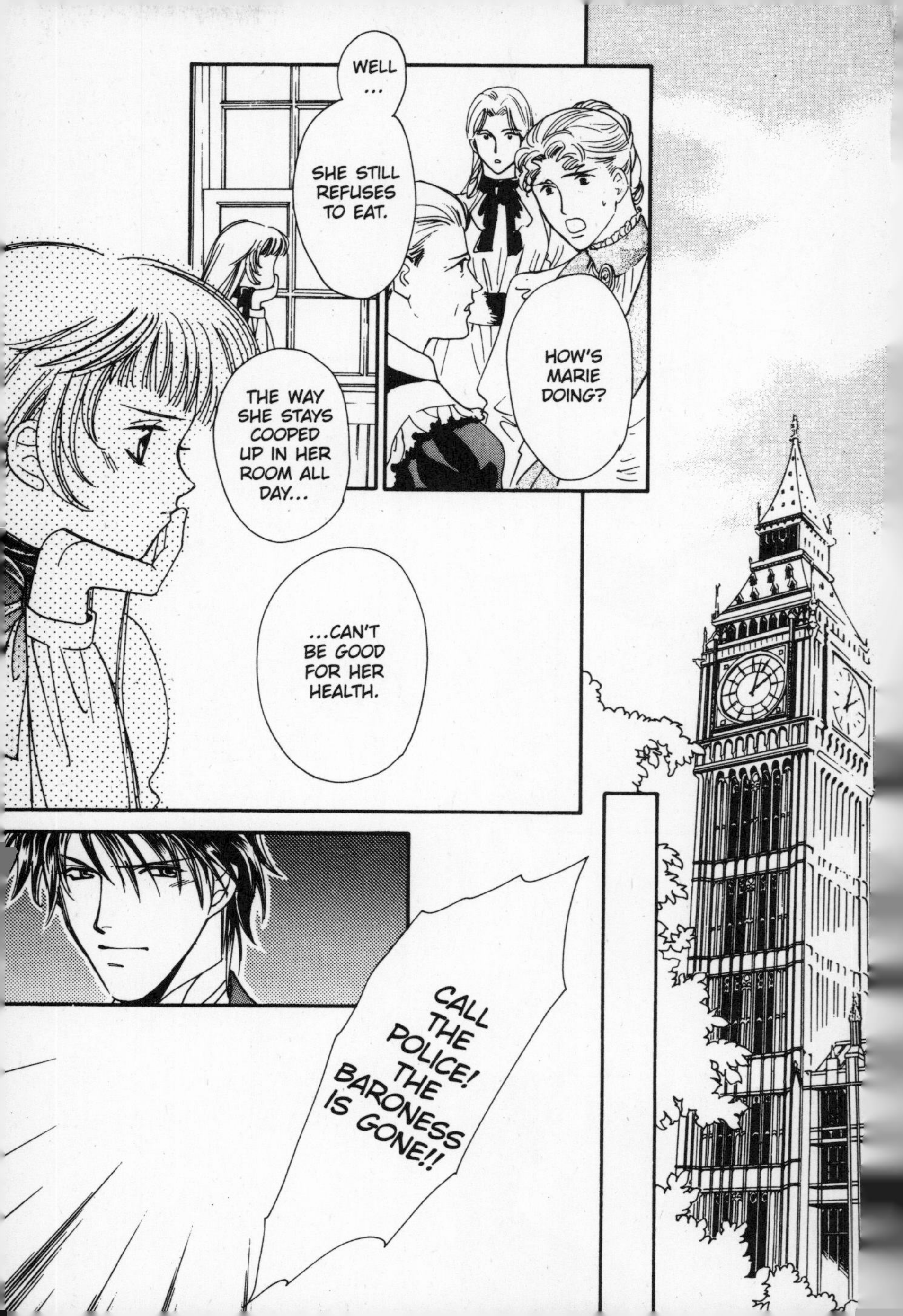
HOW'S MARIE DOING?
WELL...
SHE STILL REFUSES TO EAT.
THE WAY SHE STAYS COOPED UP IN HER ROOM ALL DAY...
...CAN'T BE GOOD FOR HER HEALTH.
CALL THE POLICE! THE BARONESS IS GONE!!

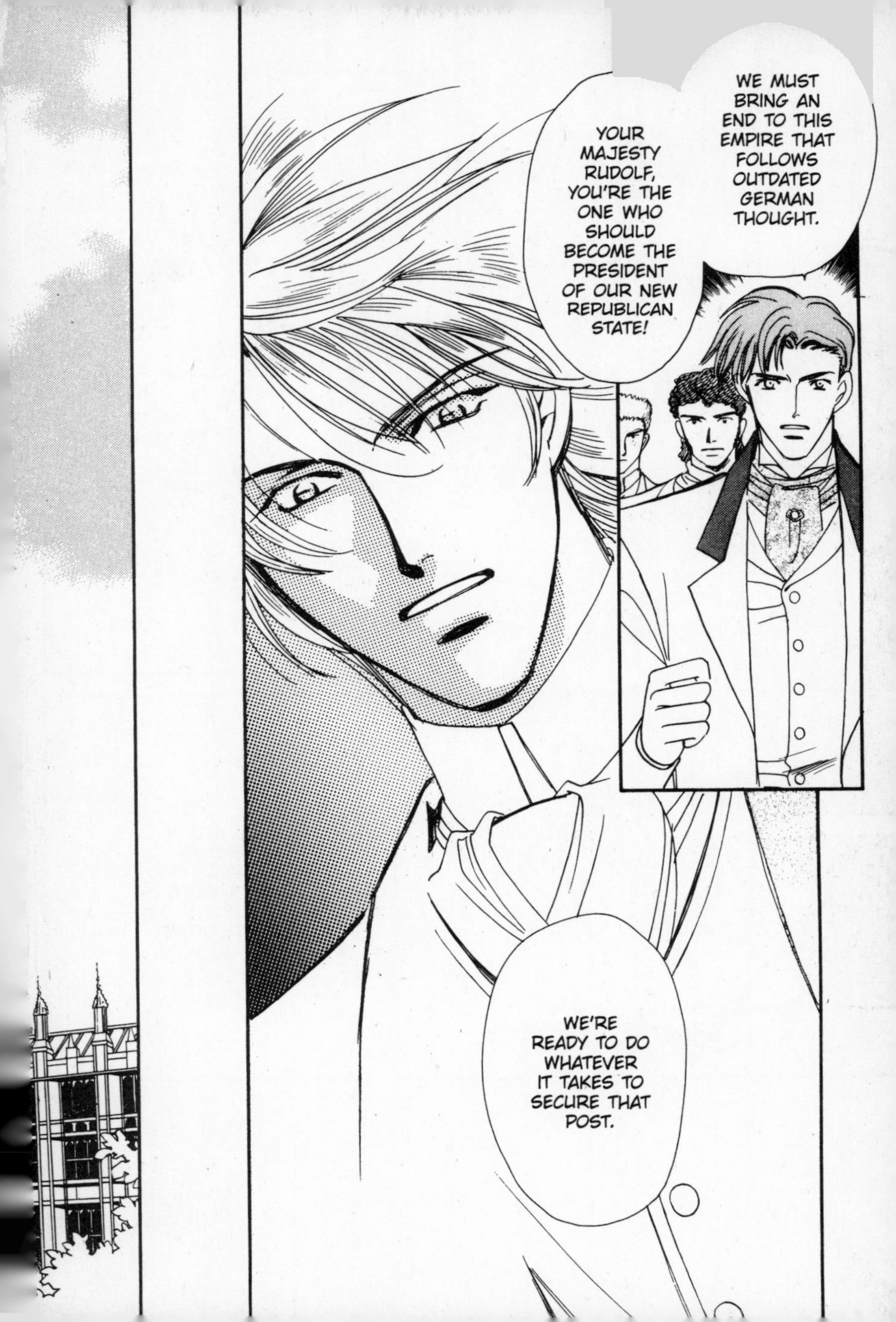
WE MUST BRING AN END TO THIS EMPIRE THAT FOLLOWS OUTDATED GERMAN THOUGHT.
YOUR MAJESTY RUDOLF, YOU'RE THE ONE WHO SHOULD BECOME THE PRESIDENT OF OUR NEW REPUBLICAN STATE!
WE'RE READY TO DO WHATEVER IT TAKES TO SECURE THAT POST.

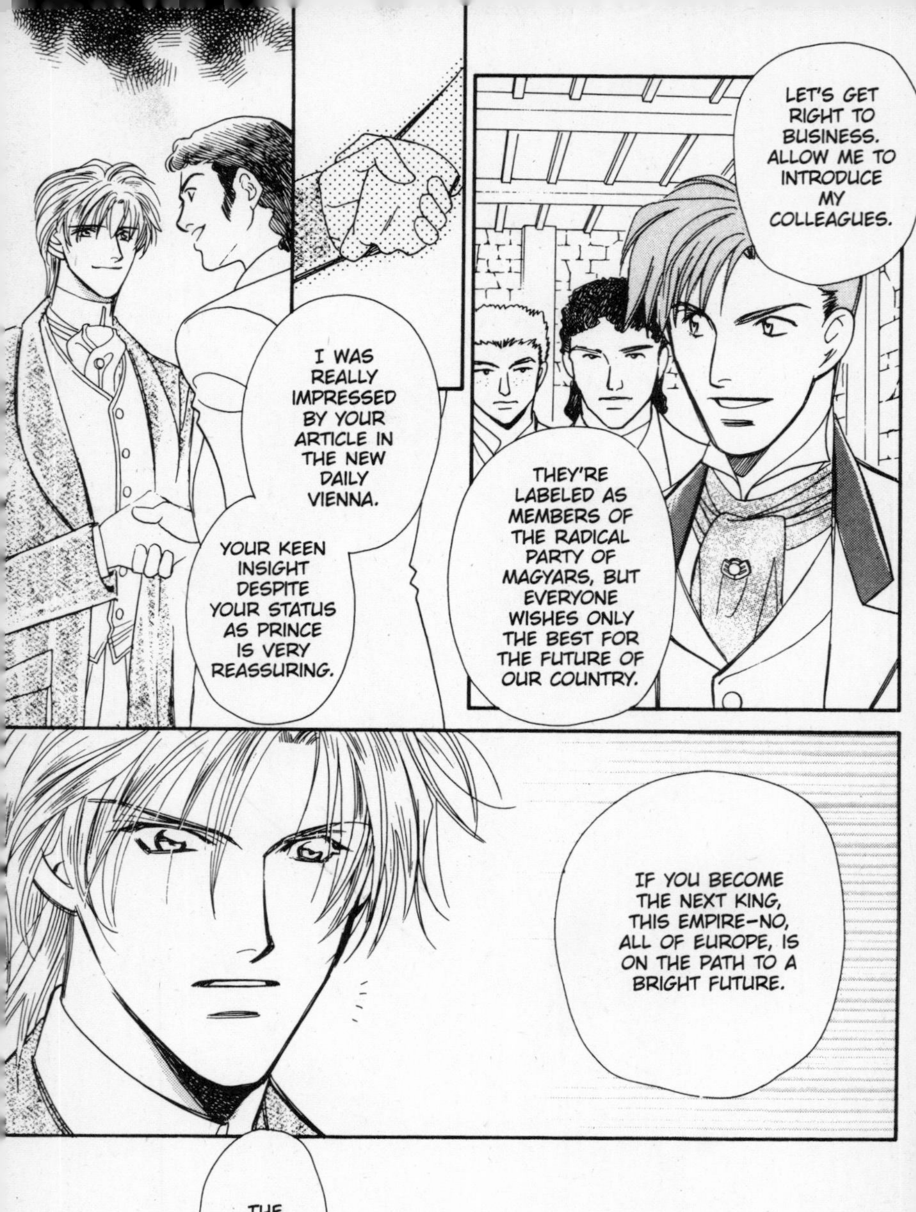
LET'S GET RIGHT TO BUSINESS. ALLOW ME TO INTRODUCE MY COLLEAGUES.
THEY'RE LABELED AS MEMBERS OF THE RADICAL PARTY OF MAGYARS, BUT EVERYONE WISHES ONLY THE BEST FOR THE FUTURE OF OUR COUNTRY.
I WAS REALLY IMPRESSED BY YOUR ARTICLE IN THE NEW DAILY VIENNA.
YOUR KEEN INSIGHT DESPITE YOUR STATUS AS PRINCE IS VERY REASSURING.
IF YOU BECOME THE NEXT KING, THIS EMPIRE—NO, ALL OF EUROPE, IS ON THE PATH TO A BRIGHT FUTURE.
THE NEXT... KING?

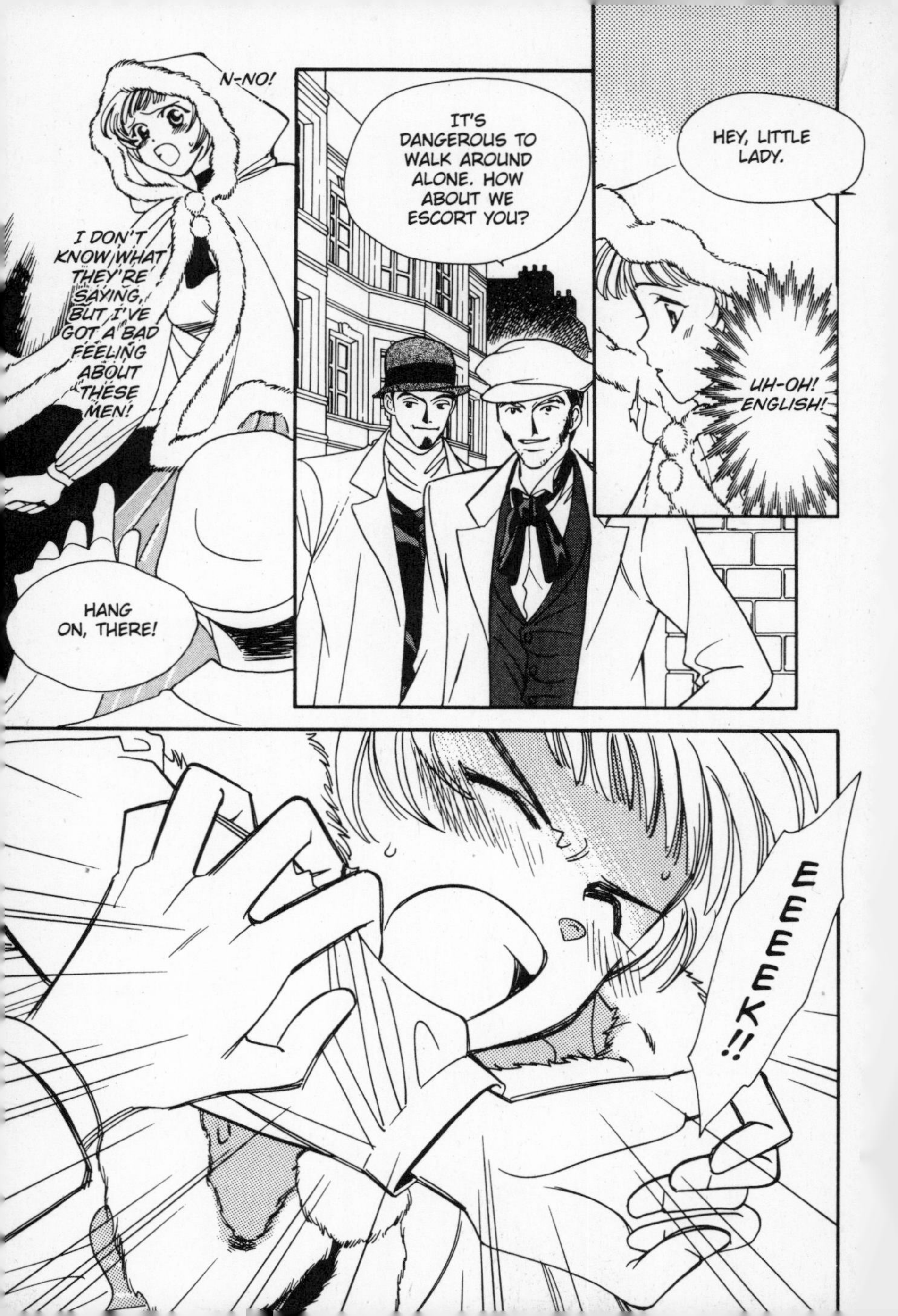
HEY, LITTLE LADY.
UH-OH! ENGLISH!
IT'S DANGEROUS TO WALK AROUND ALONE. HOW ABOUT WE ESCORT YOU?
N-NO!
I DON'T KNOW WHAT THEY'RE SAYING, BUT I'VE GOT A BAD FEELING ABOUT THESE MEN!
HANG ON, THERE!
EEEEEK!!

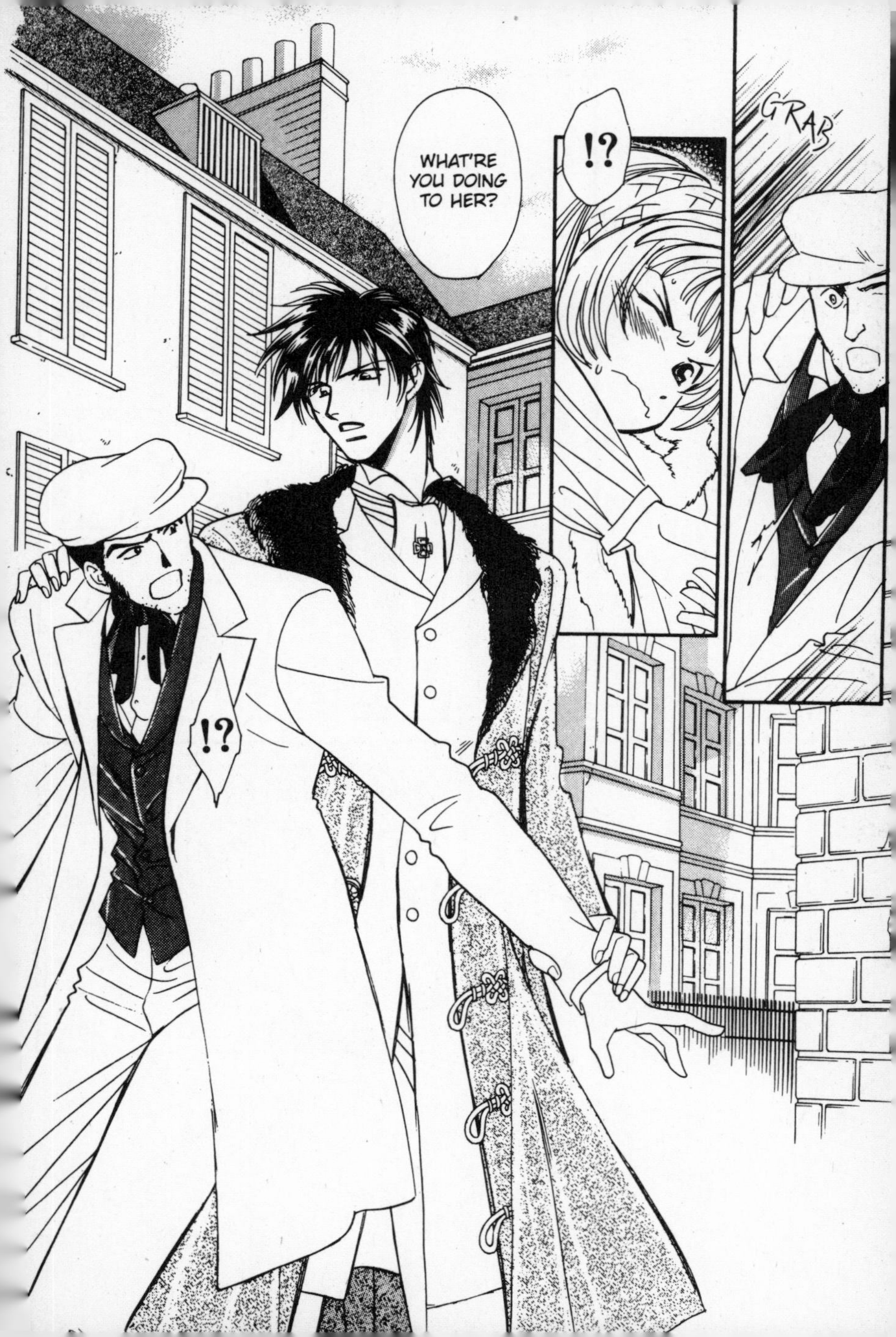
GRAB
!?
WHAT'RE YOU DOING TO HER?
!?

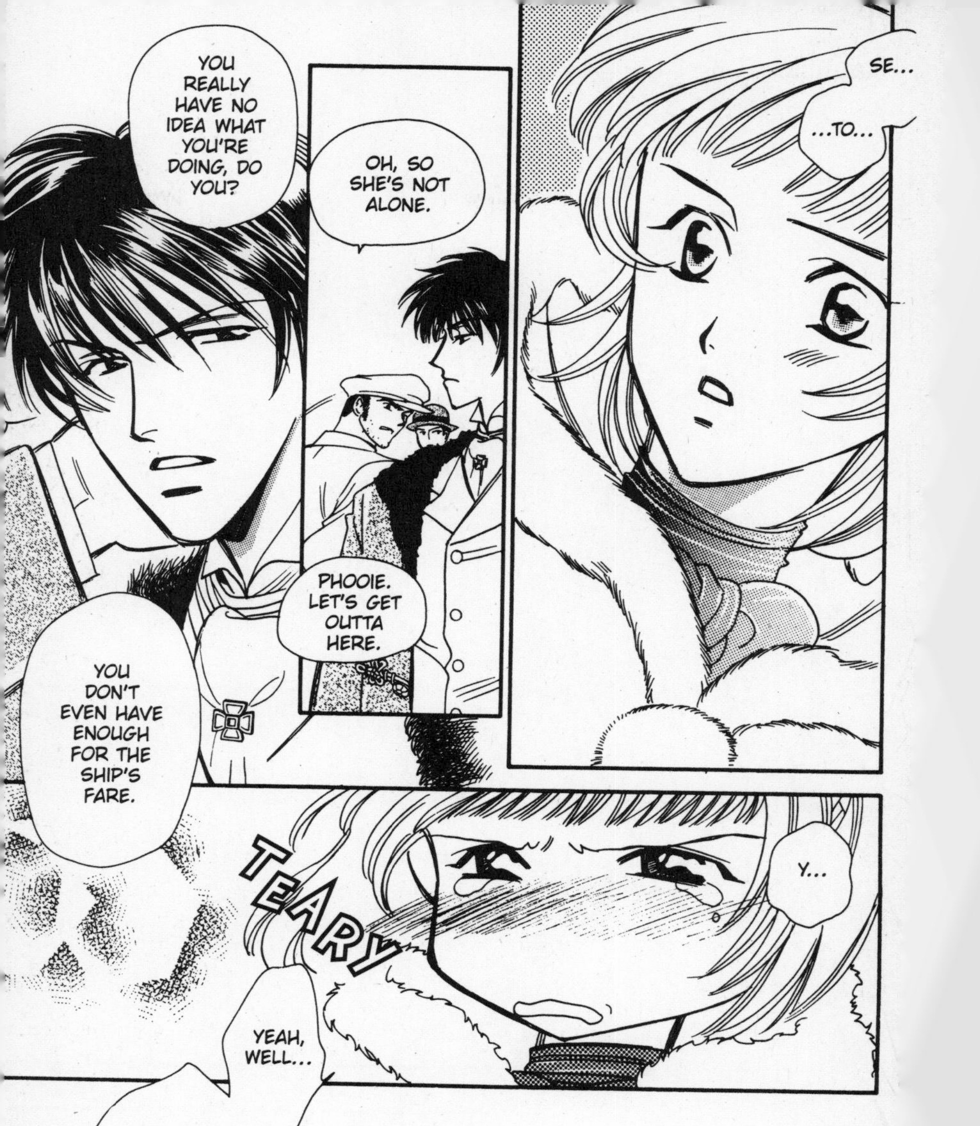
SE...
...TO...
OH, SO SHE'S NOT ALONE.
PHOOIE. LET'S GET OUTTA HERE.
YOU REALLY HAVE NO IDEA WHAT YOU'RE DOING, DO YOU?
YOU DON'T EVEN HAVE ENOUGH FOR THE SHIP'S FARE.
Y...
TEARY
YEAH, WELL...
WHAT ELSE AM I SUPPOSED TO DO!?

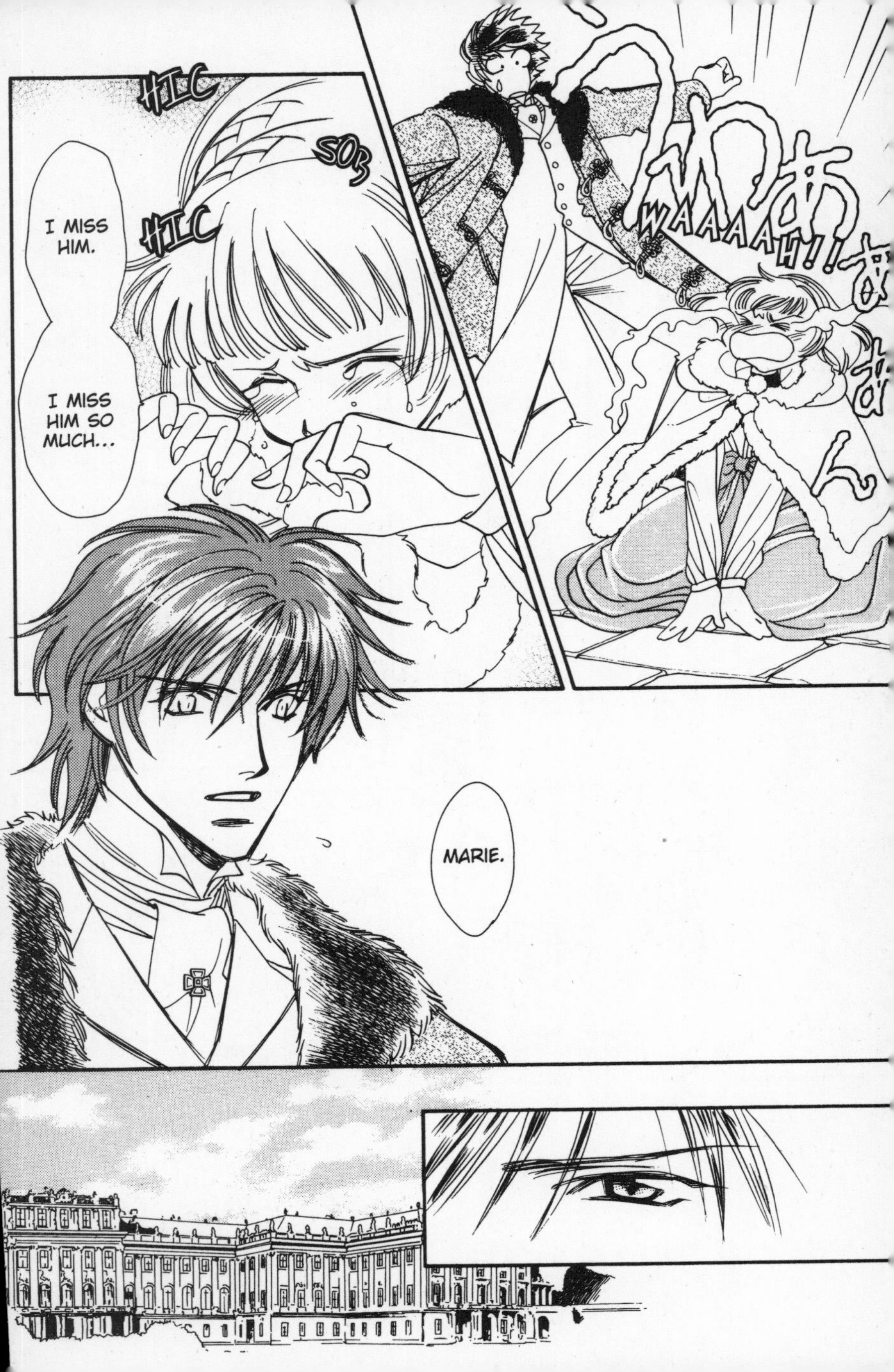
わあ
WAAAAAH!!
おおん
HIC
SOB
HIC
I MISS HIM.
I MISS HIM SO MUCH...
MARIE.

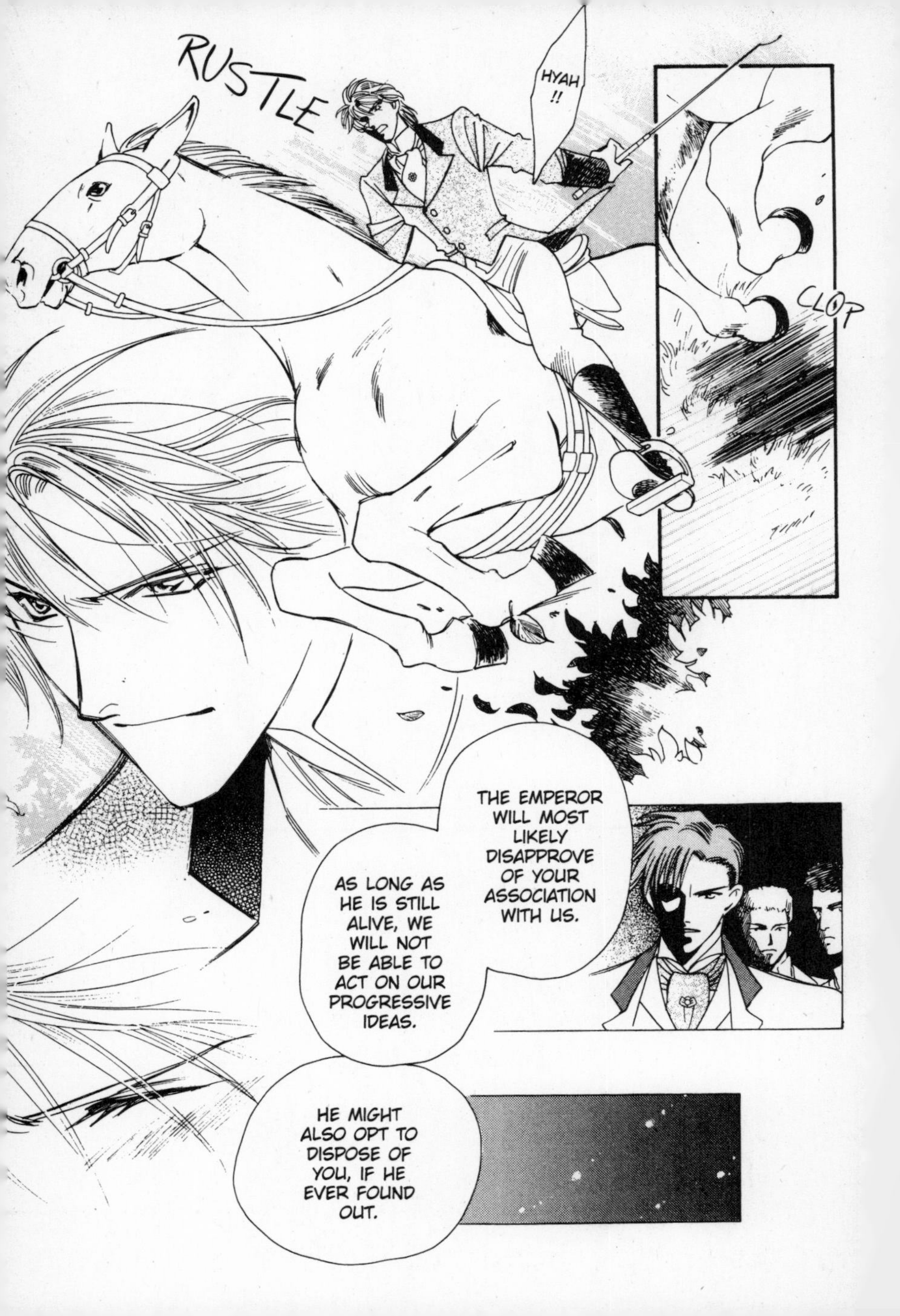
CLOP
HYAH !!
RUSTLE
THE EMPEROR WILL MOST LIKELY DISAPPROVE OF YOUR ASSOCIATION WITH US.
AS LONG AS HE IS STILL ALIVE, WE WILL NOT BE ABLE TO ACT ON OUR PROGRESSIVE IDEAS.
HE MIGHT ALSO OPT TO DISPOSE OF YOU, IF HE EVER FOUND OUT.

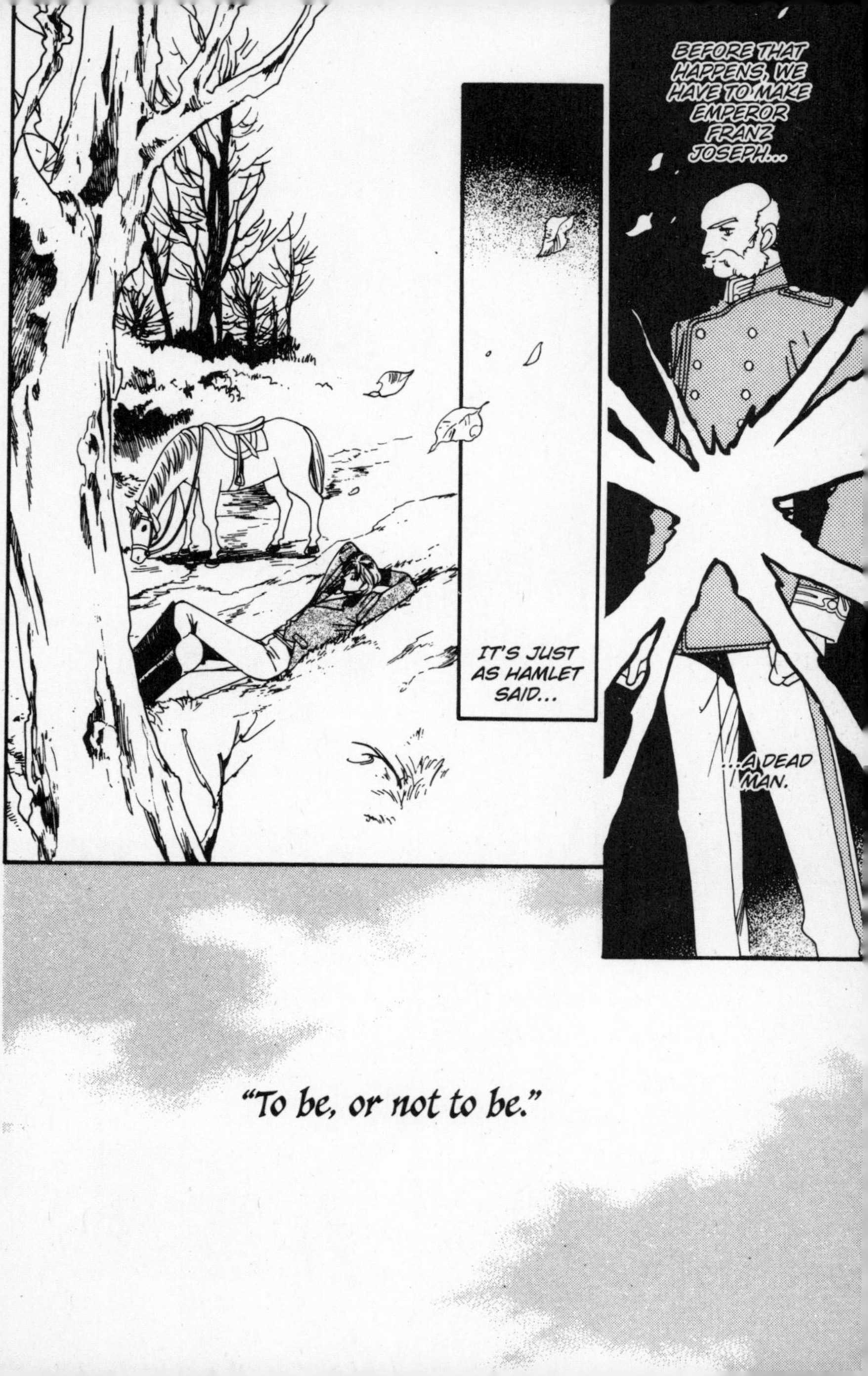
BEFORE THAT HAPPENS, WE HAVE TO MAKE EMPEROR FRANZ JOSEPH...
...A DEAD MAN.
IT'S JUST AS HAMLET SAID...
"To be, or not to be."

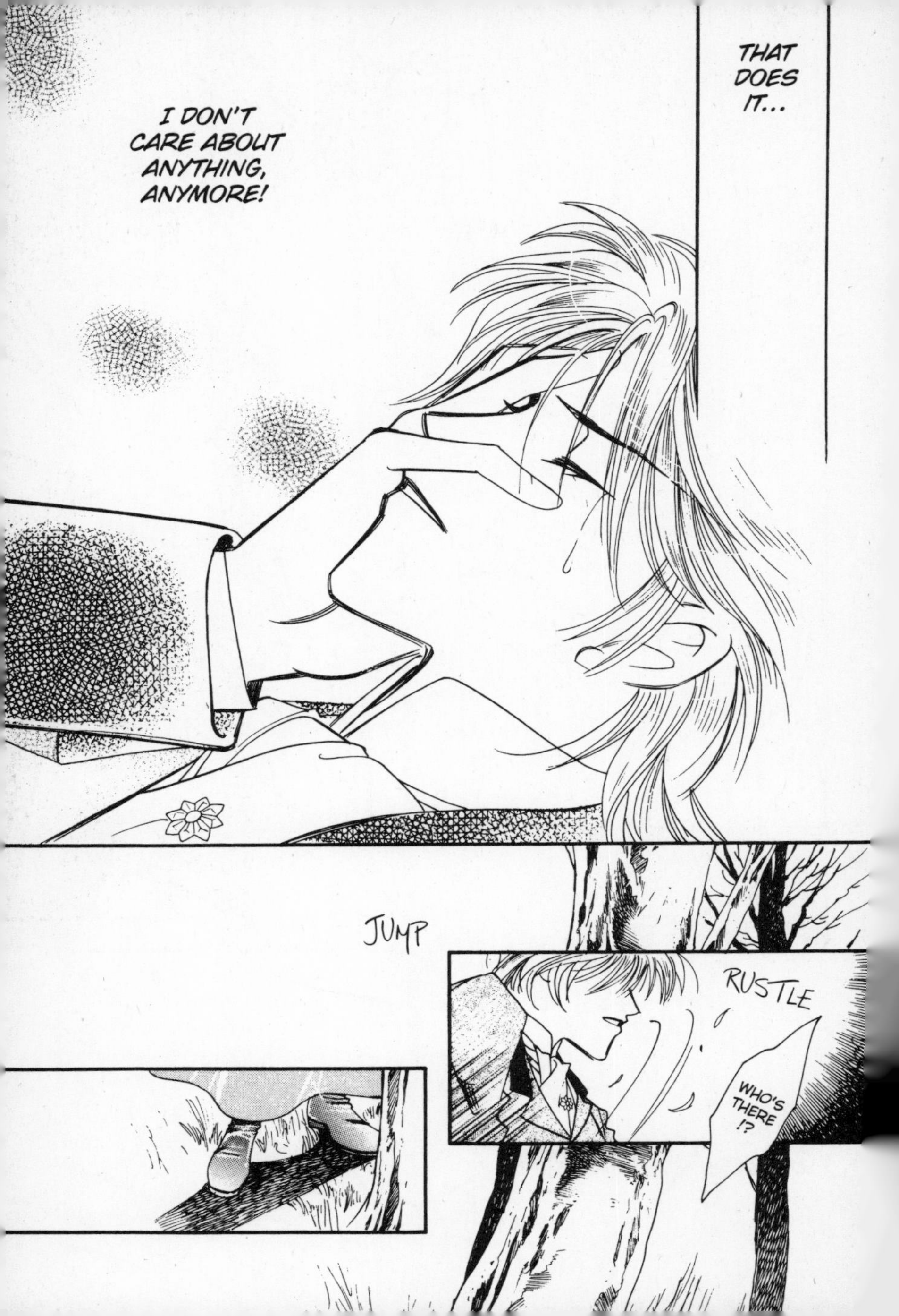
THAT DOES IT...
I DON'T CARE ABOUT ANYTHING, ANYMORE!
RUSTLE
WHO'S THERE !?
JUMP

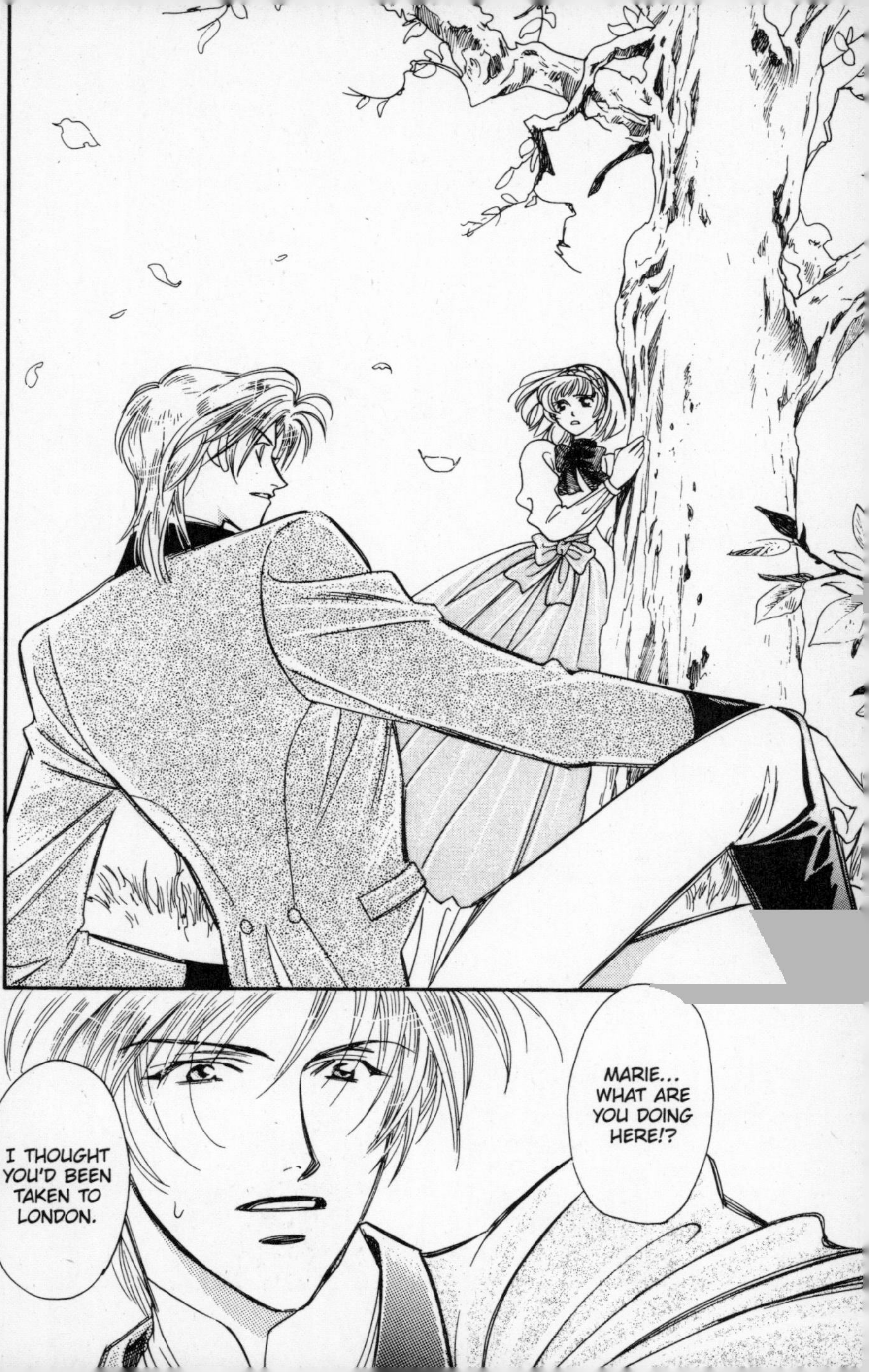
MARIE... WHAT ARE YOU DOING HERE!?
I THOUGHT YOU'D BEEN TAKEN TO LONDON.

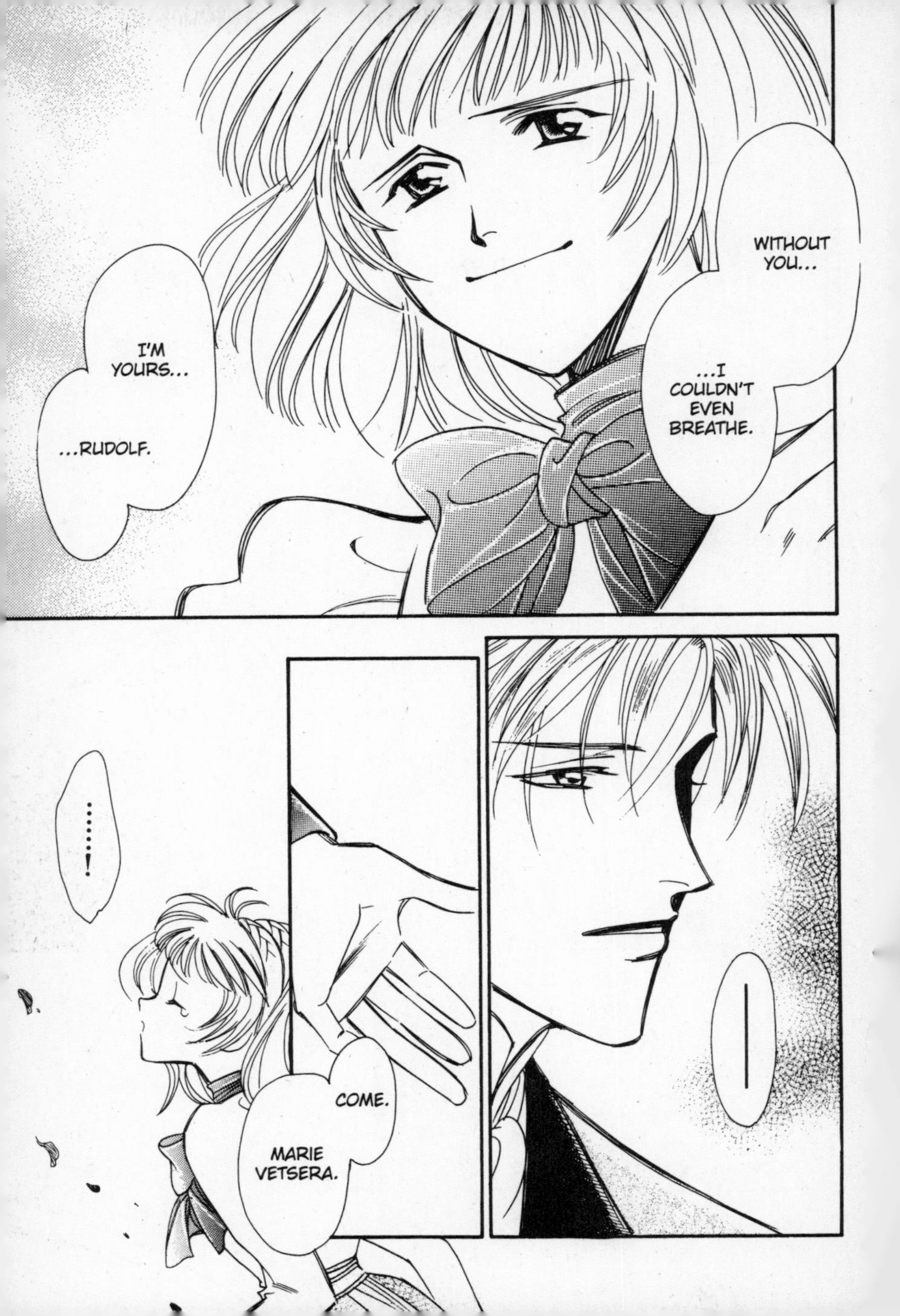
WITHOUT YOU...
...I COULDN'T EVEN BREATHE.
I'M YOURS...
...RUDOLF.
—
COME.
MARIE VETSERA.
......!

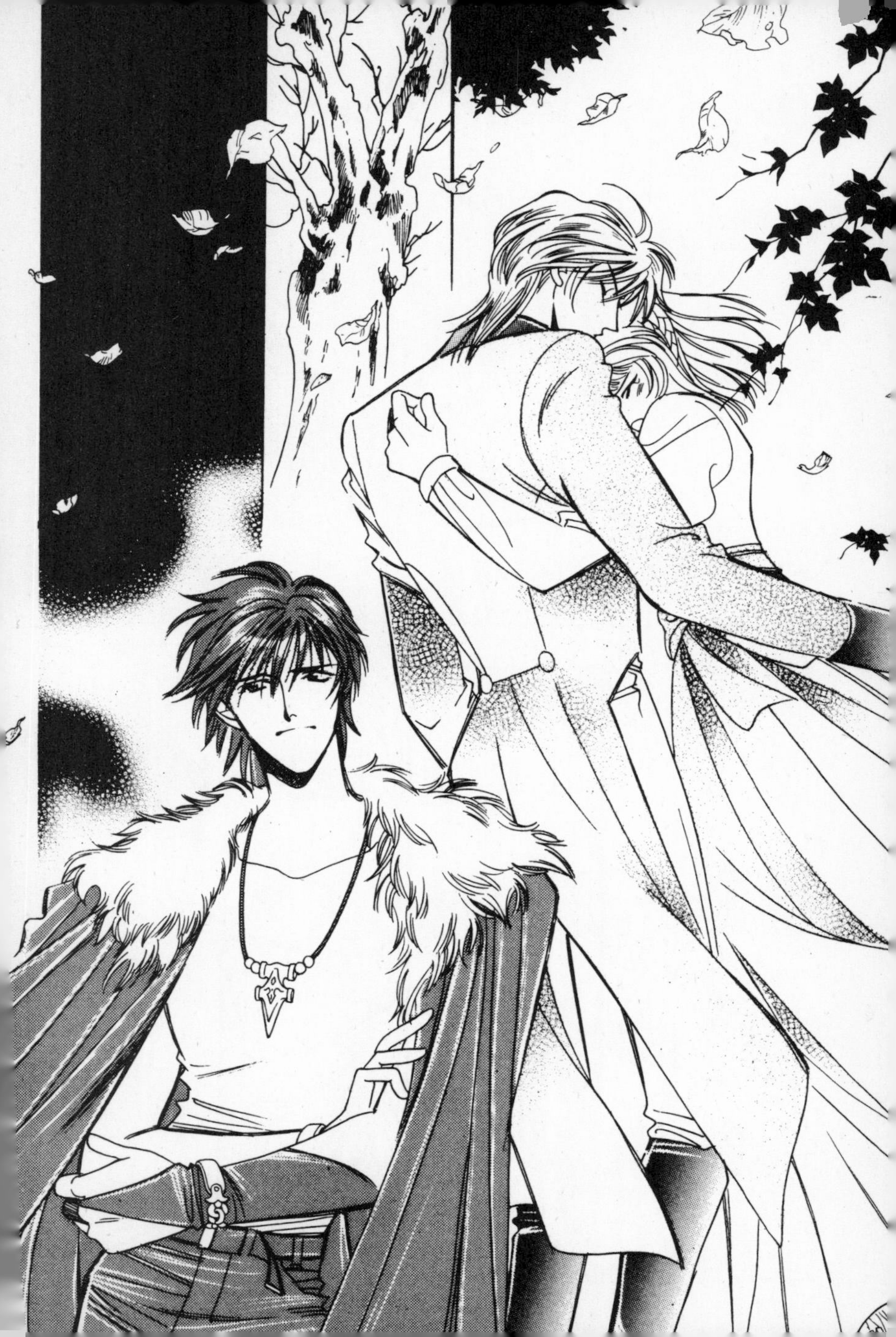

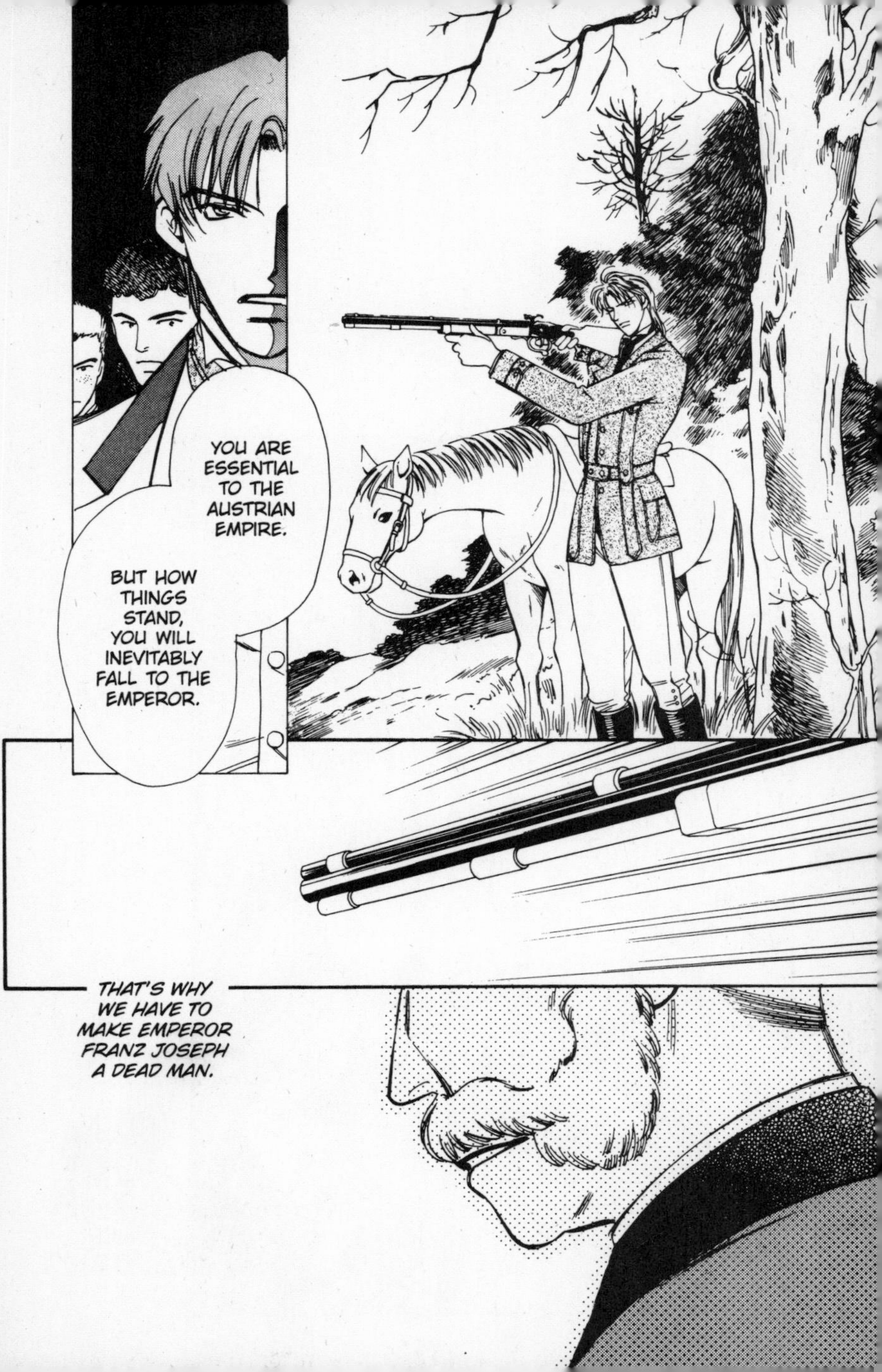
YOU ARE ESSENTIAL TO THE AUSTRIAN EMPIRE.
BUT HOW THINGS STAND, YOU WILL INEVITABLY FALL TO THE EMPEROR.
THAT'S WHY WE HAVE TO MAKE EMPEROR FRANZ JOSEPH A DEAD MAN.

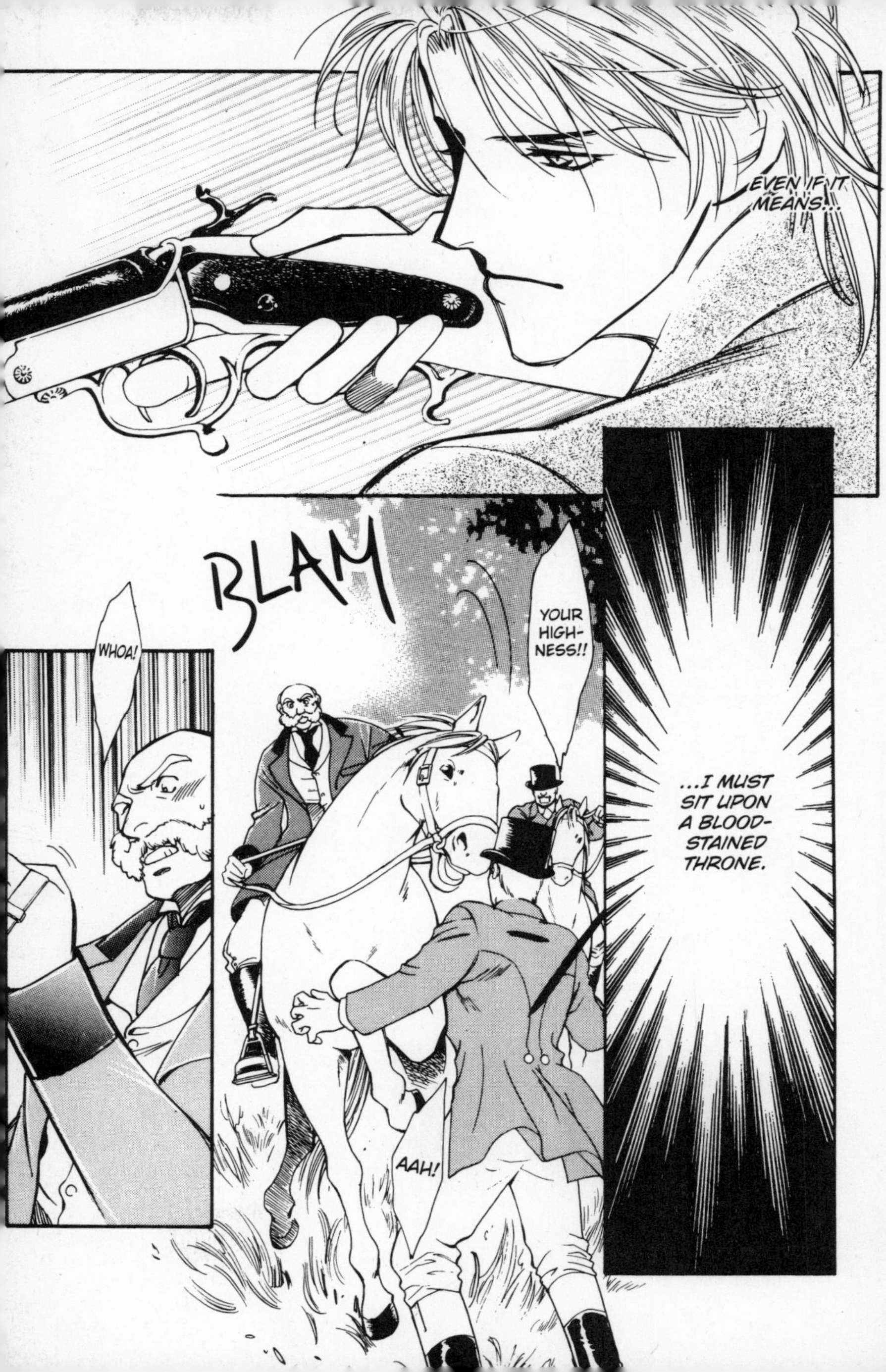
EVEN IF IT MEANS...
...I MUST SIT UPON A BLOOD-STAINED THRONE.
BLAM
YOUR HIGHNESS!!
AAH!
WHOA!

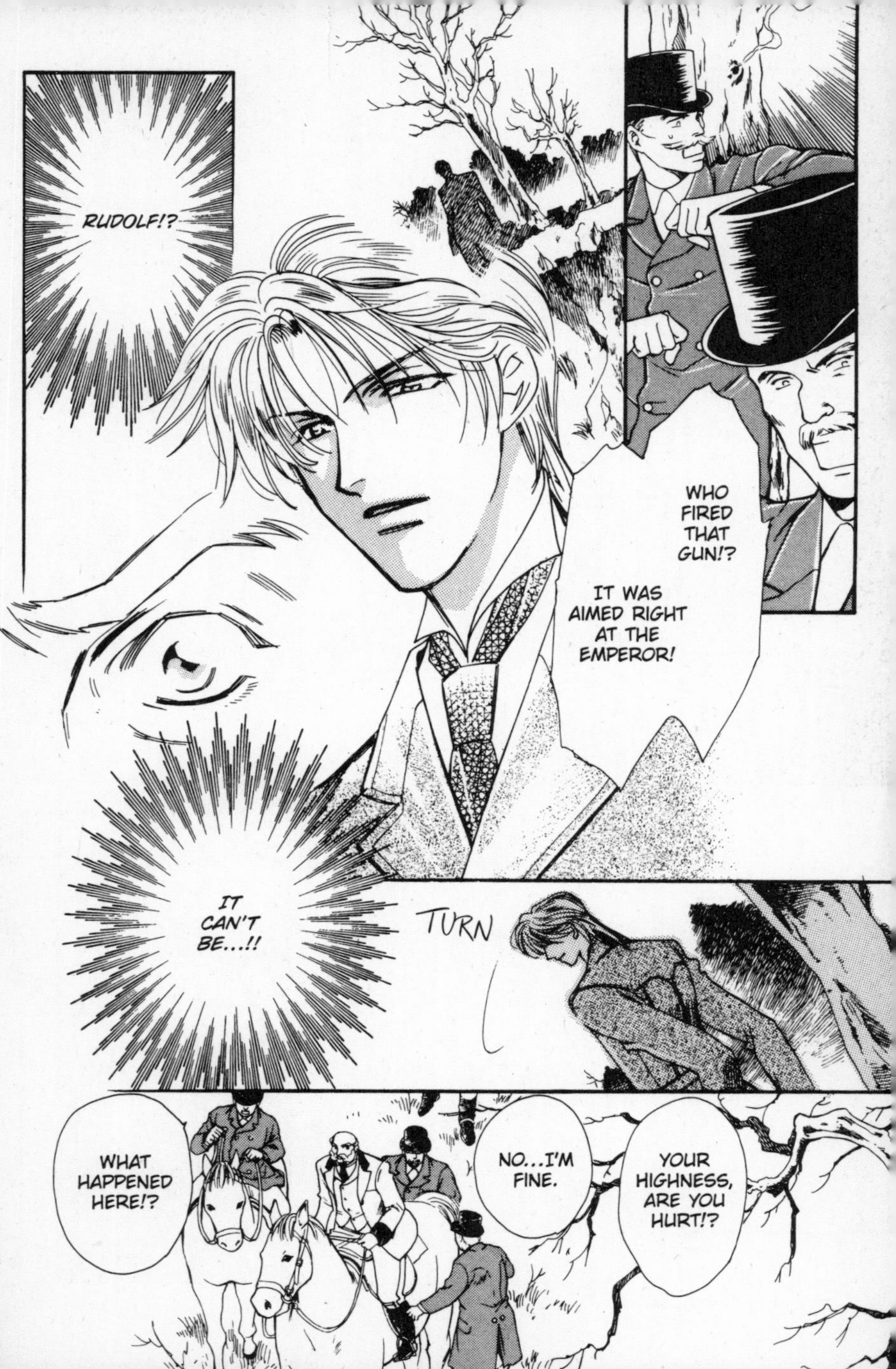
WHO FIRED THAT GUN!?
IT WAS AIMED RIGHT AT THE EMPEROR!
RUDOLF!?
IT CAN'T BE...!!
TURN
YOUR HIGHNESS, ARE YOU HURT!?
NO...I'M FINE.
WHAT HAPPENED HERE!?

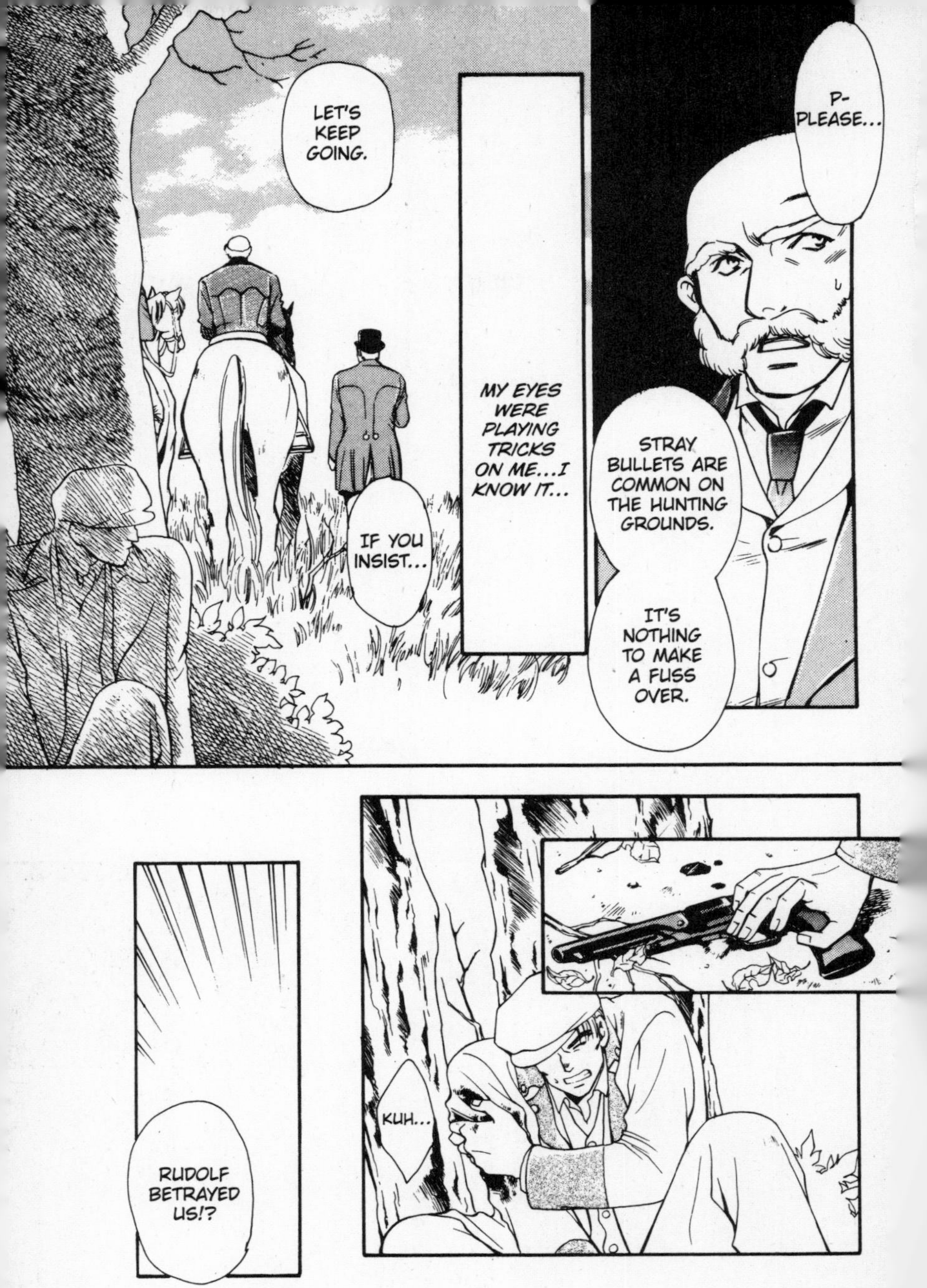
P-PLEASE...
STRAY BULLETS ARE COMMON ON THE HUNTING GROUNDS.
IT'S NOTHING TO MAKE A FUSS OVER.
MY EYES WERE PLAYING TRICKS ON ME...I KNOW IT...
LET'S KEEP GOING.
IF YOU INSIST...
KUH...
RUDOLF BETRAYED US!?

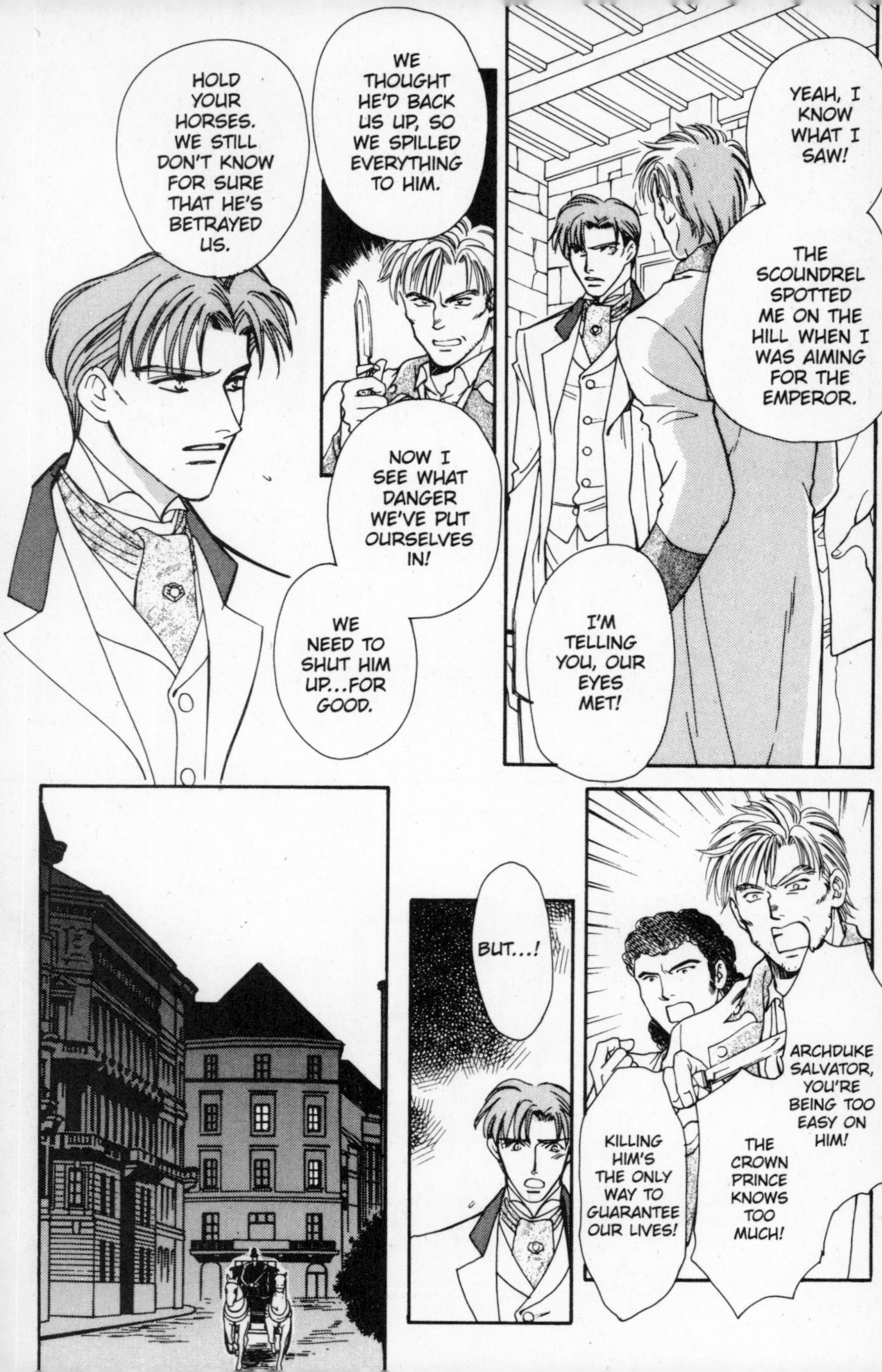
YEAH, I KNOW WHAT I SAW!
THE SCOUNDREL SPOTTED ME ON THE HILL WHEN I WAS AIMING FOR THE EMPEROR.
I'M TELLING YOU, OUR EYES MET!
WE THOUGHT HE'D BACK US UP, SO WE SPILLED EVERYTHING TO HIM.
NOW I SEE WHAT DANGER WE'VE PUT OURSELVES IN!
WE NEED TO SHUT HIM UP...FOR GOOD.
HOLD YOUR HORSES. WE STILL DON'T KNOW FOR SURE THAT HE'S BETRAYED US.
ARCHDUKE SALVATOR, YOU'RE BEING TOO EASY ON HIM!
THE CROWN PRINCE KNOWS TOO MUCH!
KILLING HIM'S THE ONLY WAY TO GUARANTEE OUR LIVES!
BUT...!

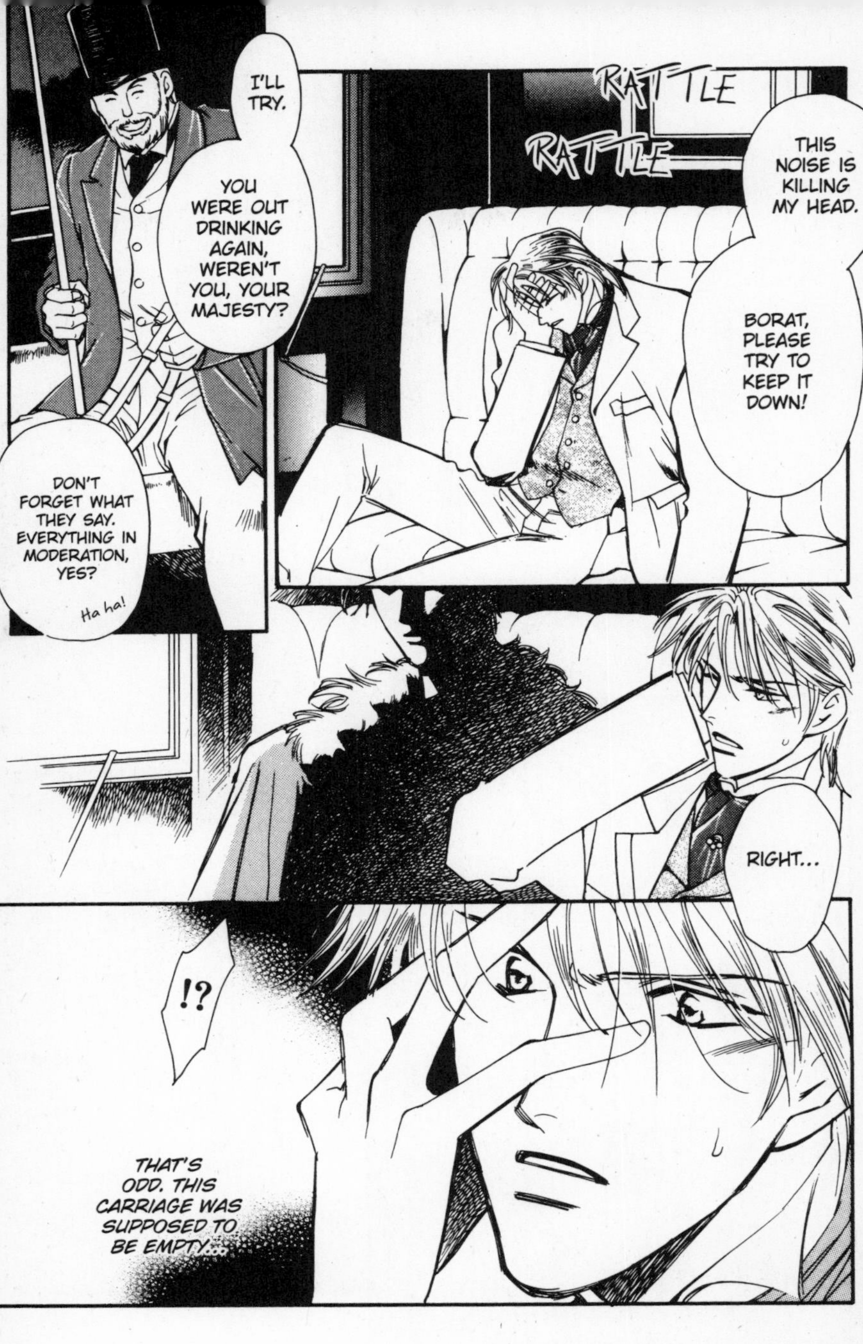
RATTLE
RATTLE
THIS NOISE IS KILLING MY HEAD.
BORAT, PLEASE TRY TO KEEP IT DOWN!
I'LL TRY.
YOU WERE OUT DRINKING AGAIN, WEREN'T YOU, YOUR MAJESTY?
DON'T FORGET WHAT THEY SAY. EVERYTHING IN MODERATION, YES?
Ha ha!
RIGHT...
!?
THAT'S ODD. THIS CARRIAGE WAS SUPPOSED TO BE EMPTY...

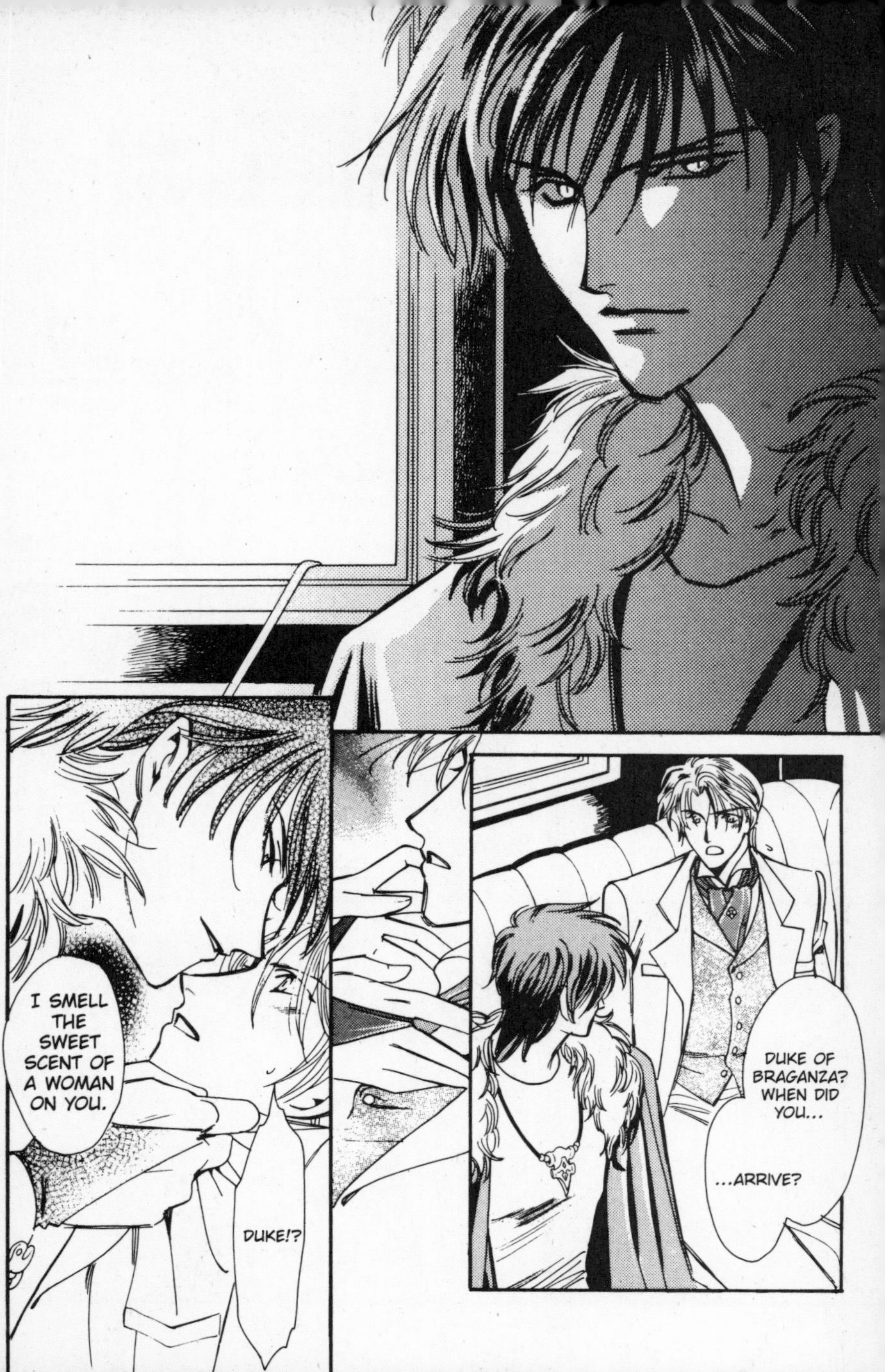
DUKE OF BRAGANZA? WHEN DID YOU...
...ARRIVE?
I SMELL THE SWEET SCENT OF A WOMAN ON YOU.
DUKE!?

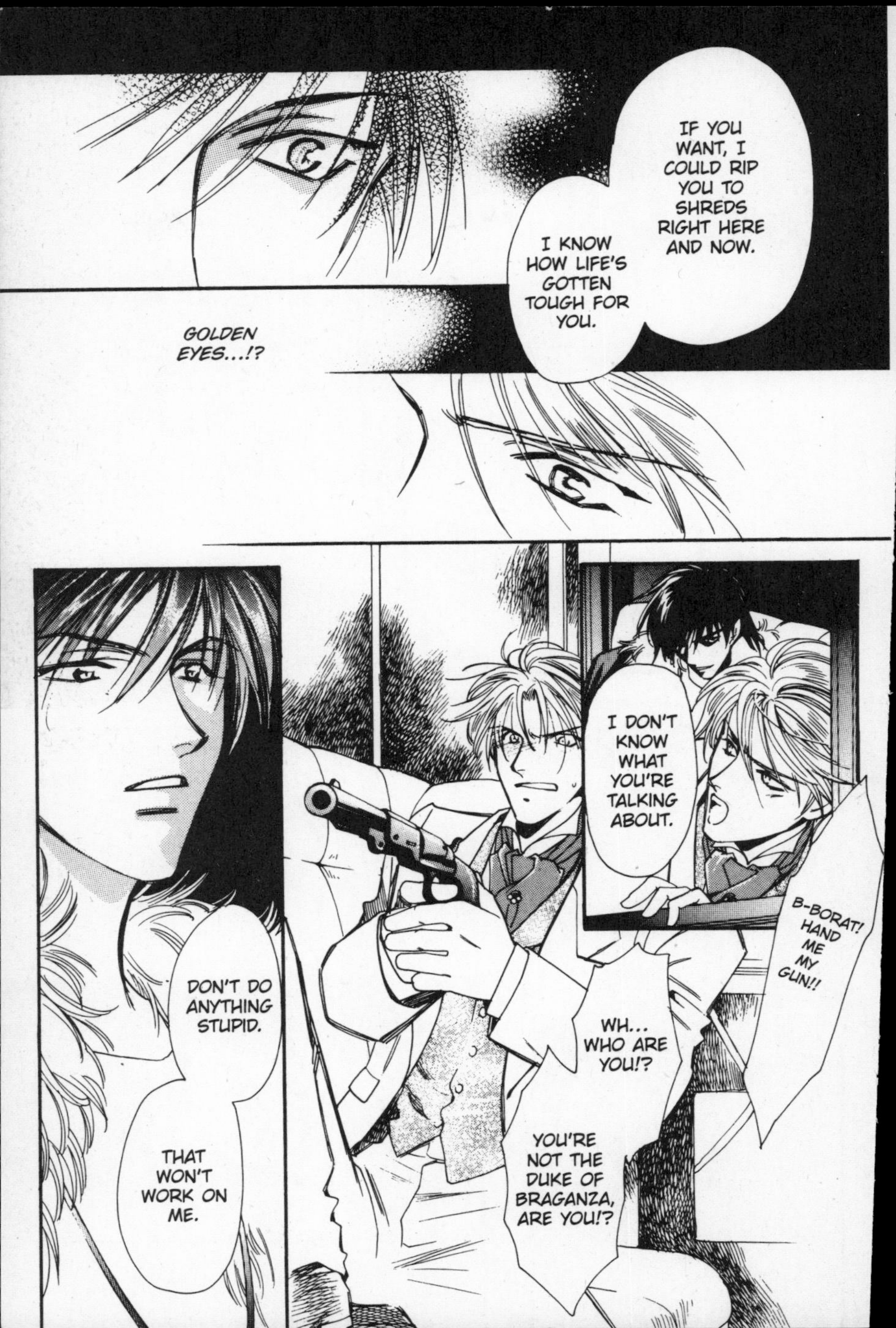
IF YOU WANT, I COULD RIP YOU TO SHREDS RIGHT HERE AND NOW.
I KNOW HOW LIFE'S GOTTEN TOUGH FOR YOU.
GOLDEN EYES...!?
I DON'T KNOW WHAT YOU'RE TALKING ABOUT.
B-BORAT! HAND ME MY GUN!!
WH... WHO ARE YOU!?
YOU'RE NOT THE DUKE OF BRAGANZA, ARE YOU!?
DON'T DO ANYTHING STUPID.
THAT WON'T WORK ON ME.

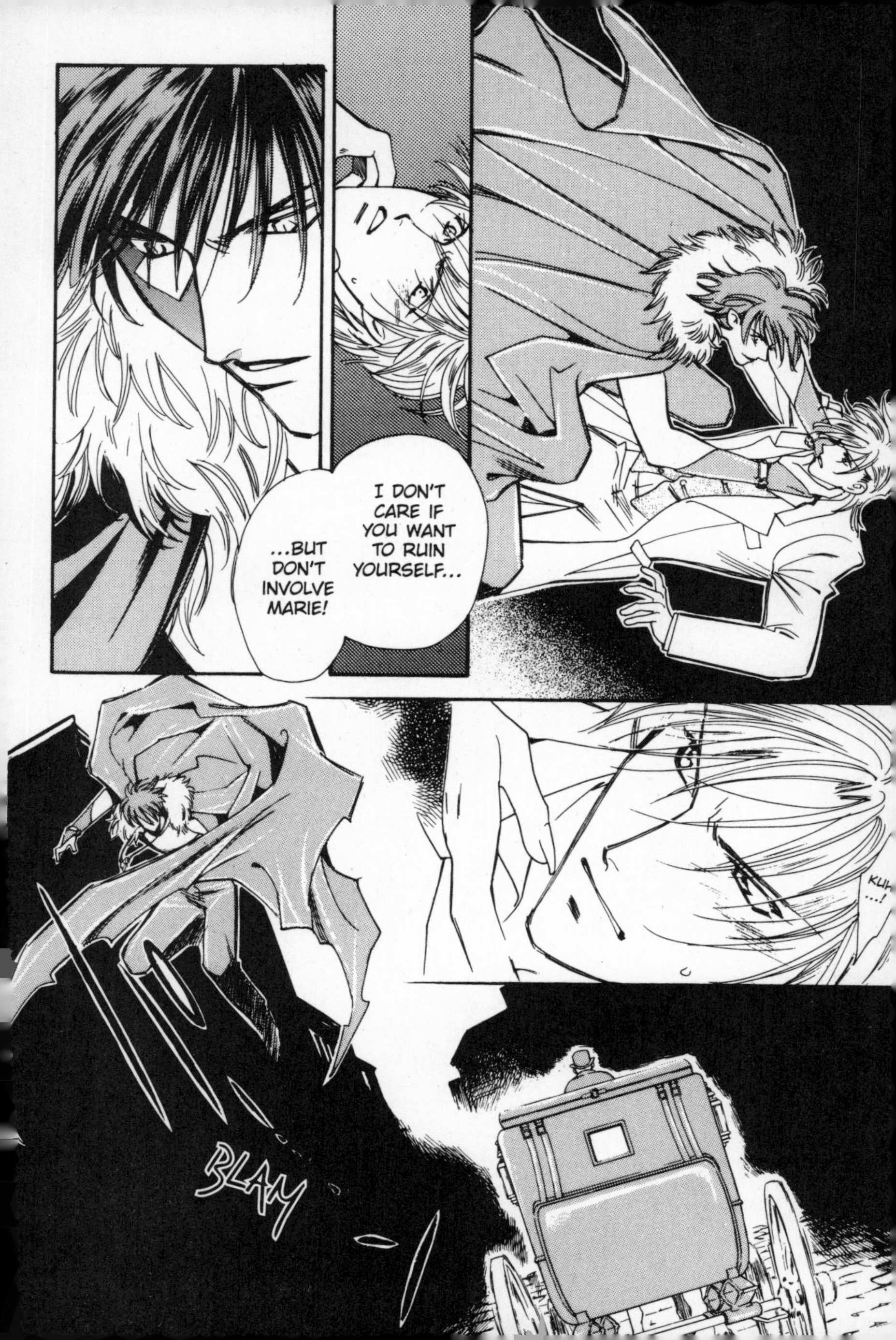
I DON'T CARE IF YOU WANT TO RUIN YOURSELF...
...BUT DON'T INVOLVE MARIE!
KUH ...!
BLAM

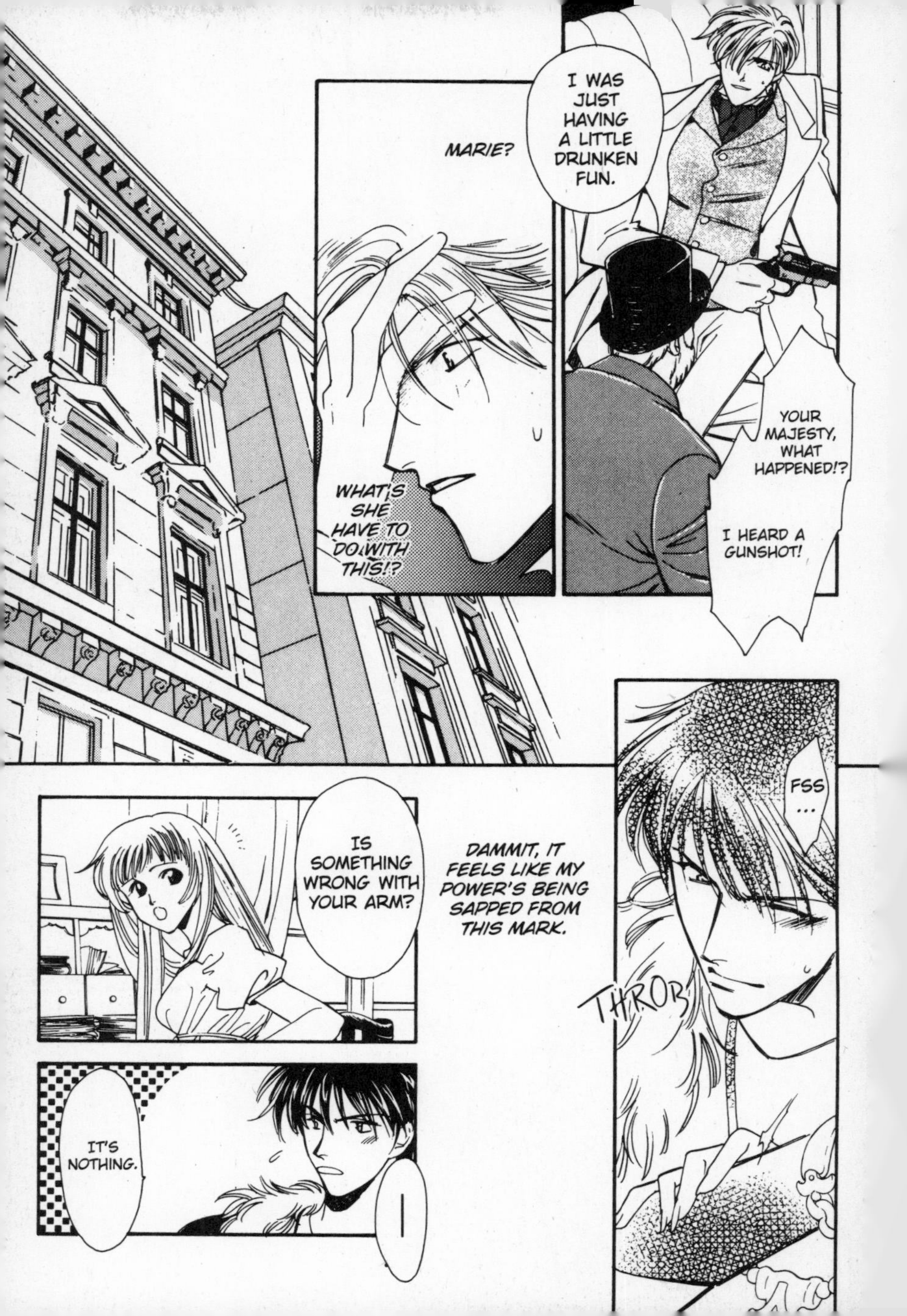
YOUR MAJESTY, WHAT HAPPENED!?
I HEARD A GUNSHOT!
I WAS JUST HAVING A LITTLE DRUNKEN FUN.
MARIE?
WHAT'S SHE HAVE TO DO WITH THIS!?
FSS...
THROB
DAMMIT, IT FEELS LIKE MY POWER'S BEING SAPPED FROM THIS MARK.
IS SOMETHING WRONG WITH YOUR ARM?
IT'S NOTHING.

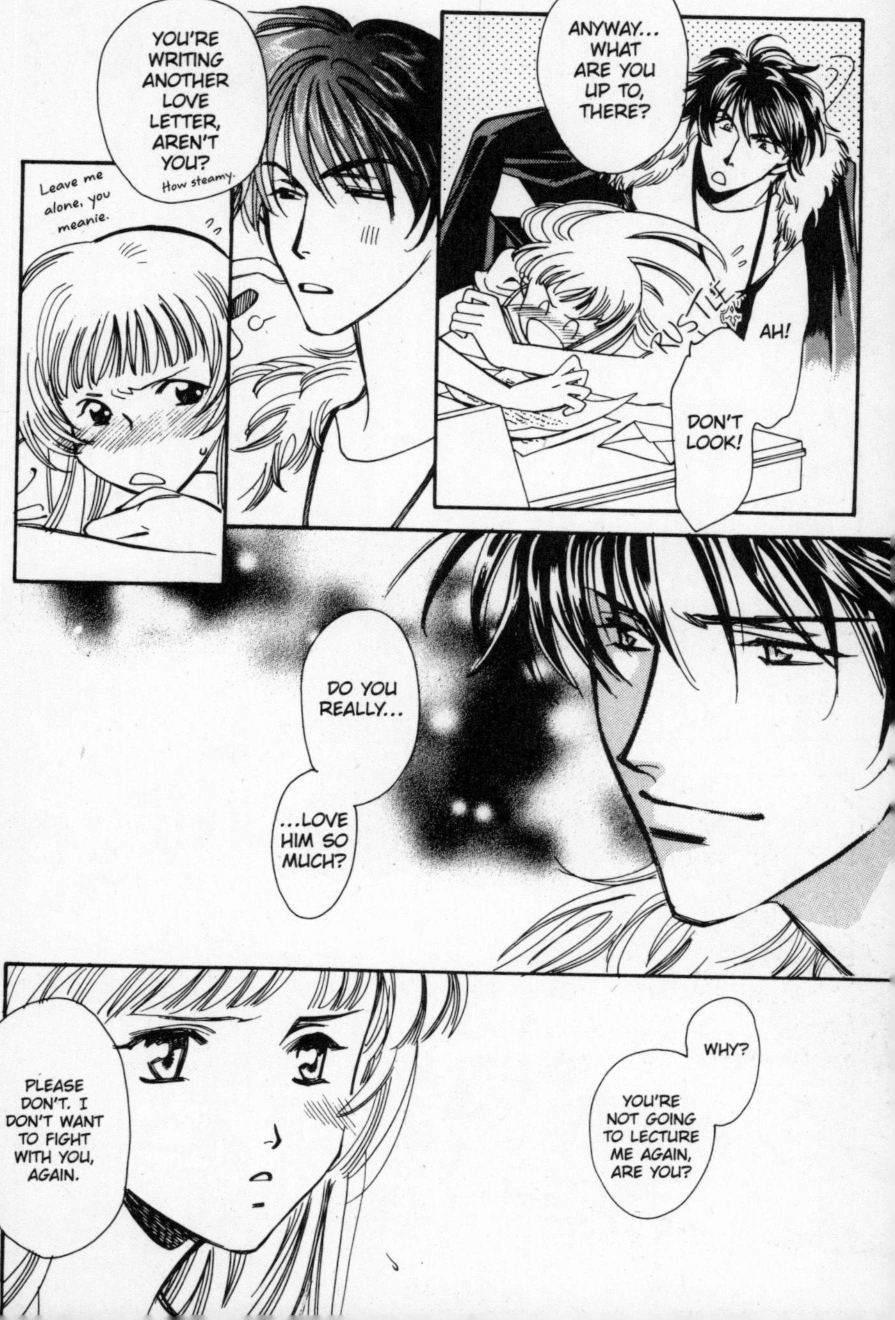
ANYWAY... WHAT ARE YOU UP TO, THERE?
RUSTLE
AH!
DON'T LOOK!
YOU'RE WRITING ANOTHER LOVE LETTER, AREN'T YOU?
How steamy.
Leave me alone, you meanie.
DO YOU REALLY...
...LOVE HIM SO MUCH?
WHY?
YOU'RE NOT GOING TO LECTURE ME AGAIN, ARE YOU?
PLEASE DON'T. I DON'T WANT TO FIGHT WITH YOU, AGAIN.

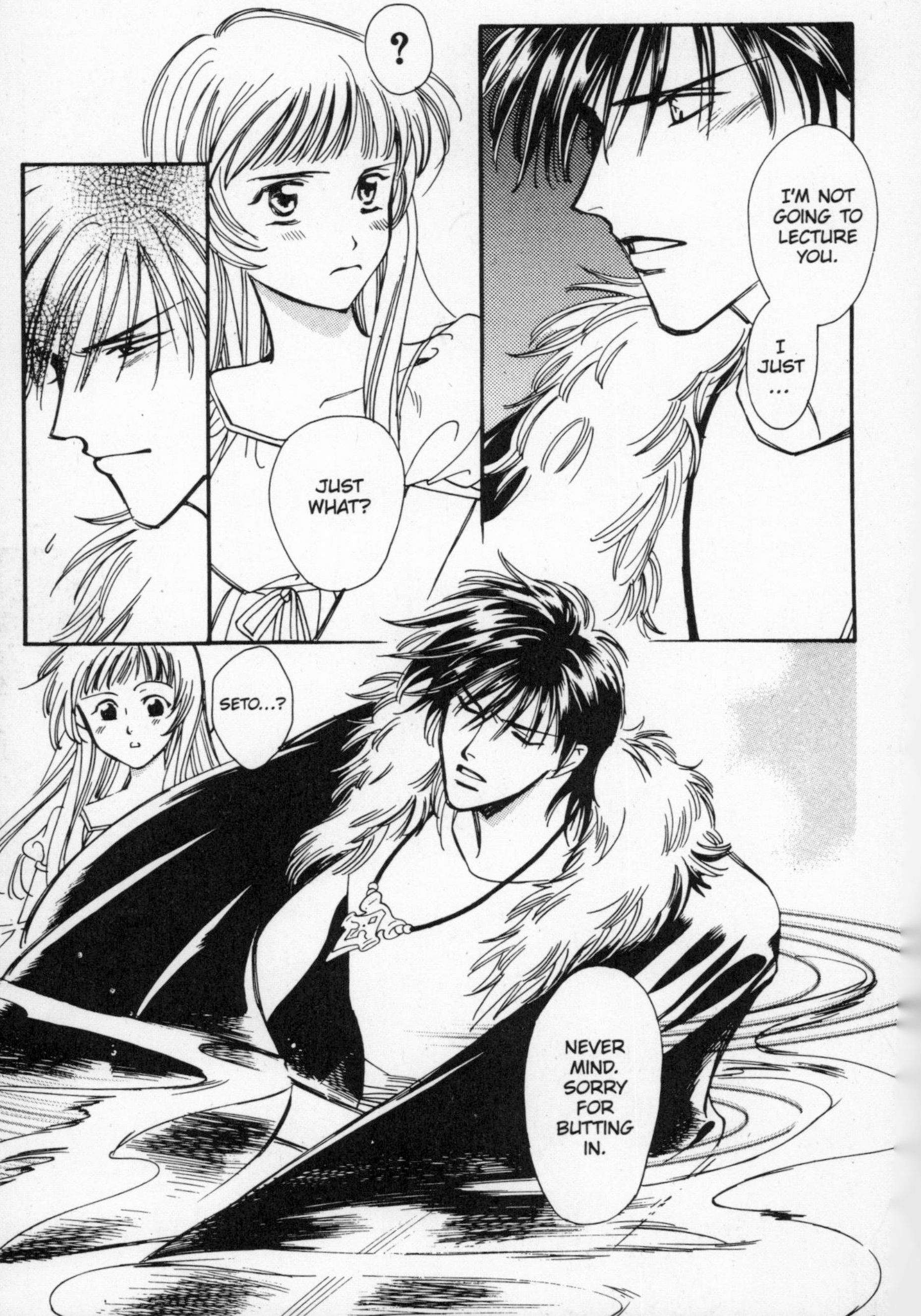
I'M NOT GOING TO LECTURE YOU.
I JUST ...
?
JUST WHAT?
SETO...?
NEVER MIND. SORRY FOR BUTTING IN.

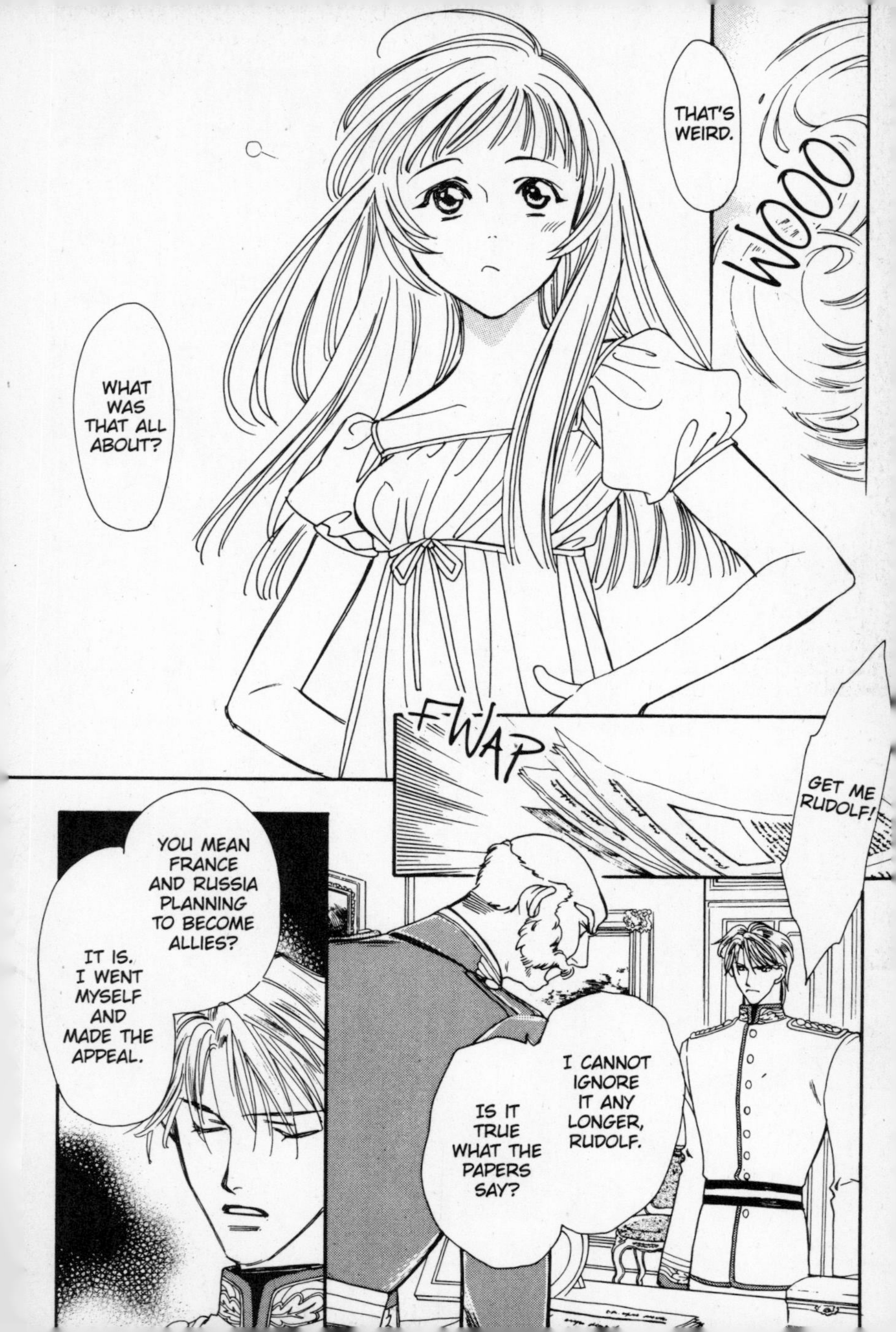
WOOO
THAT'S WEIRD.
WHAT WAS THAT ALL ABOUT?
FWAP
GET ME RUDOLF!
I CANNOT IGNORE IT ANY LONGER, RUDOLF.
IS IT TRUE WHAT THE PAPERS SAY?
YOU MEAN FRANCE AND RUSSIA PLANNING TO BECOME ALLIES?
IT IS. I WENT MYSELF AND MADE THE APPEAL.

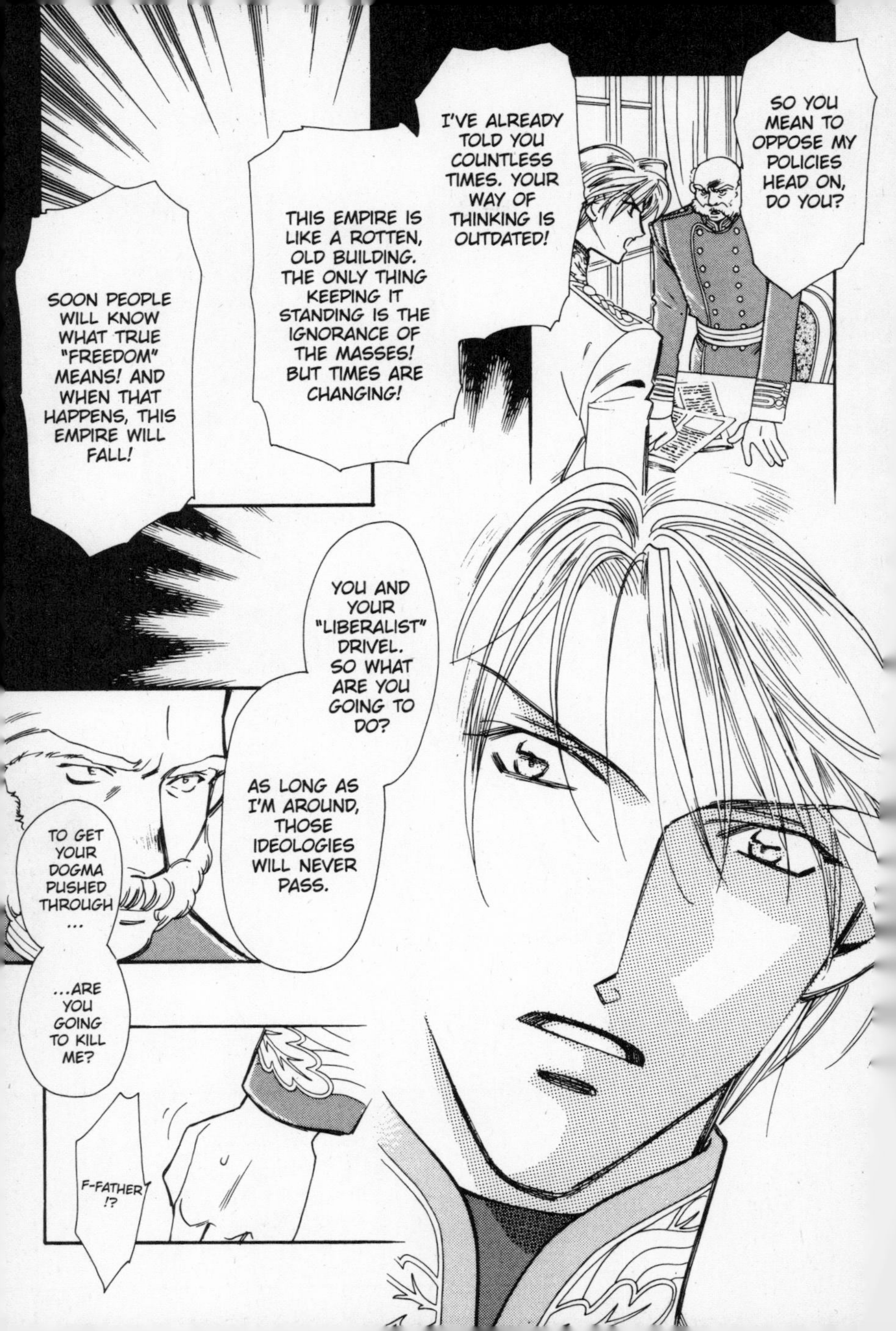
SO YOU MEAN TO OPPOSE MY POLICIES HEAD ON, DO YOU?
I'VE ALREADY TOLD YOU COUNTLESS TIMES. YOUR WAY OF THINKING IS OUTDATED!
THIS EMPIRE IS LIKE A ROTTEN, OLD BUILDING. THE ONLY THING KEEPING IT STANDING IS THE IGNORANCE OF THE MASSES! BUT TIMES ARE CHANGING!
SOON PEOPLE WILL KNOW WHAT TRUE "FREEDOM" MEANS! AND WHEN THAT HAPPENS, THIS EMPIRE WILL FALL!
YOU AND YOUR "LIBERALIST" DRIVEL. SO WHAT ARE YOU GOING TO DO?
AS LONG AS I'M AROUND, THOSE IDEOLOGIES WILL NEVER PASS.
TO GET YOUR DOGMA PUSHED THROUGH ...
...ARE YOU GOING TO KILL ME?
F-FATHER !?

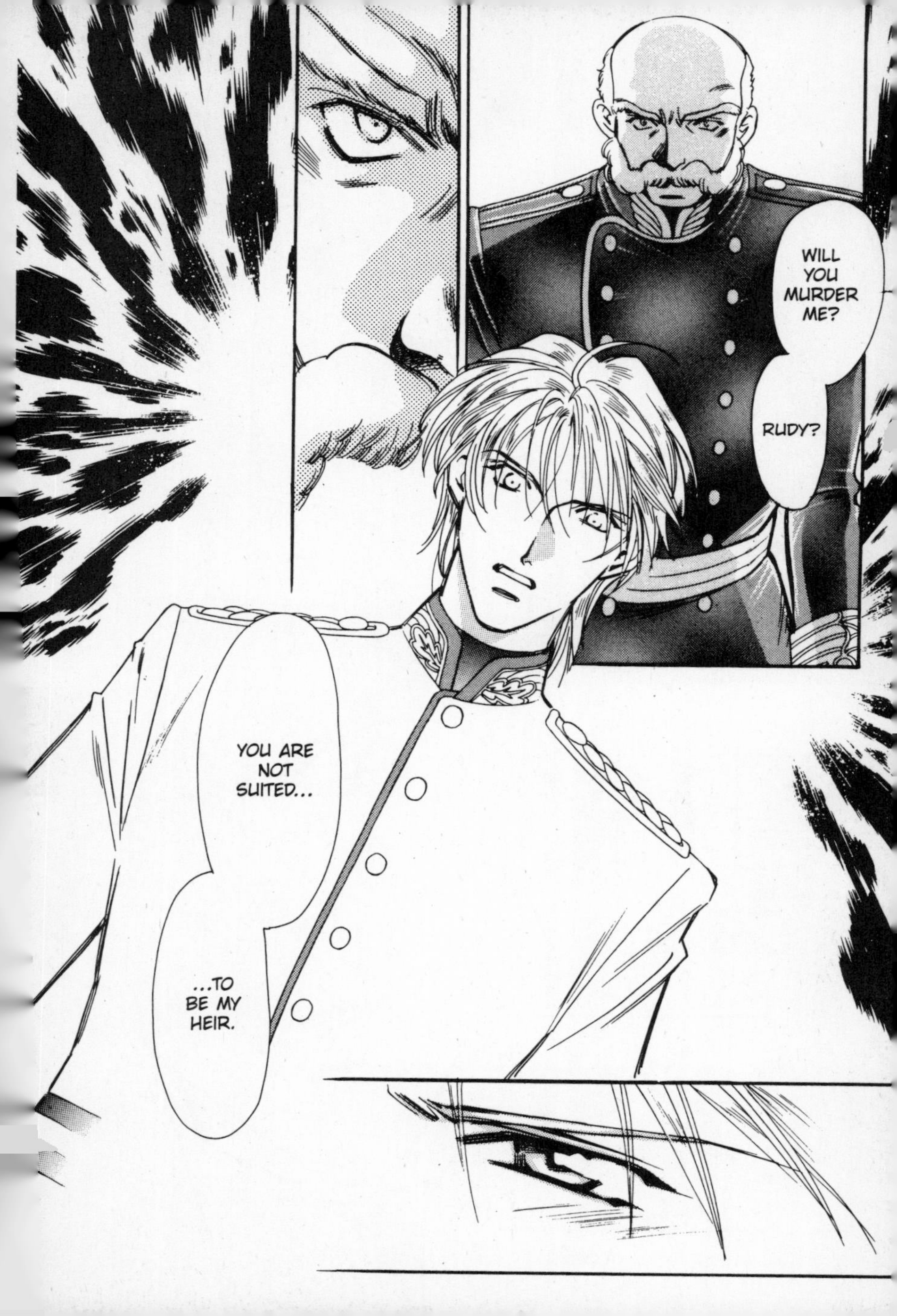
WILL YOU MURDER ME?
RUDY?
YOU ARE NOT SUITED...
...TO BE MY HEIR.

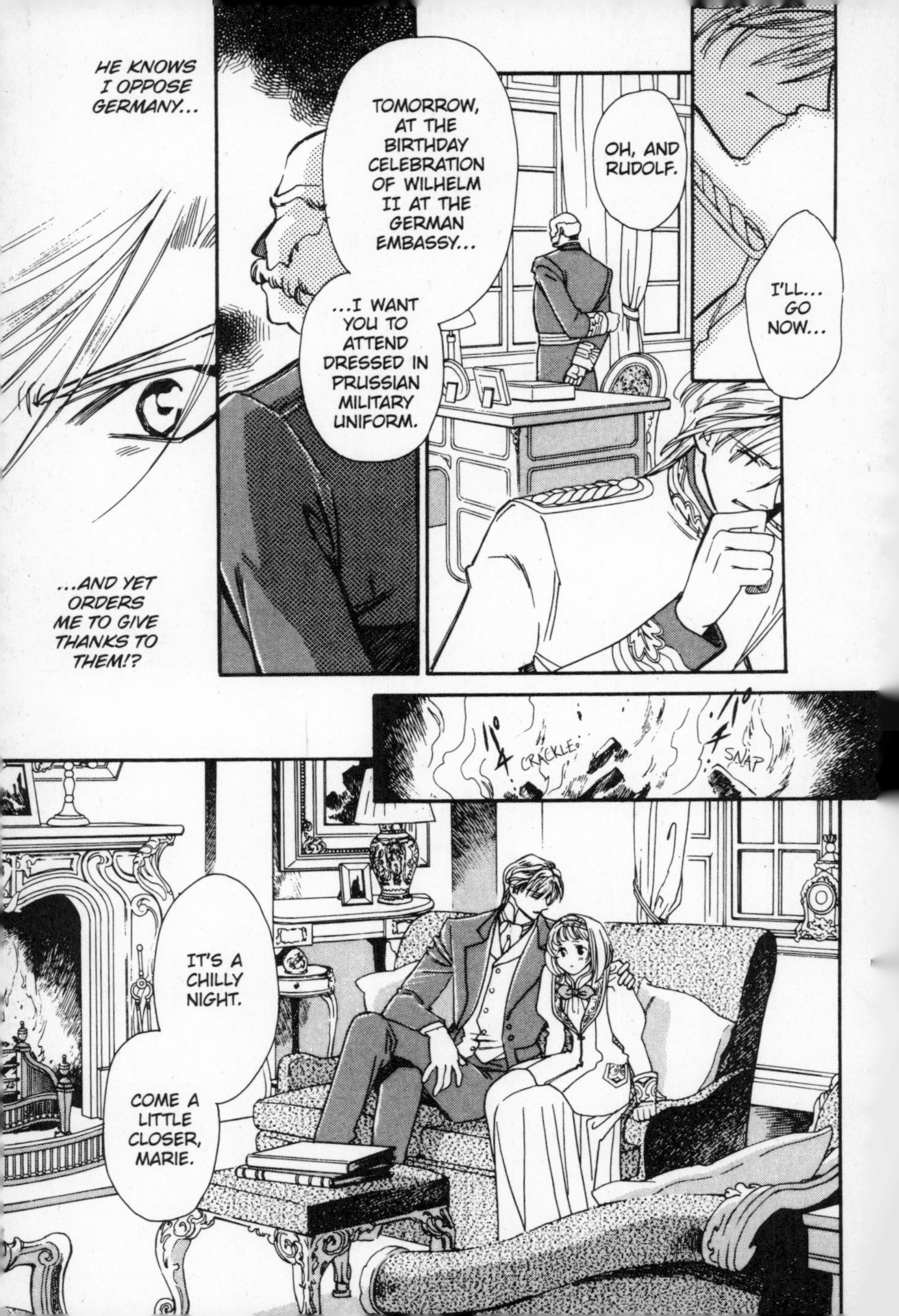
OH, AND RUDOLF.
TOMORROW, AT THE BIRTHDAY CELEBRATION OF WILHELM II AT THE GERMAN EMBASSY...
...I WANT YOU TO ATTEND DRESSED IN PRUSSIAN MILITARY UNIFORM.
I'LL... GO NOW...
HE KNOWS I OPPOSE GERMANY...
...AND YET ORDERS ME TO GIVE THANKS TO THEM!?
SNAP
CRACKLE
IT'S A CHILLY NIGHT.
COME A LITTLE CLOSER, MARIE.

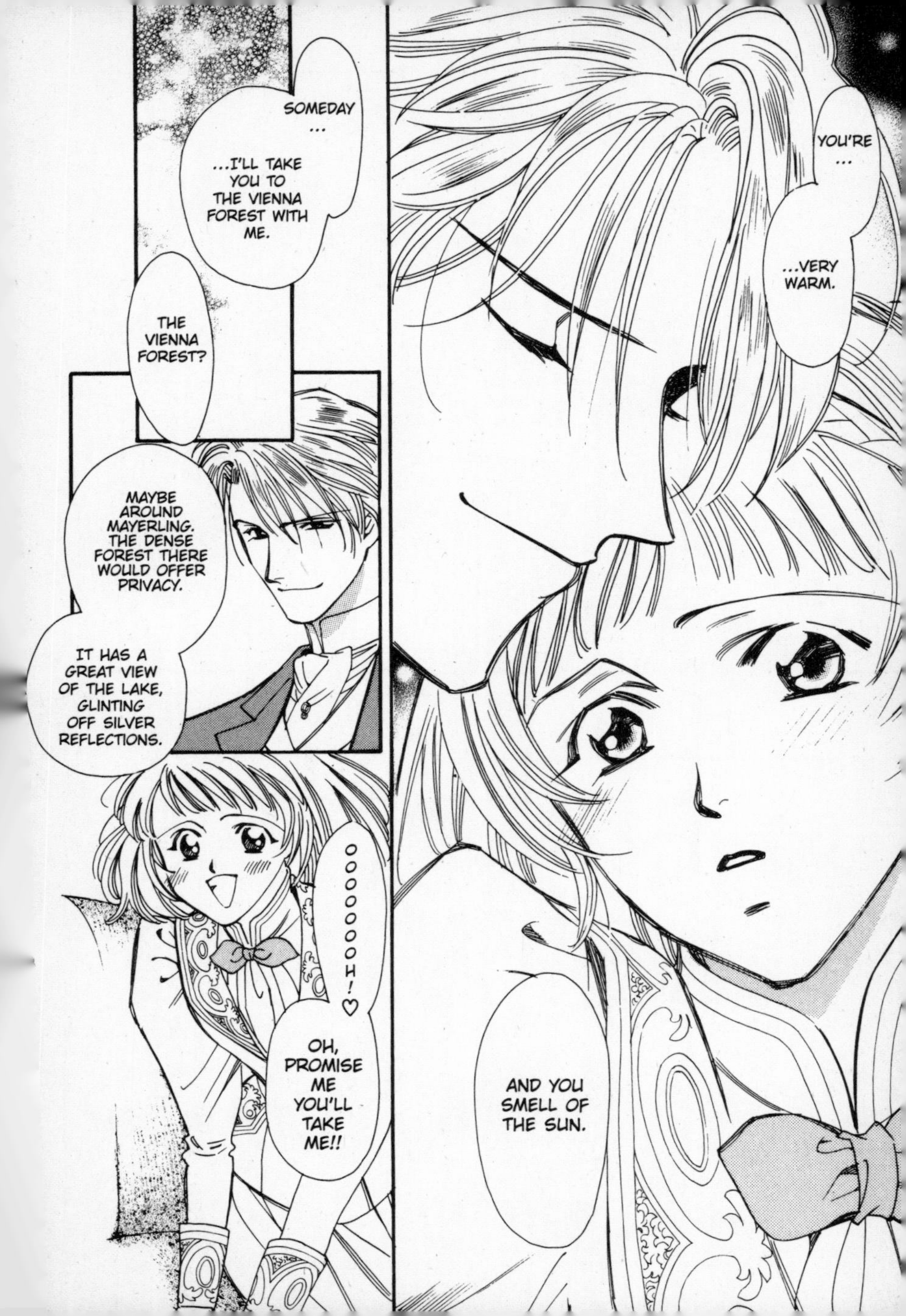
SOMEDAY ...
...I'LL TAKE YOU TO THE VIENNA FOREST WITH ME.
THE VIENNA FOREST?
MAYBE AROUND MAYERLING. THE DENSE FOREST THERE WOULD OFFER PRIVACY.
IT HAS A GREAT VIEW OF THE LAKE, GLINTING OFF SILVER REFLECTIONS.
OOOOOOOOH!♡
OH, PROMISE ME YOU'LL TAKE ME!!
YOU'RE ...
...VERY WARM.
AND YOU SMELL OF THE SUN.

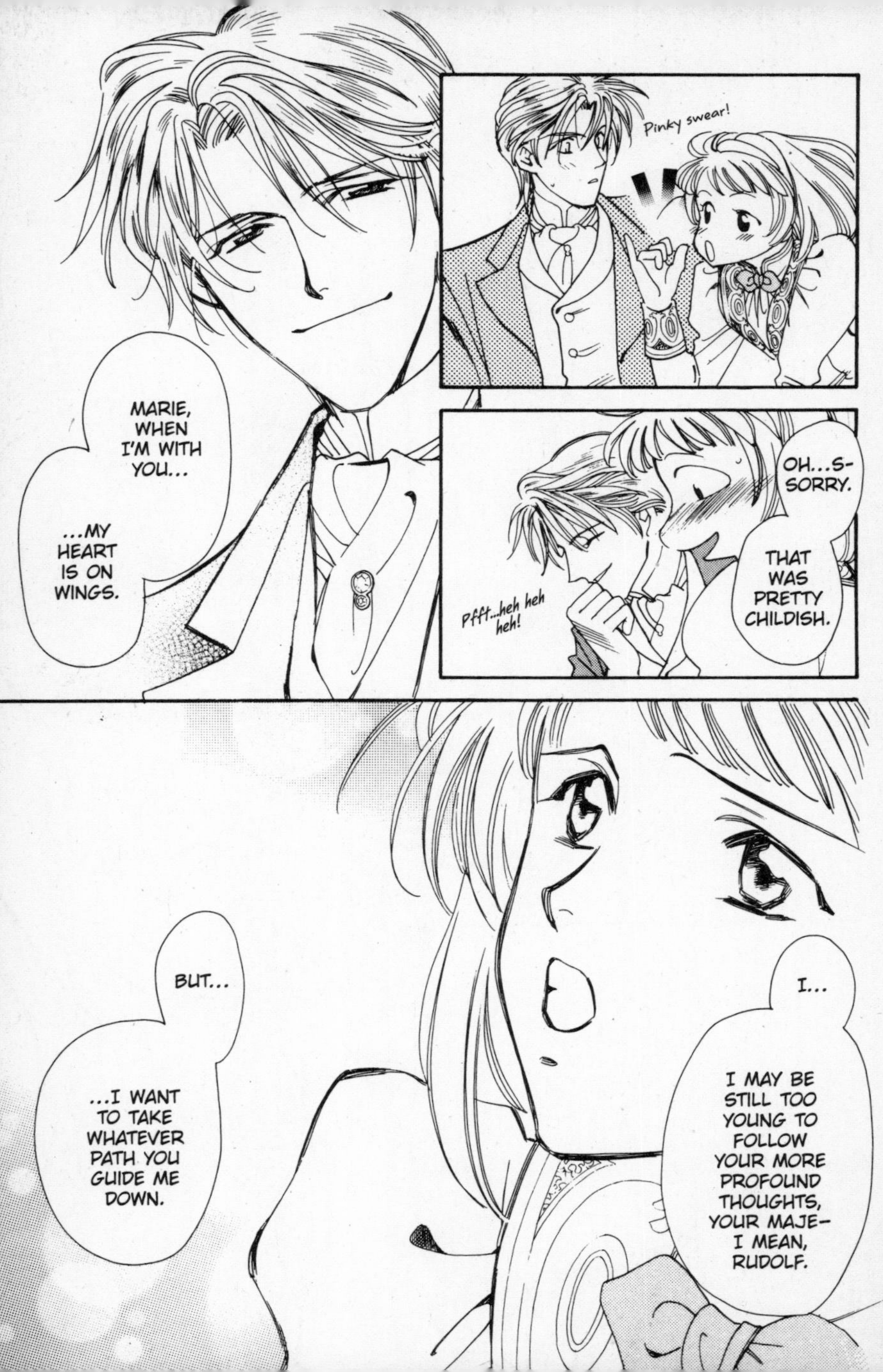
Pinky swear!
OH...S-SORRY.
THAT WAS PRETTY CHILDISH.
Pfft...heh heh heh!
MARIE, WHEN I'M WITH YOU...
...MY HEART IS ON WINGS.
I...
I MAY BE STILL TOO YOUNG TO FOLLOW YOUR MORE PROFOUND THOUGHTS, YOUR MAJE– I MEAN, RUDOLF.
BUT...
...I WANT TO TAKE WHATEVER PATH YOU GUIDE ME DOWN.

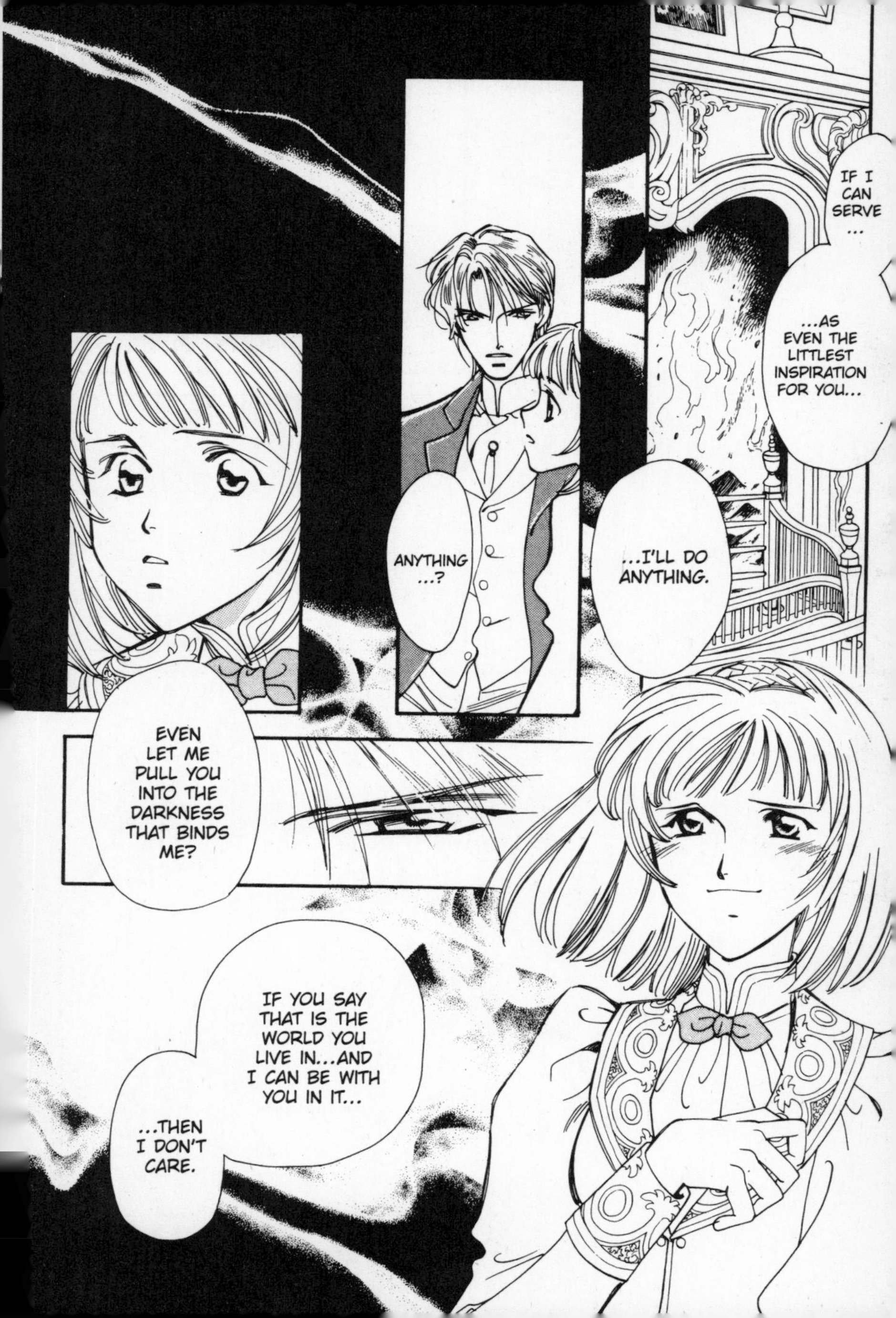
IF I CAN SERVE ...
...AS EVEN THE LITTLEST INSPIRATION FOR YOU...
...I'LL DO ANYTHING.
ANYTHING ...?
EVEN LET ME PULL YOU INTO THE DARKNESS THAT BINDS ME?
IF YOU SAY THAT IS THE WORLD YOU LIVE IN...AND I CAN BE WITH YOU IN IT...
...THEN I DON'T CARE.

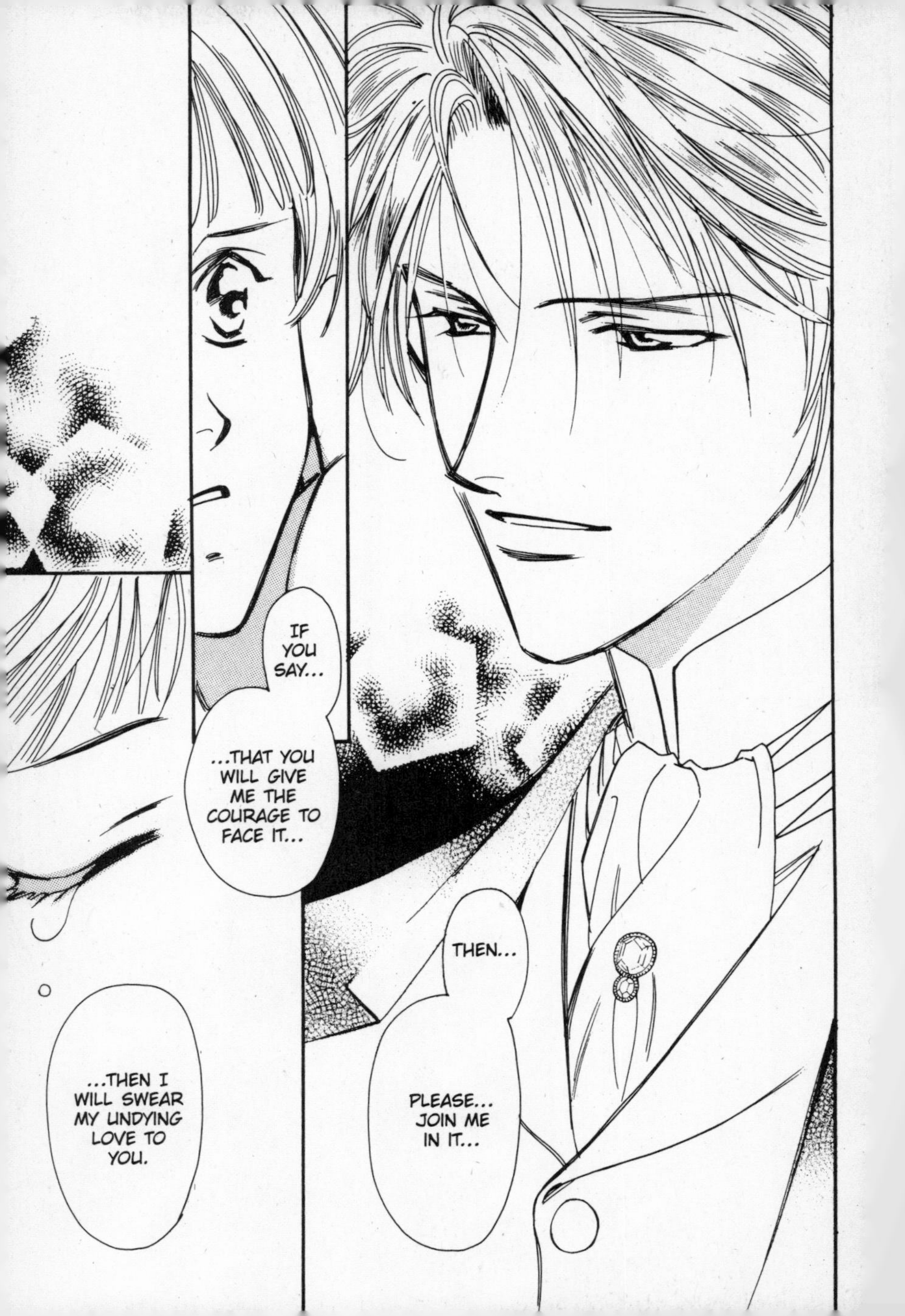
IF YOU SAY...
...THAT YOU WILL GIVE ME THE COURAGE TO FACE IT...
THEN...
PLEASE... JOIN ME IN IT...
...THEN I WILL SWEAR MY UNDYING LOVE TO YOU.

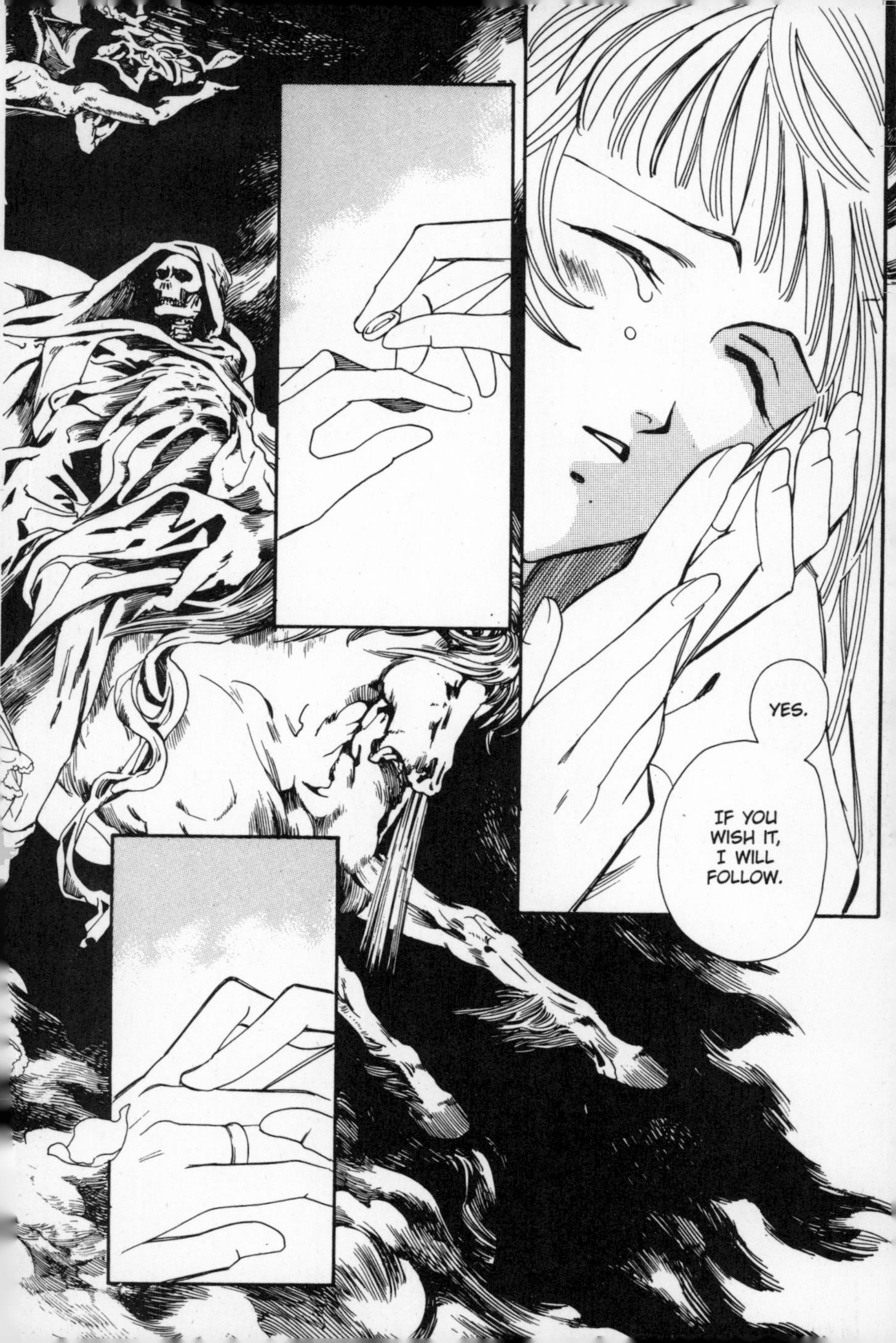
YES.
IF YOU WISH IT, I WILL FOLLOW.

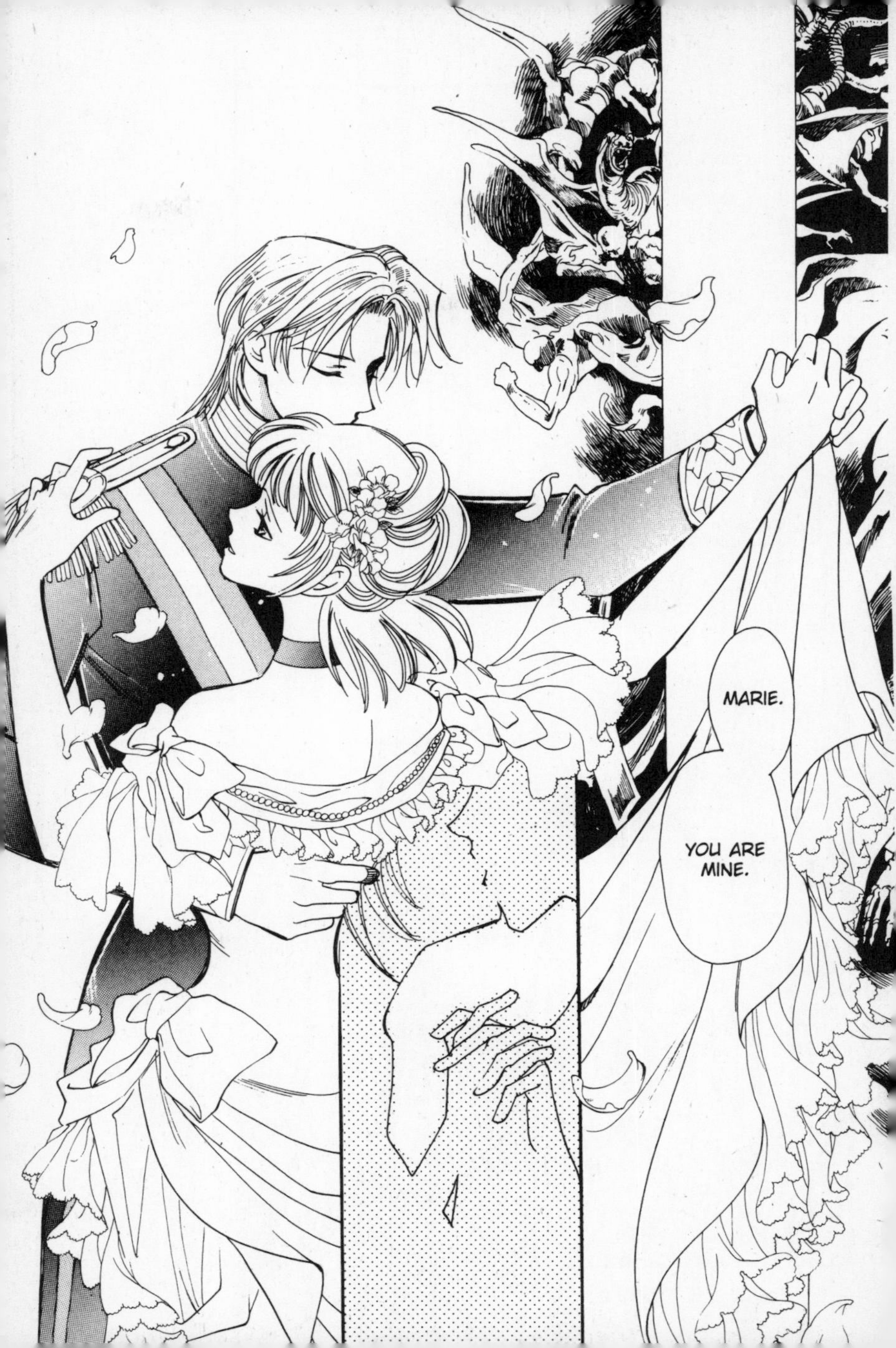
MARIE.
YOU ARE MINE.

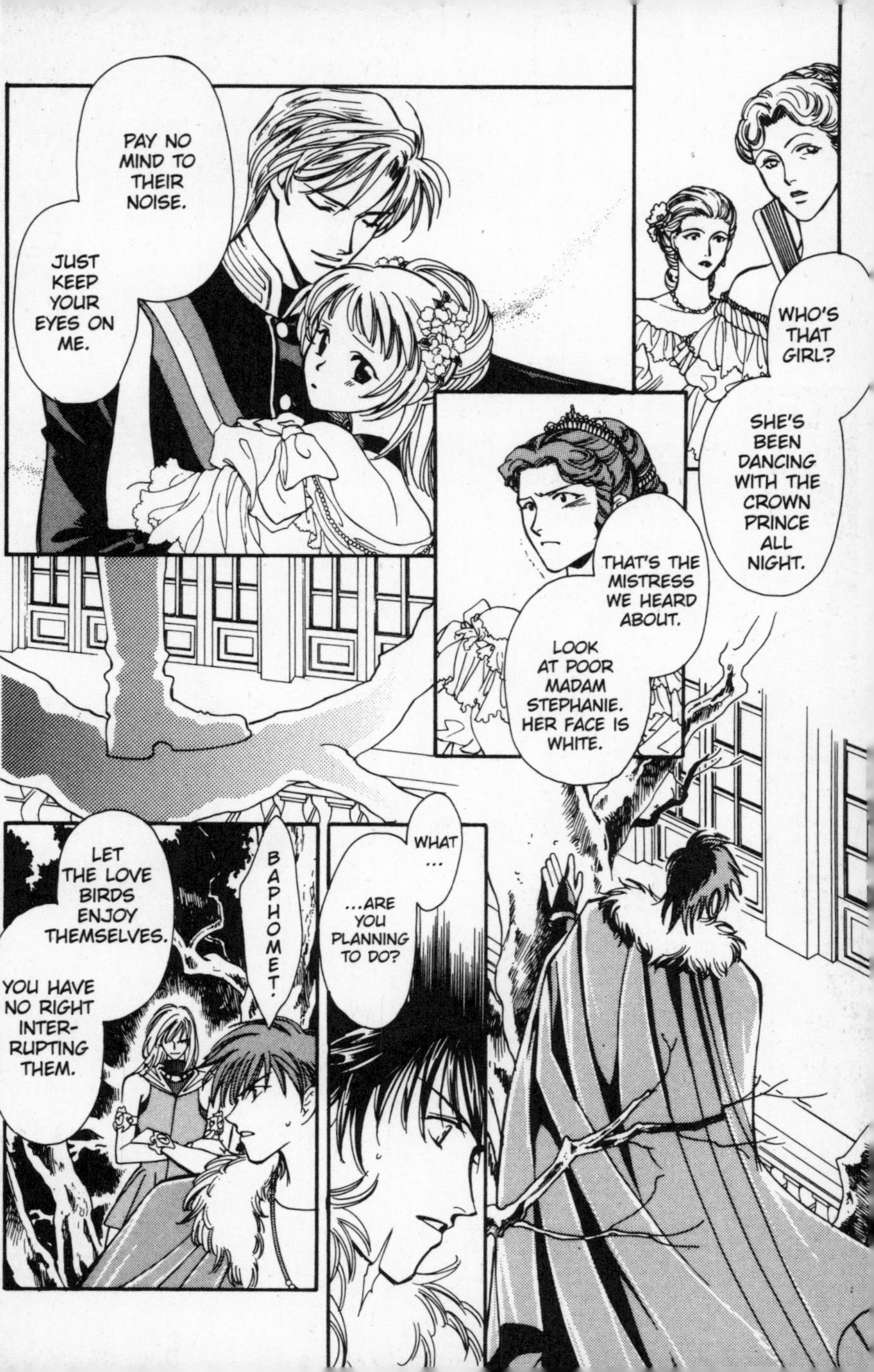
WHO'S THAT GIRL?
SHE'S BEEN DANCING WITH THE CROWN PRINCE ALL NIGHT.
THAT'S THE MISTRESS WE HEARD ABOUT.
LOOK AT POOR MADAM STEPHANIE. HER FACE IS WHITE.
PAY NO MIND TO THEIR NOISE.
JUST KEEP YOUR EYES ON ME.
WHAT...
...ARE YOU PLANNING TO DO?
BAPHOMET.
LET THE LOVE BIRDS ENJOY THEMSELVES.
YOU HAVE NO RIGHT INTERRUPTING THEM.

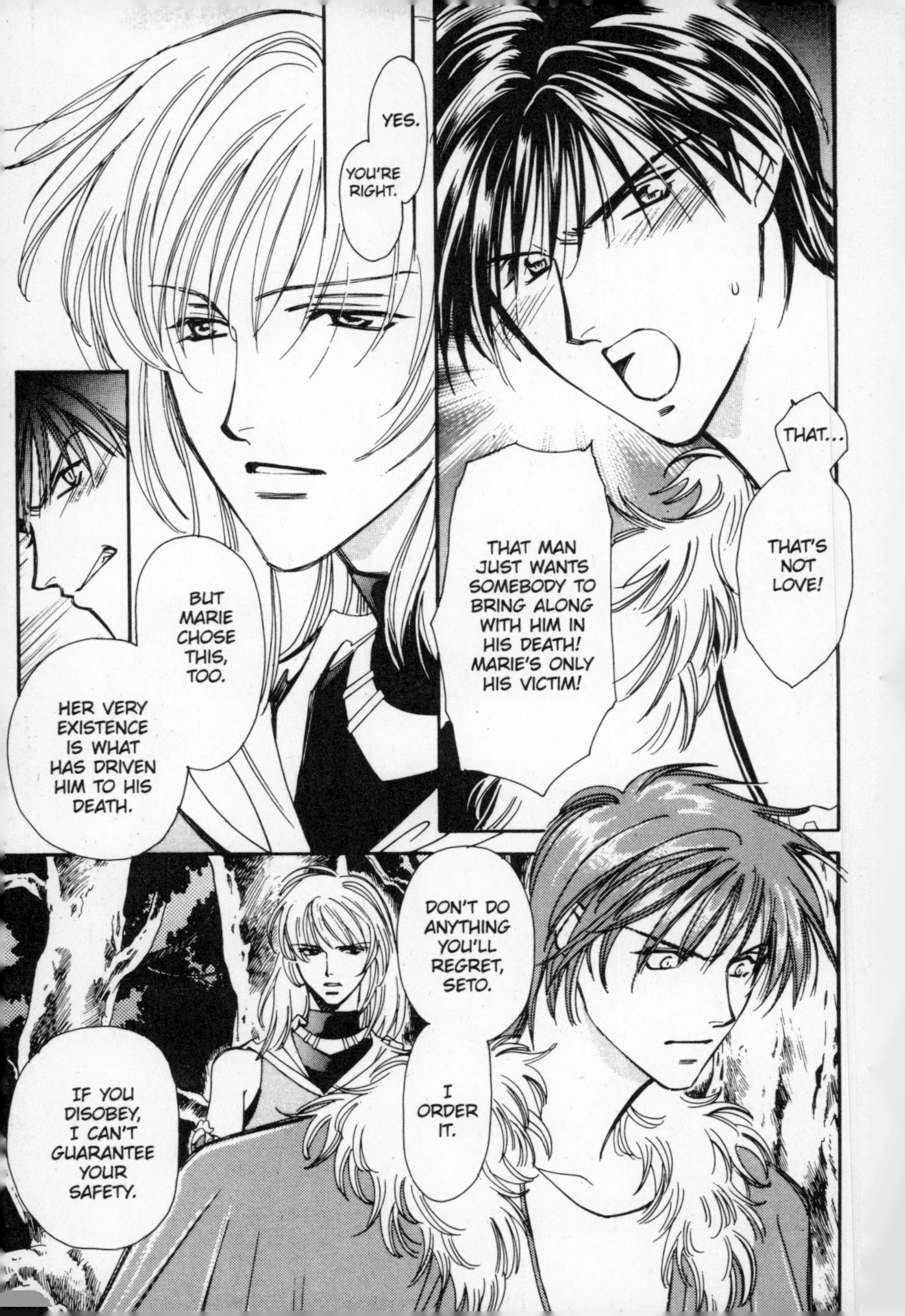
THAT...
THAT'S NOT LOVE!
THAT MAN JUST WANTS SOMEBODY TO BRING ALONG WITH HIM IN HIS DEATH! MARIE'S ONLY HIS VICTIM!
YES.
YOU'RE RIGHT.
BUT MARIE CHOSE THIS, TOO.
HER VERY EXISTENCE IS WHAT HAS DRIVEN HIM TO HIS DEATH.
DON'T DO ANYTHING YOU'LL REGRET, SETO.
I ORDER IT.
IF YOU DISOBEY, I CAN'T GUARANTEE YOUR SAFETY.

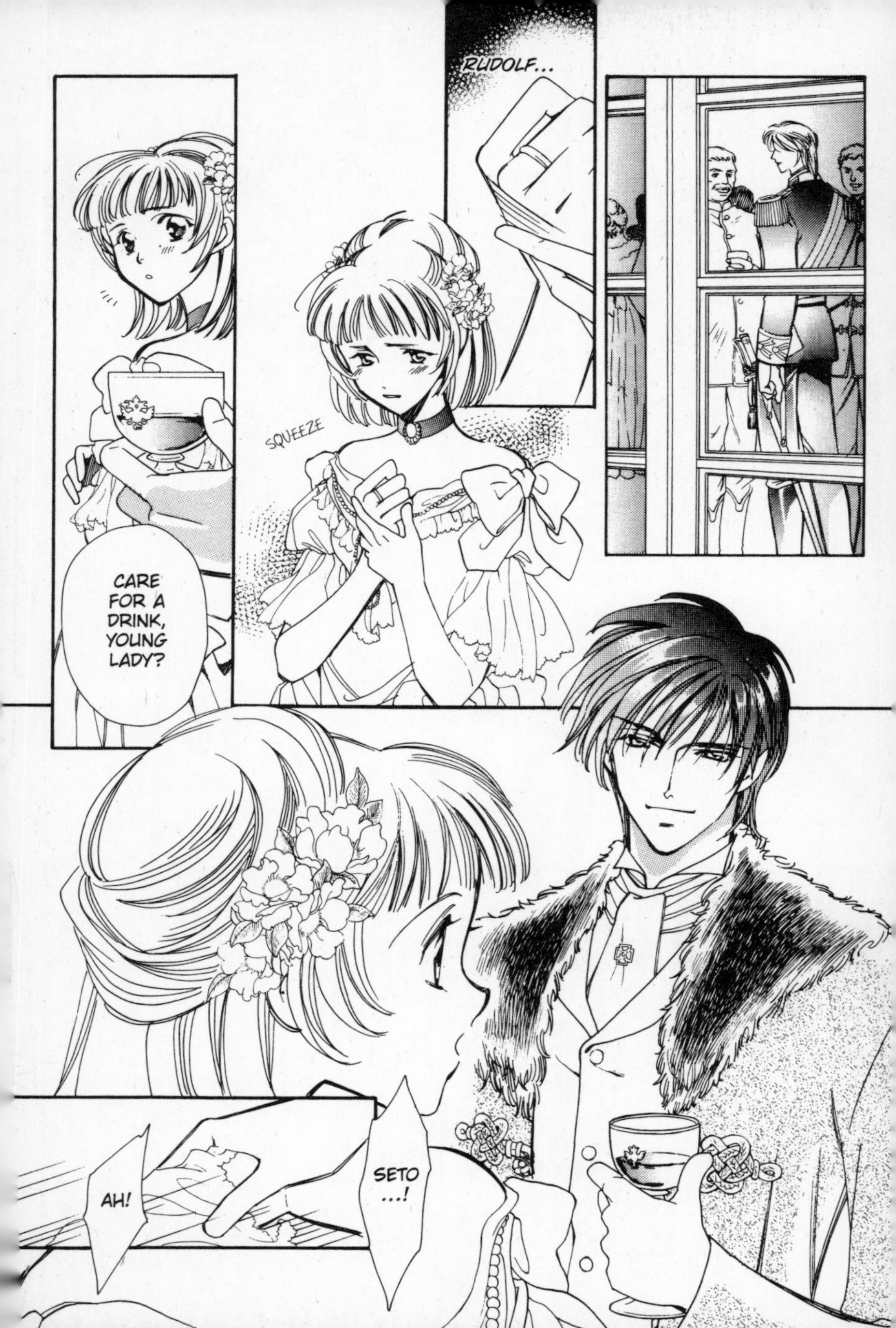
RUDOLF...
SQUEEZE
CARE FOR A DRINK, YOUNG LADY?
SETO ...!
AH!

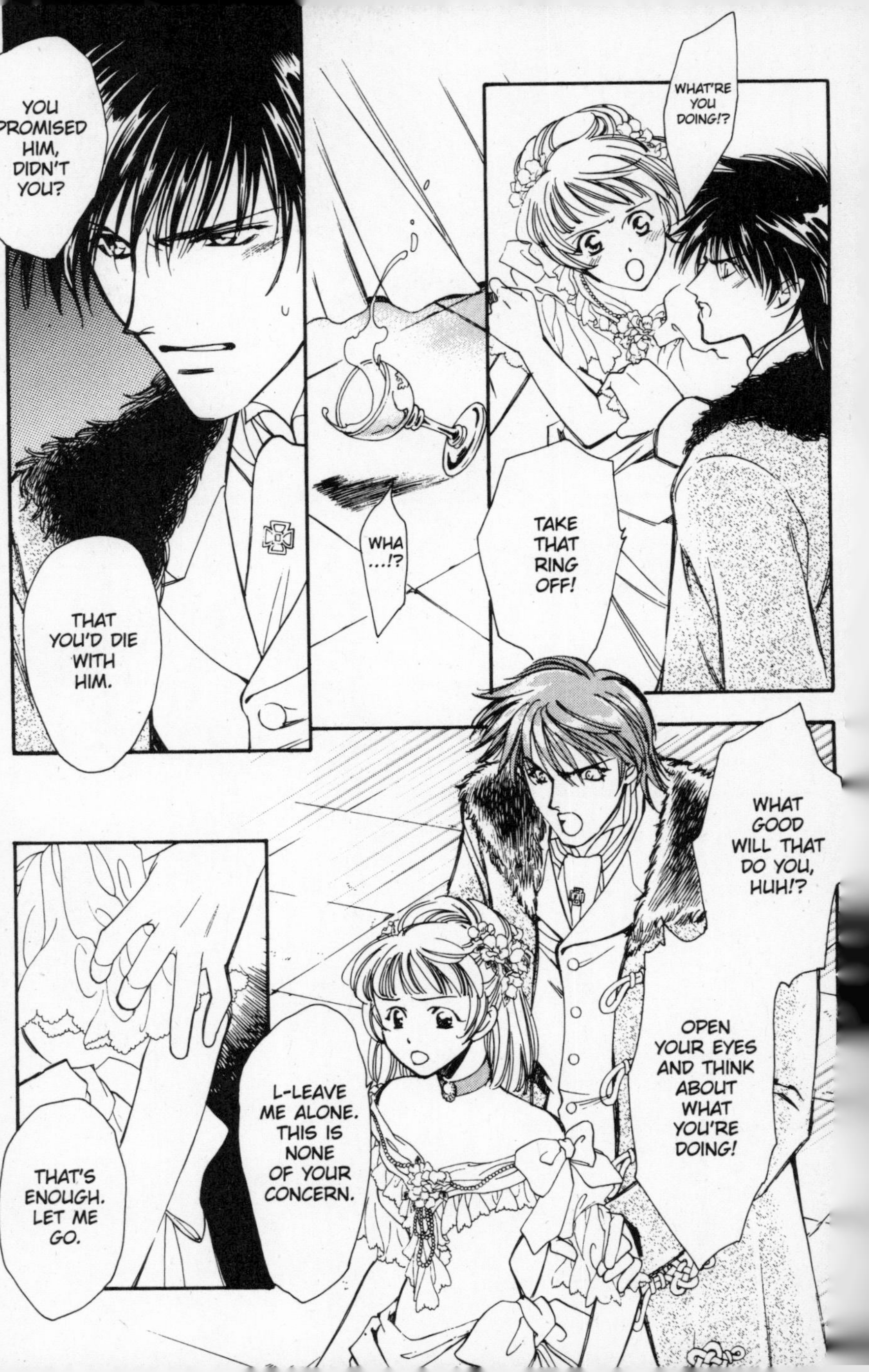

WHAT'RE YOU DOING!?
TAKE THAT RING OFF!
WHA ...!?
YOU PROMISED HIM, DIDN'T YOU?
THAT YOU'D DIE WITH HIM.
WHAT GOOD WILL THAT DO YOU, HUH!?
OPEN YOUR EYES AND THINK ABOUT WHAT YOU'RE DOING!
L-LEAVE ME ALONE. THIS IS NONE OF YOUR CONCERN.
THAT'S ENOUGH. LET ME GO.

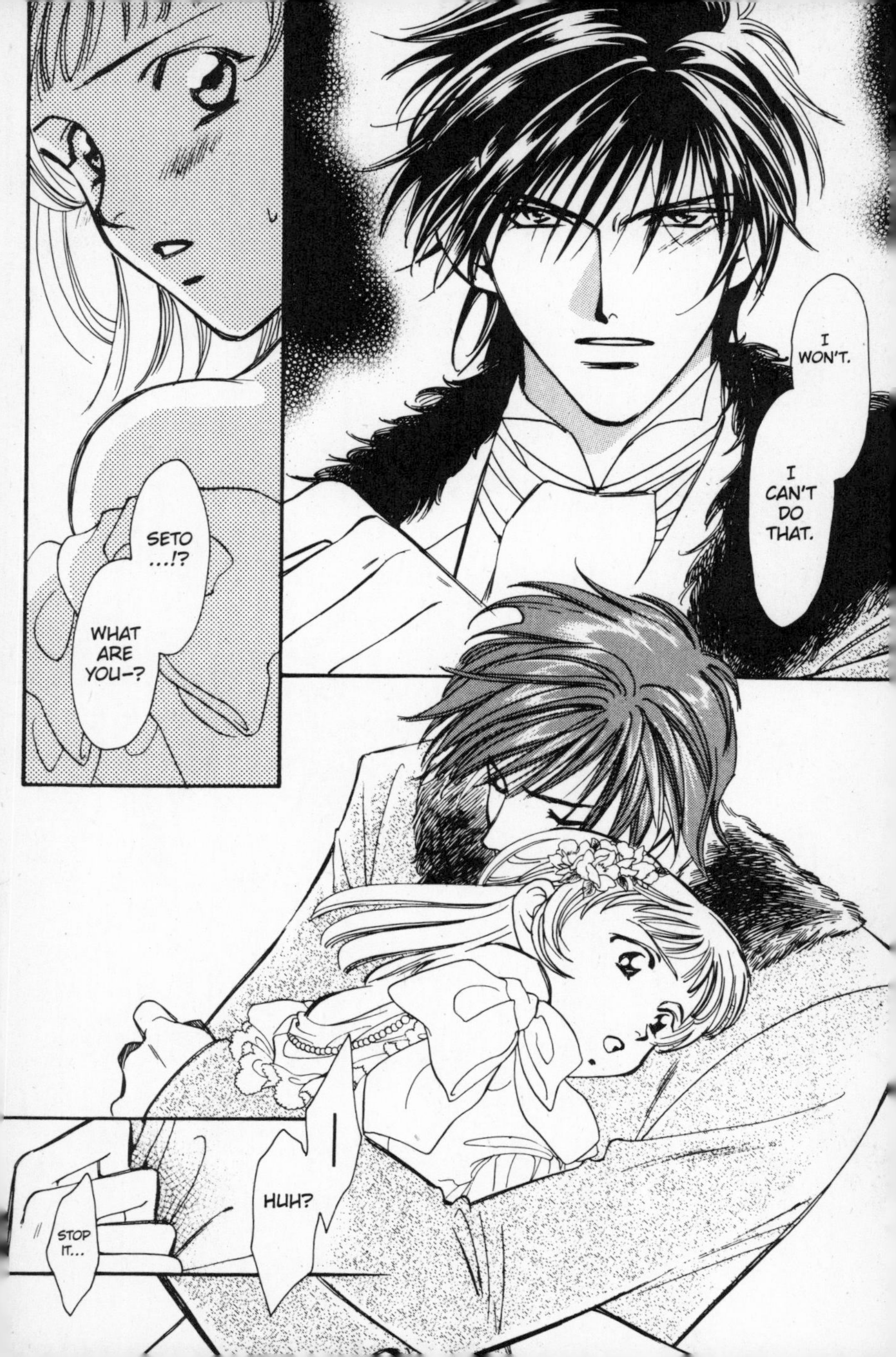
I WON'T.
I CAN'T DO THAT.
SETO ...!?
WHAT ARE YOU-?
HUH?
STOP IT...

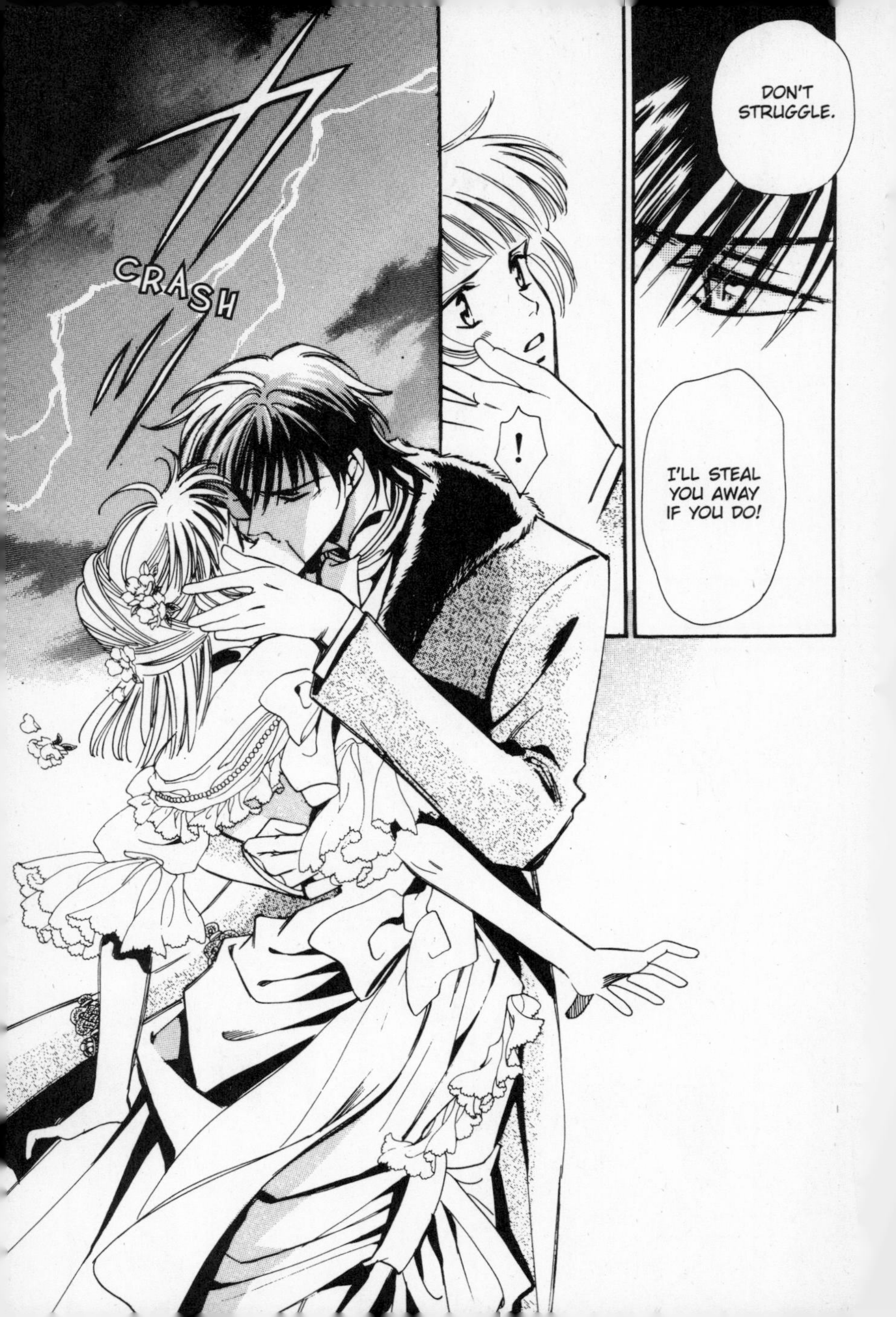
DON'T STRUGGLE.
I'LL STEAL YOU AWAY IF YOU DO!
!
CRASH

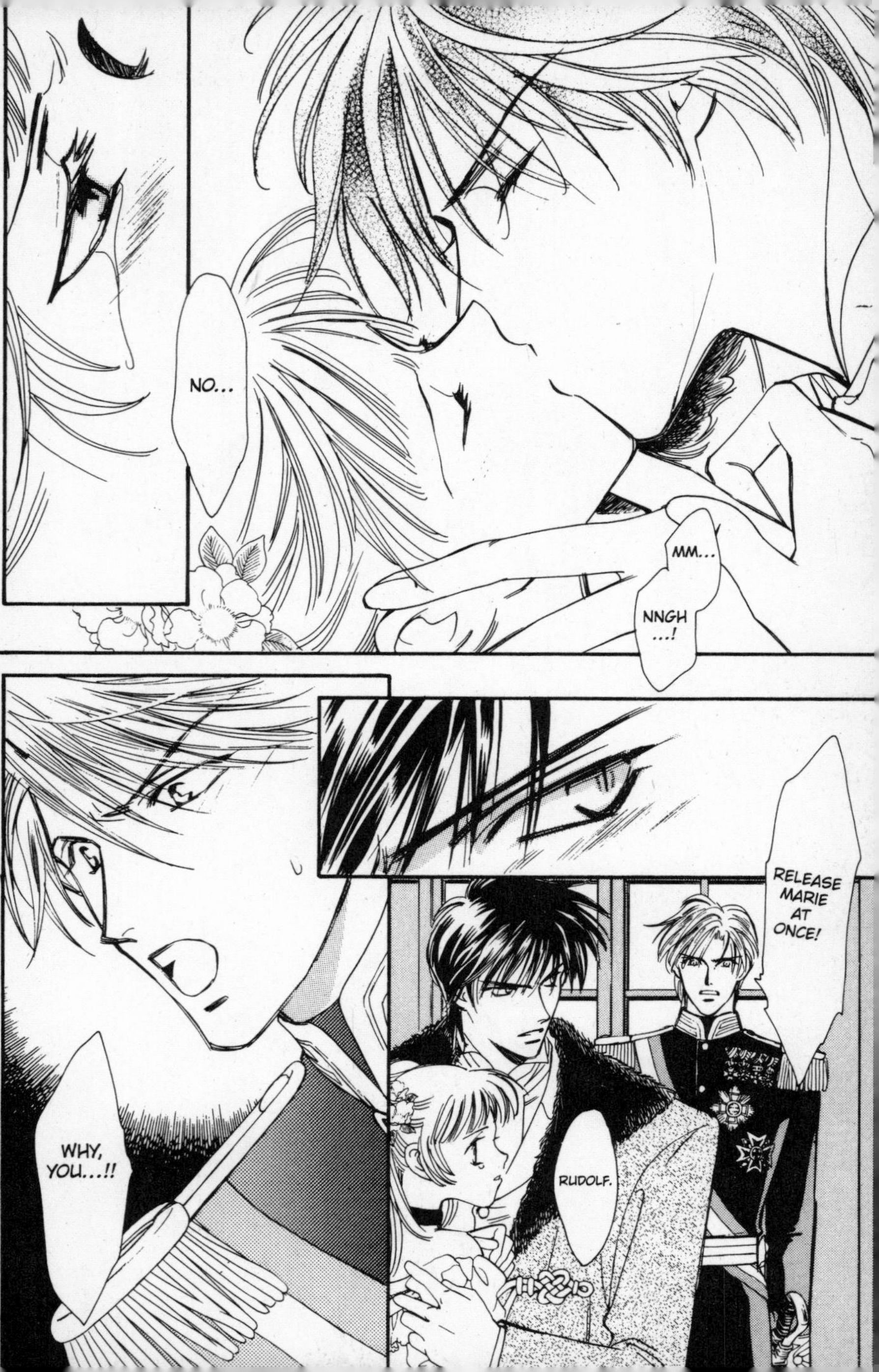
MM...
NNGH...!
NO...
RELEASE MARIE AT ONCE!
RUDOLF.
WHY, YOU...!!

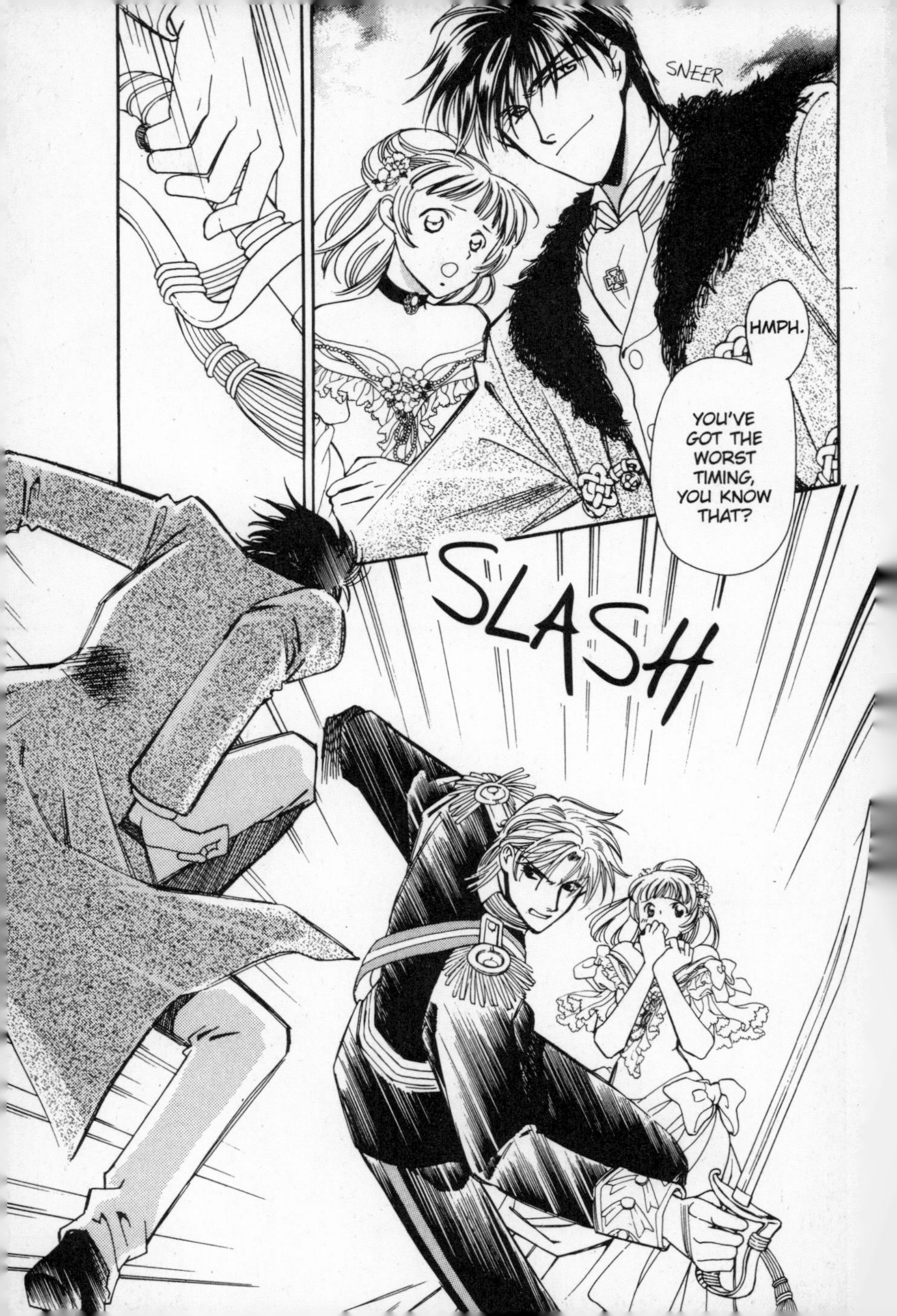
SNEER
HMPH.
YOU'VE GOT THE WORST TIMING, YOU KNOW THAT?
SLASH

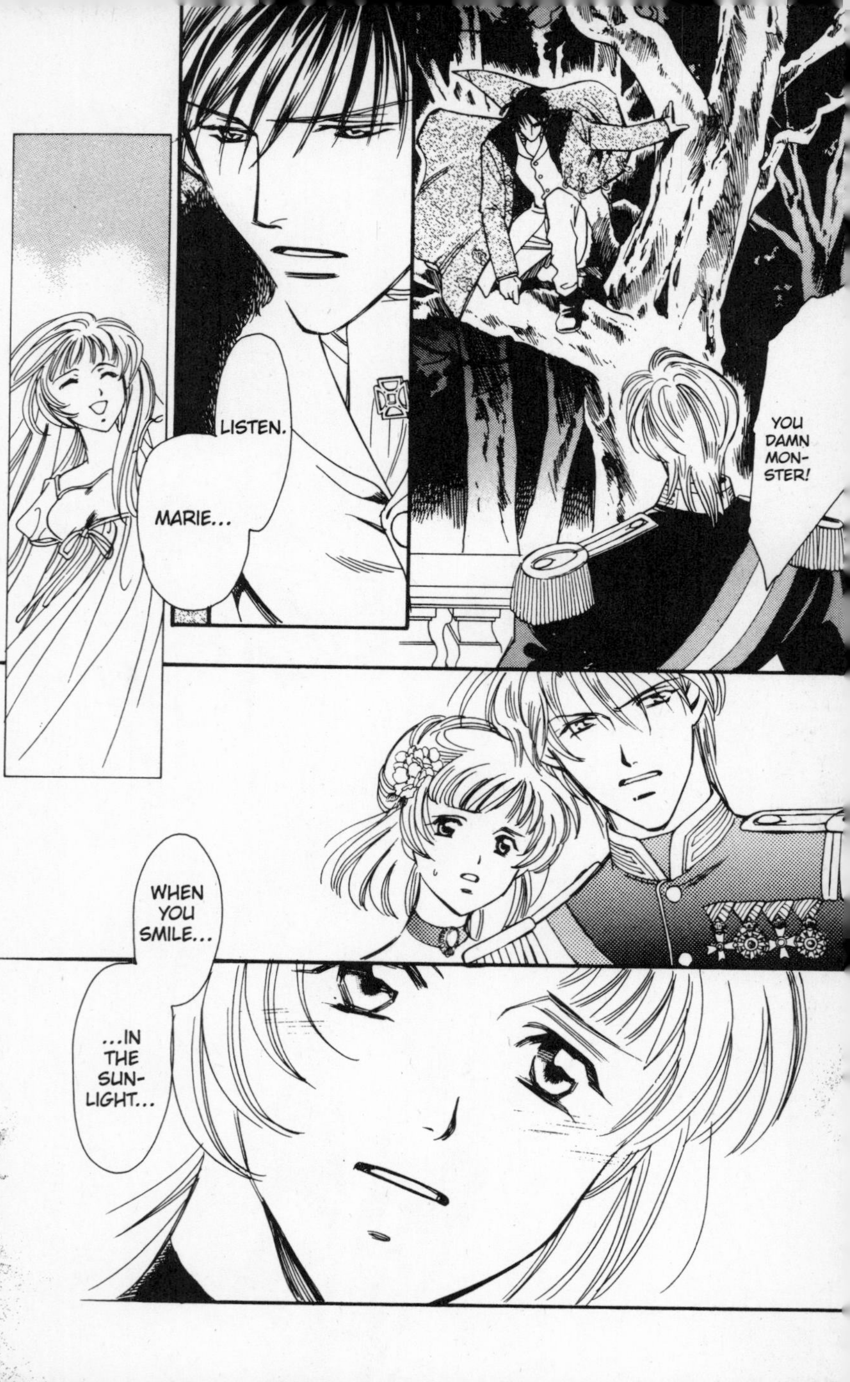
YOU DAMN MONSTER!
LISTEN.
MARIE...
WHEN YOU SMILE...
...IN THE SUNLIGHT...

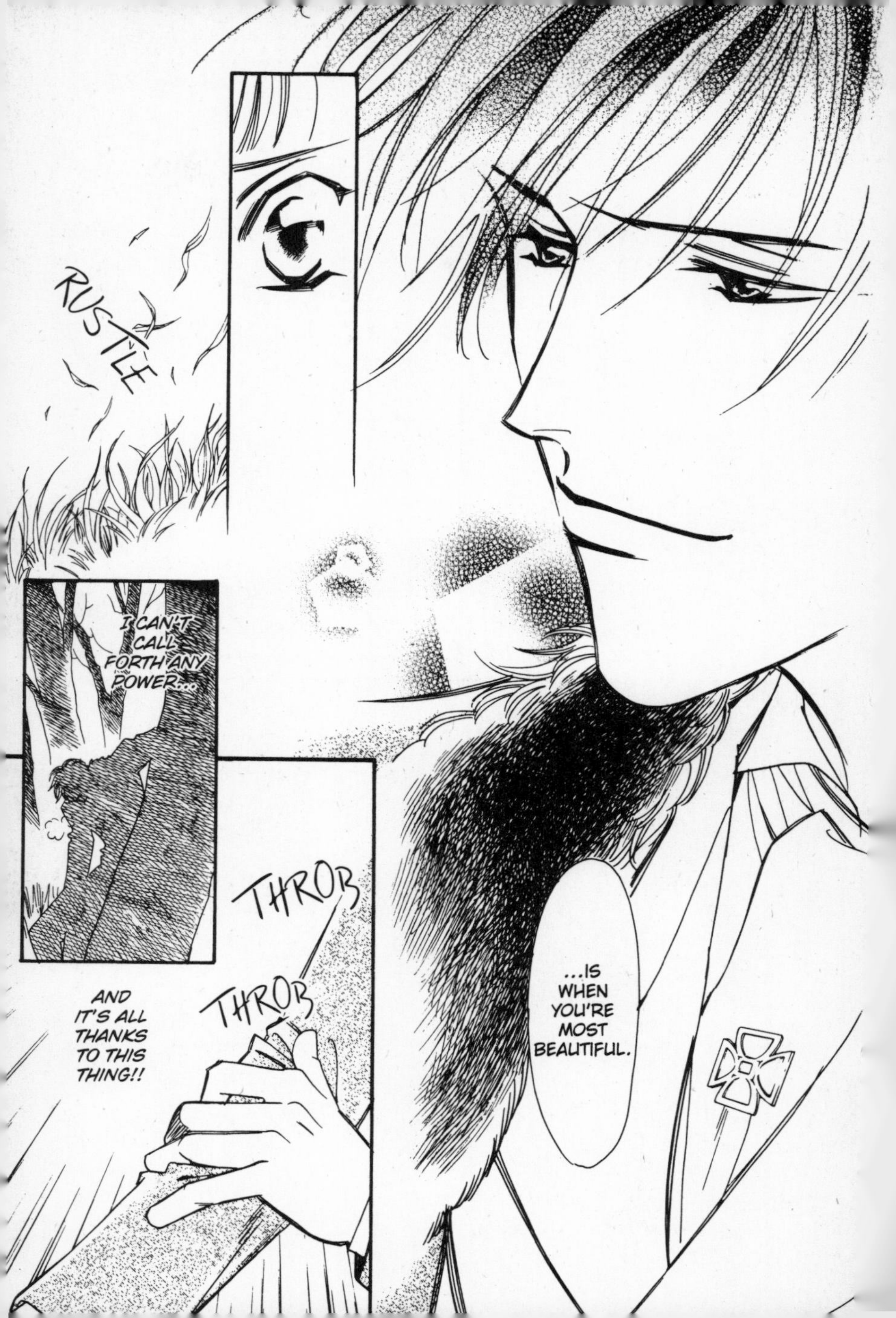
RUSTLE
I CAN'T CALL FORTH ANY POWER...
...IS WHEN YOU'RE MOST BEAUTIFUL.
THROB
THROB
AND IT'S ALL THANKS TO THIS THING!!

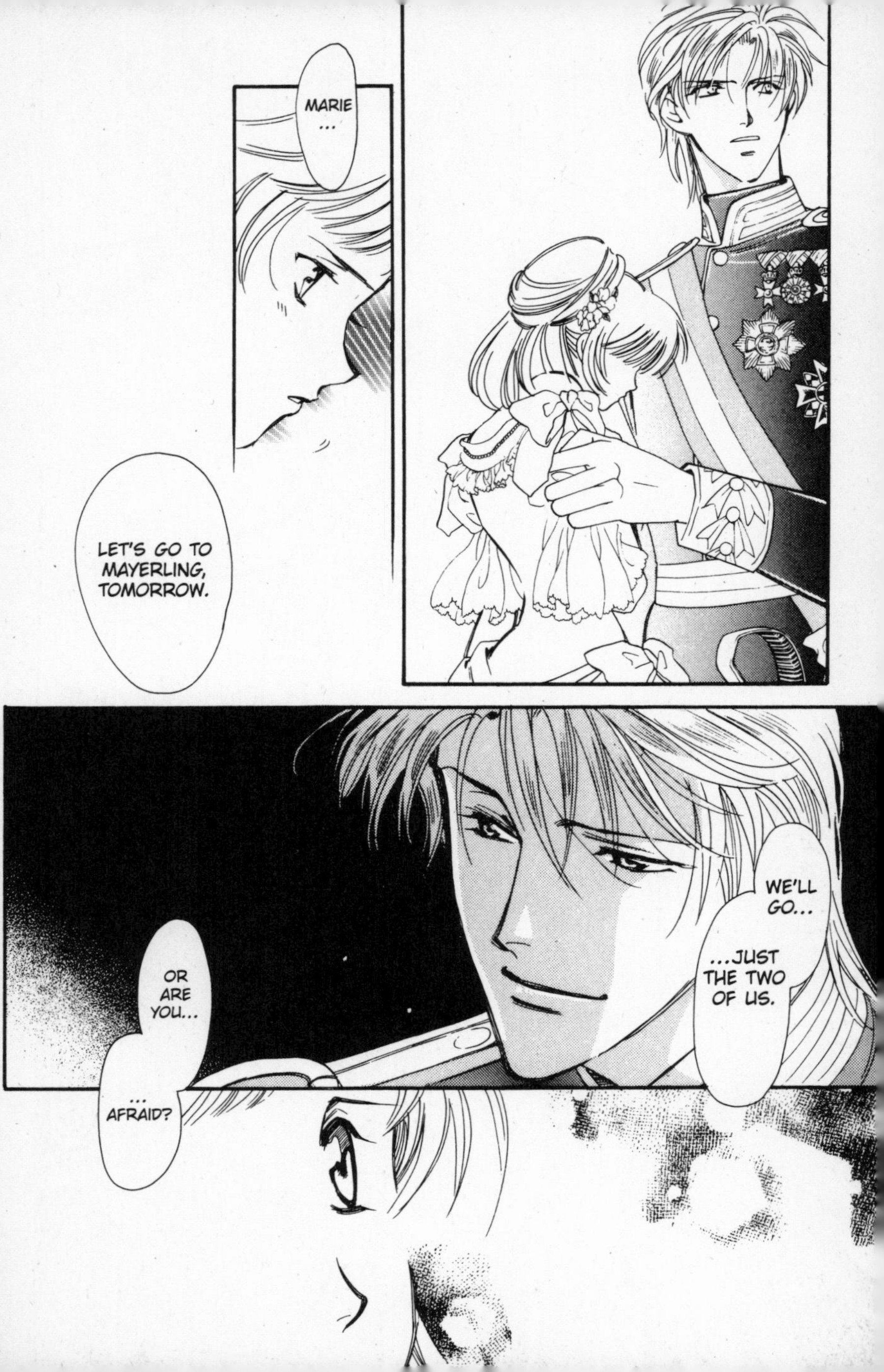
MARIE ...
LET'S GO TO MAYERLING, TOMORROW.
WE'LL GO...
...JUST THE TWO OF US.
OR ARE YOU...
... AFRAID?

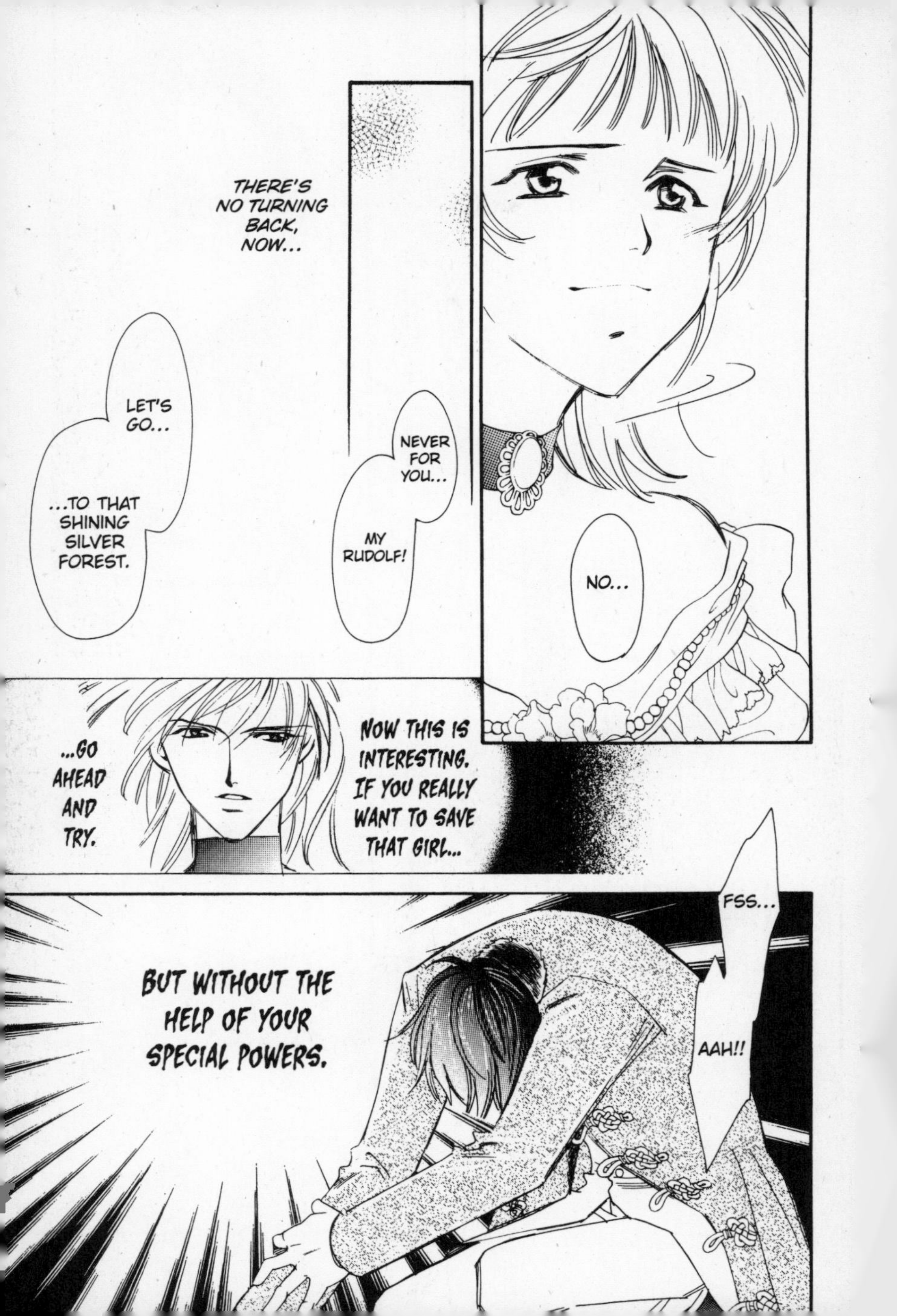
NO...
THERE'S NO TURNING BACK, NOW...
NEVER FOR YOU...
MY RUDOLF!
LET'S GO...
...TO THAT SHINING SILVER FOREST.
NOW THIS IS INTERESTING. IF YOU REALLY WANT TO SAVE THAT GIRL...
...GO AHEAD AND TRY.
FSS...
AAH!!
BUT WITHOUT THE HELP OF YOUR SPECIAL POWERS.

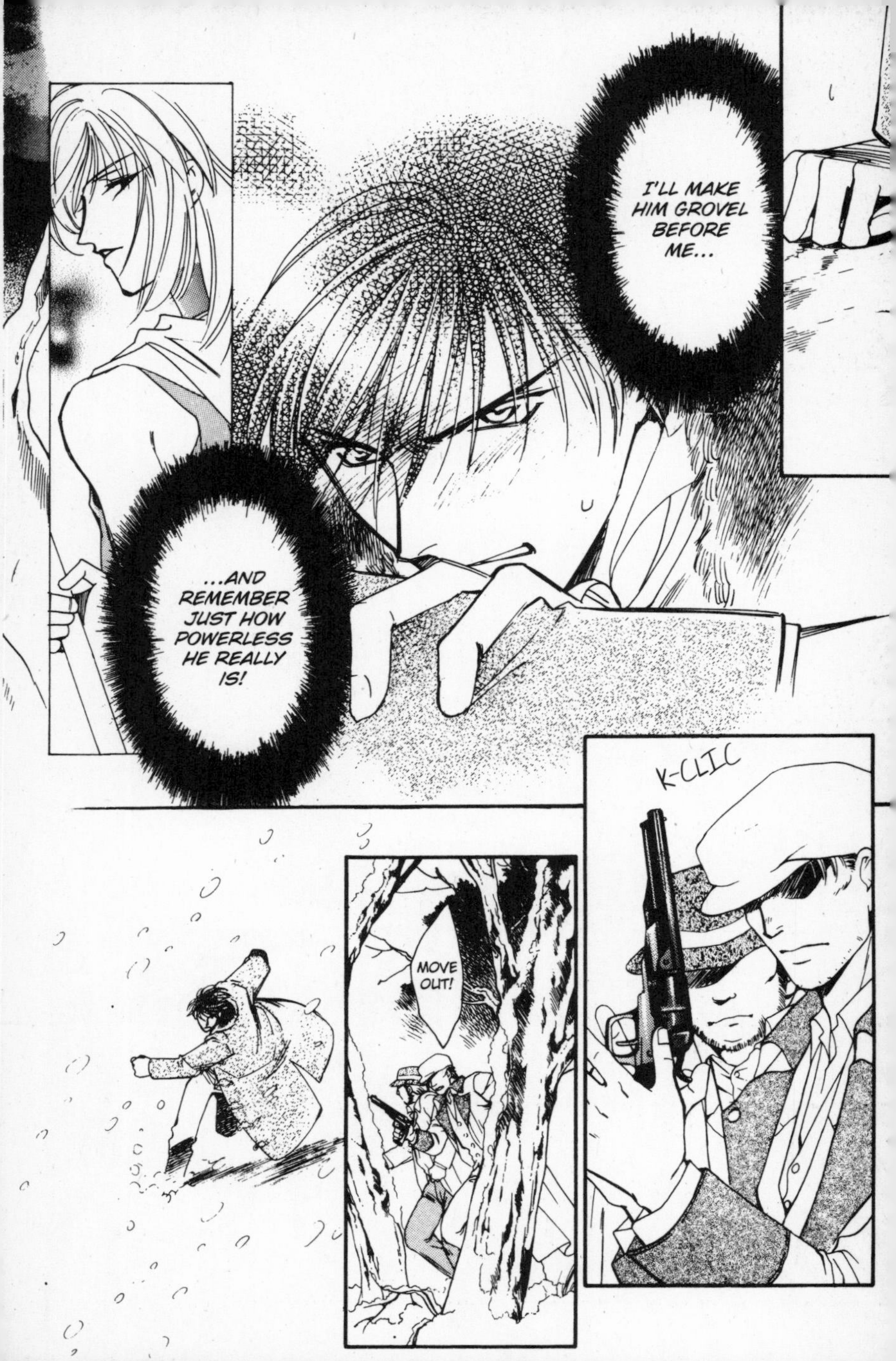
I'LL MAKE HIM GROVEL BEFORE ME...
...AND REMEMBER JUST HOW POWERLESS HE REALLY IS!
K-CLIC
MOVE OUT!

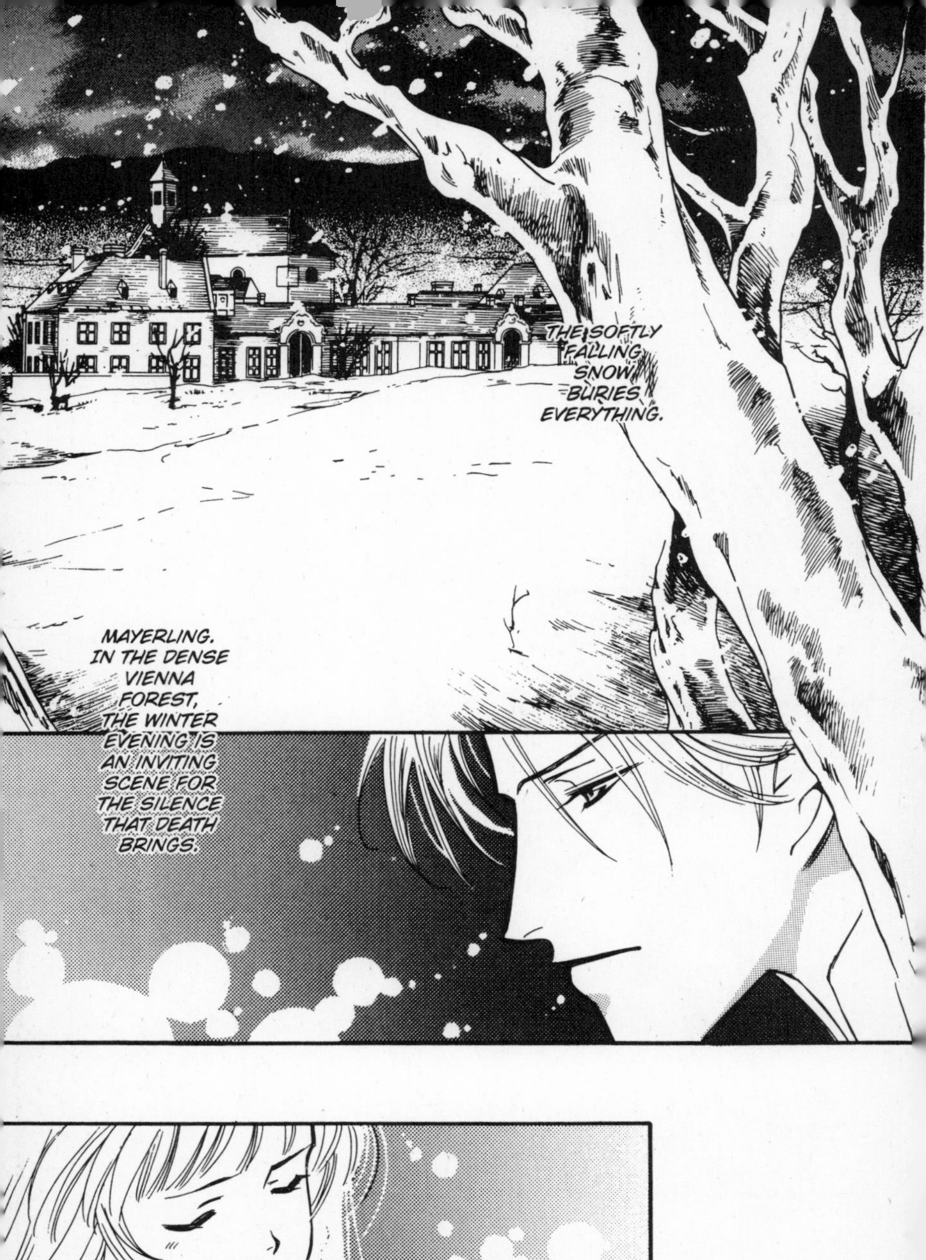
THE SOFTLY FALLING SNOW BURIES EVERYTHING.
MAYERLING. IN THE DENSE VIENNA FOREST, THE WINTER EVENING IS AN INVITING SCENE FOR THE SILENCE THAT DEATH BRINGS.

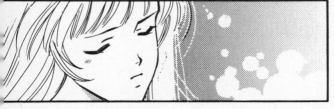

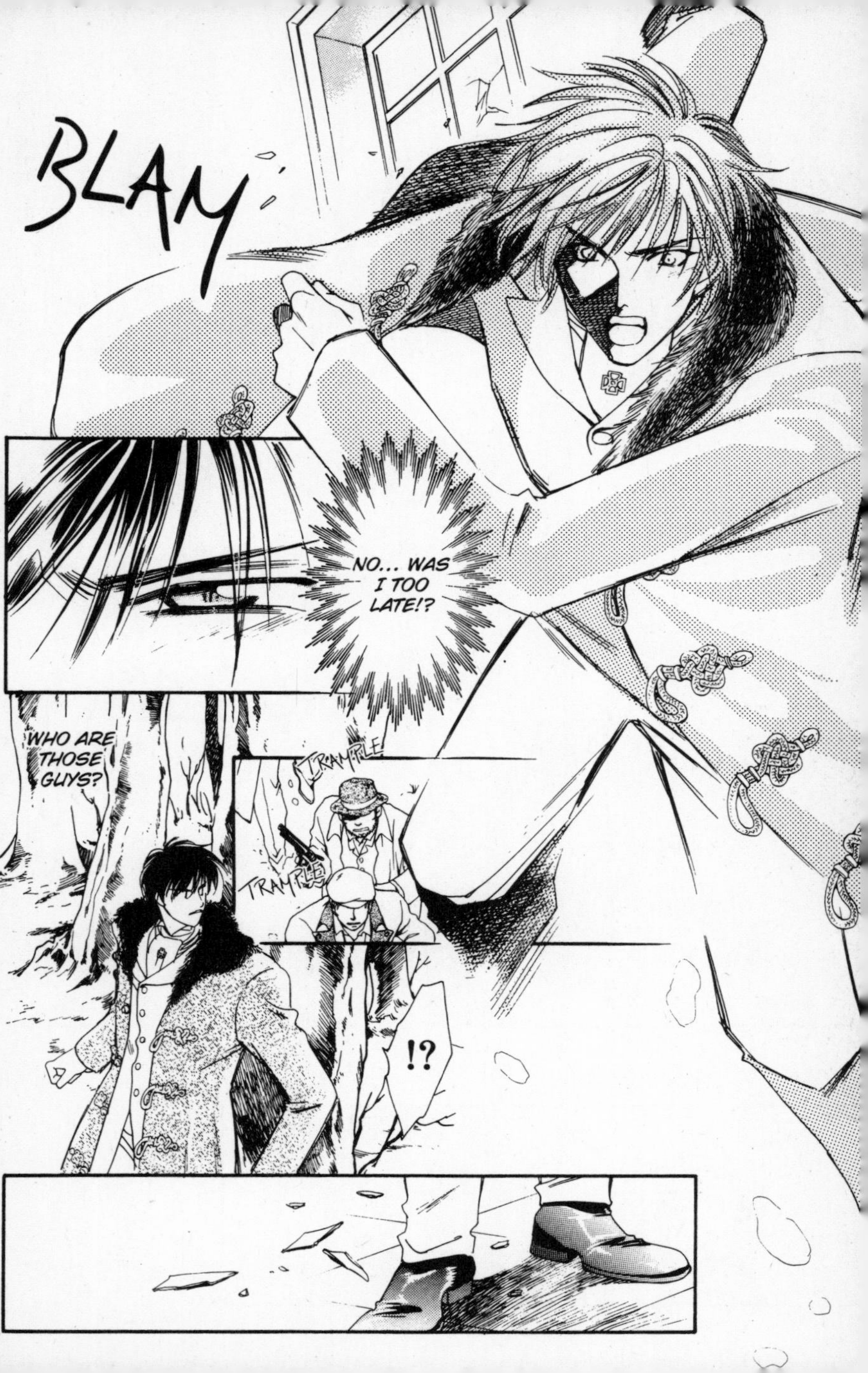
BLAM
NO... WAS I TOO LATE!?
TRAMPLE
TRAMPLE
WHO ARE THOSE GUYS?
!?

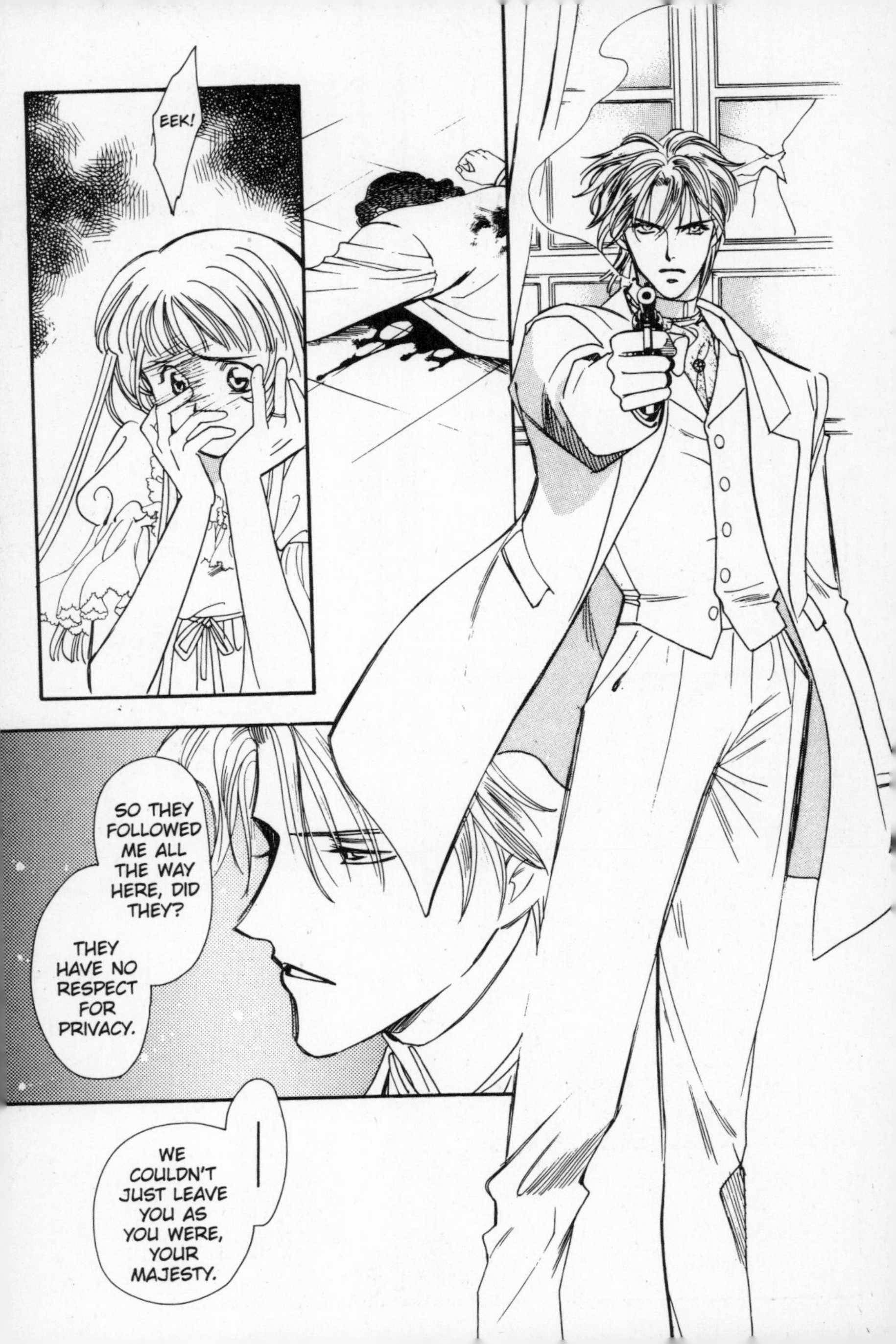
WE COULDN'T JUST LEAVE YOU AS YOU WERE, YOUR MAJESTY.
EEK!
SO THEY FOLLOWED ME ALL THE WAY HERE, DID THEY?
THEY HAVE NO RESPECT FOR PRIVACY.

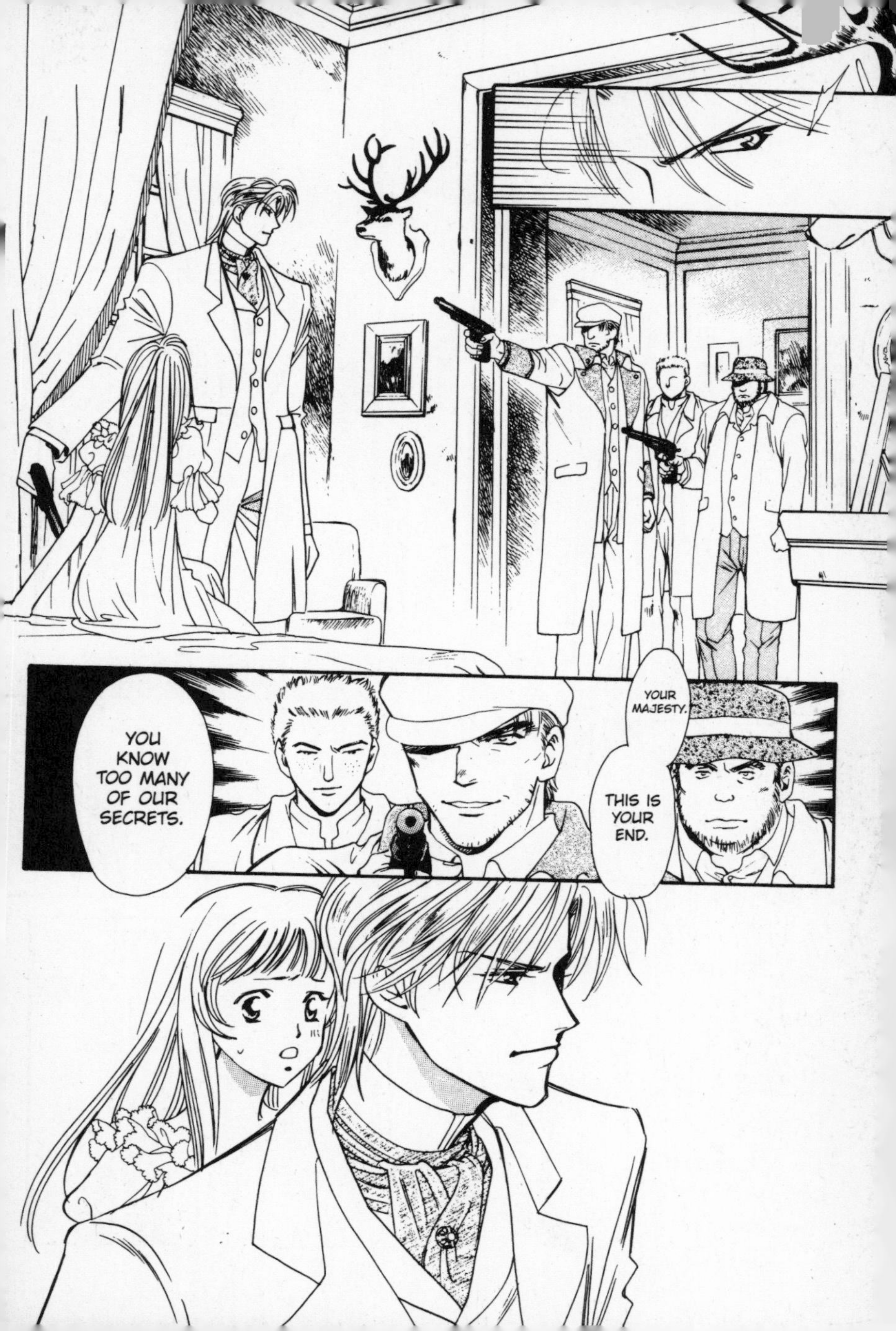
YOUR MAJESTY.
THIS IS YOUR END.
YOU KNOW TOO MANY OF OUR SECRETS.

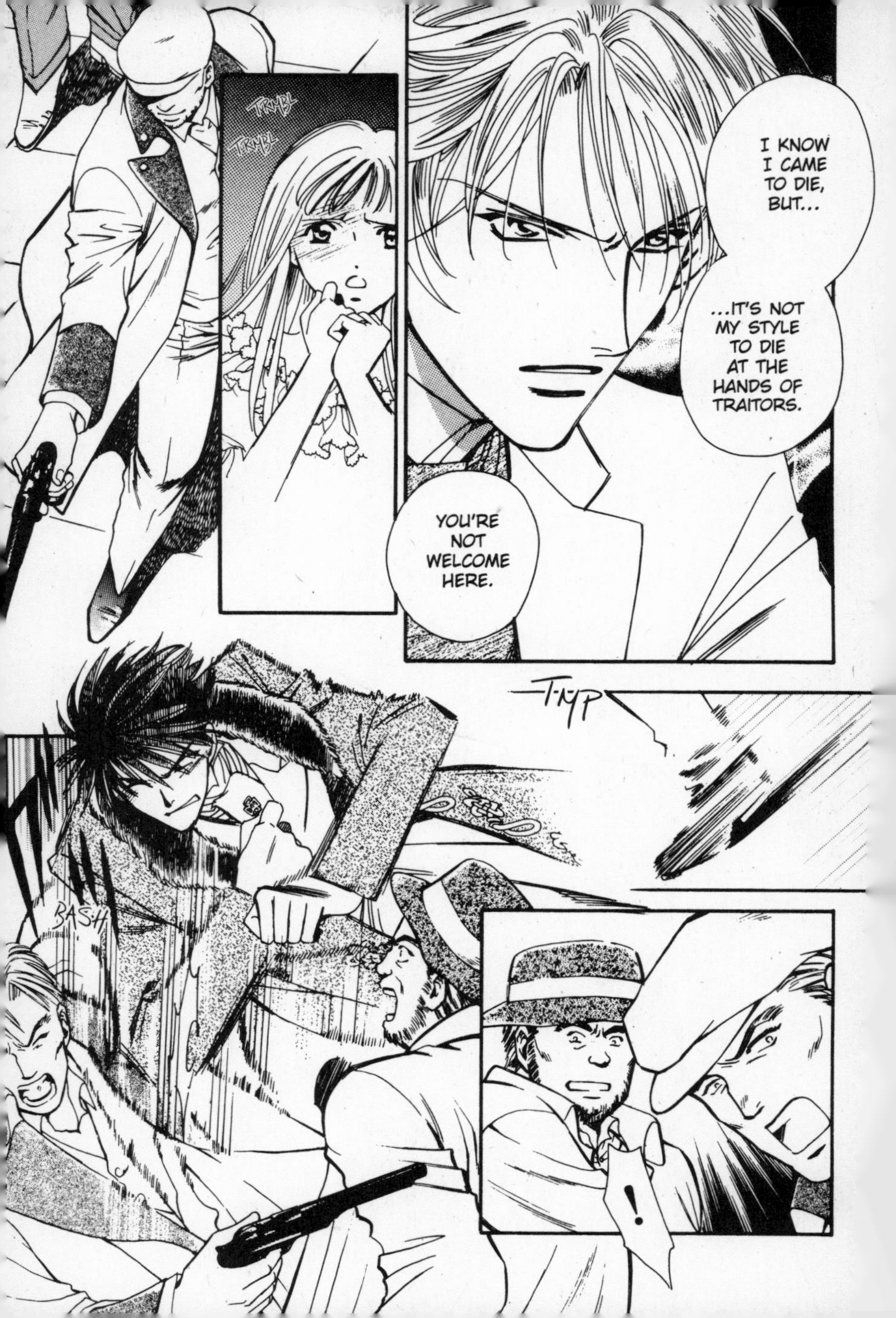
I KNOW I CAME TO DIE, BUT...
...IT'S NOT MY STYLE TO DIE AT THE HANDS OF TRAITORS.
YOU'RE NOT WELCOME HERE.
TRMBL
TRMBL
T-MP
!
BASH

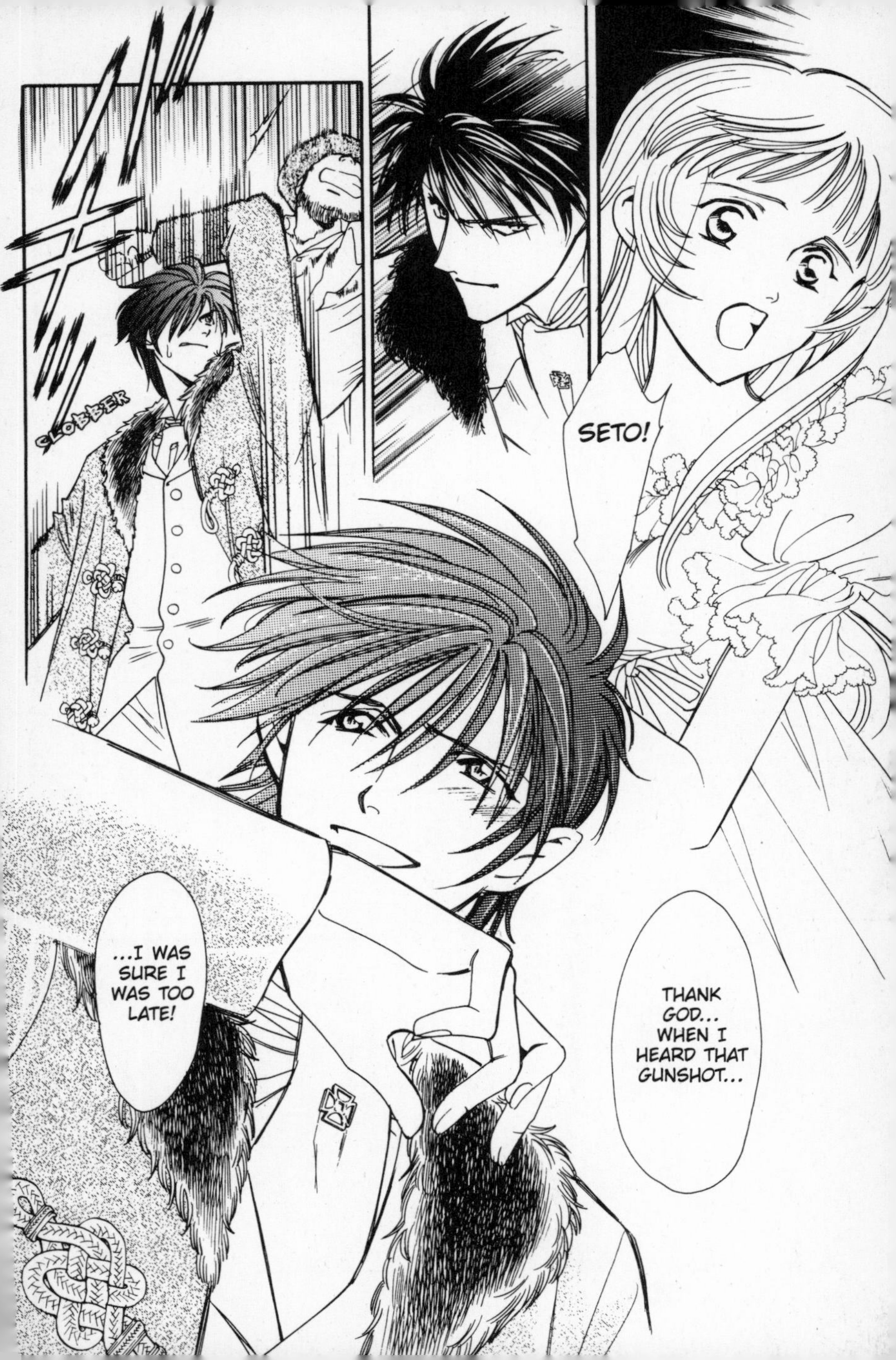

SETO!
CLOBBER
THANK GOD... WHEN I HEARD THAT GUNSHOT...
...I WAS SURE I WAS TOO LATE!

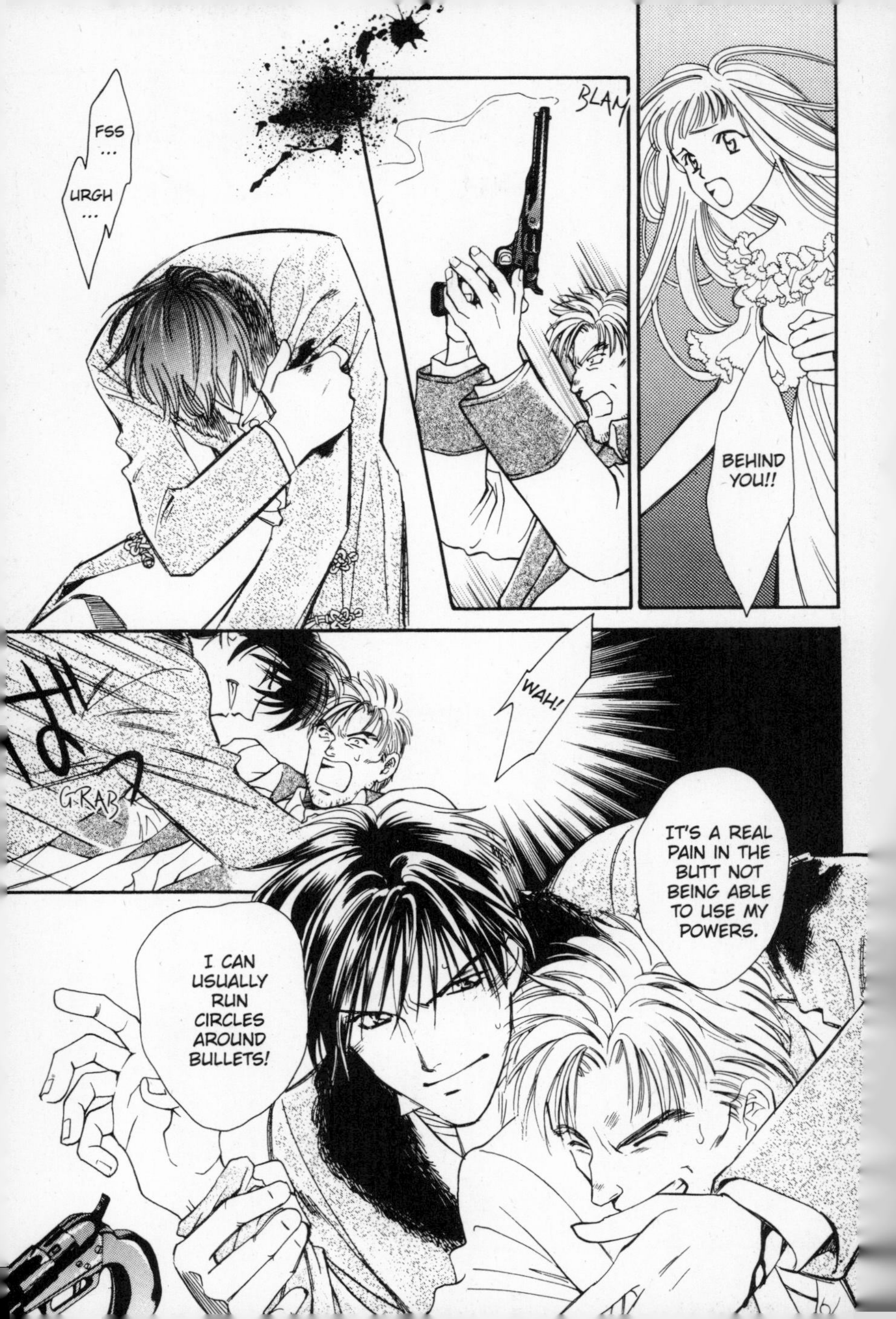
BEHIND YOU!!
BLAM
FSS ...
URGH ...
WAH!
GRAB
IT'S A REAL PAIN IN THE BUTT NOT BEING ABLE TO USE MY POWERS.
I CAN USUALLY RUN CIRCLES AROUND BULLETS!

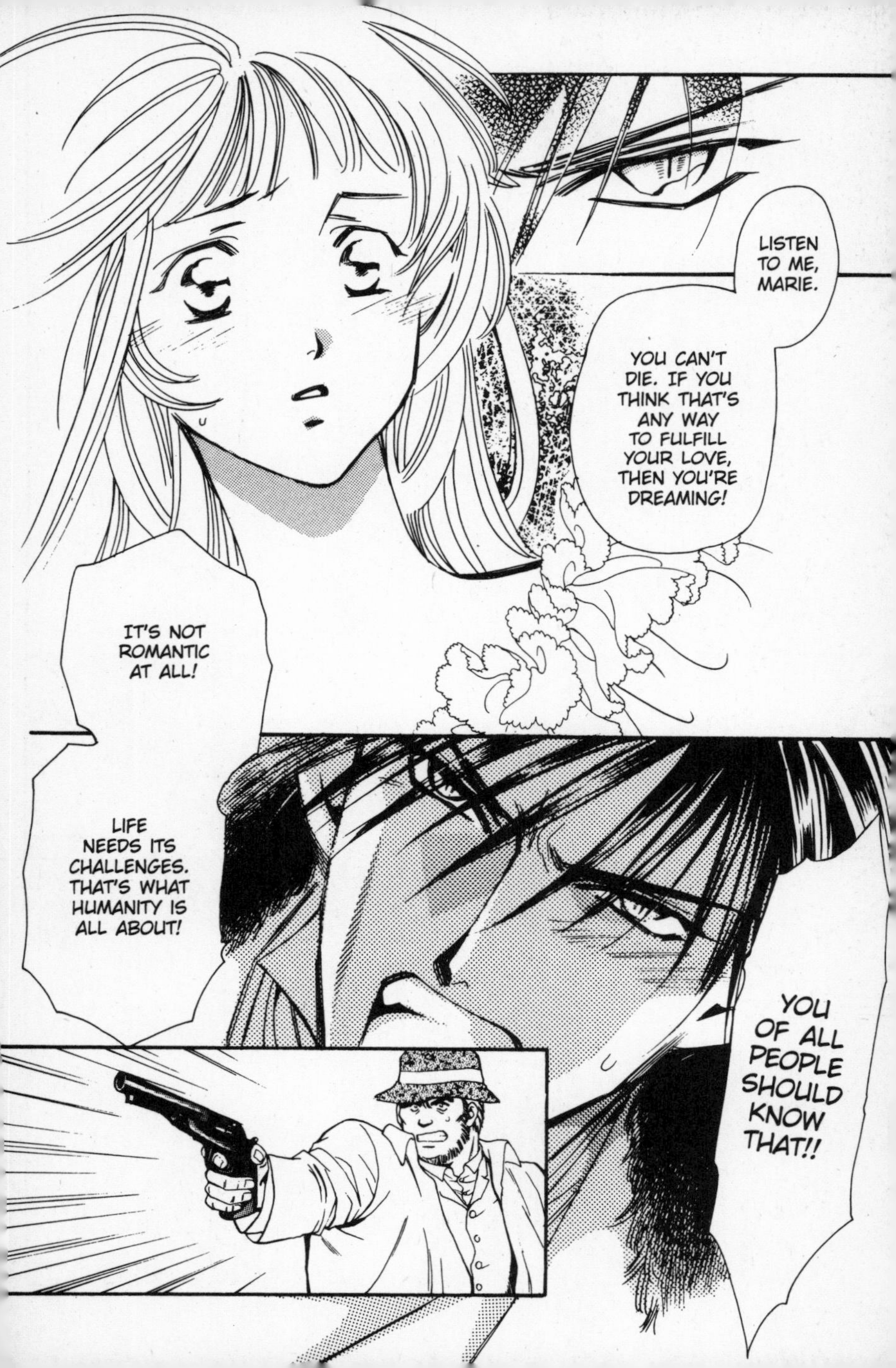
LISTEN TO ME, MARIE.
YOU CAN'T DIE. IF YOU THINK THAT'S ANY WAY TO FULFILL YOUR LOVE, THEN YOU'RE DREAMING!
IT'S NOT ROMANTIC AT ALL!
LIFE NEEDS ITS CHALLENGES. THAT'S WHAT HUMANITY IS ALL ABOUT!
YOU OF ALL PEOPLE SHOULD KNOW THAT!!

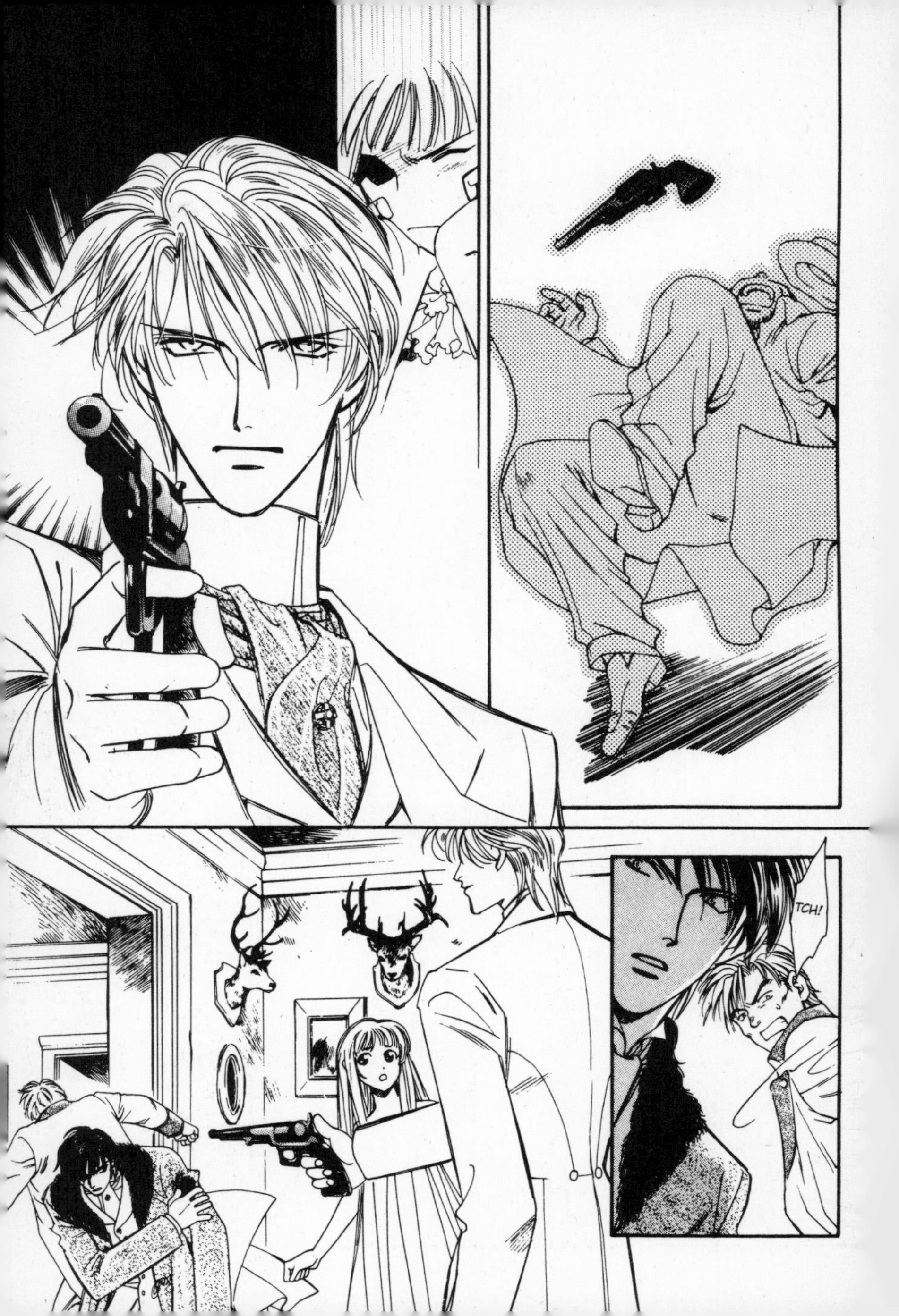
TCH!

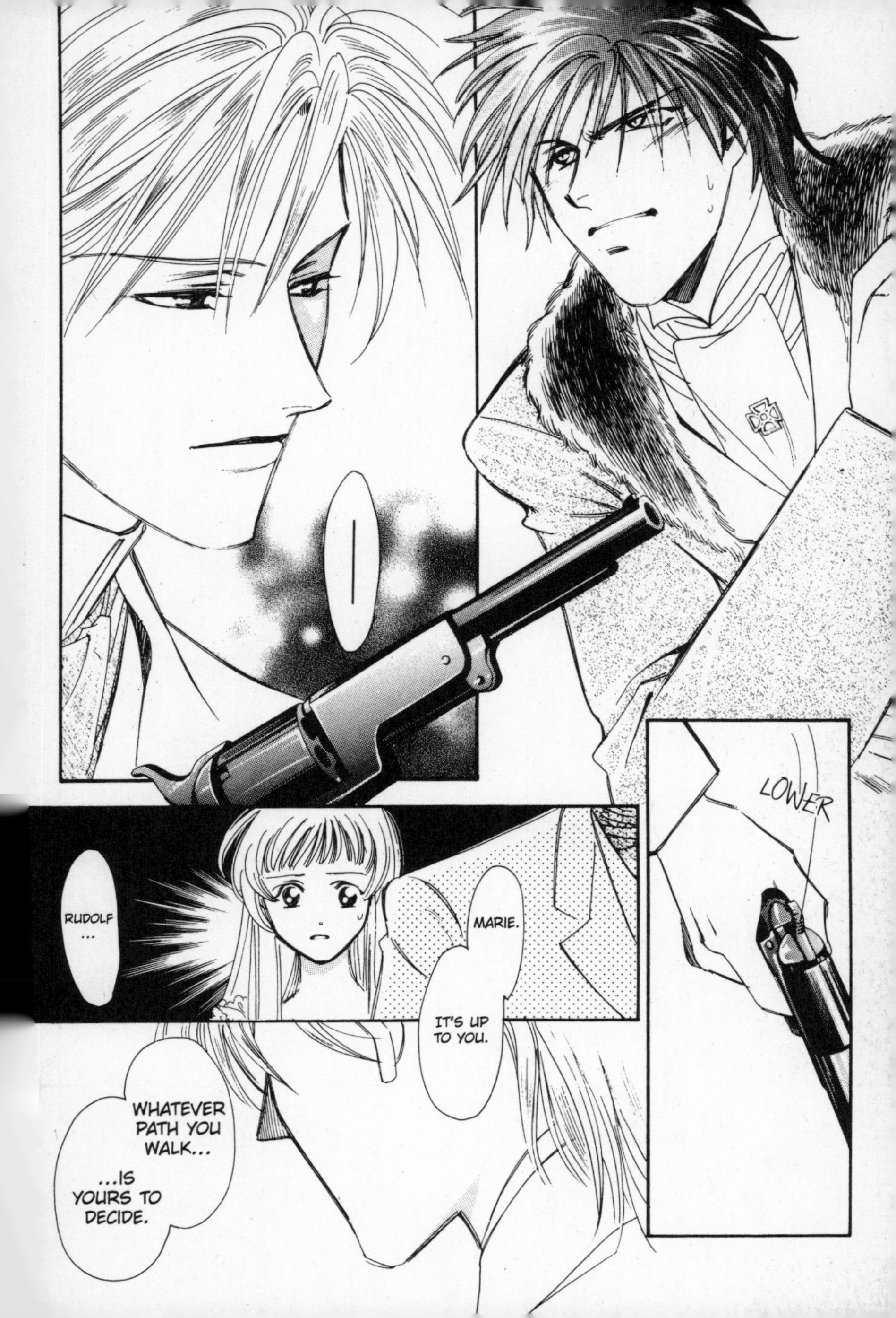
LOWER
MARIE.
IT'S UP TO YOU.
RUDOLF ...
WHATEVER PATH YOU WALK...
...IS YOURS TO DECIDE.

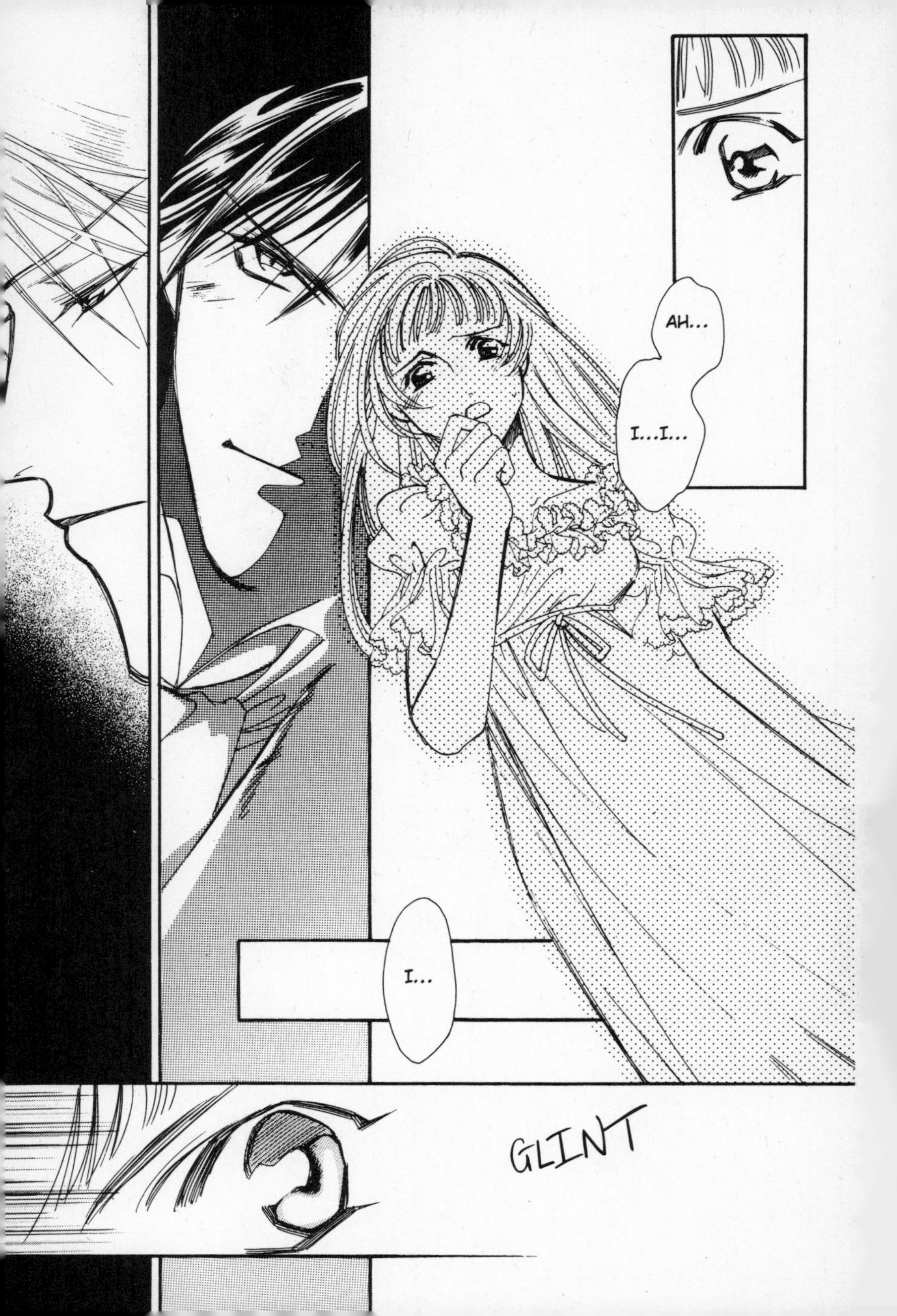
AH...
I...I...
I...
GLINT

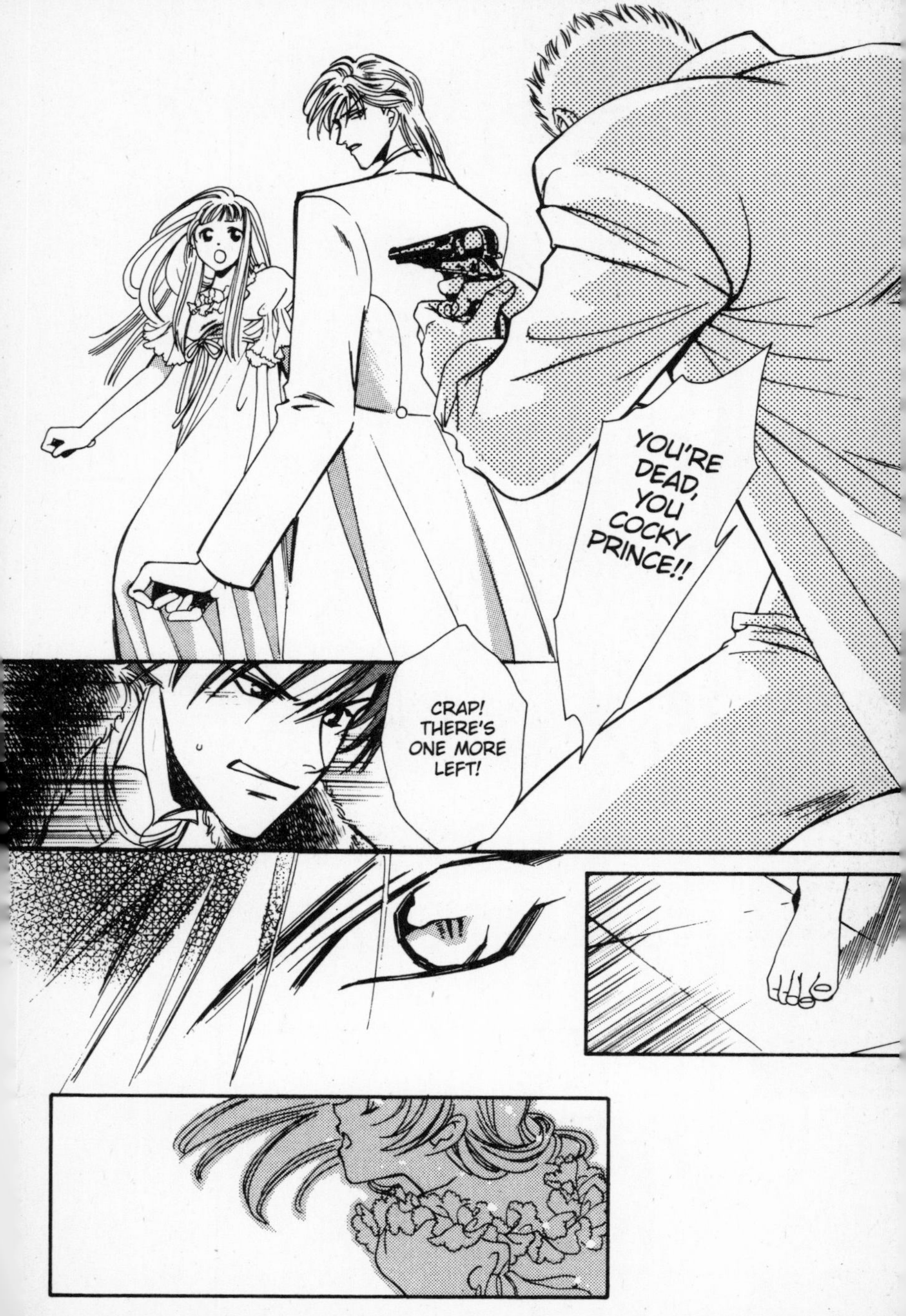
YOU'RE DEAD, YOU COCKY PRINCE!!
CRAP! THERE'S ONE MORE LEFT!

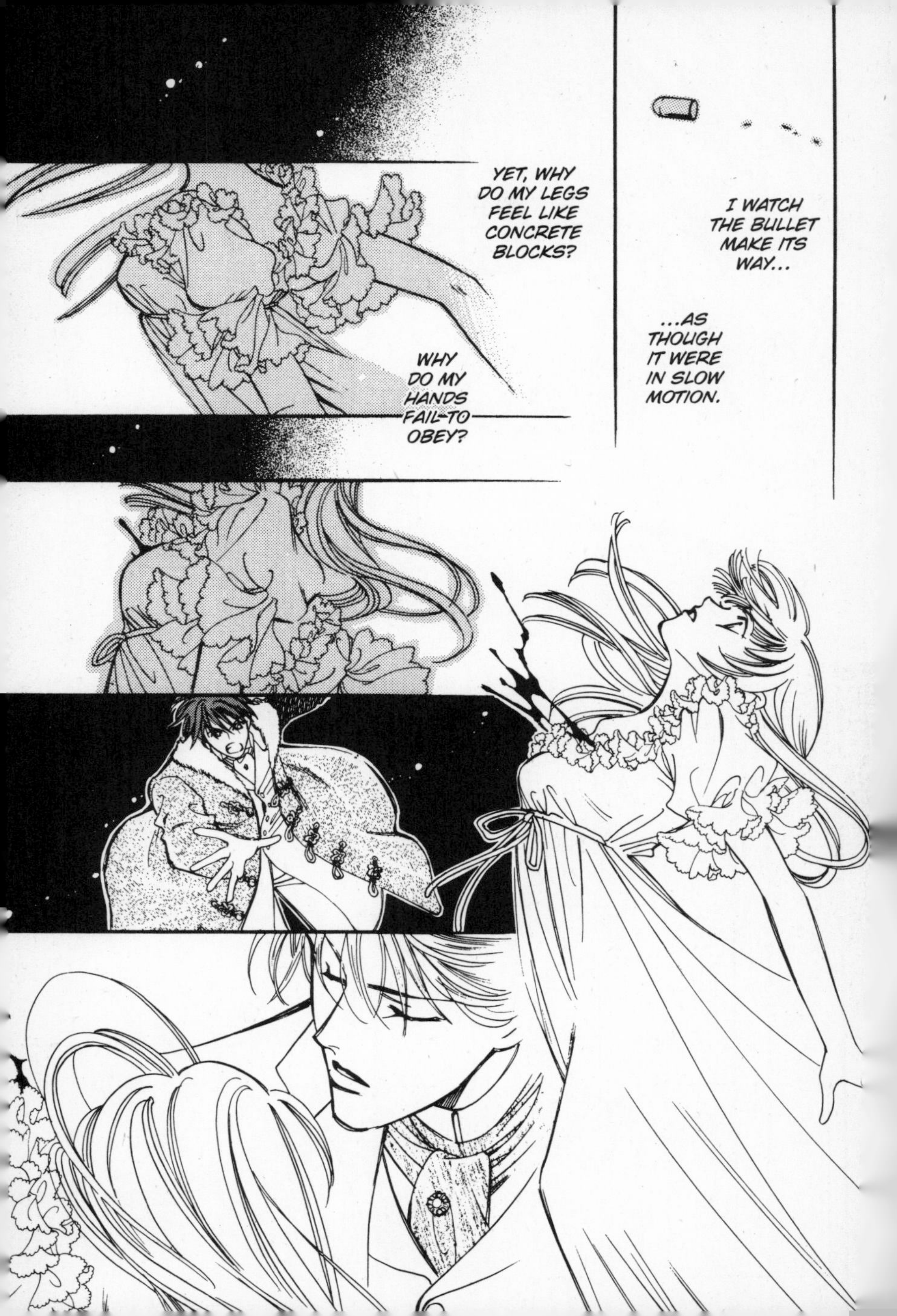
I WATCH THE BULLET MAKE ITS WAY...
...AS THOUGH IT WERE IN SLOW MOTION.
YET, WHY DO MY LEGS FEEL LIKE CONCRETE BLOCKS?
WHY DO MY HANDS FAIL TO OBEY?

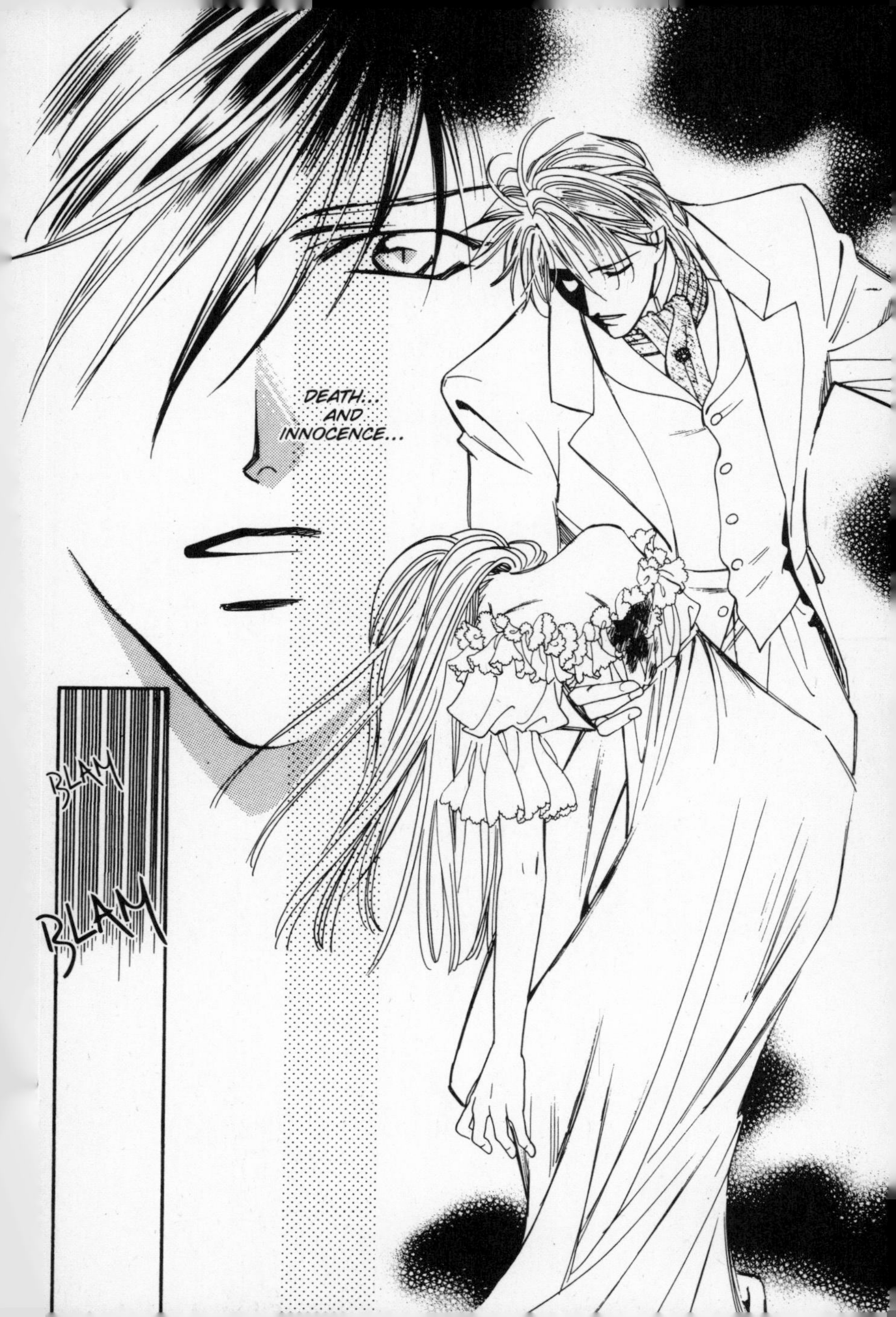
DEATH... AND INNOCENCE...
BLAM
BLAM

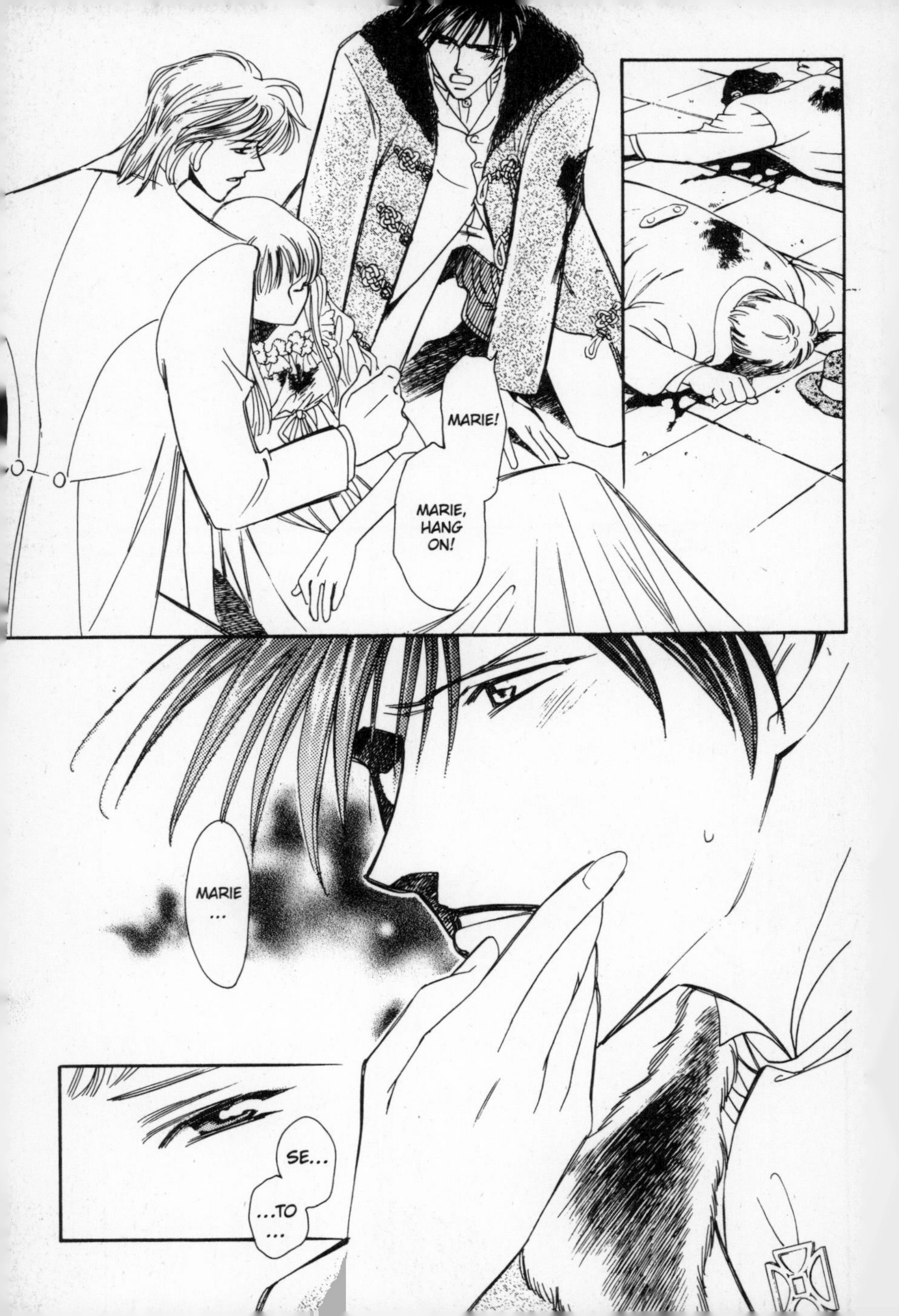
MARIE!
MARIE, HANG ON!
MARIE ...
SE...
...TO ...

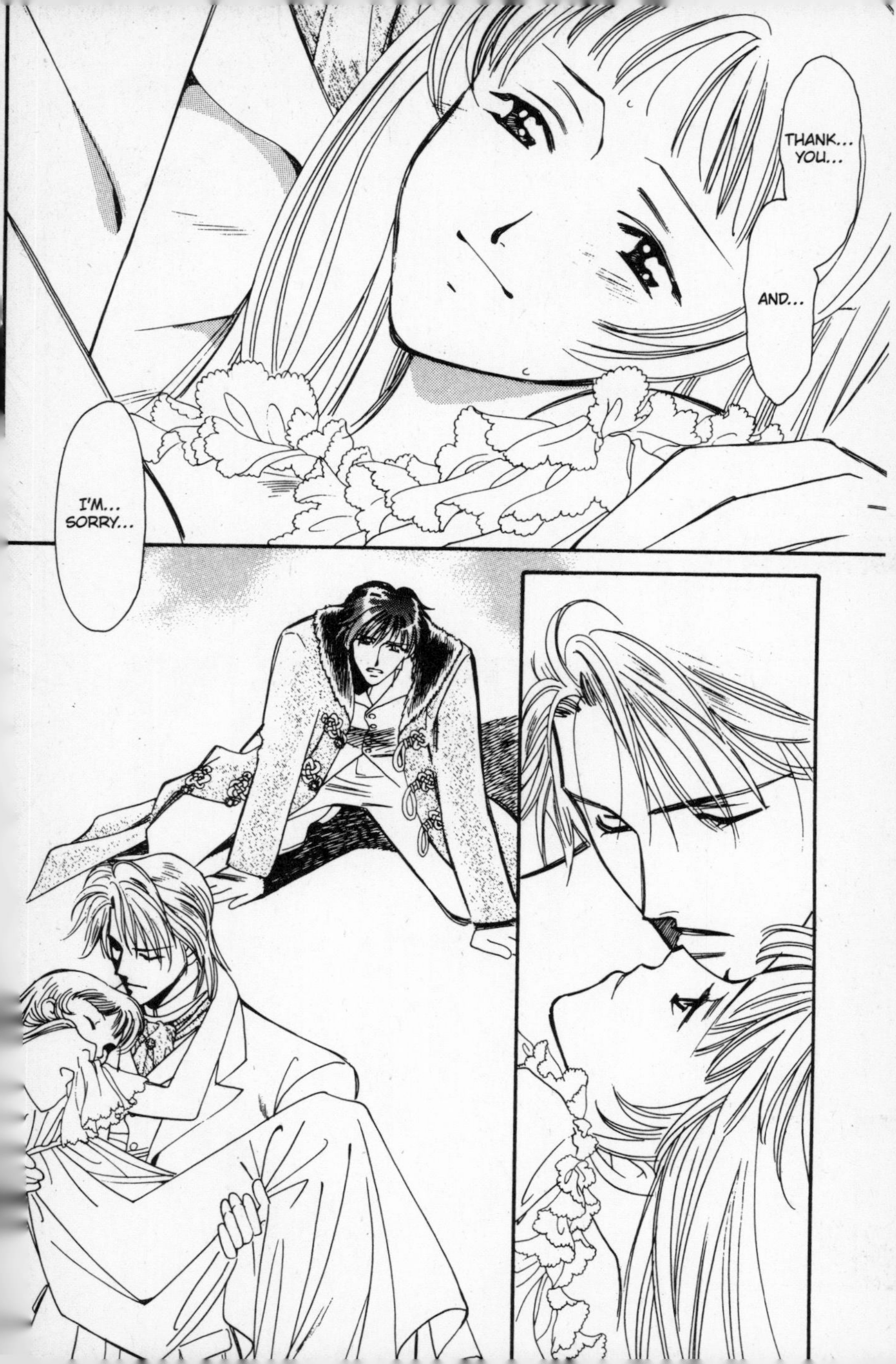
THANK... YOU...
AND...
I'M... SORRY...

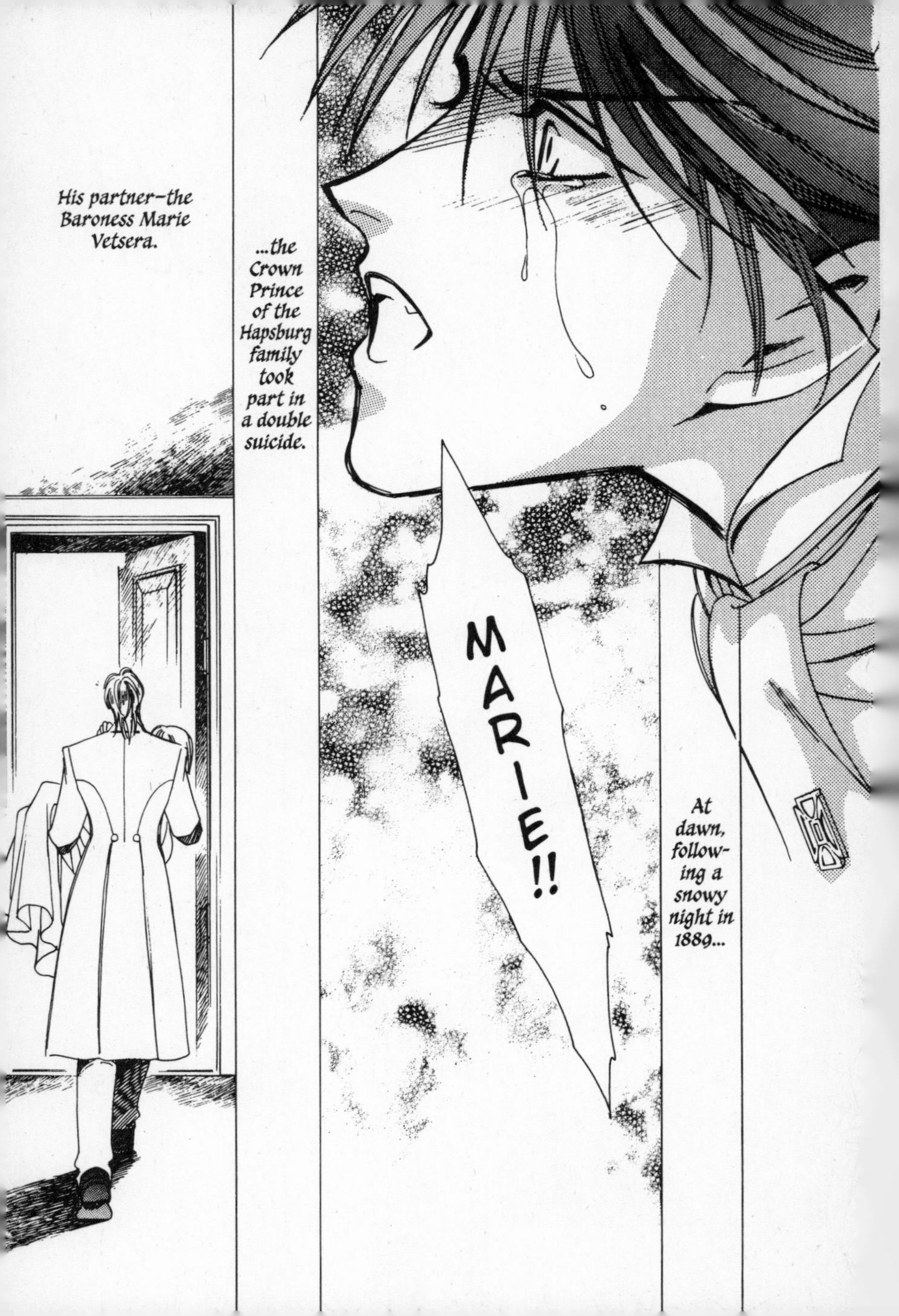
At dawn, following a snowy night in 1889...
MARIE!!
...the Crown Prince of the Hapsburg family took part in a double suicide.
His partner—the Baroness Marie Vetsera.

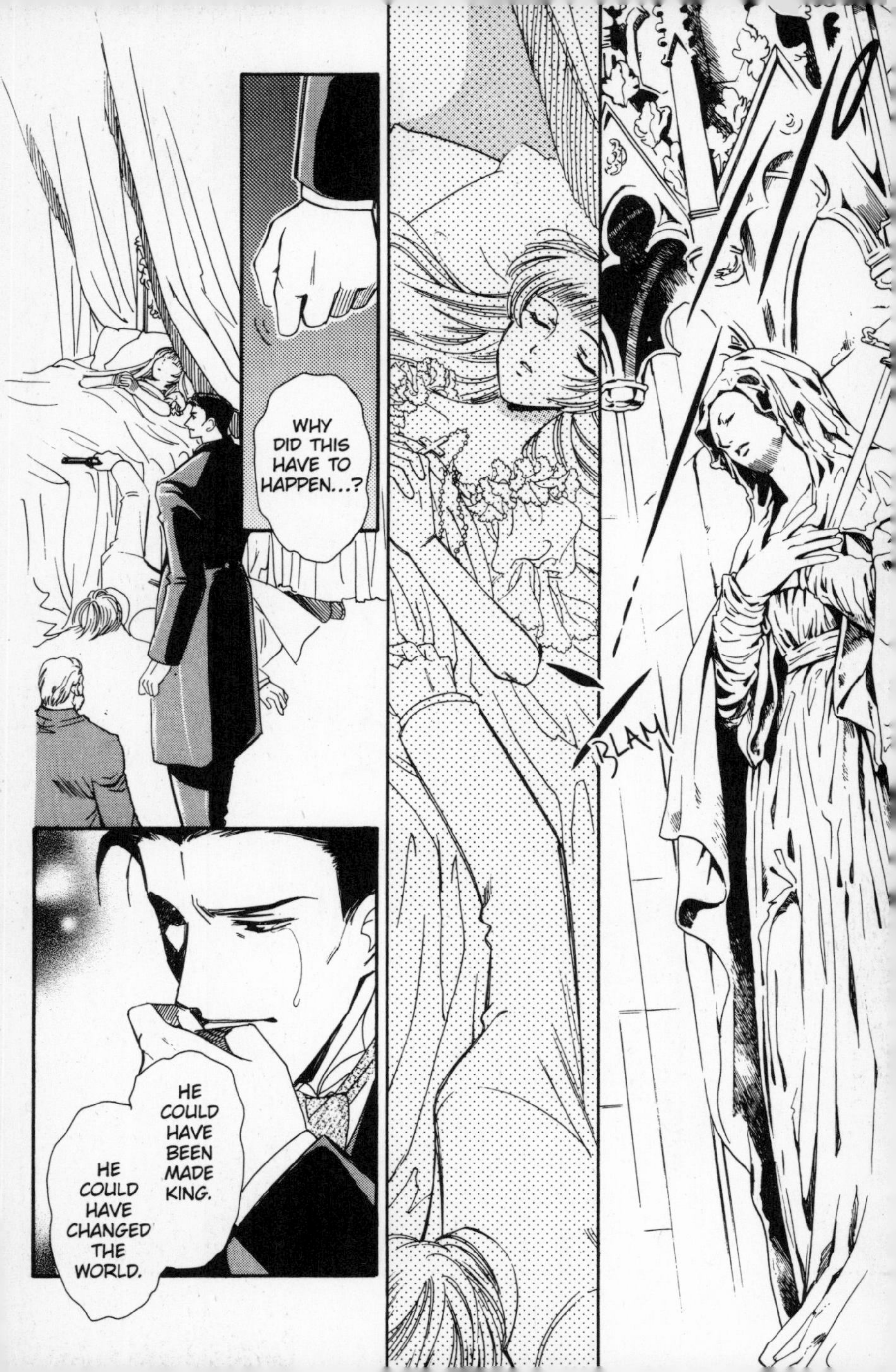
BLAM
WHY DID THIS HAVE TO HAPPEN...?
HE COULD HAVE BEEN MADE KING.
HE COULD HAVE CHANGED THE WORLD.

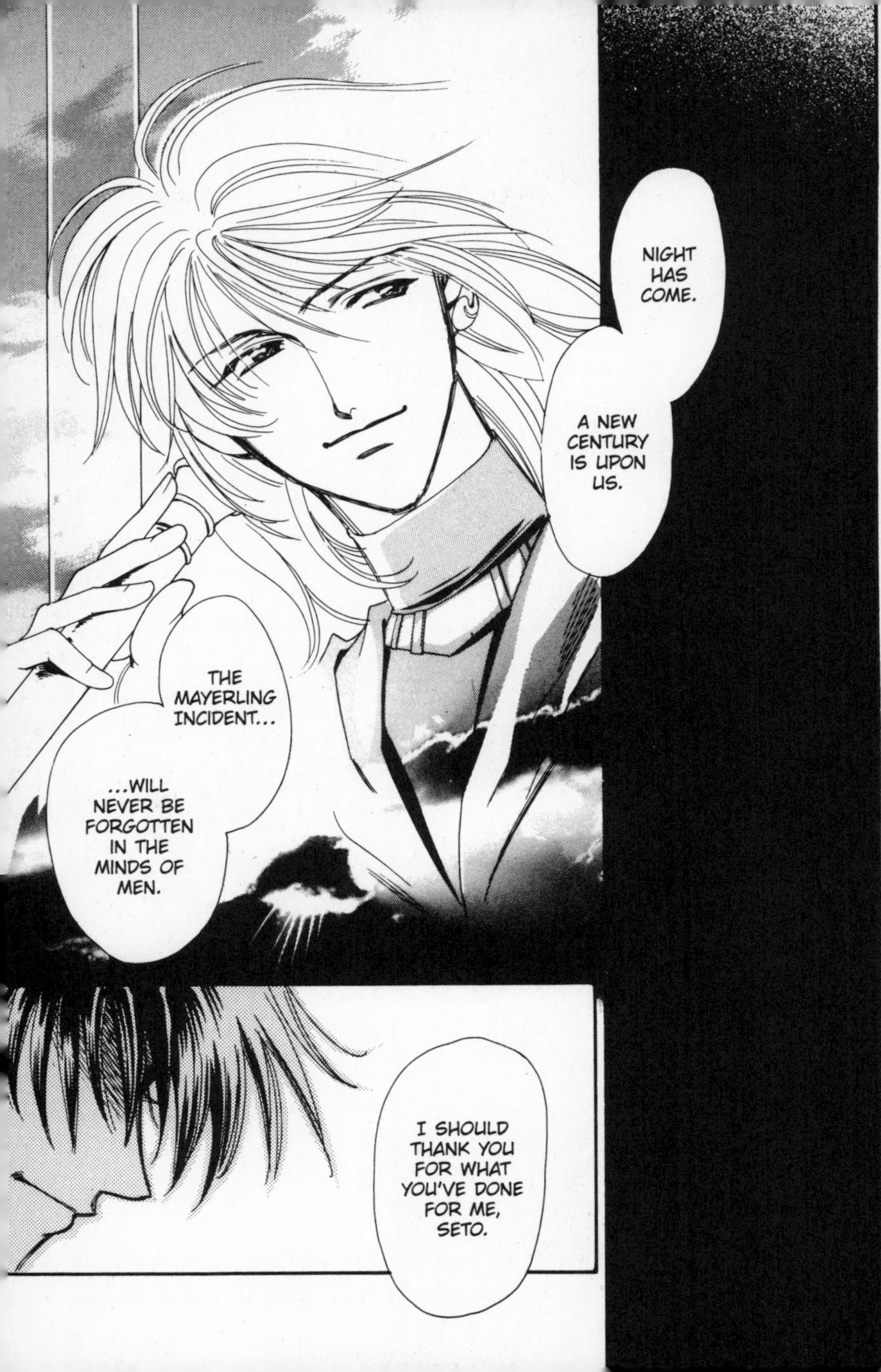
NIGHT HAS COME.
A NEW CENTURY IS UPON US.
THE MAYERLING INCIDENT...
...WILL NEVER BE FORGOTTEN IN THE MINDS OF MEN.
I SHOULD THANK YOU FOR WHAT YOU'VE DONE FOR ME, SETO.

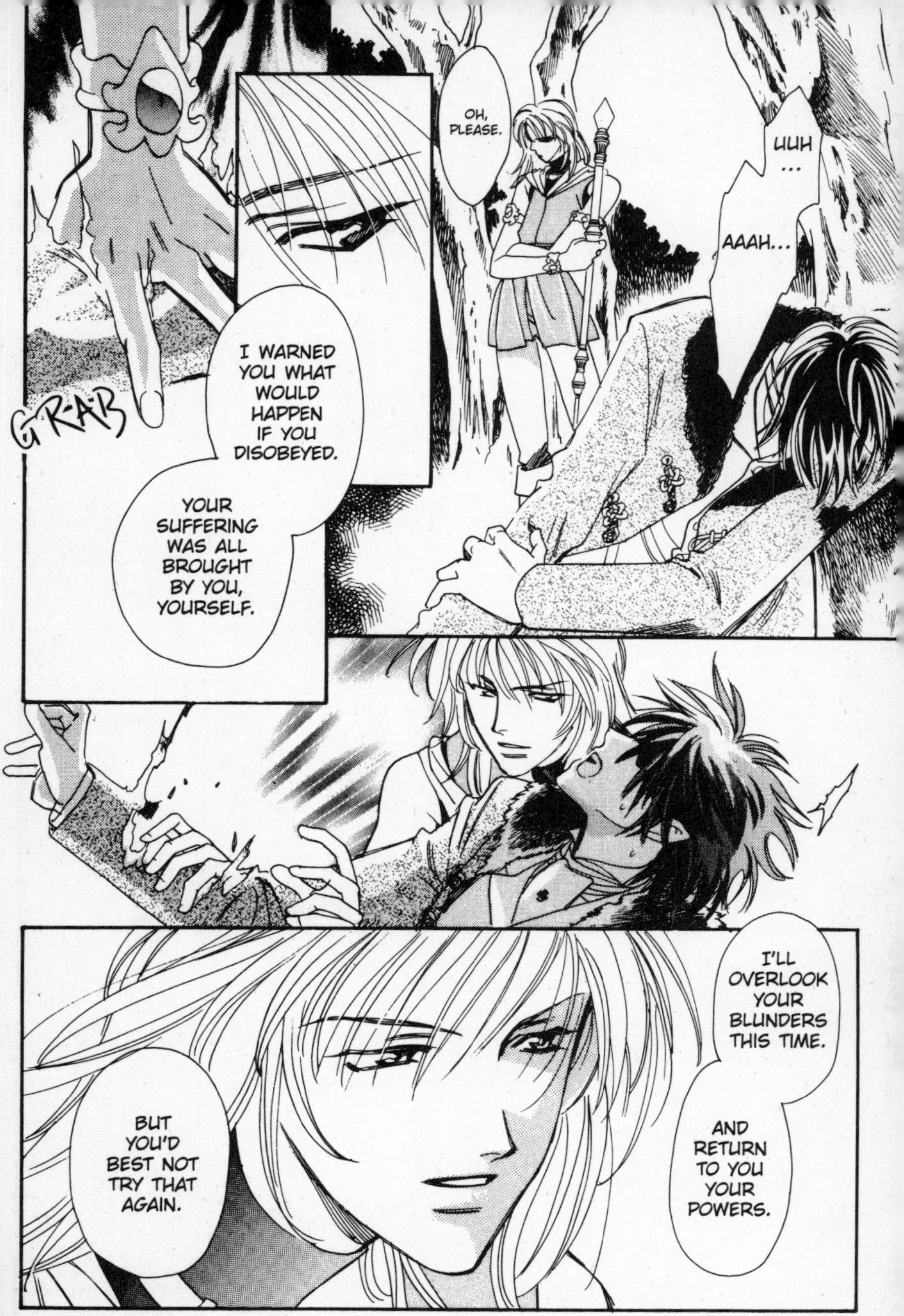
UUH ...
AAAH...
OH, PLEASE.
I WARNED YOU WHAT WOULD HAPPEN IF YOU DISOBEYED.
YOUR SUFFERING WAS ALL BROUGHT BY YOU, YOURSELF.
G-R-A-B
I'LL OVERLOOK YOUR BLUNDERS THIS TIME.
AND RETURN TO YOU YOUR POWERS.
BUT YOU'D BEST NOT TRY THAT AGAIN.

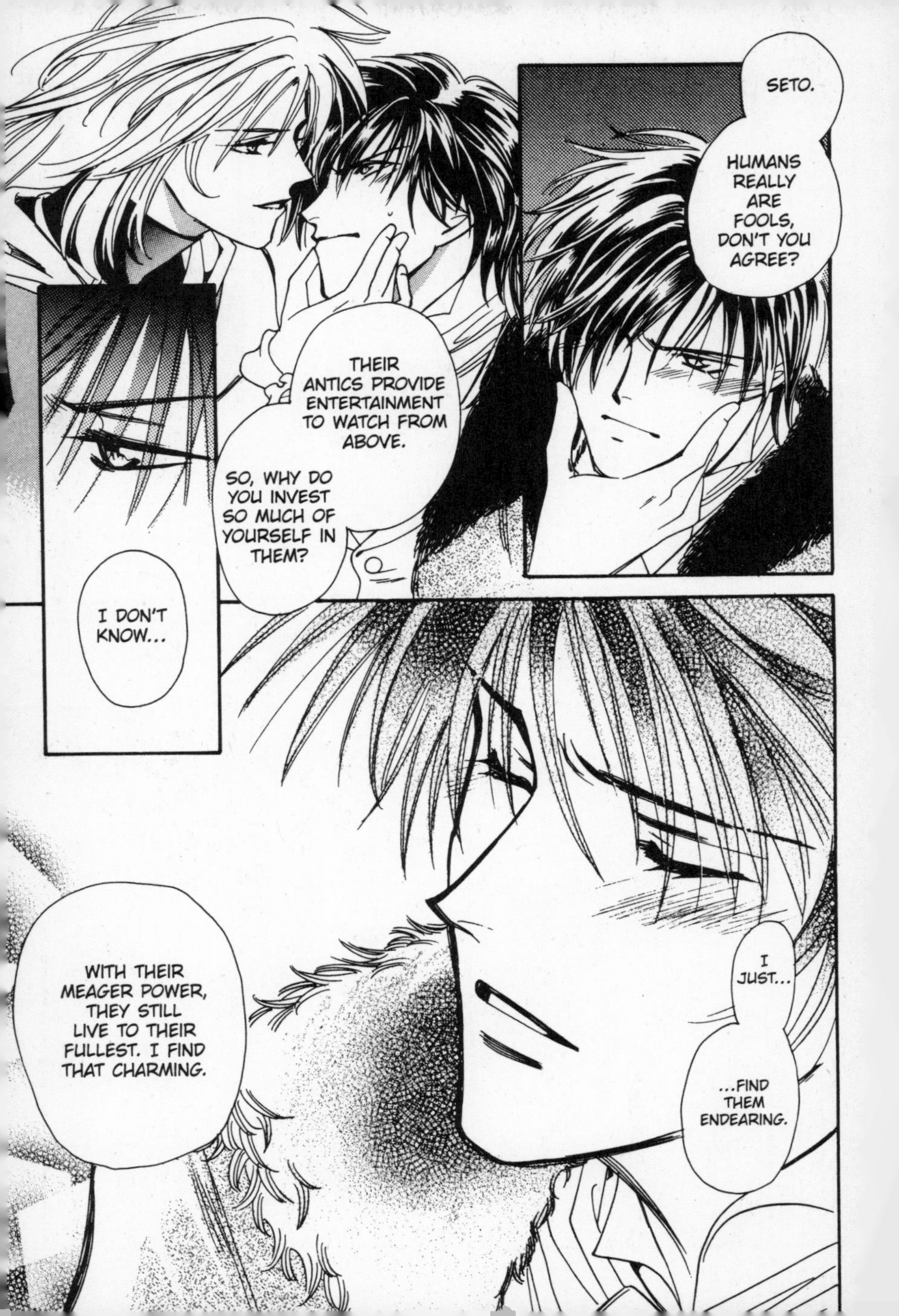
SETO.
HUMANS REALLY ARE FOOLS, DON'T YOU AGREE?
THEIR ANTICS PROVIDE ENTERTAINMENT TO WATCH FROM ABOVE.
SO, WHY DO YOU INVEST SO MUCH OF YOURSELF IN THEM?
I DON'T KNOW...
I JUST...
...FIND THEM ENDEARING.
WITH THEIR MEAGER POWER, THEY STILL LIVE TO THEIR FULLEST. I FIND THAT CHARMING.

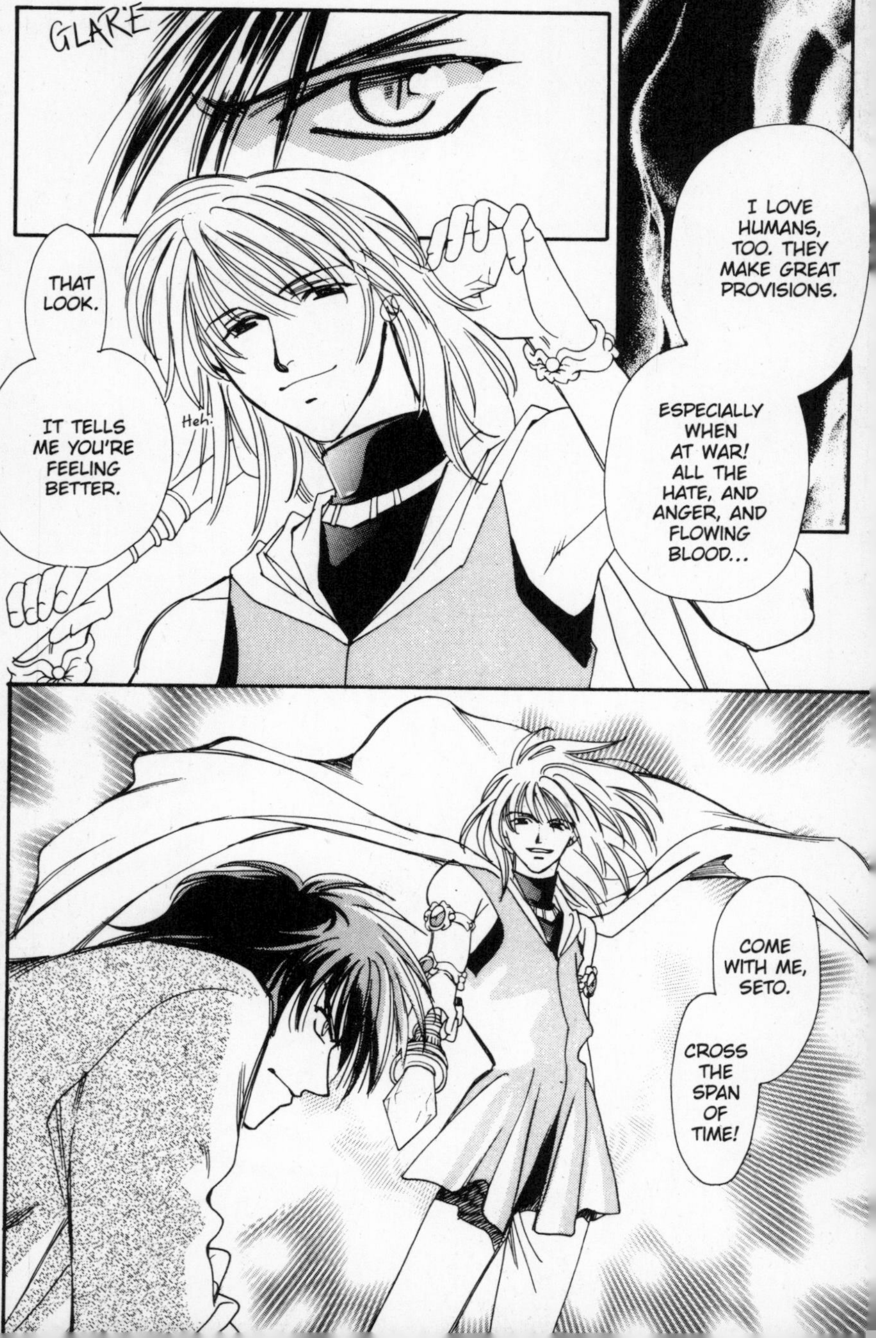
I LOVE HUMANS, TOO. THEY MAKE GREAT PROVISIONS.
ESPECIALLY WHEN AT WAR! ALL THE HATE, AND ANGER, AND FLOWING BLOOD...
GLARE
Heh.
THAT LOOK.
IT TELLS ME YOU'RE FEELING BETTER.
COME WITH ME, SETO.
CROSS THE SPAN OF TIME!

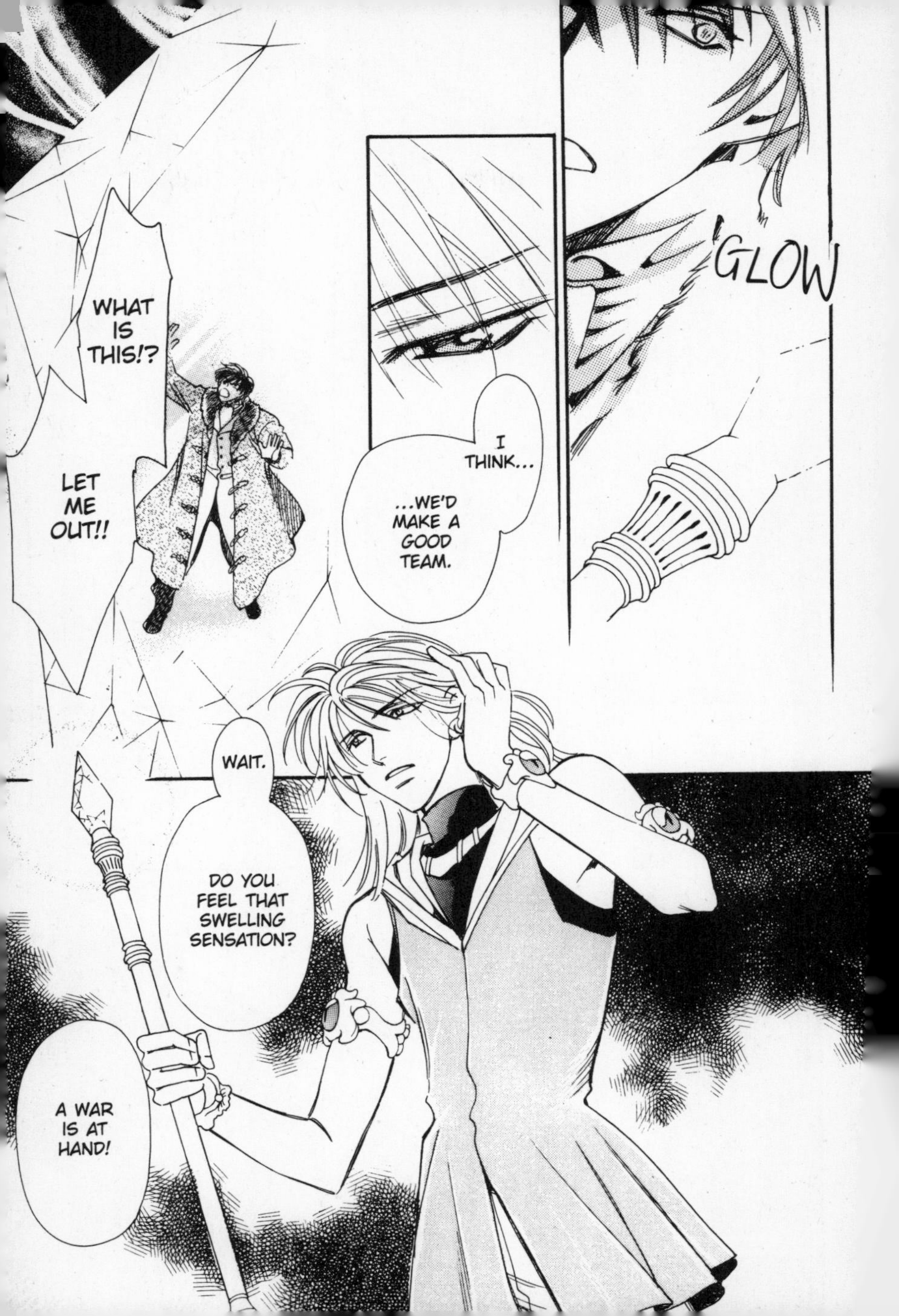
GLOW
I THINK...
...WE'D MAKE A GOOD TEAM.
WHAT IS THIS!?
LET ME OUT!!
WAIT.
DO YOU FEEL THAT SWELLING SENSATION?
A WAR IS AT HAND!

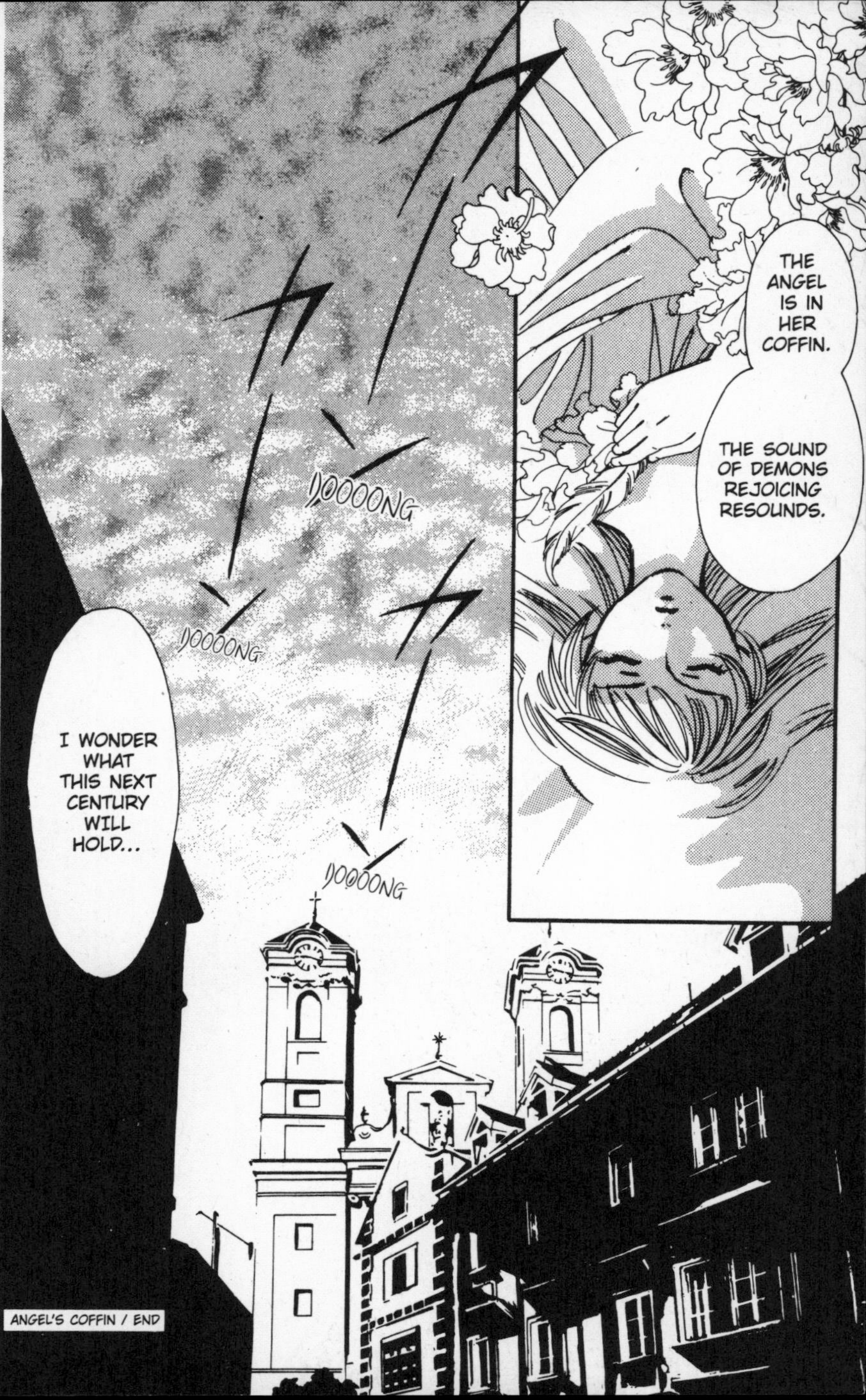
THE ANGEL IS IN HER COFFIN.
THE SOUND OF DEMONS REJOICING RESOUNDS.
DJOOOONG
DJOOOONG
I WONDER WHAT THIS NEXT CENTURY WILL HOLD...
DJOOOONG
ANGEL'S COFFIN / END

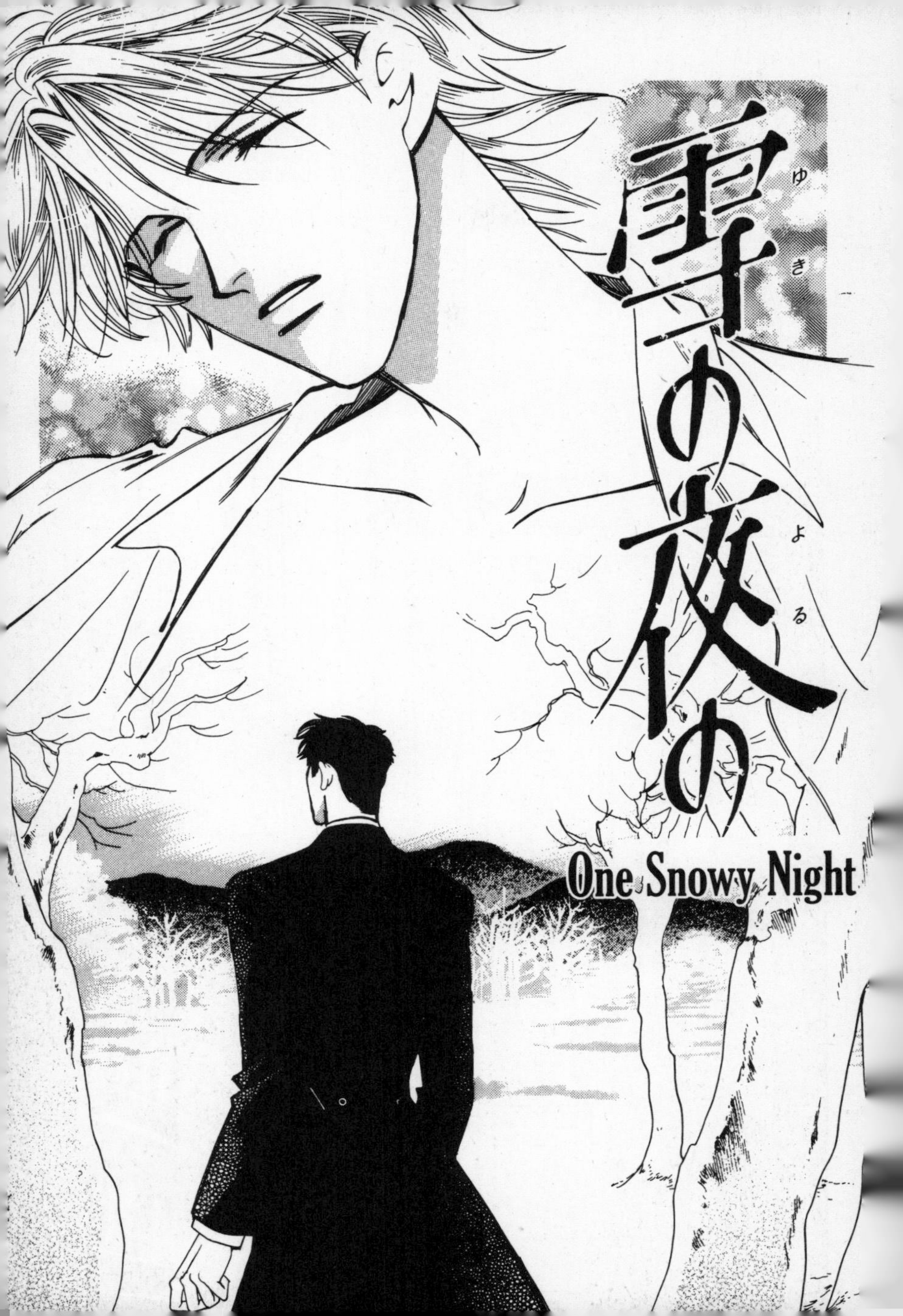
雪の夜の
One Snowy Night

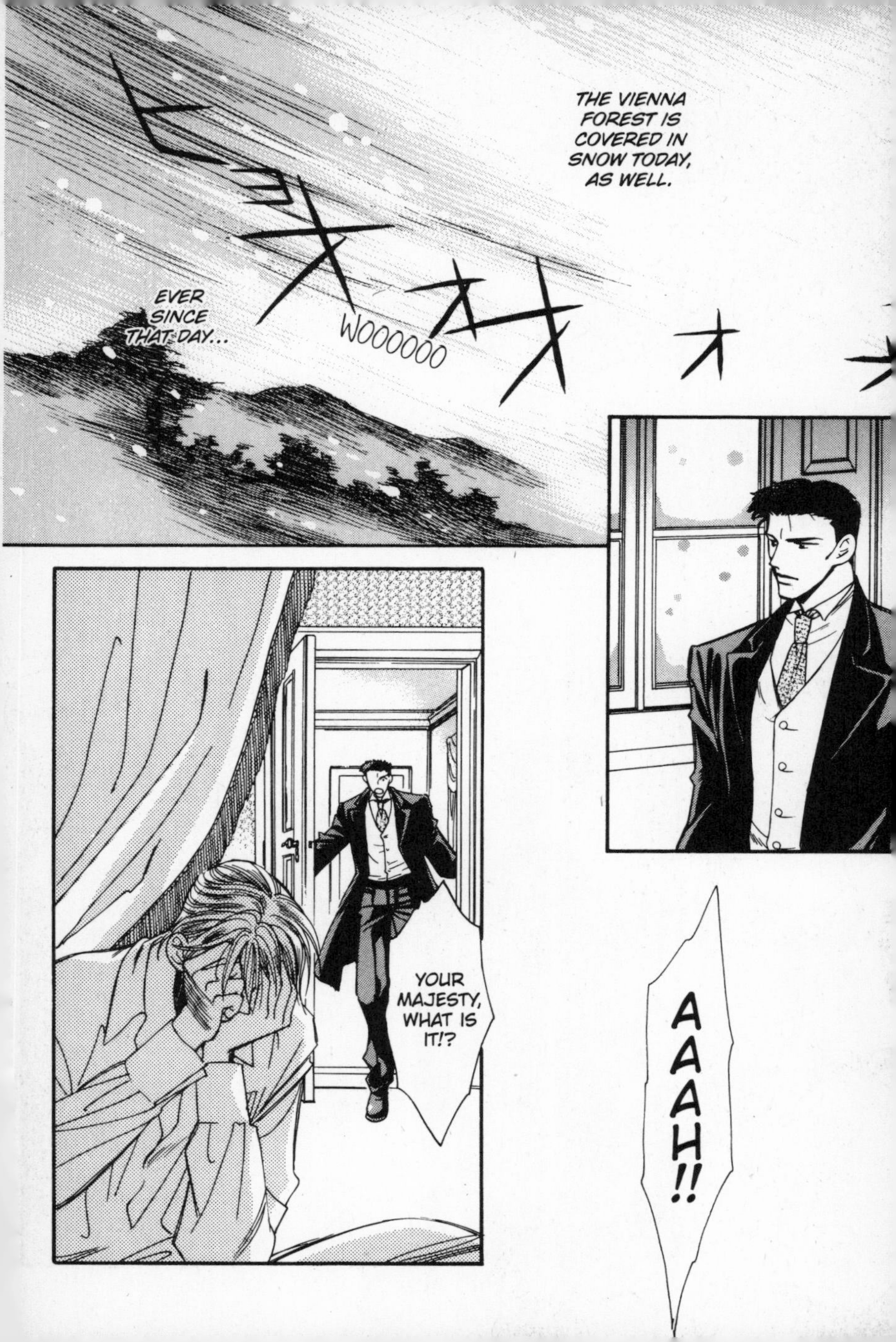
THE VIENNA FOREST IS COVERED IN SNOW TODAY, AS WELL.
WOOOOOO
EVER SINCE THAT DAY...
AAAH!!
YOUR MAJESTY, WHAT IS IT!?

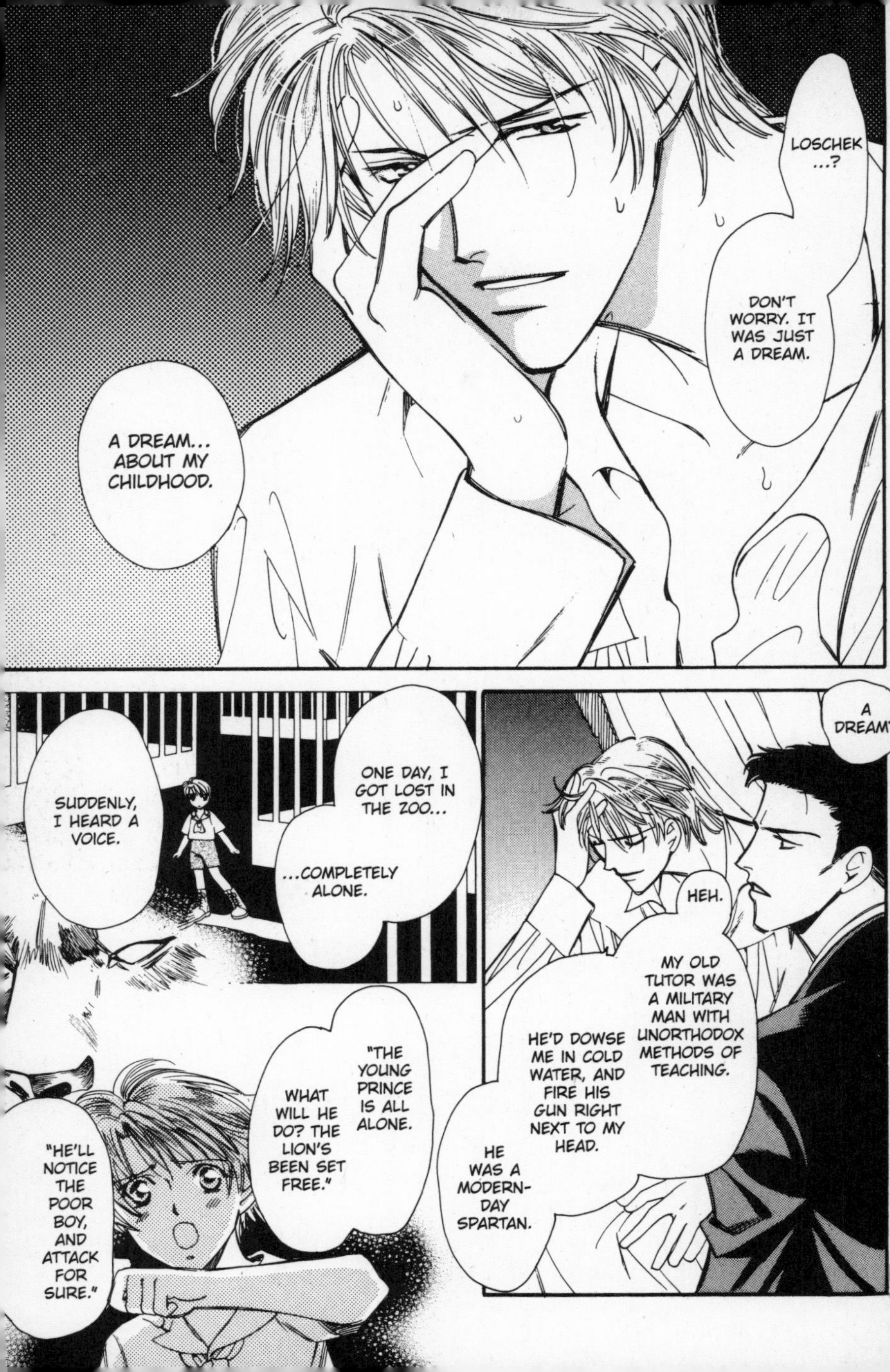
LOSCHEK ...?
DON'T WORRY. IT WAS JUST A DREAM.
A DREAM... ABOUT MY CHILDHOOD.
A DREAM?
HEH.
MY OLD TUTOR WAS A MILITARY MAN WITH UNORTHODOX METHODS OF TEACHING.
HE'D DOWSE ME IN COLD WATER, AND FIRE HIS GUN RIGHT NEXT TO MY HEAD.
HE WAS A MODERN-DAY SPARTAN.
ONE DAY, I GOT LOST IN THE ZOO...
...COMPLETELY ALONE.
SUDDENLY, I HEARD A VOICE.
"THE YOUNG PRINCE IS ALL ALONE.
WHAT WILL HE DO? THE LION'S BEEN SET FREE."
"HE'LL NOTICE THE POOR BOY, AND ATTACK FOR SURE."

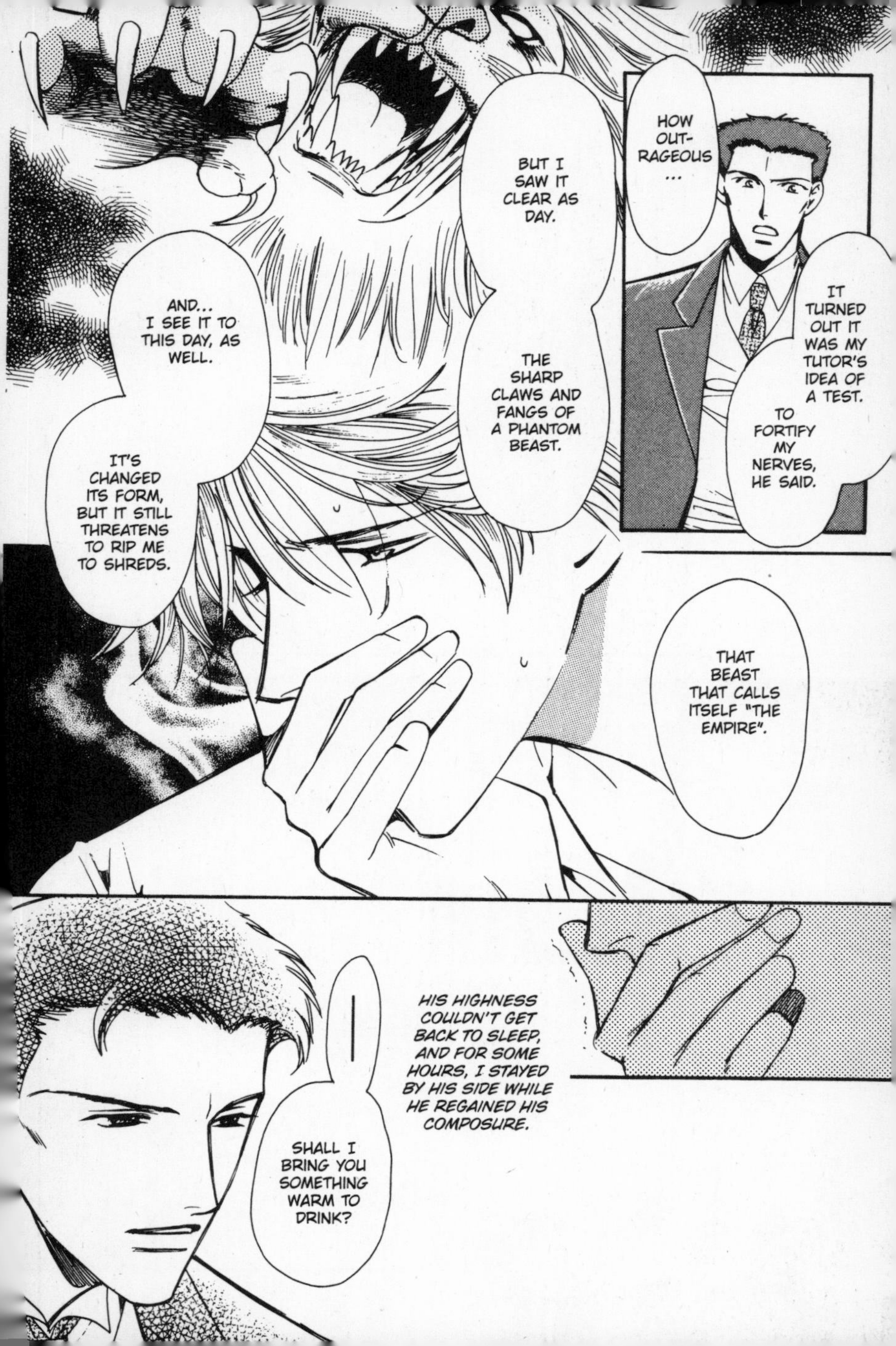
HOW OUT-RAGEOUS ...
IT TURNED OUT IT WAS MY TUTOR'S IDEA OF A TEST.
TO FORTIFY MY NERVES, HE SAID.
BUT I SAW IT CLEAR AS DAY.
THE SHARP CLAWS AND FANGS OF A PHANTOM BEAST.
AND... I SEE IT TO THIS DAY, AS WELL.
IT'S CHANGED ITS FORM, BUT IT STILL THREATENS TO RIP ME TO SHREDS.
THAT BEAST THAT CALLS ITSELF "THE EMPIRE".
HIS HIGHNESS COULDN'T GET BACK TO SLEEP, AND FOR SOME HOURS, I STAYED BY HIS SIDE WHILE HE REGAINED HIS COMPOSURE.
—
SHALL I BRING YOU SOMETHING WARM TO DRINK?

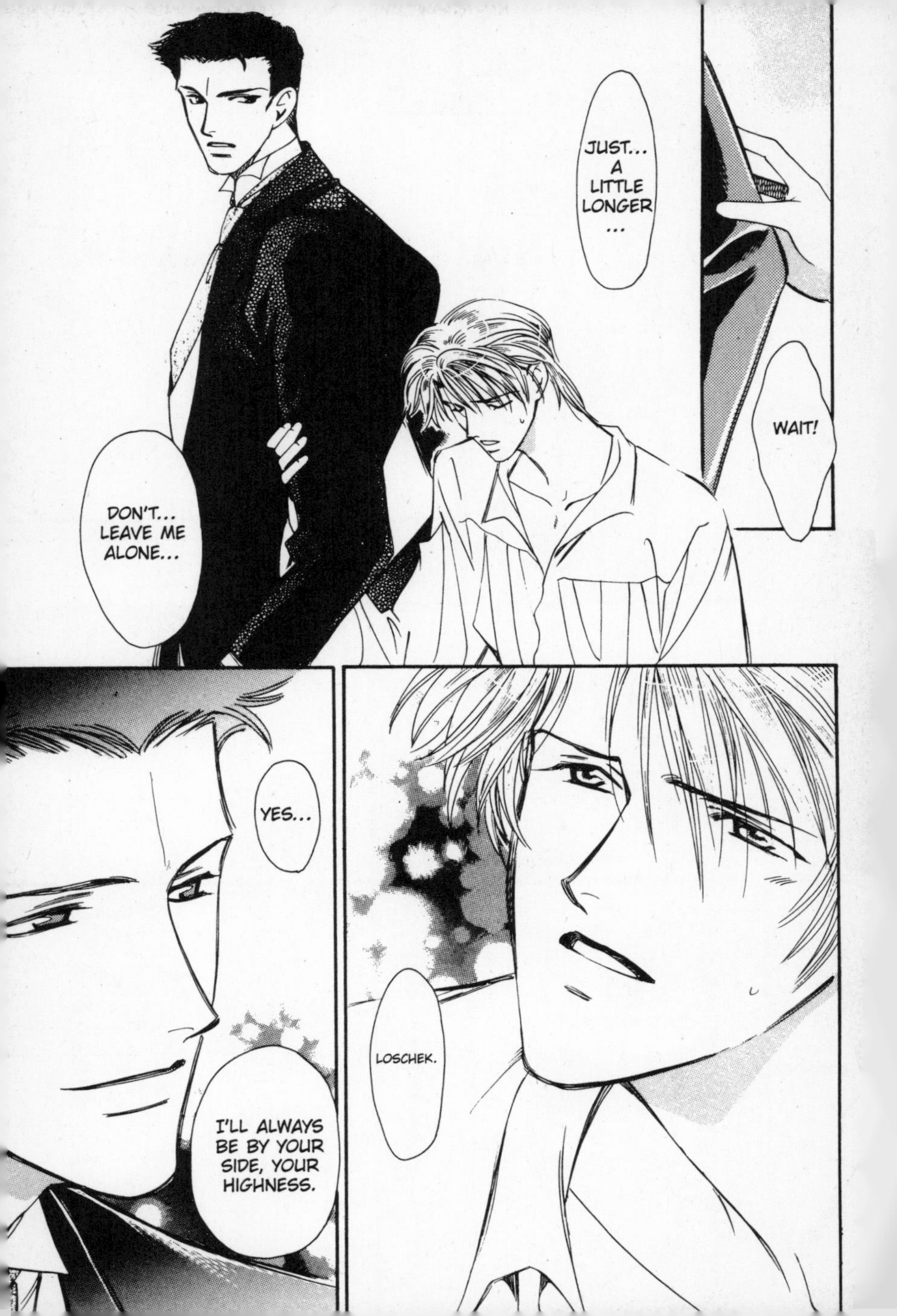
WAIT!
JUST... A LITTLE LONGER...
DON'T... LEAVE ME ALONE...
LOSCHEK.
YES...
I'LL ALWAYS BE BY YOUR SIDE, YOUR HIGHNESS.

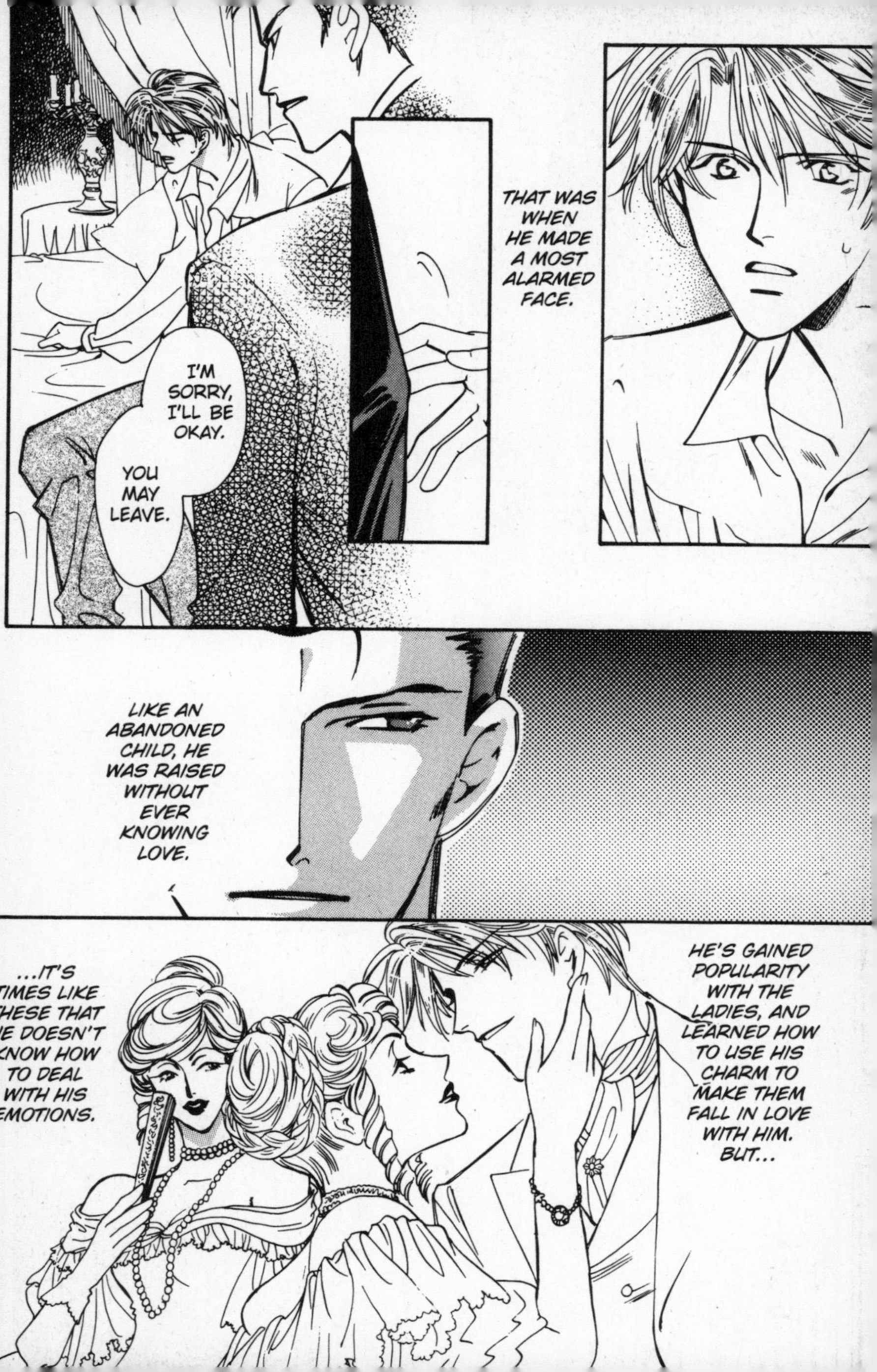
THAT WAS WHEN HE MADE A MOST ALARMED FACE.
I'M SORRY, I'LL BE OKAY.
YOU MAY LEAVE.
LIKE AN ABANDONED CHILD, HE WAS RAISED WITHOUT EVER KNOWING LOVE.
HE'S GAINED POPULARITY WITH THE LADIES, AND LEARNED HOW TO USE HIS CHARM TO MAKE THEM FALL IN LOVE WITH HIM. BUT...
...IT'S TIMES LIKE THESE THAT HE DOESN'T KNOW HOW TO DEAL WITH HIS EMOTIONS.

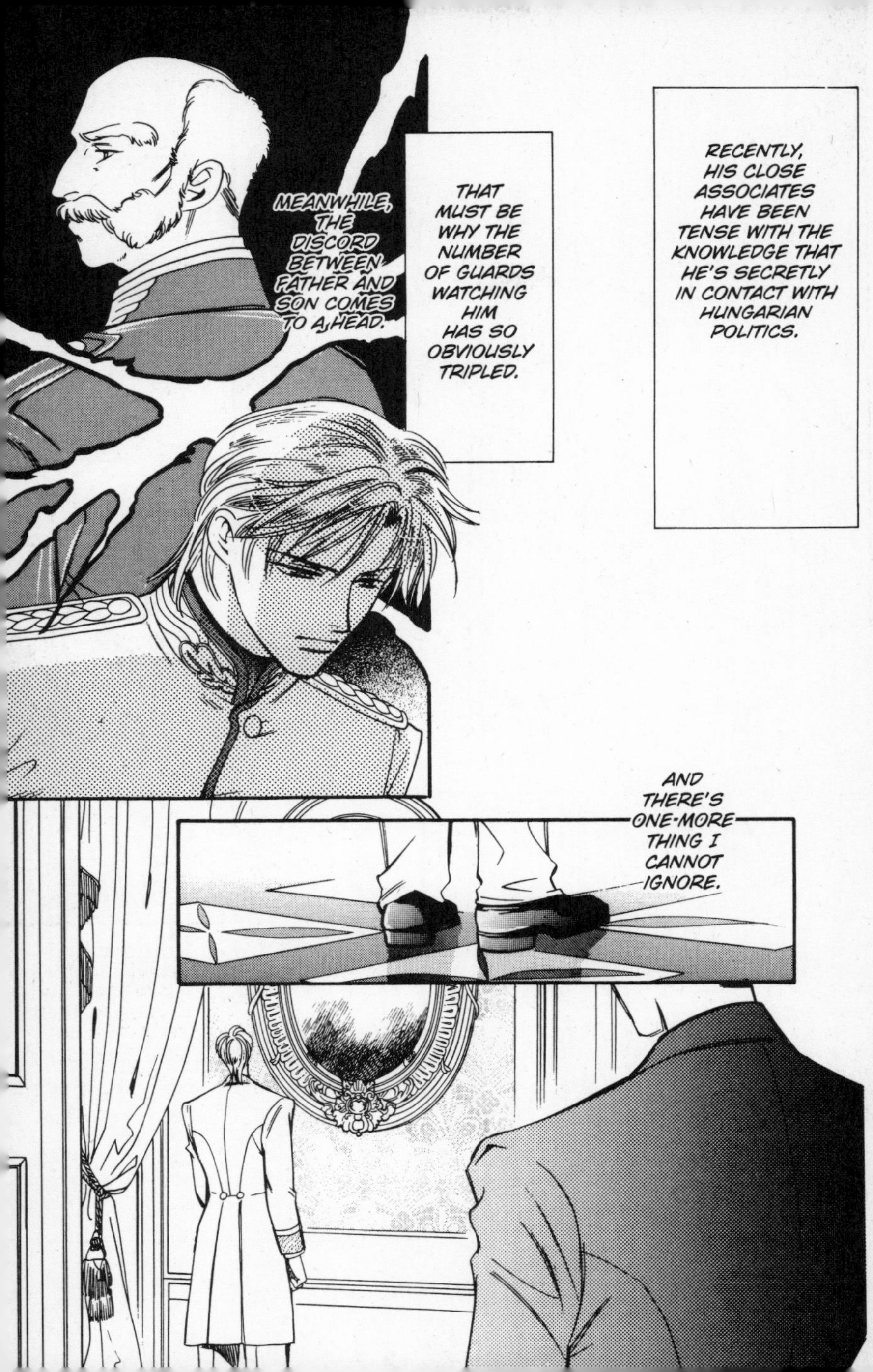
RECENTLY, HIS CLOSE ASSOCIATES HAVE BEEN TENSE WITH THE KNOWLEDGE THAT HE'S SECRETLY IN CONTACT WITH HUNGARIAN POLITICS.
THAT MUST BE WHY THE NUMBER OF GUARDS WATCHING HIM HAS SO OBVIOUSLY TRIPLED.
MEANWHILE, THE DISCORD BETWEEN FATHER AND SON COMES TO A HEAD.
AND THERE'S ONE MORE THING I CANNOT IGNORE.

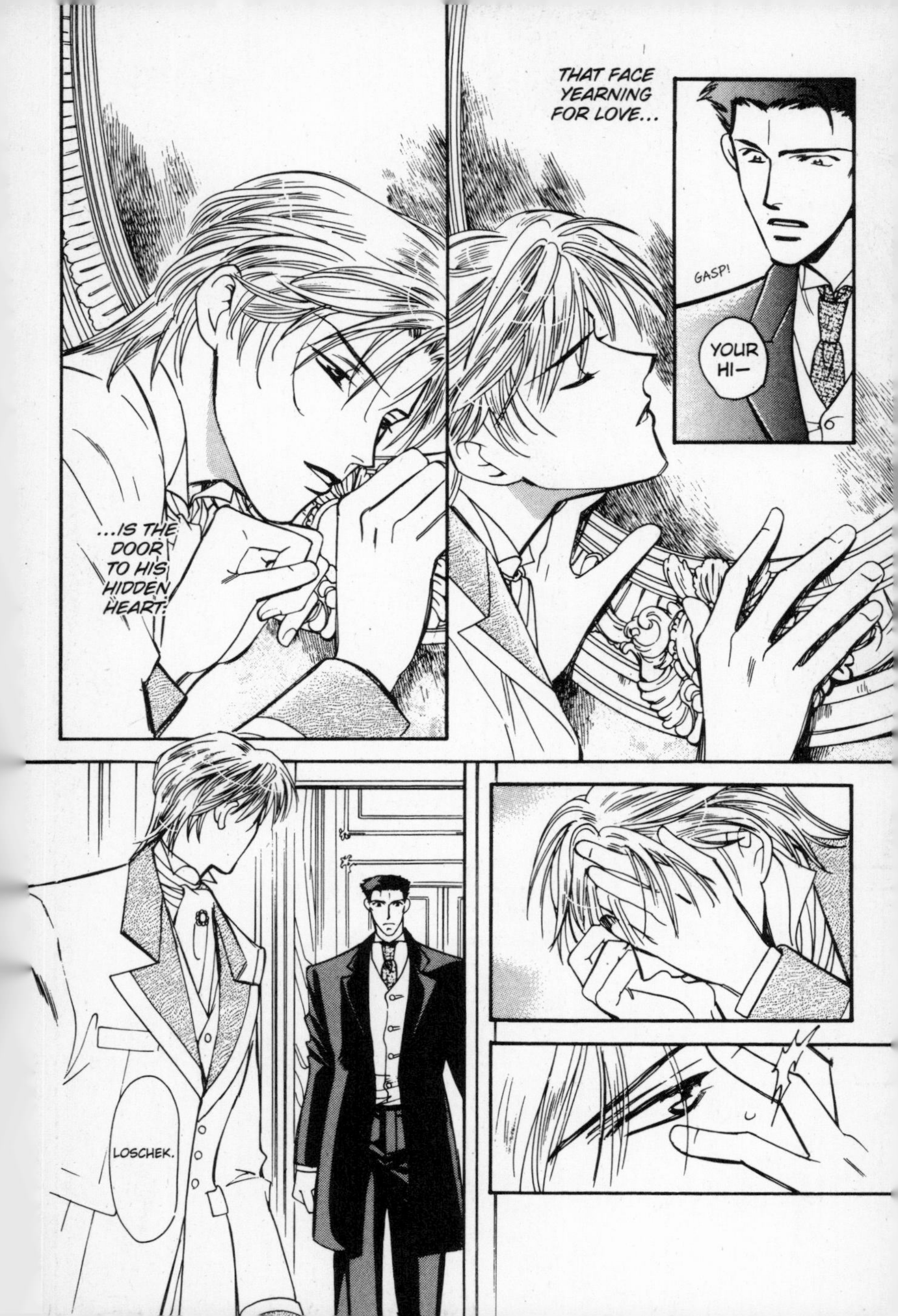
THAT FACE YEARNING FOR LOVE...
GASP!
YOUR HI—
...IS THE DOOR TO HIS HIDDEN HEART.
LOSCHEK.

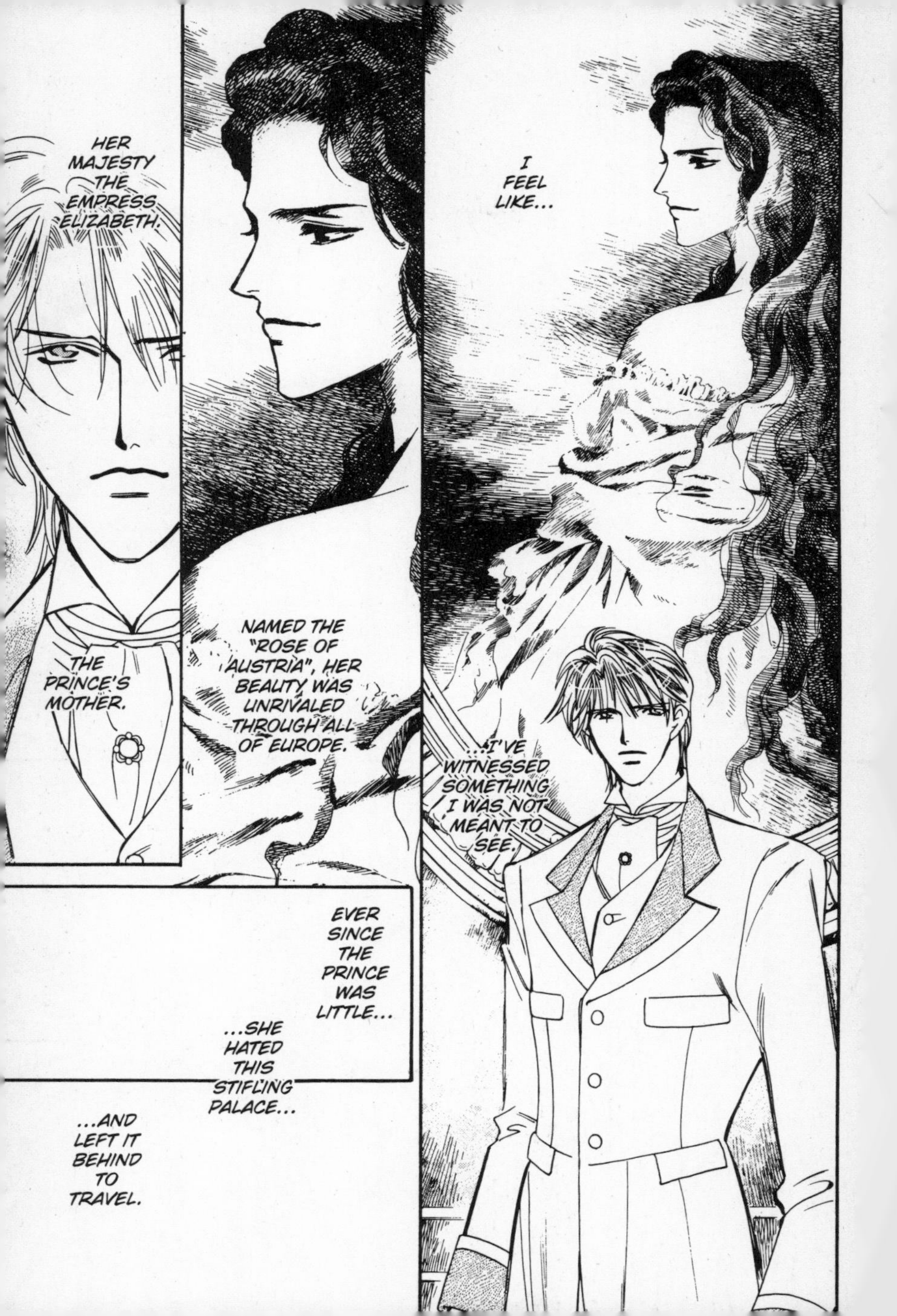
I FEEL LIKE...
...I'VE WITNESSED SOMETHING I WAS NOT MEANT TO SEE.
NAMED THE "ROSE OF AUSTRIA", HER BEAUTY WAS UNRIVALED THROUGH ALL OF EUROPE.
HER MAJESTY THE EMPRESS ELIZABETH.
THE PRINCE'S MOTHER.
EVER SINCE THE PRINCE WAS LITTLE...
...SHE HATED THIS STIFLING PALACE...
...AND LEFT IT BEHIND TO TRAVEL.

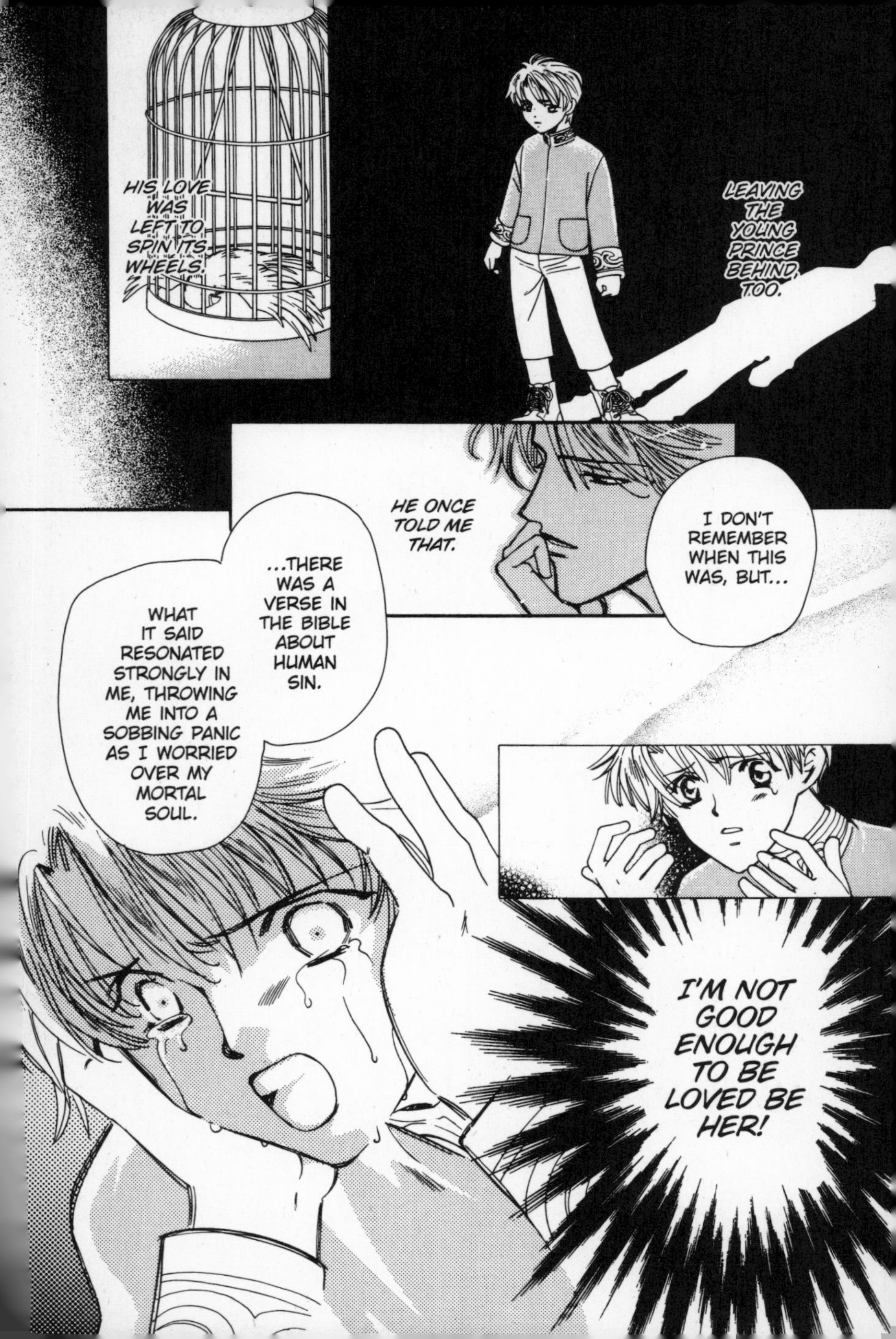
LEAVING THE YOUNG PRINCE BEHIND, TOO.
HIS LOVE WAS LEFT TO SPIN ITS WHEELS.
I DON'T REMEMBER WHEN THIS WAS, BUT...
HE ONCE TOLD ME THAT.
...THERE WAS A VERSE IN THE BIBLE ABOUT HUMAN SIN.
WHAT IT SAID RESONATED STRONGLY IN ME, THROWING ME INTO A SOBBING PANIC AS I WORRIED OVER MY MORTAL SOUL.
I'M NOT GOOD ENOUGH TO BE LOVED BE HER!

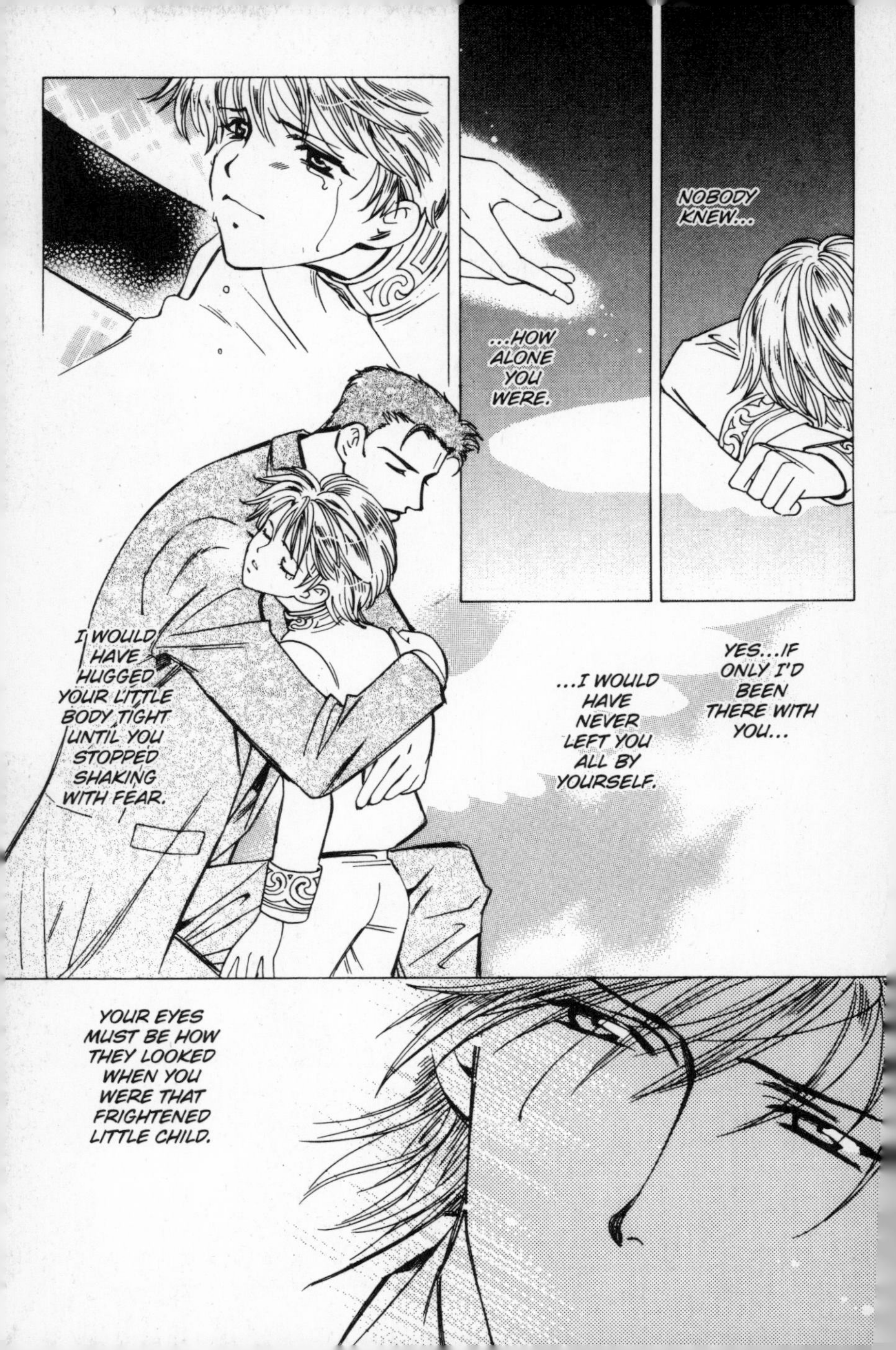
NOBODY KNEW...
...HOW ALONE YOU WERE.
YES...IF ONLY I'D BEEN THERE WITH YOU...
...I WOULD HAVE NEVER LEFT YOU ALL BY YOURSELF.
I WOULD HAVE HUGGED YOUR LITTLE BODY TIGHT UNTIL YOU STOPPED SHAKING WITH FEAR.
YOUR EYES MUST BE HOW THEY LOOKED WHEN YOU WERE THAT FRIGHTENED LITTLE CHILD.

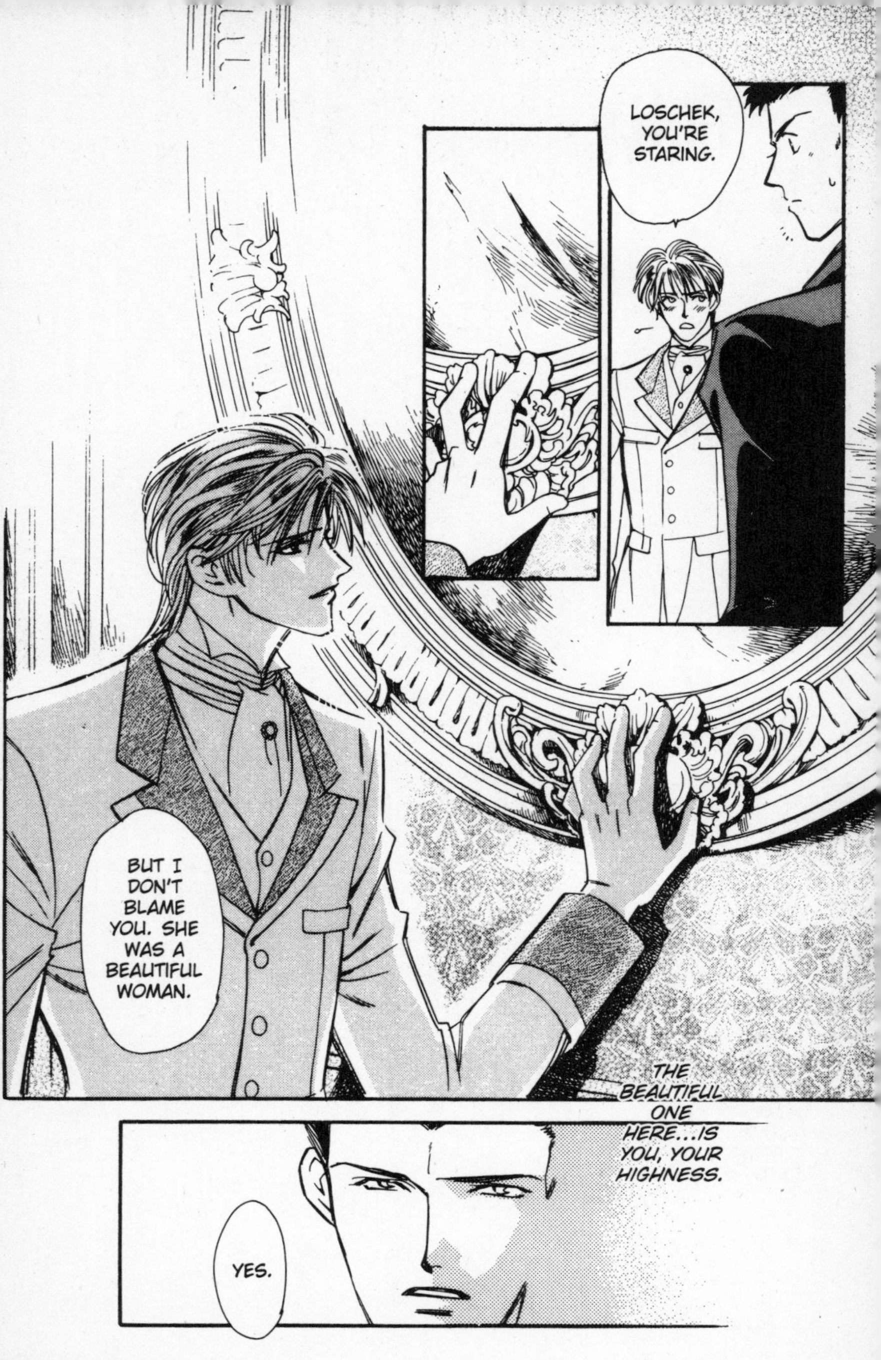
LOSCHEK, YOU'RE STARING.
BUT I DON'T BLAME YOU. SHE WAS A BEAUTIFUL WOMAN.
THE BEAUTIFUL ONE HERE...IS YOU, YOUR HIGHNESS.
YES.

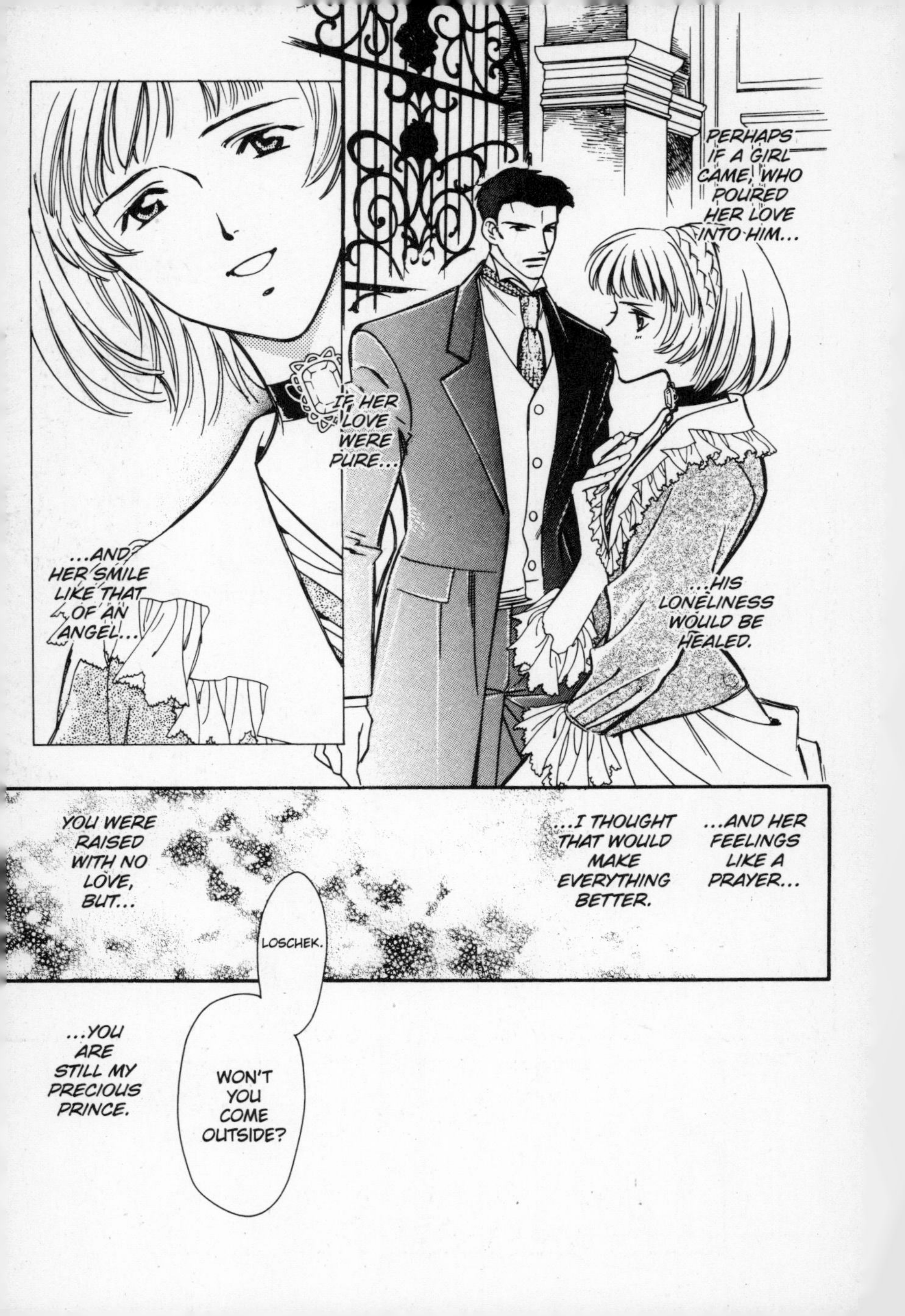
PERHAPS IF A GIRL CAME, WHO POURED HER LOVE INTO HIM...
...HIS LONELINESS WOULD BE HEALED.
IF HER LOVE WERE PURE...
...AND HER SMILE LIKE THAT OF AN ANGEL...
...AND HER FEELINGS LIKE A PRAYER...
...I THOUGHT THAT WOULD MAKE EVERYTHING BETTER.
YOU WERE RAISED WITH NO LOVE, BUT...
LOSCHEK.
WON'T YOU COME OUTSIDE?
...YOU ARE STILL MY PRECIOUS PRINCE.

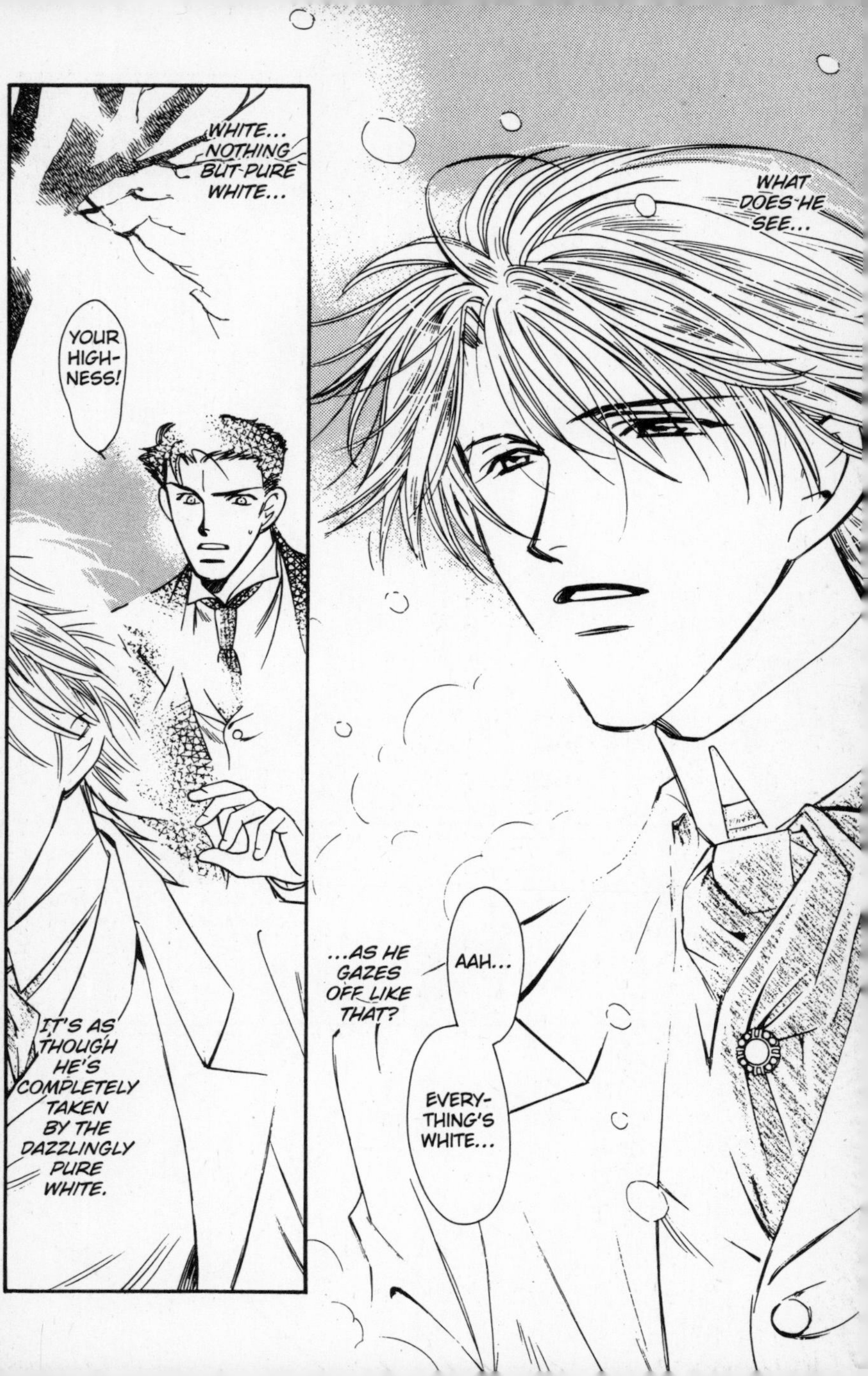
WHAT DOES HE SEE...
...AS HE GAZES OFF LIKE THAT?
AAH...
EVERY-THING'S WHITE...
WHITE... NOTHING BUT PURE WHITE...
YOUR HIGH-NESS!
IT'S AS THOUGH HE'S COMPLETELY TAKEN BY THE DAZZLINGLY PURE WHITE.

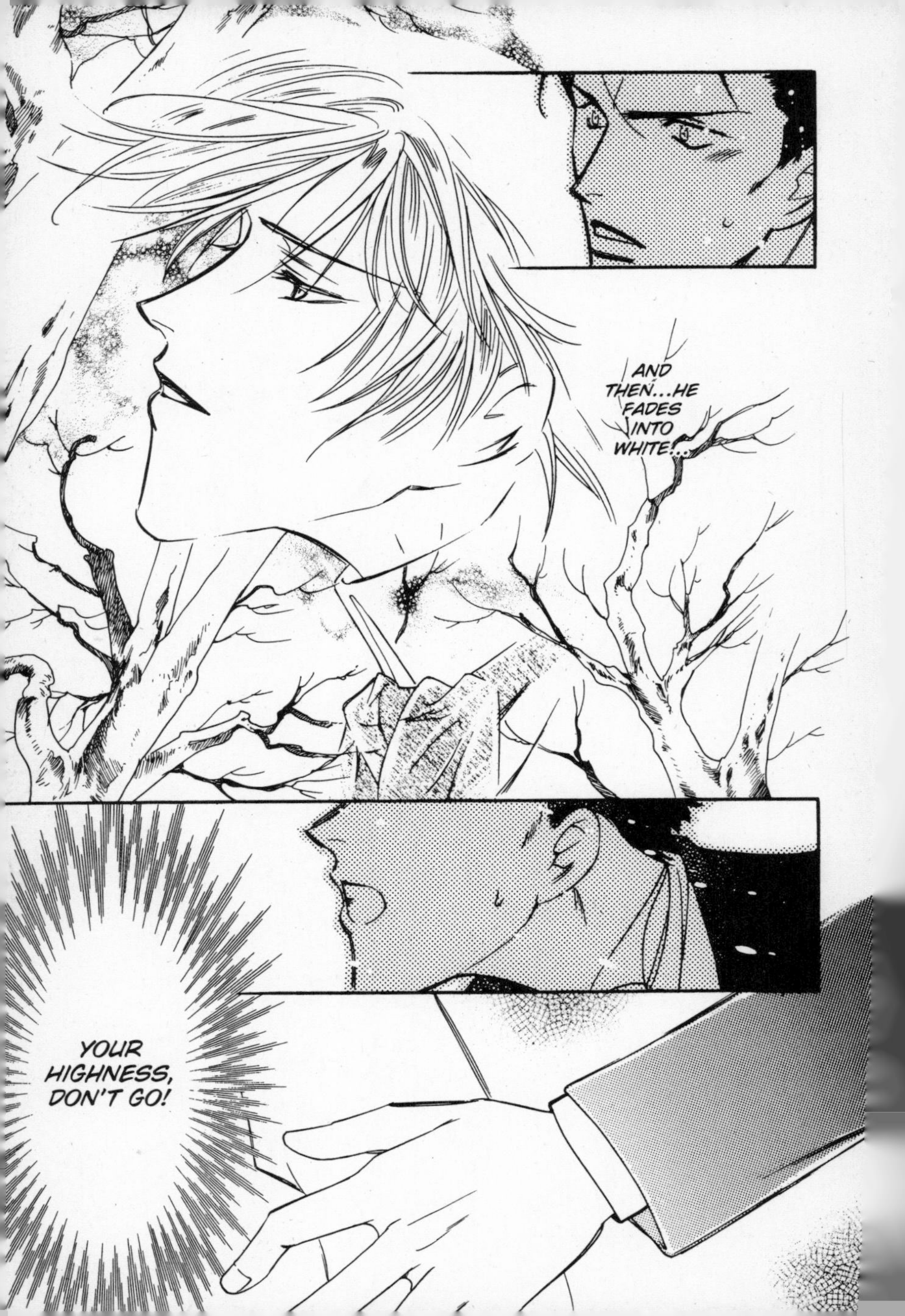
AND THEN...HE FADES INTO WHITE!...
YOUR HIGHNESS, DON'T GO!

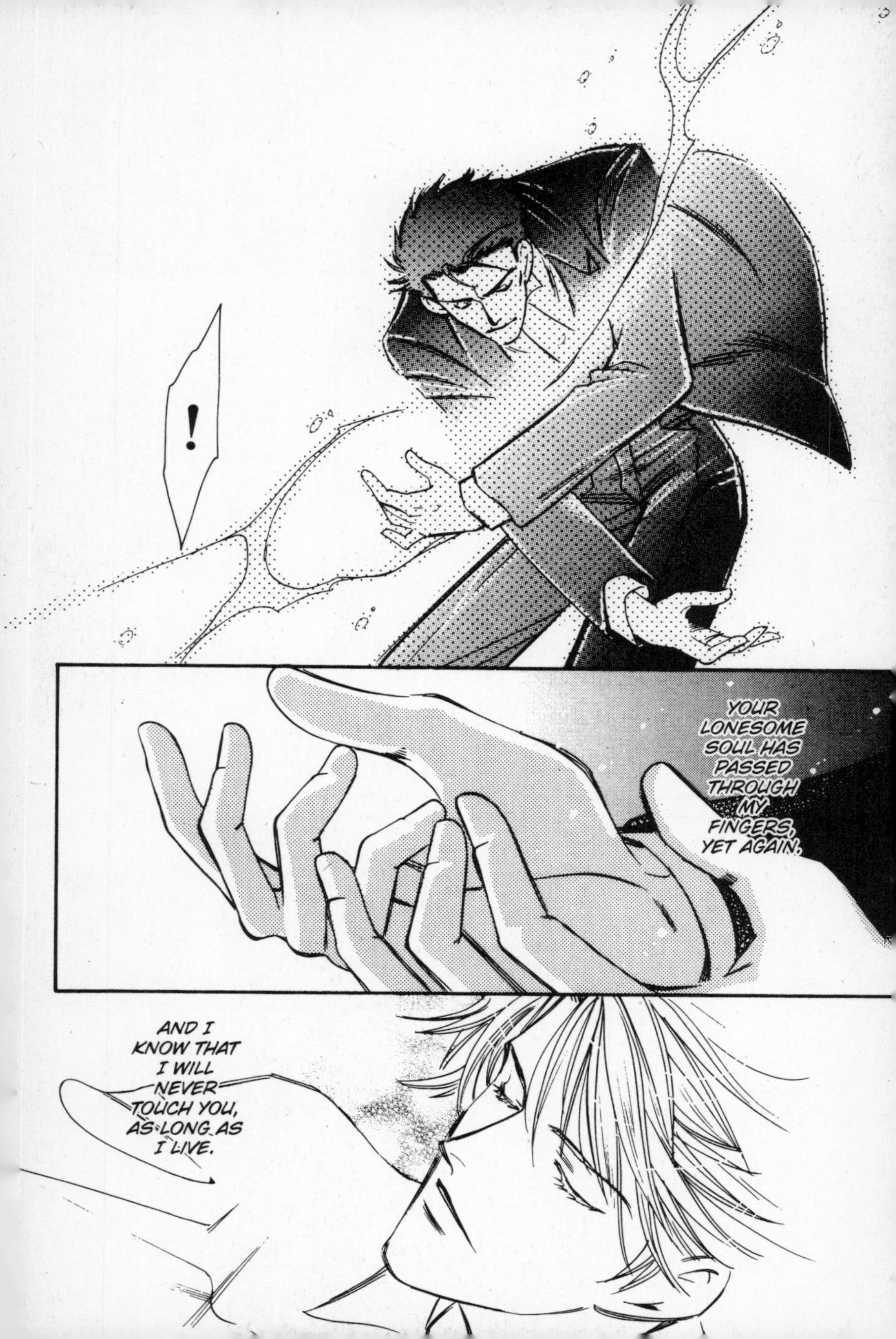
!
YOUR LONESOME SOUL HAS PASSED THROUGH MY FINGERS, YET AGAIN.
AND I KNOW THAT I WILL NEVER TOUCH YOU, AS LONG AS I LIVE.

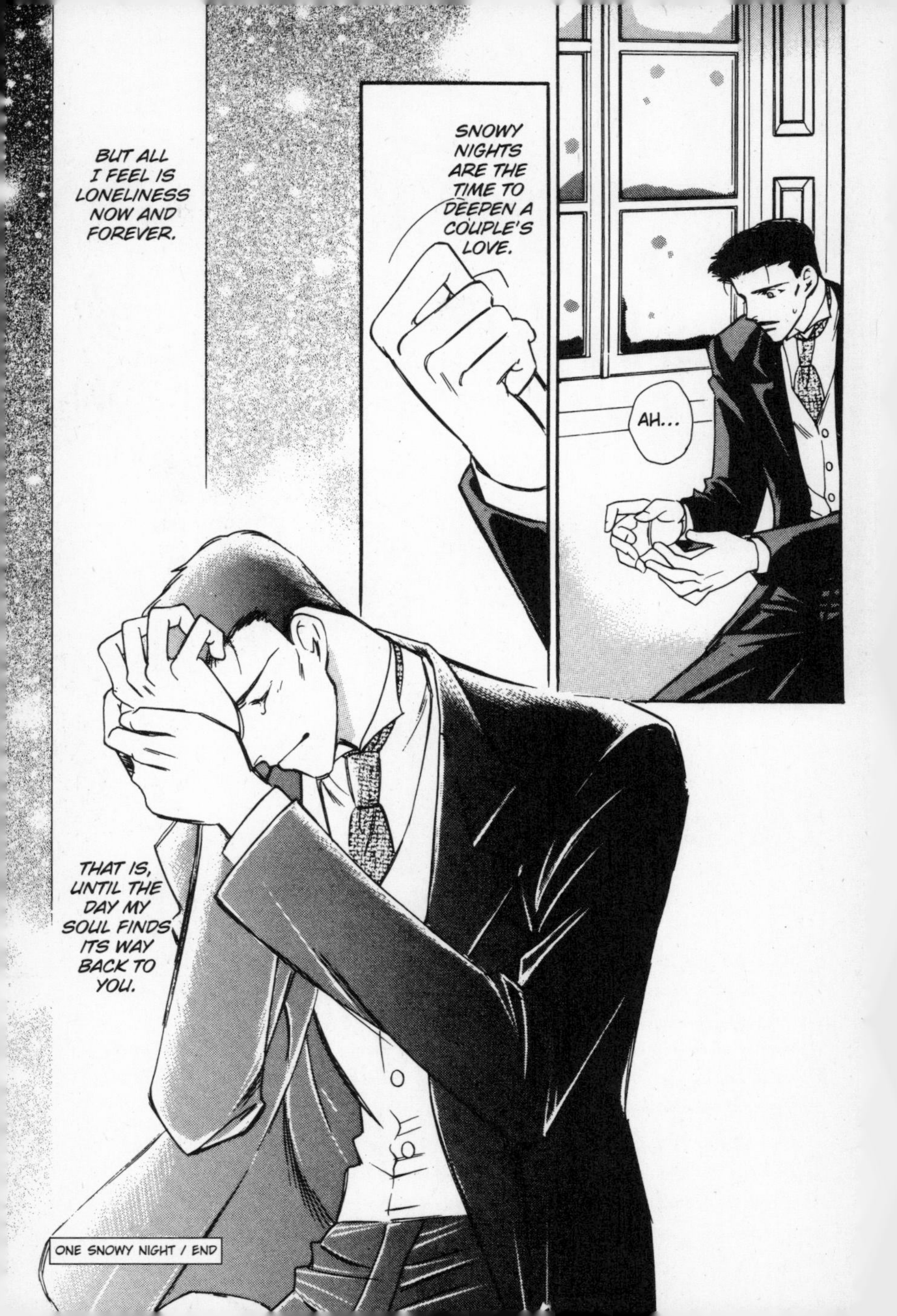
AH...
SNOWY NIGHTS ARE THE TIME TO DEEPEN A COUPLE'S LOVE.
BUT ALL I FEEL IS LONELINESS NOW AND FOREVER.
THAT IS, UNTIL THE DAY MY SOUL FINDS ITS WAY BACK TO YOU.
ONE SNOWY NIGHT / END

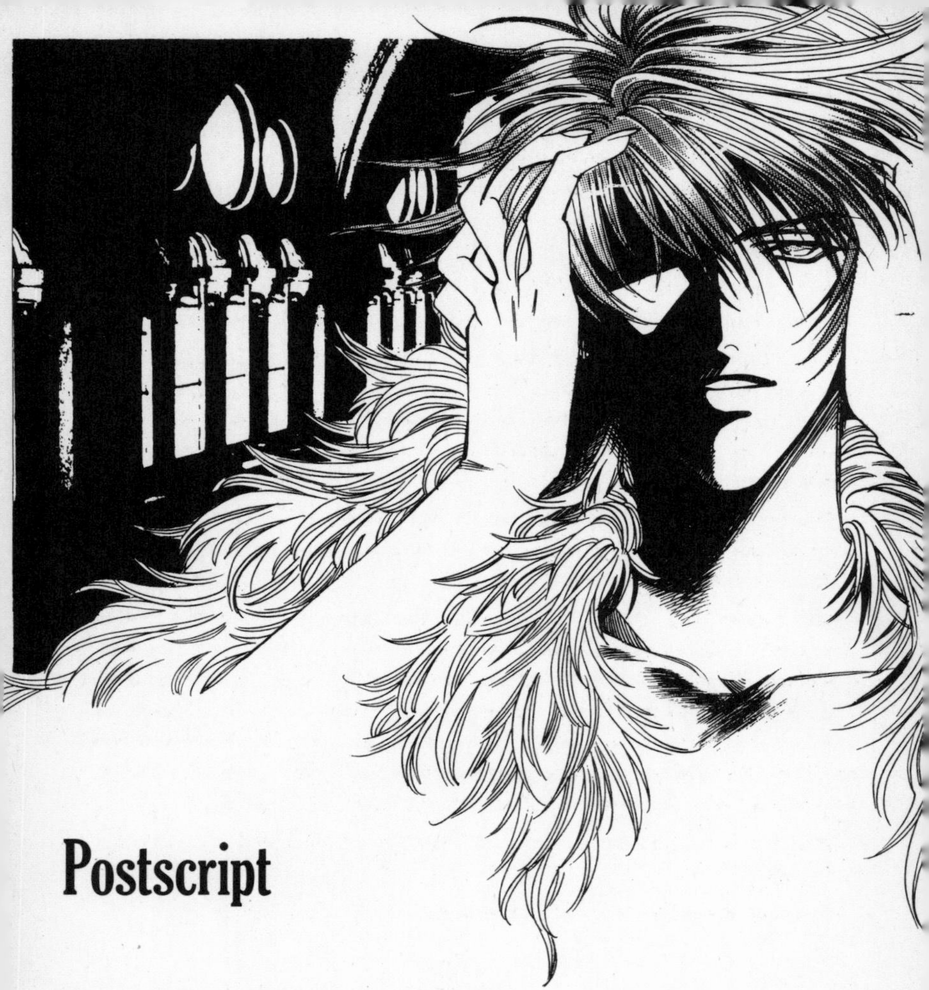

# Postscript

*Hello, and nice to meet you. This is You Higuri.*
*Thank you very much for picking up Angel's Coffin! This is the first full-length manga I've released from Princess Comics.*
*It really is moving to me. After all, the first shojo manga I ever bought was from the Princess Comics line. So for my own work to get published by them, too...it is both a stirring and bewildering feeling.*

*When making this story, I knew that I wanted to portray the shift in Europe that happened at the end of the 19th century, and since I'd already done a story on the Bavarian King Ludwig II with another publisher, I had plenty of historical references to work from. So I knew that portraying the neighboring country of Austria would be a piece of cake.*

Rudolf's mother Elizabeth was actually Ludwig II's older cousin, so it was easy to get information on her through the resources I had on him. But to gather more resource material on the country of Austria itself, I traveled there to take photos and whatnot, and even went to Mayerling during the winter season. In the gloomy Vienna Forest that was slightly shadowed by the overcast sky, stood the hunting lodge that has since then been turned into a monastery.

When I told our guide that I was there to take photos for my manga, he let me take some shots even though photography inside the building is usually forbidden. Thanks!

Then I tried to see the ruins of Marie Vetsera's family's house, it'd been turned into a window for bath and body products. It's odd, because even though most of the buildings on the street are almost completely unchanged from when they were first built, only this one was changed in an almost gratuitous way. It's the first I felt there of how time can change things.

In any case, since all the history books are just a parade of fascinating characters, I never get sick of looking at it all. If I ever get the chance again, I'd like to make another historical fiction manga.

Now to make all my "thank yous"! To my assistants who helped me get this book out: Hijiri Izumi-san, Naoko Nakatsuji-san, Misaki Kitazawa-san, Kaori Miyakoshi-san, Wakusa-san, Kazuki Mari-san, Fuyutsuki Mitsuru-san, Nari Kazuki-san, Megumi Fujikata-san, Michiko Ebara-san, Michiko Iwahashi-san, and Hiroko Wakimura-san. And Chika Shiomi-sensei who helped me despite her own busy schedule (you're too kind)! To my editor I'hashi-san whom I was always troubling with turning in my manuscripts just before the deadline. And last but not least, to my chief assistant Ryoka Oda. Good work, all of you.

Also, to all of you readers who bought this book, my undying gratitude is more than I can handle.

If you can, please send me your impressions in writing. Thank you very much!

**Yu Higuri**
**c/o Go Comi**
**28047 Dorothy Drive**
**Suite 200**
**Agoura Hills, Ca 91301**

**Visit The Digital Higurin at www.youhiguri.com**

Angel's Coffin / END

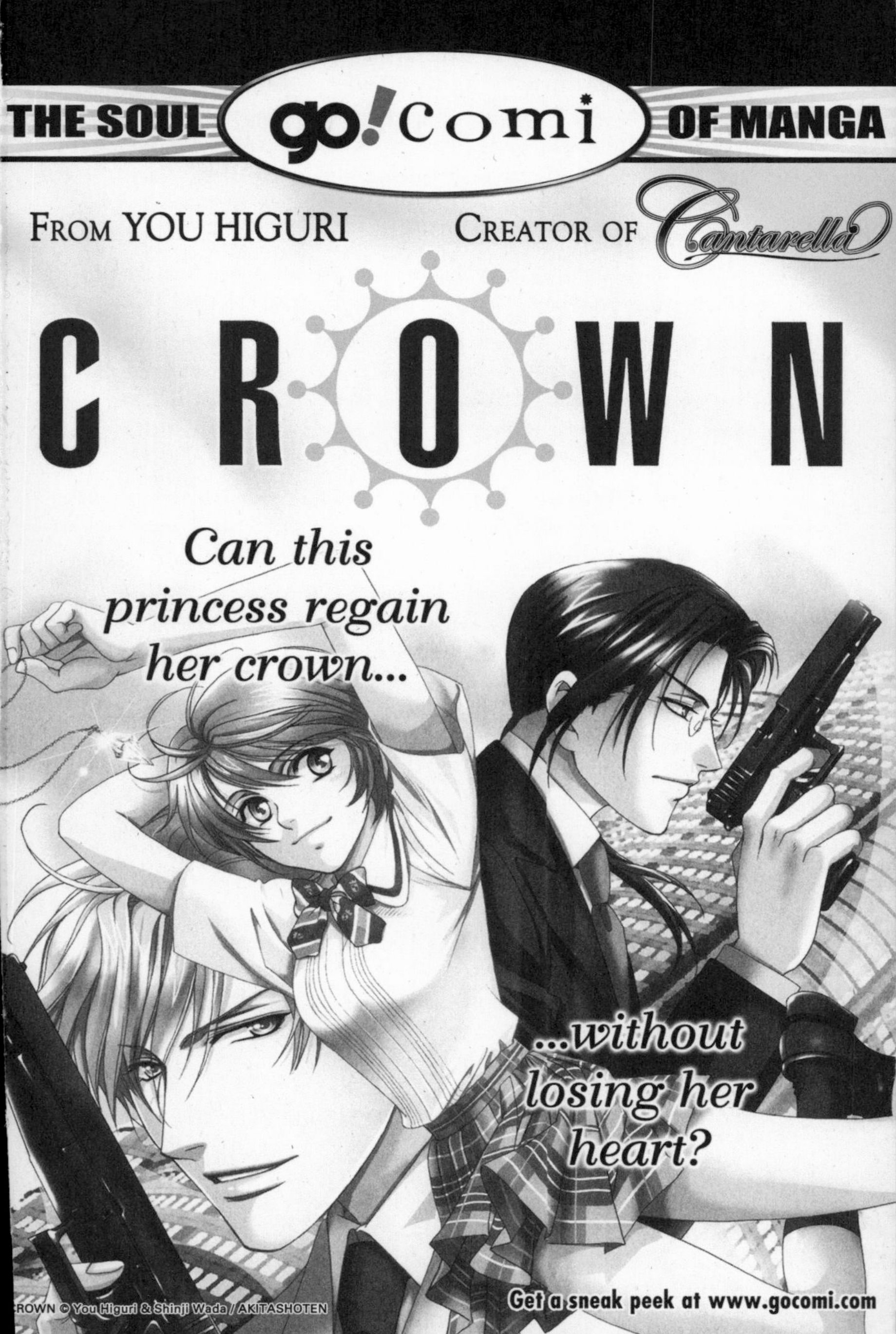
THE SOUL go!comi OF MANGA
FROM YOU HIGURI CREATOR OF Cantarella
CROWN
Can this princess regain her crown...
...without losing her heart?
CROWN © You Higuri & Shinji Wada / AKITASHOTEN
Get a sneak peek at www.gocomi.com